BRITISH ORIENTALISMS, 1759–1835

How did Britons understand their relationship with the East in the late eighteenth and early nineteenth centuries? James Watt's new study remaps the literary history of British Orientalisms between 1759, the 'year of victories' in the Seven Years' War, and 1835, when T. B. Macaulay published his polemical 'Minute on Indian Education'. It explores the impact of the war on Britons' cultural horizons, and the different and shifting ways in which Britons conceived of themselves and their nation as 'open' to the East across this period. Considering the emergence of new forms and styles of writing in the context of an age of empire and revolution, Watt examines how the familiar 'Eastern' fictions of the past were adapted, reworked, and reacted against. In doing so he illuminates the larger cultural conflict which animated a nation debating with itself about its place in the world and relation to its others.

JAMES WATT is a former director of the University of York's interdisciplinary Centre for Eighteenth Century Studies. His previous publications include *Contesting the Gothic: Fiction, Genre, and Cultural Conflict, 1764–1832* (Cambridge University Press, 1999) and an edition of Clara Reeve's *The Old English Baron* (2003). He has published numerous essays and articles in edited collections and in journals including *Eighteenth Century Life* and *The Eighteenth Century: Theory and Interpretation*.

This series aims to foster the best new work in one of the most challenging fields within English literary studies. From the early 1780s to the early 1830s, a formidable array of talented men and women took to literary composition, not just in poetry, which some of them famously transformed, but in many modes of writing. The expansion of publishing created new opportunities for writers, and the political stakes of what they wrote were raised again by what Wordsworth called those 'great national events' that were 'almost daily taking place': the French Revolution, the Napoleonic and American wars, urbanization, industrialization, religious revival, an expanded empire abroad, and the reform movement at home. This was an enormous ambition, even when it pretended otherwise. The relations between science, philosophy, religion, and literature were reworked in texts such as *Frankenstein* and *Biographia Literaria*; gender relations in *A Vindication of the Rights of Woman* and *Don Juan*; journalism by Cobbett and Hazlitt; and poetic form, content, and style by the Lake School and the Cockney School. Outside Shakespeare studies, probably no body of writing has produced such a wealth of commentary or done so much to shape the responses of modern criticism. This indeed is the period that saw the emergence of those notions of literature and of literary history, especially national literary history, on which modern scholarship in English has been founded.

The categories produced by Romanticism have also been challenged by recent historicist arguments. The task of the series is to engage both with a challenging corpus of Romantic writings and with the changing field of criticism they have helped to shape. As with other literary series published by Cambridge University Press, this one will represent the work of both younger and more established scholars on either side of the Atlantic and elsewhere.

See the end of the book for a complete list of published titles.

BRITISH ORIENTALISMS, 1759–1835

JAMES WATT

University of York

CAMBRIDGE
UNIVERSITY PRESS

CAMBRIDGE
UNIVERSITY PRESS

Shaftesbury Road, Cambridge CB2 8EA, United Kingdom

One Liberty Plaza, 20th Floor, New York, NY 10006, USA

477 Williamstown Road, Port Melbourne, VIC 3207, Australia

314–321, 3rd Floor, Plot 3, Splendor Forum, Jasola District Centre, New Delhi – 110025, India

103 Penang Road, #05–06/07, Visioncrest Commercial, Singapore 238467

Cambridge University Press is part of Cambridge University Press & Assessment, a department of the University of Cambridge.

We share the University's mission to contribute to society through the pursuit of education, learning and research at the highest international levels of excellence.

www.cambridge.org
Information on this title: www.cambridge.org/9781108460101

DOI: 10.1017/9781108560924

First published 2019
First paperback edition 2022

A catalogue record for this publication is available from the British Library

ISBN   978-1-108-47266-1   Hardback
ISBN   978-1-108-46010-1   Paperback

Contents

Acknowledgements

Three research assessment exercises have passed since the job interview at which I said that this book would probably be ready for the next one. The time that it took to complete it has given me a much clearer sense of my many debts than when I published the book of my PhD thesis, and I would firstly like to offer a belated but sincere thanks to all of my teachers at Goffs School, Cheshunt, and Cambridge University. I was fortunate enough to be able to return to St Catharine's College following the generous award of a Junior Research Fellowship (during which I began preliminary research in the field of Orientalism and empire), and I warmly remember my time back there as a postdoc.

At York it has been a privilege to work in the Department of English and Related Literature and the interdisciplinary Centre for Eighteenth Century Studies (CECS), and I am lucky to be able to count as my current departmental and CECS colleagues Mary Fairclough, Emma Major, Jon Mee, Alison O'Byrne, Deborah Russell, and Chloe Wigston Smith. When I started at York, the experience of working with John Barrell and Harriet Guest made me realize how much I didn't know about the eighteenth century, and John and Harriet – much missed – are still a source of inspiration. I have learned a huge amount from all of my colleagues in CECS, past and present, and it has been very rewarding to work with so many talented MA and PhD students. For their stimulating discussion of some of the subject matter covered by this book, I would like to thank all of the students who took my British Orientalisms MA module and my Empire and British Identities undergraduate module.

I am extremely grateful to Linda Bree for her initial support for this project. Linda, Bethany Thomas, and Tim Mason were very helpful throughout the process of seeing it to completion. Cambridge University Press's anonymous reviewers provided constructive and helpful comments on my manuscript and, among other things, alerted me to my tendency to cite lack of space as an excuse for not discussing a particular writer or work or pursuing a particular argument further. There wasn't space to include discursive footnotes in this book, which means that my engagement with the work of other scholars in this field sometimes appears truncated (or even non-existent). It is a matter of regret that I haven't been able to cite the work of others more extensively (or in some cases at all), and wherever possible I hope to be able to make good this deficiency in person.

The full list of scholars who have in one way or another influenced me during the writing of this book would certainly take me over the Press's word limit. I was enormously fortunate to be supervised as an undergraduate and PhD student by Nigel Leask, and the impact of his groundbreaking work on what follows is obvious. Among others (in addition to those named earlier here) who have offered advice, feedback, help, suggestions, and/or ideas, I would also like to thank Ros Ballaster, Greg Dart, Alun David, Pete Denney, Nick Dew, Markman Ellis, Kevin Gilmartin, Joanna de Groot, Paul Hartle, David Higgins, Peter Kitson, Adam Perchard, Shaun Regan, Jane Rendall, and Daniel Sanjiv Roberts. Although not scholars in the traditional sense of the term, Rogers and Edison deserve to be named here as my most frequent interlocutors during the writing process.

I can't really begin to do adequate justice to the love and support shown by family and friends outside of academic circles during the production of this book. My father, Alex Watt, a graduate of the Open University, didn't live to see its completion, but his example remains with me in numerous ways and many of his enthusiasms have become my own. My wife, Alison O'Byrne, has been a loving companion more or less since I started working on this project, and finishing it has made the everyday life that we share with our wonderful son, Fraser, all the more enjoyable. I dedicate this book with love and affection to Alison and Fraser, albeit in the knowledge that the latter will be slightly disappointed by its lack of train-related content.

Introduction
Britain, Empire, and 'Openness' to the East

In 1761 Richard Owen Cambridge published *An Account of the War in India*, telling the story of a decade of conflict between British and French forces in the south of the subcontinent. While this work says nothing about the 1757 battle of Plassey and the subsequent revolution that led to the East India Company (hereafter EIC) gaining sovereign power in Bengal, it testifies to 'the great reputation which the nation, and so many individuals have acquired in the East-Indies'.[1] Cambridge suggested that those, like him, without first-hand experience of India might already be primed to receive news of Britons' fantastic exploits there because of the 'Eastern' fictions to which they were accustomed: 'It will not appear strange that the generality of the world, through the habits of reading novels, and works of the imagination, should expect from an history of the East (. . . the scene of most of their ideal stories) a tale of adventures full of wonder and novelty, and nearly bordering upon romance.'[2] Even as he recorded the improbable story of how 'a handful of Europeans' had been able to dominate 'a multitude of Asiatics', however, Cambridge emphasized that his own narrative was soberly factual.[3] He also sought to mediate what he presented as – for himself and his audience – a hitherto unknown reality, prefacing his text with a 'Glossary of Persic and Indian Names', from 'Arzee' ('a request, or petition') to 'Vakeel' ('an agent or minister for the Moors').[4] Cambridge therefore identified two different and apparently opposing registers of representation in and through which 'the East' might be apprehended by Britons – the fictional extravagance of 'ideal stories' and a new lexicon of more precise and detailed reference that was the product of an ongoing global conflict.

The relationship between a generic 'Orientalism' and more specific understandings of historical, geographical, and/or cultural difference provides a key point of focus for this book, and I return throughout my introduction to the suggestive though unstable distinction between the

I

'ideal' and the real which Cambridge drew in his history of the present. Before outlining my larger concerns, however, it is first of all necessary to consider some recent developments in the critical analysis of 'British Orientalisms' which also demonstrate the capaciousness of the much disputed term 'Orientalism' itself. (I do not rehearse the now familiar debates surrounding Edward Said's justly famous work; my own reference to 'Orientalism' follows the inclusive usage of the period under discussion.) Two stimulating studies have explored the production and reception of what might be regarded, following Cambridge, as the 'old' domain of Eastern fictions, in circulation before the imperial turn that his work anticipates. Ros Ballaster's *Fabulous Orients* addresses the eighteenth-century sense of 'the East' as 'a (sometimes *the*) source of story', paying particular attention to sequences of tales associated with Persia, Turkey, China, and India.[5] Ballaster argues that the 'transport' of audiences captivated by these fictions should not be seen as a momentarily pleasurable escapism, but rather as a transformative experience of 'imaginary projection into the psyche and culture of an other', where the reading subject's 'sovereignty' is abandoned.[6] Srinivas Aravamudan's *Enlightenment Orientalism* examines instead a miscellany of 'pseudoethnographies, sexual fantasies, and political utopias', but it likewise accentuates the broadly liberatory possibilities offered by Easts of the imagination, 'nine parts invented and one part referential'.[7] Aravamudan recovers an 'archive' of playfully reflexive works that is the product of 'a transcultural, cosmopolitan ... Orientalism', which rejects the emergent novel's 'monoculture' by aspiring to 'mutual understanding across cultural differences'.[8]

Aravamudan defines 'Enlightenment Orientalism' as 'a fictional mode for dreaming with the Orient', reworking Said's terminology but accepting his claim that the turn to empire was a watershed with enduring consequences: 'Imperial conquest turned Orientalism malefic.'[9] Recently, however, it has been suggested that Britain's Eastern empire, in the EIC's late eighteenth-century 'Orientalist' phase, may have inspired in agents of colonial authority something akin to the openness to the other that Ballaster and Aravamudan regard as characteristic of an earlier period. In broad terms, as Cambridge recognized, empire confronted Britons with the unfamiliar, and as is evident in the influential work of the polymath Sir William Jones, it could provide an impetus to projects of cultural translation too. In his inaugural address to the Asiatic Society of Bengal in 1784, for example, Jones described how exposure both to 'eventful histories' and to 'agreeable fictions' sparked his interest in 'the eastern world', making him particularly receptive to his auspicious situation en route to Bengal, as '*India* lay before us, and *Persia* on our left, while a breeze from *Arabia* blew nearly on our stern.'[10]

The collective endeavour inaugurated by Jones represents an intellectual engagement with an 'infinitely diversified' Asia rather than an amorphous 'East', but the idiom of wonder – which Cambridge had associated with the 'ideal' – nonetheless endures in Jones's palpable exhilaration at the scale of this undertaking.[11] His 'Discourse' anticipates the extraction of scholarly treasure from an 'immense mine in which we might labour with equal delight and advantage', and it memorably defines the purview of the Asiatic Society as 'MAN and NATURE: whatever is performed by the one, or produced by the other'.[12] Although knowledge is clearly in the service of power here, Jones conceives of colonial encounter as a process that appears as horizon-expanding as the private readerly transport discussed by Ballaster and Aravamudan. Jones may be seen as 'provincializing' Europe, because even as he assumes a privileged way of seeing, he invites his audience to take '*Hindostan* as a centre' and, from the vantage point of Bengal, to survey the diversity of a vast continent that makes Europe, still more so Britain itself, insignificant in comparison.[13] Jones's scholarly project commonly appealed to human universals and shared pasts – for example by suggesting that different systems of mythology were versions of one another, or by identifying a 'familial' affinity between Sanskrit and European languages – and Jones played a key part in a larger European 'rediscovery' of India and the East which Raymond Schwab would call 'the Oriental Renaissance'.

While Schwab's main focus is the belated 'reconciliation' of hemispheres that this 'second' renaissance afforded, however, he also sometimes presented cultural contact as potentially more problematic in its implications, noting that it was 'logically inevitable that a civilization believing itself unique would find itself drowned in the sum total of civilizations'.[14] David Simpson has recently pursued this claim while also stressing that if the world seemed 'much bigger in 1800 than it had in 1750', that was the result both of successive global conflicts beginning with the Seven Years' War and of the second age of exploration associated in Britain with figures such as Captain Cook. For Simpson, this sense of connection to a 'bigger world' provided metropolitan Britons with a new apprehension of 'significant otherness' that was too multifarious to be immediately assimilable, and it in turn generated an ethical and imaginative challenge to which diverse literary works of the period responded. I go on in what follows to say more about Robert Southey's long poem *Thalaba the Destroyer* (1801), which Simpson regards as a paradigmatic text in this respect, but here I just want to emphasize the contrast between *Thalaba*'s dense apparatus of footnotes and Cambridge's straightforwardly functional glossary.[15] Where the latter explains an unfamiliar nomenclature in order to help its audience follow a narrative of British military success, the 'thick field of historical and anthropological material' attached to *Thalaba*'s main text is as likely to produce a kind of vertigo on the part of readers as to enhance comprehension of the poem.[16]

So far, then, I have outlined some twenty-first-century critical approaches to diverse eighteenth-century British Orientalisms, from tale cycle and experimental fiction to scholarly essay and long poem. There are obvious and significant differences between the critics referred to, with regard to both their methodology and their coverage: whereas Simpson considers a dialectic of responses to the other-as-stranger that is traceable back to the Bible and the Classics but especially prominent in Romantic writing, Ballaster and Aravamudan primarily look at an earlier period and present the idea of textual and readerly openness to the other in for the most part benign and even utopian terms. It is broadly accurate to say, nonetheless, that in their analysis of cultural encounter these critics testify to how, at varying levels of theorization, the concept of 'hospitality' has percolated into literary studies from the philosophical writings of Derrida and Levinas. It is also fair to say that they offer an implicit reframing, if not contestation, of Nigel Leask's influential argument about Britons' 'anxieties of empire'. For Leask, even as Romantic-period culture testified to a '*demand* for orientalism' a residually authoritative civic discourse of nationhood equated openness to the other with a susceptibility to contamination, so that (for example) Byron in his Turkish tales (1813–16) depicted the 'allure of the East' as a 'fatal attraction', corrosive of order and virtue.[17] In criticism of the past decade or so, generally speaking, more attention is given instead to a rather different history of contemporary imaginative and/or intellectual engagement with the East. Alternatively, as in Simpson's work, an anxious relation to otherness is understood as an enduringly disabling predicament that is in need of remedying in the present too.

It goes without saying that this attention to the ramifications of cultural encounter has been determined by the pressures and imperatives of our current moment, 'after 9/11'. In a climate that has produced intensified imaginings of external threat, any analysis of the history of reckoning with others is inextricable from a process of reflection on our civic responsibilities. Simpson emphasizes elsewhere that 'the challenge of the other' in Romantic-period writing comes from within as well as beyond the boundaries of 'home', and he argues powerfully for the political necessity of cultural translation, as an effort to combat the baneful suspicion of outsiders characteristic of our age.[18] The identification of various kinds of seemingly 'good' Orientalisms by recent critics is potentially as important as this call for greater 'translational effort', because it recovers the productivity of what Suvir Kaul terms an 'international, inter-cultural, inter-racial, colonial imagination' – the antithesis of the irreducible antagonism between opposing camps presupposed by the rhetoric of a 'clash of civilizations'.[19] Contemporary criticism has yielded additional gains of a scholarly nature, whether by thus helping to rewrite literary-historical narratives such as that of the Anglocentric 'rise of the novel', or by making previously marginalized texts such as Southey's epics much less easy to dismiss.

If this wide-ranging emphasis on encounter and its consequences has been extremely valuable, however, it has additionally generated some rather inflated claims about the nature and impact of past forms or instances of openness to the East. The argument that eighteenth-century audiences enthusiastically surrendered themselves to fictions of the East, for example, somewhat takes for granted that the pleasurable activity of reading these works brought about a significant confounding of cultural identities.[20] More problematic is a related argument that the Orientalism of Jones and others sparked a metropolitan fascination with India, and especially Hindu mythology, which resulted in not just a momentary loss of self-government on the part of Britons but also 'a kind of colonization-in-reverse'.[21] The idea that imperial powers end up themselves being metaphorically or even literally conquered would have been familiar to many eighteenth-century Britons, but critical analysis of the British taste for the exotic in this period nonetheless has to distinguish between the effects of cultural dissemination and political dominion. It is necessary too to situate Jones squarely within the messy complexities of his time rather than to present him as a straightforwardly 'exemplary' figure, possessed of positive attitudes or characteristics that are lacking today.[22] Such celebration of enlightened precursors is evident not just in some recent work on Jones but also in accounts of Leigh Hunt and his circle as generously disposed authors whose writings 'open out onto the world' and thereby manifest a 'Cockney cosmopolitanism'.[23] While the recovery of past cosmopolitanisms may help us now to reimagine 'conditions of commensurability' between Europe and its others, as David Porter suggests, the concept of 'cosmopolitanism' itself requires interrogation, and is perhaps most helpfully understood in 'prospective' terms rather than as the description of a state from which we have fallen.[24]

This book is indebted to scholarship on the expansion of intellectual and cultural horizons that accompanied the extension of British interests in the decades after the Seven Years' War. It acknowledges that global history and the 'new imperial history' have enriched the study of cultures of empire by focusing on the movement of people, ideas, and things, and thus showing how the world transformed Britain even as Britain increasingly imposed itself on the world. While there is no space to cite all of the excellent work that has been done here, the critical reorientation afforded by this perspective is demonstrated by a book such as Wendy Louise Belcher's *Abyssinia's Samuel Johnson*, which explores how Johnson was 'discursively possessed' by his early encounter with Ethiopian thought.[25] Numerous scholars have considered the formative impact of global commerce on British subjectivity, at the level of everyday social and cultural practices, for example with reference to the widespread consumption of Chinese and Chinese-style goods.[26] Miles Ogborn and others have addressed the increasing interconnection between Britain and the rest of the world over the course of this period by tracing the geographical mobility of individuals leading 'global lives'.[27] Literary critics such as Daniel White meanwhile have attended to how the transnational exchange between London and Calcutta, metropolitan 'centre' and colonial 'periphery', produced not only forms of intercultural dialogue but also a common print culture and even a 'global culture of Romanticism', marked by an inventively 'citational' creative practice.[28]

If we can take as a given the reality of an increasingly 'networked' Britain in this period, however, it is also important to emphasize that contemporaries did not always see or describe the relationship between Britain and its others in such terms. The main objective of this study is to historicize the different and shifting modes through and ways in which Britons may have conceived of themselves and their nation as 'open' to the East across the late eighteenth and early nineteenth centuries. It is useful again to refer to Cambridge's work in this context, because for all its evident opportunism it provides a prescient sense of some of the larger implications of national extroversion, broaching a debate that was just beginning in British culture about the possibility or otherwise of being, as Catherine Hall and Sonya Rose put it, '"at home" with an empire and with the effects of imperial power'.[29] Cambridge's 'Glossary of Persic and Indian Names' recognizes the new level of imaginative effort required to comprehend Britain's recently attained position of global pre-eminence. Even as Cambridge's work encourages its readers to celebrate the 'great reputation' accruing to the nation from its feats in distant lands, this glossary confronts its audience with an obtrusively alien lexicon, thereby hinting at the potential difficulty of reckoning with the new kinds of entanglement with the wider world that followed in the wake of military victory overseas.

By examining the period from the 1759 'year of victories' through to the mid-1830s moment of Macaulay's 'Minute on Indian Education', this study offers a long view of how, in an increasingly globalized and imperial nation, in fact if not always in self-image, primarily (but not exclusively) British metropolitan writers responded to and sought to negotiate the greater openness to the world and the plural and diverse encounters with otherness – sometimes already heavily mediated – that were a corollary of Eastern empire. Although extending this study's chronological focus to encompass the First Afghan War and the First Opium War of 1839–42 would have allowed me to end as well as begin by thinking about the ramifications of military conflict, Macaulay serves as a fitting end point since the ethnocentrism of his 'Minute' ostensibly signals a decisive transformation in British self-understanding: rather than thinking of Britons as in any way disoriented by colonial contact, it instead calls for the nation to wield its civilizational authority so as to afford moral direction to its colonies.[30] Among recent critics Saree Makdisi places particular emphasis on the wider significance of Macaulay's arguments, which he reads as instantiating an 'Occidentalism' that was as concerned to define the West as 'Western' as it was to modernize the East.[31]

While accepting the basic validity of this narrative of a cultural shift exemplified by Macaulay's 'Minute', what I especially want to do here, however, is to restore a richer sense of conflict to critical discussion of Britain's Eastern imaginary. Doing this makes it possible, for example, to appreciate Jones's scholarly achievements, but additionally to recognize that his work resonated differently in different contexts, and that the meanings of the relativizing comparisons it pursued were subject to contest. Thinking about the contestation of the idea of 'openness' itself helps us to recognize too that if later writers including Byron and Southey disclosed 'anxieties of empire', other contemporaries – I develop this point with reference to Charles Lamb and his essay 'The South-Sea House' (1820) – sought to contain the civic humanist critique of empire as a conduit of corruption by disputing (or submerging) the mutually constitutive relationship of metropole and colony. It is an obvious point to make that from the time of the Seven Years' War if not before, imaginative explorations of the impact of global affairs on domestic life also addressed the metropolitan implications of overseas expansion and conquest. As I hope to show, a more historically grounded approach to the concept of openness helps to provide new perspectives on the vexed question of Britons' lived relation to empire, as well as on the shifting parameters of the collective imaginary of the East over the course of the period.

Needless to say this imaginary was formed in part at least by the way in which particular historical events, and moments of crisis or rupture, brought specific sites, episodes, and actors into Britons' consciousness. At the same time, however, it is necessary to reiterate that the British imaginary of the East was not simply a function of expansionism and empire, since – whatever they knew about India or anywhere else – Britons were, as Cambridge understood, already possessed of an established set of 'Eastern' reference points, 'through the habits of reading novels, and works of the imagination'. One argument of this book is that while levels of interest in the 'ideal stories' identified by Cambridge remained more or less constant, the history of 'British Orientalisms, 1759–1835' additionally involves the processes by which the familiar fictions of the past were adapted, reworked, and (sometimes) reacted against. As I now demonstrate in more detail, attention to the formal diversity and innovation of this field of literary production richly illuminates the larger cultural conflict which animated a nation debating with itself about its place in the world and relation to its others.

British Orientalisms in an Age of Empire and Revolution

The broad-based and predominantly literary history outlined earlier in this introduction may seem to run counter to the direction taken by some of the best recent scholarship in the area of Orientalism and empire (much of it referred to in this introduction), which has tended to explore more precisely delineated topics. For reasons of space this book cannot claim to provide the same kind of close contextualization and finely grained reading that these studies display, or to engage directly with their arguments; though wide-ranging in coverage, this book has its own omissions too, on which I comment in my chapter outline. Its focus on the – primarily – metropolitan imaginary of the East across a period of seventy-five years does bring several advantages, however. Moving from the late 1750s to the mid-1830s makes it possible to run together periods which are often discretely classified, with accompanying critical baggage, as 'eighteenth century' and 'Romantic'. This time span also forces familiar texts into contact with writings which have so far been little analysed but which are (I argue) of some importance – for example, the picaresque fictions after Thomas Hope's *Anastasius, or Memoirs of a Greek* (1819), which adapted the older figure of the informant narrator and responded to the poetry of Byron, Thomas Moore, and others. Remapping the field of British Orientalisms in such a manner offers further ways of illuminating the dynamics of cultural contestation in the period too, helping to thicken accounts of the influence of scholars such as Jones, or of the reception of the *Arabian Nights* and other 'tales of the East'. Whether in relation to Jones's expression of a will-to-knowledge in his 1784 'Discourse' or to the *Nights'* frame tale of Sultan Schahriar and Princess Scheherazade, the historical range of this study facilitates scrutiny of significant but often neglected processes of rewriting and revision. The discussion that follows begins to develop a fuller sense of the diversity of broadly 'Orientalist' representation across the period, considering the emergence of new forms and styles of writing in the larger context of an age of empire and revolution.

Although at the start of this period numerous works with nominally Eastern settings addressed the domestic ramifications of imperial expansion, it was not until the early to mid-1770s that novels – whether by being set in India or by including Indian episodes – began to acknowledge the increasingly close connection between Britain and Bengal consequent upon the EIC's new sovereignty, and the problems as well as possibilities which this entailed. It is instructive here to juxtapose Charles Johnstone's *The Pilgrim: Or, A Picture of Life* (1775) and Phebe Gibbes's *Hartly House, Calcutta* (1789), both written by authors without direct experience of the subcontinent: whereas *The Pilgrim* features a wandering Chinese narrator who makes a sea voyage to Britain via 'Mogulstan', *Hartly House*, comprising its heroine's letters to a friend in England, closely renders the particulars of its Indian setting, appearing to align itself with a 'Jonesian' scholarly Orientalism. It would be misleading to suggest that fictions 'about' British India straightforwardly became more ethnographically specific, however, since many of these works are both formally uneven and intriguingly diverse in their range of reference, and the realization of India is not always their primary purpose. Two works published in 1782, Robert Bage's sprawling *Mount Henneth* and Helenus Scott's it-narrative *Adventures of a Rupee*, for example, demonstrate the way in which the necessity of responding to the ideological fallout of Britain's disastrous war in America to some extent determined the content of literary Orientalism at this time, as generalizing constructions of 'the East' (which subsumed India) came to provide a means of stabilizing the idea of 'British liberty'.

Even as works such as these manifestly reflected on Britons' sense of themselves more than on the domestic and colonial 'effects of imperial power' (in Hall and Rose's phrase), it remains fair to say that defeat in America helped to sharpen metropolitan scrutiny of the EIC; as Daniel O'Quinn shows so well, popular drama was central to this process of bringing empire home to Britons.[32] The diverse 'Eastern' materials with which poets began to engage at this time – even as they could be understood as 'new' – were not always so directly the product of colonial encounter, however. While the 'discovery' of Hinduism in which Jones participated after arriving in India in 1784 was certainly a source of inspiration for subsequent writers, Jones outlined another extensive domain of literary possibility in the much-cited 'manifesto' calling for greater engagement with 'the principal writings of the Asiaticks' – the conclusion to his 'Essay on the Poetry of the Eastern Nations', appended to *Poems Consisting Chiefly of Translations from the Asiatick Languages* (1772).[33] Southey's *Thalaba* might be regarded as the exemplary Romantic long poem, as Simpson suggests, because the thick cultural reference of its main text and its footnotes at once provides a virtual encounter with 'significant otherness' and demonstrates a response to Jones which at least matches his omnivorous intellectual curiosity.

Described by Marilyn Butler as 'an eclectic historical pastiche', *Thalaba* was partly inspired by a story in the 'pseudo-Oriental' collection of *Arabian Tales* (1792), but also responded to William Beckford's narrative of imperial decadence in an Arabian milieu, *Vathek* (1786).[34] While 'a tale of adventures full of wonder and novelty' in Cambridge's terms, then, *Thalaba* is also clearly rooted in the politics of the present, its verse narrative setting its Muslim hero, an agent of revolution, against forces of luxury, corruption, and superstition. The revolutionary decade of the 1790s constitutes another pivotal moment in the history of British Orientalisms, and *Thalaba* was one of numerous contemporary works which found in 'the East' – whether through the generic tropes of sultan and seraglio or, as Humberto Garcia argues, with more specific reference to Islam and the prophet Mohammed – a congenial medium for reflecting on the condition of Britain itself.[35] What Gerard Cohen-Vrignaud identifies as the 'radical Orientalism' flourishing between Waterloo and the 1832 Reform Act accentuated this alignment of Oriental despotism and Britain's old regime, likewise appealing to the 'function of Otherness . . . as a potent and ambivalent figure through which national publics rehearse and adjudicate their shared and excluded values'.[36]

Against a Saidian conjoining of Orientalism and empire, much recent criticism therefore emphasizes the reflexivity of Romantic-period engagements with the East, especially in works of poetry. Focusing on the distinctive formal and rhetorical procedures of Byron, Percy Shelley, and Keats (all of whom generally eschewed Southey's practice of footnoting source material), Andrew Warren, for example, argues that a poem such as Shelley's *Alastor, or, The Spirit of Solitude* (1816) ironizes the distorting operations of Orientalist discourse as it is defined by Said: in the '*Alastor*-poet's fantasizing, Warren states, 'Orientalism … becomes a kind of turning away from the realities of human life towards an abstraction or ideal'.[37] If *Alastor* does not recuperate any notion of liberatory imaginative transport (of the kind discussed by Ballaster and Aravamudan), it might be seen to constitute a non-dominative literary Orientalism nonetheless, to the extent that it presents its protagonist's quest as only drawing him back to himself – thus interrogating the very foundations of encounter and rendering the idea of openness to the other as 'perpetually fraught' rather than productive of a Jonesian 'delight and advantage'.[38] Frequently echoed in *Alastor*, another canonical poem, Coleridge's 'Kubla Khan' (1816, composed in 1797), comparably demonstrates how Romantic Orientalism often appears to establish a self-contained – intertextual rather than 'referential' – rhetorical economy of its own, at a remove from any direct reckoning with specific forms of cultural difference. 'Kubla Khan' has influentially been read as a work in which 'all realism … about locations and distances falls away', and as an exemplification of Romantic irony, where the poet's attempt to revive his vision of the Abyssinian maid belatedly strives after the transporting experience associated with eighteenth-century fictions of the East.[39]

Even as it evokes a dream landscape and displays a self-consciousness akin to *Alastor*'s, however, 'Kubla Khan', as Deirdre Coleman notes, 'flickers between the literal and the mythical'.[40] Kubla Khan himself was a historical figure, and the poem has latterly been situated as a 'post-Macartney' text, informed by works published in the aftermath of the 1792–4 British diplomatic embassy to China which provided Coleridge and his contemporaries with an awareness of (among other things) the self-fashioning of Emperor Qianlong, who claimed descent from Kubla Khan; this is a poem 'about the garden of a Chinese Emperor', Leask states.[41] The key point here therefore is that even an ostensibly anti-mimetic text such as 'Kubla Khan' can be seen both as embedded in inescapably politicized modes of representation (the idea of the 'Chinese' garden was already freighted, having been identified by William Mason twenty-five

years earlier as an expression of Tory despotism), and as to some extent
made possible by the transmission of new forms of culturally specific
knowledge. For reasons of space I am unable in this book to engage at
length with the place of China in Britain's Eastern imaginary (the subject
of fine recent studies such as Peter J. Kitson's *Forging Romantic China*). It is
useful briefly to consider Coleridge and China here, though, because –
perhaps better than any other writer's – Coleridge's work exemplifies the
diverse contextual connections and creative/political possibilities of
'Orientalism', inclusively conceived: in addition to seizing on the figure
of Kubla Khan, in the 1790s he appealed to the example of the prophet
Mohammed as a reforming legislator, and was drawn to the overlap
between the Hindu concept of an essential 'oneness' (as mediated by
scholars including Jones) and the Unitarian doctrine of 'one life'.[42]
As I show now, it is further instructive to refer to Coleridge because even
as his writings can be seen directly and indirectly to engage with contemporary scholarship and travel writing, and with the politics of the present,
in the 1790s and after he also associated the East with the seemingly
timeless and apolitical realm of pleasing fiction too.

'The Araby and Persia of Books'

Coleridge claimed that he 'became a dreamer' after his father burnt his
copy of the *Arabian Nights* to put an end to his reading of the tales, and he
later celebrated the 'pure imagination' evident in its story of a bewildered
merchant charged by a genie with having casually discarded a date shell
which put out the eye of his son; just as this tale's appeal for Coleridge had
to do with its staging of an abstract idea, the apparently arbitrary logic of
cause and effect, so Coleridge's 1816 revision of 'Kubla Khan' signalled an
effort to 'universalize' the meaning of his own work, now framed as an
opium-tinged curiosity and detached from its earlier allegorical
resonance.[43] If, as Ballaster argues, a generalized notion of the East could
be understood as 'a (sometimes *the*) source of story' in the eighteenth
century, Coleridge's example suggests that such an understanding
extended into the Romantic period and beyond, and that the 'East' in
question could be regarded as a space that was more or less insulated from
any encroachment of the realities of Eastern empire. While one story to tell
about British Orientalisms in the period covered by this study concerns the
emergence of new forms of writing that were essentially responsive, to
political crisis and/or cultural stimuli (which could include other literary
works), another is that the presence in British culture of the 'works of the

imagination' referred to by Cambridge in 1761, at the time of his own virtual encounter with India, remained enduring and ubiquitous. Many others besides Coleridge recalled their early experiences of the *Nights*, and Henry Weber's testimonial, in his introduction to *Tales of the East* (1812), describes a kind of shared literary memory, and a process of internalization by which the *Nights*' tales especially may almost have become so familiar as to cease to astonish: 'there are few who do not recollect with pleasure … the golden dreams of happiness and splendour which the fairy palaces and exhaustless treasures of the east presented to their imagination.'[44] Marina Warner's history of 'charmed states and the *Arabian Nights*' emphasizes above all the universality of the *Nights*' appeal, founded on the basic truth that '*Homo narrans* observes no ethnic divisions.'[45]

While Warner remains primarily interested in the *Nights* because of the manifold and – in their own right – brilliant kinds of 'magical thinking' that the collection inspired, however, she also identifies the 'disavowal' of such transformative potential as a cultural counter-current. If, from the eighteenth century to the present, the *Nights*' diverse tales have most often been read as 'laying open infinite possibilities of fantastic invention and fabrication', Warner argues, they have also sometimes been taken to 'reveal the Orient' and to 'represent the customs, beliefs, and passions actually held and experienced in the countries where the stories are set'; some of the tales indeed tend as much to social realism as to fabulous Orientalism.[46] With this point about the potential 'referentiality' of tales in the *Nights* and elsewhere in mind, I want now to return to my earlier claim about the way in which familiar stories were adapted, reworked, and reacted against over the period under discussion. It is useful again in this context to attend to three particular moments in British culture – the period during and after the war in America, the revolutionary decade of the 1790s, and the post-1815 years which saw a renewal of radical attacks on the repressive government personified by the Prince Regent.

While 'Eastern' fictions, whatever their actual origin, were widely associated with a realm of enchantment and wonder throughout our period, from around the late 1770s onwards they began to be viewed by some as collectively offering a misleadingly benign impression of life in the East, particularly where relations between the sexes were concerned. Around this time too similarly unspecified tales and romances conversely came to be credited with evidential value, as they were seen to circulate already established truths, again most often regarding the condition of women, with a recurrent slippage between supposedly 'Muslim' and more broadly 'Eastern' customs and manners. The editor of *Arabian Tales*, Robert

Heron, for example, stated that its stories displayed the 'strange and singular' spectacle of 'Beauties, cooped up together . . . in a Haram, all for the amusement of one man' (though a man 'fitter to repose in the grave or the hospital, than to riot on the nuptial couch').[47] This kind of sceptical detachment further took the form of a creative revisionism which, especially in popular drama, rewrote the *Nights'* frame tale by transferring the free-speaking Scheherazade's reformist agency to British women, while depicting as culturally typical the vengeance-seeking Sultan Schahriar's 'fatal prejudice'.[48] From the mid-1770s to the 1790s at least, numerous different works, invariably in comic terms, staged the confrontation between free-born Britons, or their proxies, and (usually) 'Turkish' despots – the latter shocked by, though also sometimes finally receptive to, audacious challenges to their authority.

The fixation on harems and seraglios in these decades may be read as a function of what Christopher Leslie Brown refers to, in his persuasive account of the origins of the abolitionist movement, as 'the crisis of liberty that made its vindication necessary'.[49] Certainly in the 1780s the cultural work performed by seraglio discourse probably had less to do with legitimizing empire than with negotiating the loss of empire: in other words, if 'British liberty' was antithetical to Oriental despotism then it could be understood as possessed of a stable meaning, and therefore as uncompromised by defeat at the hands of American colonists who had fought to free themselves from British tyranny. The rhetoric of Oriental despotism was highly mobile too, however, and as Makdisi argues, reformers in the 1790s identified the seraglio as the 'ideal surrogate target' for domestic critique. More directly than the Orientalized versions of 'old corruption' depicted by Coleridge and Southey, the seraglio provided, in Makdisi's words, 'an imaginary space on which to project all the supposed faults of the old regime, and then subject them to attack'.[50] As already noted, reformist writers of the 1810s and 1820s in turn exploited the potential of such 'radical Orientalism' in attacks upon a despotic state and alien ruling class.

As I show in what follows, the literary Orientalisms of the 1810s and 1820s exemplify especially well the cultural conflict which is a major concern of this book. While contemporaries were characterizing modern Britain as an 'Eastern' despotism, Thomas Moore's *Lalla Rookh* (1817), steeped in the Regency culture symbolized by the Royal Pavilion at Brighton, was enjoying great commercial success. Its two longest constituent tales are allegorically resonant, like Southey's epics, and the poem as a whole is clearly rooted in the scholarly Orientalism of Jones and others. All the same, what reviewers recognized as the luxurious and splendidly 'ornamental' idiom of Moore's verse meant that *Lalla Rookh* could be seen to provide 'poetical "Arabian Nights' Entertainments"', and, in an echo of Weber's introduction to *Tales of the East,* 'a renewal of the delicious moments of our childhood, when we first read those wondrous and golden tales'.[51] Moore's pastiche of such tales was so popular partly because of the way in which it supplied its audience with familiar and undemanding pleasures – recall again Cambridge's point about the '*habits* of reading novels, and works of the imagination' (my emphasis) – rather than any more challenging encounter with 'significant otherness'. Although Leigh Hunt deployed a 'radical Orientalist' idiom in his satirical representation of the Prince Regent in the early 1810s (as Moore did too), he subsequently offered a Cockney inflection of *Lalla Rookh*-style exoticism in some of his poetry, while drawing attention to his own fondness for, in Aravamudan's phrase, 'dreaming with the Orient'.

The great popularity of *Lalla Rookh* and Hunt's carefree appeal to a 'gorgeous East' emphasize the enduring presence of 'fabulous Orients' in the British imaginary, even as Britain continued to extend its worldly interests in Asia and elsewhere.[52] Situating this apparent recuperation of romance within a larger cultural context, however, also reveals that *Lalla Rookh* generated a considerable amount of critical hostility, because of its apparent occlusion of the 'real' East: if Moore's work could be seen by its admirers as repackaging past pleasures for the present, others understood it as mired in wilful delusion, pitting its 'Asiatic' idiom against the mundane actuality of which it appeared wilfully ignorant. Towards the end of the period under discussion in this book, it is arguable indeed that the new style of self-consciously corrective fiction initiated by Hope's *Anastasius* became the dominant mode of representing the East. Novels such as James Morier's *The Adventures of Hajji Baba* (1824) and William Browne Hockley's *Pandurang Hari, or Memoirs of a Hindoo* (1826) were written by men with first-hand experience of travel, and sometimes diplomacy and colonial administration, but the 'knowledge' that they transmitted had more to do with a quasi-racialized notion of Oriental 'character' than with cultural difference. To the extent that they focus on 'character' rather than 'culture', these works help us now to recognize at once the changing contours of the Orientalist imaginary and a larger shift in Britons' under-standing of themselves in relation to their others over the course of our period. Since, as fictionalized autobiographies, they can be seen to adapt an older tradition of informant narrative associated with Oliver Goldsmith or Elizabeth Hamilton, they additionally invite us to think about the episte-mological and ideological functions of literary form, and the formal dimension of the cultural conflict which is one of the organizing threads of this study.

If such works bear out Uday Singh Mehta's argument that 'the imperial gaze is never really surprised by the stranger,' however, they introduce us to protagonists who sometimes appear to be incorrigibly roguish, and thus impervious to 'improvement'.[53] These protagonists are seldom presented as being beyond sympathy, but the fictions in which they appear offer their readers a position of superiority that is also a position of detachment and distance from the milieu described. Using literary history as a lens on the question raised earlier about Britons' lived relation to empire, it seems fair to say that by the end of our period, as the picaresque novels of the 1820s and after attest, any connection of the kind broached by Cambridge in 1761 between the extension of British material interests and an accompanying expansion of Britons' cultural horizons had long since been severed. One necessary caveat to this point is that the varying reception of these picaresque fictions demonstrates areas of difference as well as overlap between metropolitan and colonial literary culture, as I show later in this volume. The case of Leigh Hunt meanwhile suggests that while it was certainly possible for some to carry on 'dreaming with the Orient', their readerly pleasure may have become divorced from any aspiration to cross-cultural understanding of the kind which Aravamudan locates in an earlier 'Enlightenment Orientalism'. Hunt declared his great enthusiasm for the *Nights*, in particular, but he distinguished between 'the Araby and Persia of books' and 'the Araby and Persia of the geographer, dull to the dull, and governed by the foolish'.[54] The idea of openness to the other to some extent remains in play here, but it is exercised in a private reading space rather than a contact zone of virtual encounter, and it thus appears to be separated from social reality and ethical responsibility altogether.

Plan of the Book

My opening chapter examines in more detail the cultural significance of the Seven Years' War, focusing especially on works by Samuel Johnson, Oliver Goldsmith, and James Ridley which employ current modes of literary Orientalism – respectively the Oriental tale (*Rasselas* [1759]), the informant narrative (*The Citizen of the World* [1762]), and the story sequence (*Tales of the Genii* [1764]) – in order to assess the domestic consequences of national extroversion. I consider Johnson and Goldsmith because they are two of the most influential writers of the period, and because their works display numerous common concerns, not least regarding the difficulty in such a climate of establishing a stable position from which cultural commentary might be offered; I look at Ridley because his *Tales of the Genii* alludes to recent conflict in India and may be the first work to acknowledge Britain's empire in the East in purportedly 'Eastern' narrative. For all three writers the greater openness of Britain to the world resulting from the Seven Years' War is troubling at an abstract level rather than because of the challenge posed by the substance of otherness as such. At the same time, however, as I argue, works by these writers all demonstrate a fascination with the idea of Britons' 'impatience', conceding the impotence of critique in the face of the nation's seemingly inexorable expansionism.

Where the works addressed in the first chapter are for the most part non-referential, Chapter 2 begins by looking at Charles Johnstone's *The Pilgrim* (1775) as the prototype of a hybrid form of fiction more directly exploring Britain's newly formalized relationship with Bengal. The works I examine here are generically uneven in part because, like Robert Bage's *Mount Henneth* (1782), they combine an anti-nabob discourse which sees Britain's Indian empire as domestically corrupting with a vision of a commercial empire where openness to the East is productive both of economic opportunity and of ideological compensation for the nation's loss of its American colonies. The chapter concludes with a discussion of Phebe Gibbes's *Hartly House, Calcutta* (1789), since it was praised by some reviewers for the accuracy and quality of the local 'information' it provided, and may indeed have captured a high point of metropolitan curiosity about life on the ground in the EIC's foremost settlement. The main focus of this chapter, however, is the contemporary sense of the difficulty of bringing home (in Edmund Burke's phrase) 'Indian details' to readers in Britain.[55] Rather than look closely at Burke's much-discussed role in the impeachment of Warren Hastings, I examine, in addition to prose fiction, works such as Hugh Mulligan's poem 'The Virgins' and Mariana Starke's play *The Sword of Peace* (1788) which differently stage the epistemological and ethical issues accompanying any effort to familiarize the public with goings-on in a distant land.

Chapter 3 is organized around a received idea rather than a historical period or geographical location, and it explores how, coterminous with Burke's project to extend Britons' sympathies, a fixed sense of women's oppression across 'Asia' gained cultural traction. I return to the claim made earlier in this introduction about the responsiveness to political crisis of generalizing representations of 'the East', and I consider how, across diverse forms of writing (including literary-historical accounts of the

Arabian Nights and other Eastern fictions), seraglio discourse enabled Britons to conceive of an exceptional heritage of freedom that was still untainted despite defeat in America. This chapter provides my fullest engagement with popular theatre, and it examines the way in which, in plays reworking the *Nights'* frame tale of Schahriar and Scheherazade, the seraglio could offer a way of reflecting not only on a broadly consensual idea of British (sometimes specifically 'English') liberty but also on domestic relations of class and gender. In the 1790s, I show, this fault line in Britons' Orientalist imaginary was exposed, with numerous reformist writers identifying 'Eastern manners' as characteristic of a corrupt ruling class. After discussing the ideological mobility of fictionalized Easts in the 1790s, I conclude by reading Elizabeth Hamilton's *Letters of a Hindoo Rajah* (1796) as a work which, in its retrospect on the function of the rhetoric of sexual despotism over the previous three decades, puts pressure on the notion of a distinctly British moral virtue that it initially appears to establish.

My fourth chapter is organized around an individual, and it focuses on Sir William Jones because of the importance of his diverse work both to the process by which metropolitan Britons were confronted with 'significant otherness' and to recent critical narratives, which have returned to Schwab's *Oriental Renaissance*, about the scale and impact of that process. It situates Jones alongside his contemporaries in order to consider the relative lack of concern he displayed about the ethics of importing 'literary treasure' from India, the distinctive character of his exploration of Hindu devotional subjectivity, and the way in which, as in 'A Hymn to Ganga' (1785), his construction of mythological tradition sometimes occluded the colonial violence and native suffering registered by other writers. The emphasis of this chapter is on the plural 'Joneses' that are evident in the variety of his work and in the different contexts of its reception. The case of Jones exemplifies especially well the cultural conflict referred to earlier in this introduction, as I show, since while many poets creatively responded to his mediation of Hinduism, after his death obituarists tried to contain the implications of the comparisons that he drew between Hindu and other mythologies. Sydney Owenson's novel *The Missionary* (1811) provides a fitting conclusion because in its portrayal of its title character it at once pays tribute to an implicitly Jonesian principle of openness to the other and interrogates the purchase of exemplary individual qualities of sympathy and tolerance in a hostile environment.

Chapter 5 begins by considering Robert Southey as a poet who was inspired by, and sought to outdo, Jones. It takes Southey's *Thalaba* as a starting point because of its notable idiosyncrasy as an allegorically resonant work which displaces Southey's radicalism of the 1790s, confronts readers with the heterogeneous detail of its voluminous footnotes, and displays its conflicted relation to Orientalist poetic 'ornament'. I read Southey's *Roderick, the Last of the Goths* (1814) as a rewriting of *Thalaba* which re-familiarizes the verse form which Southey helped to establish, and which, by adopting the rhetoric of holy war, responds to Byron's *The Giaour* (1813) – albeit that it further stages 'anxieties of empire' which converge with those of Byron and others. Byron and/or Shelley and Mary Shelley could productively be brought into dialogue with Southey here, but I focus primarily on Thomas Moore alongside Southey instead, because his *Lalla Rookh* offers 'samples of the finest Orientalism' (in the phrase of Byron's *Beppo* [1818]) that are detached from any residual civic humanist perspective on the corrupting effects of Asiatic luxury.[56] *Lalla Rookh*'s longest constituent tales remain in the allegorical tradition of Southeyan Romantic Orientalism, with an obvious application to contemporary Ireland, but 'The Fire-Worshippers' strikingly combines allegory and ornament in a tale of colonial resistance which evokes, without distancing strategies, a dazzling, sensuous Orient. Moore's final tale, 'The Light of the Haram', more emphatically constructs an 'ideal' realm of romance; Francis Jeffrey regarded its 'excessive finery' as its greatest fault, yet conceded that such excess was not mere 'vulgar ostentation' but 'the extravagance of excessive wealth'.[57]

This claim about *Lalla Rookh*'s seemingly 'authentic' magnificence is the starting point for Chapter 6, which focuses on what I term the 'Cockney Orientalism' of Leigh Hunt and Charles Lamb (regrettably, there is no space to discuss Keats in any detail alongside them). Although Hunt in the 1810s participated in the 'radical Orientalist' critique of the Prince Regent, I am especially interested here in the ways in which he also exoticized a fabulous Orient in a manner that was self-consciously second-hand, and sometimes derivative of Moore's work. While Hunt often performed his own outward-looking openness to the East, I argue, his benign cosmopolitanism is best characterized by its insouciant facility of reference rather than by any reckoning with the substance of cultural difference, and it is tellingly unable to incorporate China (which, for Hunt, was not part of the 'gorgeous East').

My discussion of Lamb offers this book's closest engagement with the place of China in British imaginings of 'the East' in our period. The fantastical reverie of Lamb's Elia essay 'Old China' (1823) may be read as a Cockney parody of De Quincey's opium nightmares, but

elsewhere in his writings, I argue, Lamb often less genially parades his lack
of knowledge of the wider world. Lamb is an important figure for this
study – a kind of Cockney Jones, perhaps – because of the oblique way in
which his work explores the relationship between the material interests that
he served (as a 'writer' for the EIC) and his own imaginative horizons: even
as Lamb's letters sometimes present his employment at India House as if it
were a form of colonial subjection, his suggestive notion of the EIC's
'unseen' workings, alluded to in 'The South-Sea House', stages a new
metropolitan apprehension of an arm's-length relationship between
Britain and its expanding Eastern empire.

My final chapter examines a subgenre of fictionalized autobiographies
which revise an older mode of informant narrative and additionally define
themselves against both the scholarly example of Jones and the literary
practice of Moore, and it thus underscores the centrality of cultural conflict
to my remapping of the literary history of British Orientalisms.
In a tradition inaugurated by Thomas Hope's *Anastasius* (1819), works
such as James Morier's *Adventures of Haji Baba* (1824) signal enduring
affiliations to the *Arabian Nights* but also offer avowedly revisionist perspectives on the nature of a homogenized 'East' and the character of
a typified 'Asiatic'. Novels such as William Browne Hockley's *Pandurang
Hari* (1826), the first such work narrated by an Indian protagonist, were
sometimes rejected by metropolitan readers for offering overdrawn caricature, and the possibilities of literary Orientalism remained diverse in the
1820s and after; I briefly consider the relationship between works by
Morier, James Baillie Fraser, and Sir Walter Scott, and Scott's *Tales of
the Crusaders* – especially *The Talisman* (1825) – and Mary Shelley's
narrative of contagion *The Last Man* (1825) would reward attention alongside the picaresque fictions I discuss. I concentrate on the latter works,
however, both because they remain relatively little known and because
a strong case can be made for their significance: certainly if the approving
reactions of later readers are anything to go by, these new and professedly
experience-based tales of the East exerted a considerable cultural impact.

In my conclusion I consider T. B. Macaulay's retrospect on the history
of Britain's empire in the East since the Seven Years' War, and I return to
the previous point about how his 'Minute on Indian Education' (1835)
appears to mark a decisive shift away from the reflexive self-criticism
displayed by many of the works addressed in this book from *Rasselas*
onwards. I also seek to complicate any notion of the ascendancy of an
ideology of empire-as-improvement at this time, however, in particular by
acknowledging that improvement was a contested concept (and that the

colonial subjects who are largely silent in this book sought to define it on their own terms), and by returning to Leigh Hunt's account of his attachment to the 'gorgeous East' as 'the magic land of the child'.[58] Hunt's celebration of readerly pleasure appears to demonstrate the imaginary self-projection discussed by Ballaster and Aravamudan, but if such pleasure may carry a dissident charge, the very benignity of Hunt's sympathetic imaginings invites us to think about the content of his self-declared openness to the East – a space happily disentangled from the domain of British material interests which Richard Owen Cambridge had sought to introduce to his readers seventy-five years earlier.

Notes

1. Cambridge, *Account of the War*, preface, iv.
2. Ibid., v.
3. Ibid., introduction, iv.
4. Ibid., n.p.
5. Ballaster, *Fabulous Orients*, 17.
6. Ibid., 8.
7. Aravamudan, *Enlightenment Orientalism*, 4.
8. Ibid., 3.
9. Ibid., 8 and 11.
10. Jones, 'Discourse', 3.
11. Ibid., 4.
12. Ibid., 10 and 8.
13. Chakrabarty, *Provincializing Europe*; Jones, 'Discourse', 6.
14. Schwab, *Renaissance*, 17, 11, and 18.
15. Simpson, 'Limits of Cosmopolitanism', 148.
16. Ibid., 150.
17. Leask, *British Romantic Writers*, 8 and 10.
18. Simpson, *Stranger*, 15.
19. Kaul, *Eighteenth-Century British Literature*, 79.
20. Ibid., 34, n. 53.
21. Fulford, 'Poetic Flowers', 123.
22. Franklin, *Orientalist Jones*, 360.
23. Cox, 'Cockney Cosmopolitanism', 250.
24. Porter, 'Sinicizing Early Modernity', 305; Simpson, 'Limits of Cosmopolitanism', 148.
25. Belcher, *Abyssinia's Johnson*.
26. For example, Porter, *Chinese Taste*.
27. Ogborn, *Global Lives*.
28. White, *Little London*, 139.
29. Hall and Rose, eds., *At Home*, 1.

30. Leask, 'Romanticism', 272.
31. Makdisi, *Making England Western*.
32. O'Quinn, *Staging Governance*.
33. Jones, *Poems*, 336.
34. Butler, 'Orientalism', 413.
35. Garcia, *Islam*.
36. Cohen-Vrignaud, *Radical Orientalism*, 217.
37. Warren, *Young Romantics*, 139–40.
38. Ibid., 132.
39. Elinor Shaffer, cited in Coleman, 'Coleridge', 39.
40. Ibid., 39.
41. Leask, 'Kubla Khan', 7.
42. Garcia, *Islam*.
43. To Thomas Poole, 9 Oct. 1797, *Letters*, 1:347; *Table Talk*, 1:272–3; Fulford, 'Coleridge', 216–21.
44. Weber, *Tales of the East*, 1:i.
45. Warner, *Stranger Magic*, 8.
46. Ibid., 23–4.
47. *Arabian Tales*, 1:ix.
48. *Arabian Nights*, 892.
49. Brown, *Moral Capital*, 27.
50. Makdisi, *Blake*, 206.
51. *Asiatic Journal*, 4 (1817), 457.
52. *London Journal*, 1 (1834), 233.
53. Mehta, *Liberalism*, 31.
54. *London Journal*, 1 (1834), 233.
55. Burke, 'Speech on Fox's India Bill', *Writings and Speeches*, 5:404.
56. Warren, *Young Romantics*, 95–173, 185–230; Byron, *Complete Poetical Works* (hereafter *CPW*), 4:145, l.408.
57. *Edinburgh Review*, 57 (1817), 33.
58. *London Journal*, 1 (1834), 233.

CHAPTER I

'Those Islanders'
British Orientalisms and the Seven Years' War

Kathleen Wilson has argued that if the loss of Minorca in 1756 constituted 'the symbolic emasculation of the British nation', then later military successes across the globe were widely regarded as manifesting a true Britishness that was independent, incorruptible, and able to impose itself on the world wherever and whenever it chose.[1] As others have emphasized, however, the scale of British territorial acquisition additionally raised new problems of authority and governance, in relation to India as well as to North America, and colonial conquest was attended by anxiety that the growth of empire might trouble the integrity of the state and the meaning of home and belonging.[2] From the Treaty of Paris to the American Revolution, Britons were, in Linda Colley's words, 'captivated by, but also adrift and at odds in a vast empire abroad and a new political world at home which few ... properly understood'.[3] The enthusiastic popular response to events such as the taking of Quebec in 1759, the 'year of victories', may therefore be interpreted as evidence of an 'imperialist sensibility', but for many it was impossible to dissociate such rejoicing from consideration of the longer-term implications of Britain's new status as a global superpower.[4] Thomas Gray wrote in August 1759 that '[t]he season for triumph is at last come,' but in October of the same year he queried as to whether the nation 'will ... know how to behave itself, being just in the circumstances of a Chambermaid, that has got the 20,000£ Prize in the Lottery'.[5]

Gray's suggestion that the national experience of sudden and unexpected good fortune generated a collective intoxication – followed by, at least among some, sober reflection – provides a useful starting point for this chapter, which is organized around an exploration of the cultural climate of the Seven Years' War, and specifically Britons' engagement with the extension of their horizons during and immediately after the conflict. The main texts discussed here have been chosen because they use the then current forms of literary Orientalism, broadly defined (the Oriental tale, the informant narrative, and the story sequence), and also because in their efforts to make sense of the momentousness of the present they display common concerns. I begin by looking at Samuel Johnson's *Rasselas* (1759), which through its treatment of its title character's bewildered experience of the world outside the Happy Valley allegorizes the problem of dominion referred to earlier. In the light of Johnson's analysis of human restlessness, I then address the representation of mobility in Oliver Goldsmith's work, especially *The Citizen of the World* (1762), before discussing Goldsmith's fascination with what he took to be the distinctively English quality of 'impatience under restraint'.[6] Goldsmith's double-edged reference to Britons as 'lords of human kind' is echoed in James Ridley's *Tales of the Genii* (1764), and I conclude by considering Ridley as perhaps the first writer to acknowledge Eastern empire in 'Eastern' narrative – albeit that his East largely remained a composite domain and India still occupied a relatively marginal position in Britons' imagination of the wider world.[7]

Ridley elsewhere asked whether posterity would consider his contemporaries 'wise or foolish', and this appeal to futurity exemplifies the striving for a stable position of critical objectivity that is evident in all three authors' work.[8] As is suggested by Ridley's question as well as by the title quotation from Goldsmith's *The Citizen of the World*, the texts under discussion here are more interested in national character or the general predicament of the nation, increasingly entangled with the rest of the world, than in any particular aspect of the otherness to which Britain had become exposed. The fictional Chinese traveller who narrates *The Citizen of the World* is eccentric but benign, and rather than embody any kind of imagined threat, his function is, partly at least, to offer a detached perspective on Britons' sense of their own exceptionalism. Lien Chi Altangi says of the British that '[l]iberty is echoed in all their assemblies ... though perhaps not one of all the number understands its meaning,' and the potential difficulty – even danger – that imperial authority posed for a liberty-loving people is a recurrent concern in British culture until the mid-1780s at least.[9] Even as such self-analysis is a feature of works by Johnson, Goldsmith, and Ridley, however, these works all variously display a reflexive awareness of the impotence of critique in the face of the energies that they anatomize. As I argue in what follows, one reason why Ridley found it impossible to determine whether his countrymen were 'wise or foolish' – explaining why, in his work and others', critique is often undercut – is that while territorial empire was widely recognized as compromising national autonomy and independence, it could also be understood as instantiating a peculiar British instinct for enterprise and daring.

'A Sea Foaming with Tempests'

In his writings prior to *Rasselas* Johnson often combined a focus on human nature in the abstract with an expansive field of geographical reference. In his poem 'The Vanity of Human Wishes' (1749) Johnson invoked a universal human condition, surveying 'the busy scenes of crowded life' across the earth ('from China to Peru'), along with particular instances of the defeat of 'wavering man, betrayed by venturous pride'.[10] Johnson's experimentation with the established mode of the Oriental tale or 'apologue', popularized by *The Spectator* (1711–14), allowed him to explore similarly general thematic concerns. Numbers 204 and 205 of *The Rambler* (1752), for example, tell the story of Seged, 'Lord of Ethiopia', who, once established as 'the monarch of forty nations', decides to devote himself to the pursuit of pleasure, imagining what it might be 'to ... live without a wish unsatisfied'. Beset by a series of calamities culminating in his daughter's death, Seged comes to appreciate 'the uncertainty of human schemes', telling his story to future generations 'that no man ... may presume to say, "this day shall be a day of happiness".[11]

Like Seged's narrative, *Rasselas* appears to investigate the human condition, offering an essentially composite Eastern setting and retaining its predecessor's moral seriousness and stylistic austerity.[12] If *Rasselas* is in some ways an extended version of this 'Ethiopian' tale, however, it also interrogates the process of enquiry itself, insistently returning to the question of how, if at all, properly comprehensive forms of knowledge might be acquired.[13] Unlike Seged, Rasselas is from the outset dissatisfied with a life of pleasure, and fired with the ardour to '[do] something, though he knew not yet with distinctness, either end or means'.[14] This ambition occupies the prince in a state of 'visionary bustle' (18), rendering him susceptible to the fantasy of flight proffered by an aviation enthusiast who promises both a means of escape from the Happy Valley and an aerial survey affording an Olympian vision of the earth and its people. This episode at once invokes and undercuts the idea of an elevated prospect view, since the mechanical artist's attempt to fly succeeds only in plunging him into a lake. Rasselas's first experiences of life outside the valley provide a further ironic perspective on his dual quest for knowledge of the world and meaningful activity, since while he is fascinated with the social diversity that he encounters, he expects to be able to stand apart from the activity he witnesses, and to maintain his royal privilege.

Johnson's work emphasizes that the condition of retirement forced upon Rasselas by his upbringing is productive of naïvety rather than disinterestedness: on being told by the poet Imlac, his 'director in the *choice of life*', that even the most vigilant sovereign 'can never know all the crimes that are committed, and can seldom punish all that he knows' (32), the prince is simply uncomprehending. Even as their relationship is essentially that of teacher and pupil, however, Imlac as much as Rasselas is made to confront the limits of his knowledge. While they are still in the Happy Valley, Rasselas assumes that since he is able to find new things 'within the circuit of these mountains', his tutor must inevitably have 'left much unobserved' on his previous travels, prompting Imlac to define the poet's role as examining 'general and transcendental truths' that concern the species rather than the individual (43). Imlac goes on to explain, though, that if a poet 'must write … as a being superior to time and place', such a position is only available to one who is already well acquainted with 'variety in life' (35). For all that Imlac stresses the extensiveness of his own experience, therefore, he also recognizes that there can be no end to what poets need to know. After Rasselas concludes from what he has heard that 'no human being can ever be a poet,' Imlac summarizes in Johnsonian terms that the business of a poet is 'indeed very difficult' (46).

Imlac often rehearses the wariness about the imagination that is famously evident in Johnson's *Rambler* 4 (1750), which states that prose fiction's true province is 'to bring about natural events by easy means, and to keep up curiosity without the help of wonder'.[15] This rejection of 'wonder' clearly informs Johnson's subsequent authorial practice, since he distinguishes his own variant of the Oriental tale from *Arabian Nights*-style extravagance and improbability. While Imlac stresses that poets face the all-but-impossible task of attending to both the particular and the general, he makes a point of principle out of not trying to describe 'what I had not seen' (41). *Rasselas* begins with a narratorial caution about fiction's capacity to seduce, and Imlac warns his pupil against 'the power of fiction', said to exert its 'despotick' (152) influence over people, like the prince, whose minds are not sufficiently occupied. In keeping with this suspicion of 'the whispers of fancy' (7), *Rasselas* makes little concession to Orientalist exoticism, such that when Nekayah's maid, Pekuah, is kidnapped by a harem-keeping Arab chieftain, she presents her captor as suffering from 'intellectual famine' (140) and above all else craving stimulating conversation.

Some contemporaries complained that Johnson deceived his readers, arguing that *Rasselas*'s 'garb' did not live up to the billing of its full title, and that the insight that it provided into the human condition might have been acquired 'without going to Ethiopia'.[16] In his reading of a *Rasselas* for the present, by contrast, Clement Hawes suggests that the tale's lack of 'local colour' should be seen as signalling Johnson's recognition of an essential human sameness.[17] The terms of Macaulay's later attack on *Rasselas* seemingly bear out this point, since Macaulay was affronted by the way in which Johnson made the prince and Imlac into 'philosophers as eloquent and enlightened as himself or his friend Burke', when real Abyssinians would have been the 'filthy savages' described by the Scottish explorer James Bruce.[18] At the same time that it presents modern Abyssinians as rational and intelligent, *Rasselas* identifies ancient Egypt, 'where the sciences first dawned' (111), as the fount of world civilization. Owing partly at least to his connection to a tradition of 'Ethiopian thought' (Johnson's first publication was a translation of Jeronimo Lobo's *Voyage to Abyssinia*), his work at times unsettles a normative Eurocentrism, as in its opening reference to the Nile as 'the Father of waters' (7), or in Imlac's description of the pyramids as 'the greatest work of man, except the wall of China' (117).[19]

Johnson's treatment of Egypt is not straightforward, however, since while Imlac claims that the pyramids shame 'European magnificence' (111), he cites them as evidence both of the general vanity of human wishes and of the particular 'folly' (119) of men sated with dominion. A passage such as this exemplifies *Rasselas*'s combination of the Oriental tale's abstract ethical focus with an attention to historical questions concerning human civilization, global commerce, and the rise and fall of empire. Earlier, Imlac speaks of having encountered the present-day bearers of 'all power and all knowledge', in the form of people from 'the northern and western nations of Europe … whose armies are irresistible, and whose fleets command the remotest parts of the globe' (46). In response to Rasselas's naïve question about whether 'Asiaticks and Africans' could turn the tables on Europeans and 'invade their coasts, plant colonies in their ports, and give laws to their natural princes', Imlac tells him that Europeans are 'more powerful … because they are wiser', although 'why their knowledge is more than ours, I know not what reason can be given, but the unsearchable will of the Supreme Being' (46–7). This ambiguous reference to the uneven development of the regions of the world is interpreted by Hawes as further evidence of Johnson's rejection of any kind of racially determinist explanation of human inequality, while for Nicholas

Hudson, Imlac's acknowledgement of European superiority provides a resonantly 'providential' account of the incipient process of British imperial expansion.[20]

That Imlac's discussion of the global distribution of power has generated such divergent readings testifies to the work's at once complex and oblique engagement with its historical moment. '[T]o judge rightly of the present we must oppose it to the past' (112), Imlac tells the prince, and in passages such as this *Rasselas* broaches an ambitious enquiry into the beginnings of European colonialism and the origins of Britain's latest conflict with France. Johnson initiated this enquiry in essays that he wrote for the *Literary Magazine* in 1756, and in his 'Introduction to the Political State of Great Britain' and 'Observations on the Present State of Affairs' he traced 'the present system of English politics' back to the reign of Elizabeth, during which America first became 'the great scene of European ambition'.[21] These essays emphasize the illegitimacy of the seizure of 'distant dominions' that began in the sixteenth century, and they also at times consider how indigenous peoples might themselves see the current quarrel between Britain and France, a struggle between 'two robbers for the spoils of a passenger', in which the true interest of 'Indians' is that 'both should be destroyed'.[22] *Rasselas* makes no direct reference to this conflict, in striking contrast to Voltaire's *Candide* (published just before Johnson's tale, and often regarded as a companion to it), which famously cites the fate of Admiral Byng, executed '[b]ecause he didn't kill enough people', as an index of the war's 'madness'.[23] Instead, in his account of the debate between Imlac and the prince about the uneven distribution of power and knowledge, Johnson sought to rise still further above contemporary politics than Voltaire. In doing so he upheld Imlac's definition of the proper role of the poet – namely, 'presiding over the thoughts and manners of future generations; as a being superiour to time and place' (45) – in order better to apprehend the world-historical processes of which the war was a product.

Johnson's engagement with the present in *Rasselas* can additionally be illuminated by situating the work in relation to his essays of the late 1750s. In *Idler* 30 (1758), for example, Johnson justified not writing more about the war, styling himself as an impartial seeker after truth rather than a patriotic purveyor of 'news' about battles 'in which we and our friends . . . did all, and our enemies did nothing'.[24] If Johnson attempted to counter the journalistic manipulation of the public, however, his war-time writings shift between emphasizing the conflict's morally dubious origins and demonstrating a more worldly understanding of the interests at stake in it. What complicates any account of Johnson as an anti-imperialist is that he saw the French settlement of lands to the east of Britain's Atlantic colonies as a provocation which, he claimed, 'at length forced' the country into war.[25] As Hudson argues, a further index of Johnson's attention to 'realpolitik' is that his 1756 essays present British traders' mistreatment of native peoples as a strategic error as much as a moral injustice, making it harder to forge the local alliances from which the French appeared to be gaining, at Britain's expense.[26]

In *Idler* 81 (1759), published just after victory at Quebec, Johnson developed his earlier attempt to ventriloquize a 'native' perspective on the war in North America, amplifying his 1756 'Observations' with the statement that, since the British and the French were 'the sons of rapacity', indigenous peoples should 'look unconcerned' upon their mutual slaughter, as 'the death of every European delivers the country from a tyrant and a robber.'[27] Goldsmith in turn borrowed from *Idler* 81 in *The Citizen of the World* (1762), emphasizing the cost of war for Britain as well as for the 'savages of Canada'.[28] Johnson appears to have been more equivocal in his analysis than this, however, for among the grievances articulated by the 'chief' in *Idler* 81 is that, in addition to offering treaties 'only to deceive' and seeking to trade 'only to defraud', Europeans had 'studiously concealed' their arts and failed to communicate their 'written law'.[29] For Hudson, the narrator's profession of interest in the Christian gospel is informed by a vision of 'a better colonial relationship'.[30] The chief nonetheless also states that Europeans do not preach Christianity to 'Indians', as they know that their actions violate its precepts, and he concludes by suggesting that what Indians can most usefully learn from Europeans is how to harness their weaponry and military discipline so as eventually to free themselves from oppression. Johnson reflected just as ambivalently on the course of past, present, and future contact between the peoples of Europe and the rest of the world in his introduction to *The World Displayed*. Focusing on the fifteenth-century Portuguese exploration of Africa's West Coast, he declared in seemingly definitive fashion that '[t]he Europeans have scarcely visited any coast, but to gratify avarice, and extend corruption; to arrogate dominion without right, and practise cruelty without incentive.' Yet this statement is preceded by a short tribute to Prince Henry, the Portuguese patron of maritime exploration, which offers a non-judgemental assessment of his legacy: 'What mankind has lost and gained by the genius and designs of this Prince, it would be long to compare and very difficult to estimate.' The same paragraph concludes by expressing 'reason to hope' that whatever the grim evidence of the previous centuries, 'good may sometime be produced' out of evil, and 'the light of the gospel . . . at last illuminate the sands of Africa, and the desarts of America'.[31]

Both *Idler* 81 and Johnson's introduction to *The World Displayed* thus combined seeming optimism about the future spreading of Christianity with a more uncertain assessment of the actual consequences of past contact between Europe, Africa, and America (Asia is largely beyond Johnson's purview here). Imlac's account of the global imbalance of power likewise testifies to Johnson's apprehension of the entanglement of the regions of the world, and, in its invocation of God's 'unsearchable will' (47), further suggests that this state of affairs is now entrenched and irreversible. If Imlac might be seen here to present the superior 'power' and 'knowledge' (47) of Europeans as a product of providential design, as Hudson argues, however, he does not raise the question that Johnson posed in his other works of the same year about 'what mankind has lost and gained' as a result of this ascendancy. Indeed, the corollary of Imlac's emphasis on the near impossibility of acquiring a comprehensive social knowledge is that such a question is too large to be answered – or that there is not a sufficiently stable vantage point from which it could be addressed in the first place.[32]

It is instructive here to consider *Rasselas* alongside Johnson's *Adventurer* 67 of 1753, in which he noted that what a newcomer to London would experience as a bewildering multiplicity of sights and sounds, someone with the leisure to reflect might appreciate as the orderly 'concurrence of endeavours' that characterizes an advanced commercial society. Like *Rasselas*, this essay emphasizes that, even for the affluent, material plenty offers no guarantee of individual happiness. Where the essay and the tale clearly differ, though, is that while, for the former, the diverse activities evident within the ostensibly circumscribed bounds of a single city come together in a 'secret concatenation', for the latter, the greatly more complicated and multifarious effects of global interconnection exceed any attempt to discern in them an underlying pattern or organization.[33] Accustomed to an environment which magically offers 'consumption without production', in Anna Neill's phrase, Rasselas imagines that once he is outside the Happy Valley he will be in a position to 'review [the world] at leisure' (68).[34] Shortly before they escape, however, Imlac cautions the prince that if he expects the outside world to be 'smooth and quiet as the lake in the valley', the reality will be 'a sea foaming with tempests, and boiling with whirlpools', in which he will be 'sometimes overwhelmed by the waves of violence, and sometimes dashed against the rocks of treachery' (56). Figuring the space beyond the Happy Valley in terms of sea rather than land, Imlac hints at how *Rasselas* appears to map the current predicament of Britons, the self-styled 'island race', onto that of the prince and his party.

'Driven along the Stream of Life'

When recalling his dawning curiosity about the wider world, Imlac tells Rasselas that his first stop after leaving his father was the port of Surat, the location of the EIC's first trading post, established in 1608. Imlac does not mention encountering Europeans in India, although he claims to have 'conversed with great numbers' (46) in Palestine. The specificity of this reference to Surat solicits critical attention, nonetheless, since it connects Imlac's cosmopolitan past, along with the expedition that he leads, to a larger commercial and colonial history. Surat was taken by EIC forces shortly before *Rasselas* was written (news of this reached Britain in September), and the capture of such a 'great and opulent city', as the *Annual Register* for 1759 reported, further confirmed that Britain was going from 'success to success' in this theatre of the war.[35] Just as Johnson's introduction to *The World Displayed* emphasizes that the maritime exploration which extended 'the power of Europe' also fostered the 'acquaintance' of 'distant nations', so *Rasselas* here alludes to the material basis of the enquiry pursued by Imlac and his party, reliant on both the technologies and the networks of contact underpinning the system of global commerce.[36]

Rasselas invites the reader to recognize what makes the mobility of Imlac and his party possible, then, and moreover provides a sceptical commentary on the forms of insight provided by their survey. Its final chapter draws attention to this reflexivity, announcing itself as a 'conclusion, in which nothing is concluded', and ending ambiguously as the group resolves to 'return to Abissinia' (175–6). Whereas *Candide* finishes with the title character's entreaty that 'we must cultivate our garden,' *Rasselas* offers no call to purposive action, leaving the reader to question whether this return might also constitute a kind of retreat to the familiarity of the Happy Valley.[37] Imlac's position of authority as a tutor to the prince is again qualified here too, since in the penultimate paragraph he and the astronomer whom the group have just met are described as 'contented to be driven along the stream of life without directing their course to a particular port' (176). Although Imlac escapes the 'maladies of the mind' (150) from which the work's other philosopher figures suffer, the tale underlines that his lack of attachment to any specific profession or place is a condition of drift rather than a source of critical purchase. '[T]eachers of morality live like men' (74), Imlac counsels Rasselas when they encounter a lecturer who proves unable to live by his own stoic precepts, and Imlac himself is likewise unable to transcend the harsh inevitabilities of the human condition.

Rasselas's conclusion emphasizes Imlac's lack of any decisive influence over his pupil, as the prince restates his earlier desire to rule 'a little kingdom, in which he might administer justice in his own person, and see all the parts of government with his own eyes' (175–6). Such a realm would at once represent a denial of the social complexity he had witnessed and recreate the political conditions from which he initially sought to escape; Rasselas's restatement of this plan in fact underscores Imlac's point about 'the effects of visionary schemes', namely, that we 'familiarise them by degrees, and in time lose sight of their folly' (153). Importantly, Johnson also provides a reminder of the topicality of the idea of restlessness here, since after the reader is told about the prince's desire for a 'kingdom' of his own, the narrator adds that Rasselas's unchecked delusions encompass the dream of empire: 'he could never fix the limits of his dominion, and was always adding to his subjects' (176).

Addressing the 'politics of empire' in *Rasselas*, Stephen Scherwatzky argues that 'Johnson satirizes the conflicted nature of claims for political virtue that include imperial ambition.'[38] 'Satire' is perhaps too strong a term here, however, both because the tale's engagement with questions of empire is so indirect, and since it continually suggests that ambition of this kind is an innate human characteristic and therefore no more irrational than Imlac's wish to be 'driven along the stream of life' (176). As Carol Watts argues, 'Johnson's very language for the acquisition of knowledge and experience is shaped by the circulating desires and energies of worldly life, as if ... it cannot be imagined distinctly from them.'[39] The best-known example of this appears in Johnson's 'Plan' for his *Dictionary* (1755), in which he likened his monumental task to that of 'the soldiers of Caesar', looking on Britain as a 'new world, which it is almost madness to conquer'. Johnson expressed the hope here 'that though I should not complete the conquest, I shall at least discover the coast, civilize part of the inhabitants, [and] make it easy for some other adventurer to proceed farther' – thus 'half-mocking the loss of sense of proportion he has incurred', in John Barrell's words, yet challenging 'the scale, but not wholly the nature of the comparison'.[40]

If 'the conclusion, in which nothing is concluded', only emphasizes that restlessness in all its manifestations is an inescapable facet of the human condition, however, the end of the preceding chapter provides a rather different conclusion, with Nekayah declaring that 'the choice of eternity' now seems a more important question than 'the choice of life'. The project that Nekayah announces is not presented as any more realizable than her brother's, but her enlightened ambition to found 'a college of learned women' (175) nonetheless offers a significant counterpoint to Rasselas's visions of empire. While Nekayah initially assumes that people outside of the Happy Valley will 'prostrate themselves before her' (62), she moves beyond expecting to be obeyed, whereas the prince – his dreams of dominion still intact – does not. Nekayah's ambition to 'raise up for the next age models of prudence, and patterns of piety' (175) is especially resonant, since in attending to the domestic sphere it invokes an arena of feminine influence that is also a locus of stability, implicitly defined against the ever-shifting horizons of Rasselas's imagined sovereignty. In an earlier dialogue with her brother, Nekayah asserts that families, like kingdoms, may themselves sometimes be 'torn with factions and exposed to revolutions' (95). The tale's concluding account of the agency of women by contrast establishes the domestic sphere as a 'line of defence' that, as Watts suggests, at once offers a refuge from the world and a consolidation of home, community, and patriotic belonging.[41] This remedial perspective has no place in Johnson's other works that engage more directly with the origins or the conduct of the ongoing war, and in conjunction with Nekayah's appeal to 'eternity', its presence here helps to close off the text's previous reflections on the tempestuousness of the wider world.

Rasselas remained a difficult text for late eighteenth-century readers to assimilate, and for some it was simply a work of 'cheerless scepticism' arousing 'painful uncertainty'.[42] One index of the apparently troubling inconclusiveness of *Rasselas* is that subsequent authors chose to rewrite it – in the case of Ellis Cornelia Knight's sequel *Dinarbas* (1790), by offering a conventional 'romance' plot culminating in the marriages of the prince and his sister and a collective return to the Happy Valley. Sir Walter Scott, by contrast, thought of *Rasselas* as a 'wholesome' work, elevated above the 'poisonous' *Candide* because it encouraged readers 'to look to another and a better world for the satisfaction of [their] wishes'.[43] Such a reading of Nekayah's 'choice of eternity' (175) as an extractable moral imperative significantly ignores the way in which, elsewhere in the text, the consideration of the vanity of human wishes is inextricably bound up with specific questions concerning both the relative power and knowledge of Europeans and their others, and the contemporary situation of a globally extended Britain. '[N]othing is concluded' (175) at the close, then, because *Rasselas* offers more than one conclusion. Together with her commitment to the education of women, Nekayah's 'choice of eternity' potentially provides a form of stabilizing readerly orientation that offsets Rasselas's visions of empire and Imlac's readiness to be 'driven along the stream of life'. As much as the problem of dominion remains the same, because the prince is unable to determine the limits of his imagined authority, Nekayah makes *Rasselas* available to be read as a quietist and otherworldly text – as an abstract moral tale, in other words – that transcends history altogether. From the beginning of the period under discussion in this book, the seemingly pivotal moment of 1759, therefore, it is possible to identify signs of that disengagement and even 'amnesia' that has in different ways been read as characterizing Britons' relation to their history of empire. As I now show, the writings of Oliver Goldsmith similarly address the 'problem' of victory and national expansion while also reflecting on the possibility or otherwise of critical commentary itself.

Goldsmith's Philosophical Travellers

Goldsmith's diverse works of the late 1750s and early 1760s emphasize the potential benefits of 'philosophical' travel but also address the actual experience of mobility on which any such active process of cultural comparison would be dependent. In *The Bee* in 1759, for example, Goldsmith's peripatetic persona celebrates the possibilities of mutually improving forms of exchange, where participants take the best from each other: 'let us endeavour to imitate the good to society that our neighbours are found to practise,' he declares, 'and let our neighbours also imitate those parts of duty in which we excel.'[44] If such a quest for enlightenment is comparable to that undertaken by Rasselas, however, Goldsmith presented the business of investigation differently from Johnson, often writing from the perspective of narrators for whom mobility is involuntary – a function of penury and social marginality rather than leisurely curiosity. In the 'Letter from a Traveller' included in *The Bee*'s first issue, the author assumes the subaltern position of Rasselas's unnamed attendants, since he describes having just arrived in Poland in the train of 'the Prince of ***', among whose men he is 'regarded as an ignorant intruder'. In this particular context, mobility is a rootless state offering little to compensate for its pains. 'Secluded from all the comforts of confidence, friendship, or society,' he declares, 'I feel the solitude of a hermit, but not his ease.' That Goldsmith's traveller separates 'solitude' from 'ease' – while also downplaying the fabled 'wisdom' of the hermit – emphasizes that he is

isolated rather than independent, lacking access both to the critical authority and the cultural prestige of principled retirement.

'[O]ut of my own country,' *The Bee*'s travelling correspondent writes,
'the highest character I can ever acquire, is that of ... a philosophic
vagabond.'[45] Goldsmith's Chinese philosopher, Lien Chi Altangi, his
most developed travelling persona, similarly identifies himself as 'a poor
philosophic wanderer'.[46] Like *Rasselas, The Citizen of the World* positions
itself in an established literary tradition, informant narrative, which
stretches back at least as far as Giovanni Marana's *Letters Writ by
a Turkish Spy* (translated into English in 1687). Goldsmith's work also
signals its connection to a domestic version of this tradition, as exemplified
by Ned Ward's *The London Spy* (1698–1700). Just as Ward's text emphasizes the gullibility of its 'spy', so *The Citizen of the World* introduces
Altangi as a naïve spectator on 'a new world', where 'every object strikes
with wonder and surprise' (21): early on, for example, he mistakes inn signs
for house decorations, and falls victim to a female confidence trickster who
steals his watch after offering to mend it. Goldsmith here recycled materials
from numerous different sources, and the extent of his borrowings illustrates his predicament of 'writing for bread' as he provided copy for John
Newbery's daily *The Public Register*.[47]

Even as Goldsmith plundered other texts, however, he also adapted the
figure of the Eastern observer for his own purposes. While the 'editor' of
The Citizen of the World initially seems to set up Altangi for ridicule, he also
presents him as a polite visitor from a 'tutored' nation, and, assuming that
all such nations seek 'refined enjoyment' in comparable ways, asserts that
'the Chinese and we are pretty much alike' (13–14). This latter claim draws
attention to Altangi's distinction from other eighteenth-century spies and
informants, for while previous works had seized upon the comic and satiric
possibilities offered by the device of the foreign or provincial observer,
The Citizen of the World seems as concerned to familiarize Altangi as to
exploit the estrangement effects that he affords. Goldsmith's Chinese
philosopher often appeals to the idea of an enlightened transnational
community, as when he declares that 'it is the duty of the learned to
unite society ..., and to persuade men to become citizens of the world'
(86), a bold statement of intellectual faith which contrasts with the aphor-
istic scepticism of Johnson's Imlac or Nekayah. Altangi thus hails an at
once expansive and inclusive notion of cosmopolitan fellowship that is
differentiated both from contemporary accounts of the sociability engendered by global commerce and from the 'habitus' of an aristocratic elite. He
frequently cites Confucius as an exemplar of this philosophical ideal, and it

is clear that 'China' for Goldsmith among other things represents the long history of civilization and moral authority with which Confucius was still widely associated.

Altangi's first reference to Confucius is undercut, however, by the editor's disclaimer that his letter provides 'little more than a rhapsody of sentences borrowed from . . . the Chinese philosopher' (39). Similarly to Johnson's writings on the origins of the Seven Years' War, Goldsmith's work moreover juxtaposes a utopian ideal of cross-cultural exchange with the actual history of contact between the peoples of the world. As in Johnson's essays, there is a striking provisionality about Goldsmith's account of the consequences of this contact, a wariness of offering any claim that might appear definitive. Echoing the passage from *The Bee* cited earlier in this chapter, Altangi declares in letter 108, for example, that the 'export' of curious and open-minded European travellers would help to atone for the past conduct of those who had been motivated only by 'commerce or piety': 'To send out a traveller properly qualified for these purposes . . . would, in some measure, repair the breaches made by ambition; and might shew that there were still some who boasted a greater name than that of patriots, who professed themselves lovers of men' (421). Elsewhere, though, *The Citizen of the World* registers that Britons' energies continue to be channelled towards profit-driven innovation, ahead of any other sphere of 'improving' activity. In doing so it again follows *The Bee*, which states that while 'we are arrived at a perfect imitation of porcelain,' Britons are much less ready 'to imitate the good to society that our neighbours are found to practise'.[48]

Altangi occasionally acknowledges the economic benefits that the British demand for Chinese imports brings his country, but – maintaining his self-professed status as a trader in ideas rather than things – more often invokes the frivolous superficiality of 'Chinese' artefacts as a foil to his own good sense, a distinction that the editor announces with his prefatory declaration: 'If the Chinese have contributed to vitiate our taste, I'll try how far they can help to improve our understanding.' The editor describes how he had dreamt of a 'Fashion Fair' on the frozen Thames, where, seeing the marketability of the 'furniture, frippery, and fireworks of China', he resolved to offer 'a small cargo of Chinese morality' (15). That the ice then cracks under the weight of this cargo signals Goldsmith's ironic recognition of the limits of his work's critical purchase, and perhaps his awareness of the compromise inherent in using an imaginary Chinese philosopher to satirize the taste for, among other things, chinoiserie; though only 'a small cargo', 'Chinese morality' itself takes on the status of a commodity here.

As precarious as this opposition is, however, Altangi frequently suggests that the 'Chinese' aesthetic travesties the real China to which it obliquely refers, as is most vividly demonstrated by his experience with the two 'ladies of distinction' who summon him to visit them. In both encounters, Altangi finds that his hosts are so deeply invested in bogus notions of Chinese authenticity as to be unwilling to revise their assumptions after meeting someone who is – so the work has it – in a position to disabuse them of their errors.

What complicates any such critique of Orientalist exoticism in the work is the fact that Goldsmith sometimes has it both ways, since, as David Porter observes, he 'delights ... in his own narrative rendering of the chinoiserie aesthetic'.[49] This is especially evident in letter 33, where Altangi describes meeting an author at the house of the second 'lady of distinction'. The author sets himself up as a fount of knowledge in a way that bears out the letter's overall emphasis on metropolitan arrogance, but even as he fails to recognize the 'sameness' of Altangi, he also provides an entertainingly extravagant example of his own compositions in 'the true eastern taste', beginning:

> Eben-ben-bolo, who was the son of Ban, was born on the foggy summits of Benderabassi. His beard was whiter than the feathers which veil the breast of the Penguin; his eyes were like the eyes of doves, when washed by the dews of the morning; his hair, which hung like the willow weeping over the glassy stream, was so beautiful that it seemed to reflect his own brightness; and his feet were as the feet of a wild deer which fleeth to the tops of the mountains.

Although Altangi states that 'I could not avoid smiling to hear a native of England attempt to instruct me in the true eastern idiom' (145), his letters elsewhere incorporate tales (including that of Prince 'Bonbenin-bonbobbin-bonbobbinet' in letter 48) which similarly revel in their own absurdity. When the author in letter 33 asserts that 'Eastern tales should always be sonorous, lofty, musical, and unmeaning' (145), in other words, he makes a point that Goldsmith's work occasionally upholds. In contrast with Johnson's Oriental apologues, *The Citizen of the World* at times displays what Srinivas Aravamudan terms 'a cultivated irresponsibility towards the cultural referent', even as it also aligns China with Confucian gravity.[50]

Combining informant narrative with interpolated fictions, therefore, Goldsmith's work moves between different – stylistically and tonally varying – versions of the 'Enlightenment Orientalism' examined by Aravamudan. What these forms have in common in Goldsmith's hands is that they are alike uninterested in the 'real' China, which as in the case of Altangi's account of the ladies of distinction remains a rhetorical counter – an idea to which to appeal so as to illustrate the excesses of the groundless fantasizing that the text itself periodically enjoys. Although Goldsmith consulted the most authoritative French Jesuit sources of information about Chinese customs and manners, Altangi's purportedly 'Chinese' background is frequently manifested in bizarre ways, as in his story of his aunt Shang in letter 102. After stating that it is 'common in China . . . to see two women of fashion continue gaming, till one has won all the other's clothes, and stripped her quite naked', Altangi tells of how, having already lost all her clothing to a card sharper, his aunt 'staked her teeth' and then 'at last . . . played for her left eye' (402).

The Citizen of the World is strikingly heterogeneous, then, and it both develops and departs from the example of its predecessors. For the purposes of this chapter, however, I want especially to draw attention to the possibilities that the idea of Altangi's critical detachment offered Goldsmith. Altangi appeals to his 'Chinese' experience not just in his anecdote about his gambling aunt, but also in narrating 'The Rise and Declension of the Kingdom of Lao', an allegory about what happens 'when a trading nation begins to act the conqueror', told in response to a politician who argues that the nation's business should be with 'settling new colonies' (105–6) rather than continental wars. At certain points, Altangi's status as a Chinese philosopher enables him to offer an Olympian perspective on the 'ridiculousness' of European affairs: 'each laughs at each,' he notes, 'and the Asiatic at all' (320). This kind of position is especially apparent in letter 17, where Altangi begins by wondering how 'an Asiatic politician' would understand 'Christian princes' continually fighting wars with each other, despite their 'treaties of peace and friendship' (72). Although this observation appears naïvely oblivious to the strategic interests of the participants in the ongoing conflict, it is significant that Altangi here considers the rights of the indigenous peoples of Canada to possess the land on which they had lived 'for time immemorial' (73). He goes beyond analysing the domestic ramifications of empire (the history of Lao's emphasis), therefore, and instead broaches a principled opposition to the very idea of colonial authority. Altangi's account of Canadian 'savages' presents them as 'harmless' victims of a fundamentally illegitimate European expansionism, and, borrowing from Johnson, he declares that 'such is the contest' between the English and the French, 'that no honest man can heartily wish success to either party' (74). Goldsmith's engagement with the conduct of the war was complex, nonetheless, and in his works of the period he continually shifted between this mode of detached commentary and an exploration of the mentality of popular patriotism in which he sometimes appeared to relinquish critical distance.

'Am I Not Greater Than a Host of Slaves?'

Goldsmith's editor says of Altangi's arrival in Britain that people were 'surprised to find a man born so far from London, that school of prudence and wisdom, endued even with a moderate capacity' (13). This ironizing of metropolitan arrogance prepares the reader to think of Altangi as a generic 'outsider' as much as a Chinese philosopher, and thus perhaps as a figure deployed by Goldsmith in order to address his own experience of being regarded as an Irish exotic. Altangi later complains about 'the presumption of those islanders, when they pretend to instruct me in the ceremonies of China!': 'They lay it down as a maxim,' he states, 'that every person who comes from [China] must express himself in metaphor; swear by Alla, rail against wine, and behave, and talk and write like a Turk or Persian' (142). Goldsmith's critique of exoticizing misrepresentation is rhetorically unstable, because Altangi is at pains to project 'unlettered sympathy' onto other Eastern peoples, and since, as discussed earlier, his work some-times conceives of the East in knowingly inaccurate terms. Altangi's reference to 'islanders' in the quotation just cited remains resonant, how-ever, as it suggestively turns the charge of naïvety and unworldliness against Britons. His account of the self-assurance with which those he meets 'lay down' their opinions about China additionally captures something of Goldsmith's fascination with Britons' sense of themselves in relation to their others.

One significant way in which *The Citizen of the World* differs from its precursors is that, as in his reference to presumptuous 'islanders', its narrator offers a 'provincializing' commentary on his hosts and interlocu-tors. If Altangi rejects patriotism in the name of Confucian cosmopolitan-ism, however, he also registers the enduring force of patriotic attachment among some of those he encounters. Meditating on Goldsmith's fre-quently drawn distinction between unmerited reward and unrewarded merit, Altangi begins letter 119 by stating that while 'the misfortunes of the great ... are held up to engage our attention,' '[t]he miseries of the poor are ... entirely disregarded' (458). Yet when he describes the figure of a 'disabled soldier' (459) who had served his country around the world, Altangi notes that this man displays a disregard for his own desperate circumstances while maintaining an instinctive antipathy towards the

French; 'one Englishman', the veteran says, 'is able to beat five French at any time' (464). Goldsmith here juxtaposes the soldier's zeal for liberty, 'the property of every Englishman', with his actual experience of having been imprisoned for poaching, transported to the Caribbean as an indentured labourer, then taken by a press gang on his return to the 'Old England' (462) for which he still retains an irrational affection.

While he declares his 'regard to mankind' in general, Altangi himself elsewhere states that his time in England has made him sympathetic towards the national cause, such that, as he says in letter 85, 'I now begin to read with pleasure of their taking towns or gaining battles, and secretly wish disappointment to all the enemies of Britain' (345). Days after news of victory at Quebec reached London, Goldsmith published an essay 'On Public Rejoicings for Victory' in the *Busy Body*, written from the position of a witness to the mass celebration of national military triumph. The narrator is a quizzical observer, sarcastically referring to alehouse warriors re-enacting scenes of conflict as men 'who have ... bravely become votaries for their country, and with true patriotism not disdained to fall dead – drunk in every house'. Surveying a range of reactions to the news from Canada, Goldsmith's spectator describes a bellicose waiter who thinks that France itself is now there for the taking, and he records a dispute between a shoemaker and his wife over the cost of buying candles to illuminate their house. Significantly, though, the narrator also writes that he 'could not avoid admiring the artificial day that was formed by lights in every window', and he registers the contagiousness of the public mood, noting how easy it is 'to forget the ravages of war and human calamity, in national satisfaction'.[51] As he is seduced by 'the affective nationalism of wartime' (in Carol Watts's phrase), the narrator begins to lose his spectatorial detachment: 'How blest am I . . . who makes one in this glorious political society, which thus preserves liberty to mankind and to itself'; 'solitary as I am', he adds, 'am I not greater than an host of slaves?'[52] Watts presents this passage as staging the emergence of new forms of national belonging, generated by the increasingly euphoric climate of the 'year of victories'. Claiming to 'make one' in a 'glorious political society', and, later, that he is 'friends together' with his king and his country, the narrator embraces his subjection to the state while at the same time experiencing a compensatory, indeed self-aggrandizing, individual liberation in return – the product of his ability to recast a 'vertical' relationship in horizontal terms as 'a mutual intercourse of kindness and duty'.

The essay does not finish here, however, since even as he drinks in his 'newly acquired and conscious dignity', Goldsmith's narrator hears 'a hissing noise' in the tails of his wig and notices 'a stream of fire dashing from [his] right ear', having been struck by a rocket from the pyrotechnics around him.[53] This momentary blurring of the distinction between the pleasures of rejoicing and the perils of conflict discomposes but then reorients the narrator, who concludes with a more sober reassessment of recent military success. While acknowledging that the 'exercise of war' might provide a temporarily invigorating boost to a commercial society grown 'putrid by a long stagnation', he presents the illuminations that celebrate victory as a troubling metaphor for the longer-term health of the nation: 'A country at war resembles a flambeaux, the brighter it burns, the sooner it is often wasted.'[54] Goldsmith recycled this metaphor and returned to his accompanying claim that 'peace is the only triumph of victory' in his December 1759 'Thoughts Preliminary to a General Peace' in the *Weekly Magazine*. This essay provides a familiar caution against territorial empire, but its reference to North America makes its general claim that Britain's colonies might become 'too large ... to manage' seem particularly prescient.[55] It thus provides a still more sceptical counterpoint to 'public rejoicings' than Goldsmith's *Busy Body* piece, raising the increasingly unavoidable question about what it was that connected Britons to each other across their expanding empire.

In his writings of 1759 and 1760, therefore, Goldsmith's various narrators and authorial personae at different times share in popular exhilaration at British military triumphs and stand back from the crowd in order to warn that victory comes at a price. At the same time too, as suggested earlier, these surrogate figures enabled Goldsmith to reflect on his own position both as Irish exile and as professional author. In the first issue of *The Bee*, the editor adopts the principled stance that 'neither war nor scandal shall make any part' of his project, thereby echoing Johnson's stated refusal to play with his readers' emotions by writing about the conflict's progress.[56] He later laments his lack of success, however, claiming in the fourth issue that to reach a bigger audience he would need to change the title of the publication to 'the ROYAL BEE', or 'the ANTIGALLICAN BEE'. Goldsmith's editor considers what it would involve 'to throw off all connections with taste, and fairly address my countrymen in the same engaging style and manner with other periodical pamphlets, much more in vogue than ... mine shall ever be'. Imagining himself as the proprietor of a literary warehouse, he speaks of assembling a stock of pieces that deal with 'popular topics' – including 'invectives against ... the French', 'our undoubted sovereignty of the seas', 'a dissertation upon liberty', and 'an ode upon our victories' – in order to provide his audience with the opportunity for self-congratulation that they crave.[57]

The four related essays that Goldsmith contributed to the *Royal Magazine* in 1760 seem to cater to such a demand, since while the first of them recycles passages from *The Citizen of the World* regarding the need to 'level those distinctions which separate mankind', it also begins by – it seems – un-ironically addressing Britain as the 'happiest of countries! happy in thy climate, fertility, situation, and commerce; but still happier in the peculiar nature of thy laws and government'.[58] The last essay in this series similarly states that 'the English are not less divided from the rest of the world by the circumfluent seas, than differing from them in their manners, disposition, and turn of thinking.' Although it attributes a 'conscious importance' to 'the English', in line with the ironizing strategies of *The Citizen of the World*, this essay appears finally to uphold a mythology of 'island race' exceptionalism. Its reference to the 'superior accuracy in reasoning' of the English presents this quality as 'the consequence of their freedom', which in turn, it suggests, may be the product of environmental determinants such as climate, or an innate, racial characteristic.[59] Goldsmith glossed the national 'passion for liberty' as 'impatience under restraint', evident in the way that the English 'pursue truth wherever it may lead, regardless of the result'.[60] While Goldsmith – unlike Johnson – was insistent that this 'impatience' was a national attribute rather than a feature of the human condition, as it is in *Rasselas*, he similarly conceived of such restless energy as a force with an unstoppable momentum, which it would be all but impossible to curb.

Lords of Humankind

Goldsmith's ambiguous reference to Britons as 'the lords of human kind', in his poem 'The Traveller' (1764), nicely captures the way in which his writings sometimes appear to endorse as well as to undercut Britons' opinion of themselves. Like Goldsmith's earlier works, 'The Traveller' explores the doubleness of mobility. While the poet initially alludes to Ireland, and writes of the 'lengthening chain' that he drags during his painful absence from his brother, he thereafter invokes an Alpine prospect from which 'the philosophic mind' is provided with an Olympian survey of 'Creation's charms' in all their rich variety.[61] Pledging to interrogate 'the patriot's boast', the poet now declares that 'wisdom' finds '[a]n equal portion dealt to all mankind'.[62] As in Goldsmith's *Royal Magazine* essays, however, the 'blessings' that different nations apparently enjoy are only minimally substantiated, and the poem later seems to set up the idea that Britain might after all be uniquely favoured. Goldsmith's 'lords of human kind' make their entrance in the poem, 'Intent on high designs, a thoughtful band,/ By forms unfashioned, fresh from Nature's hand;/ Fierce in their native hardiness of soul,/ True to imagined right, above control'.[63]

The subsequent statement that 'even the peasant boasts these rights to scan,/ And learns to venerate himself as man' recalls the proud assertion of *The Citizen of the World*'s military veteran that liberty is 'the property of every Englishman' (462), and thus prepares the reader familiar with Goldsmith's work for another account of how patriotic attachment makes the poor oblivious to their degradation.[64] Anticipating Goldsmith's depiction of the independent and undisciplined inhabitants of Auburn in 'The Deserted Village' (1770), these lines hint at how 'impatience' also manifested itself, during and after the Seven Years' War, in new conceptions of popular resistance and political agency.[65] Rather than investigate this potential, however, the poem instead considers the blessings of freedom as understood and acted upon by 'self dependent lordlings' who 'stand alone,/ All claims that bind and sweeten life unknown' – their accumulation of personal fortunes destroying the social fabric, as '[f]ictitious bonds ... of wealth and law' supersede customary ties.[66] Goldsmith here returned to the subject of his essay 'The Revolution in Low Life' (1762), arguing that such a concentration of wealth was a by-product of foreign commerce and colonial expansion that hastened rural depopulation by exchanging 'useful sons' for 'useless ore'.[67] Though the idea that such an exchange might result in a net national loss is a familiar one in his writings, Goldsmith went further in this essay, bearing witness to a social transformation that he presented as an internal colonialism. Likewise describing a state of affairs where 'laws grind the poor, and rich men rule the law', 'The Traveller' appeals to 'the throne' – the institution of the monarchy rather than George III – as the only guarantor of the security of the poor and the middle orders against the increasingly powerful forces besieging them.[68]

Goldsmith stated in 'The Traveller' that the 'rich men' perpetrating this social revolution were bearers of 'The wealth of climes, where savage nations roam,/ Pillag'd from slaves, to purchase slaves at home'.[69] If Goldsmith thus circulated the image of the plundering nabob that would become so prominent, however, it is striking that in *An History of England* (1764), he accompanied his commentary on the domestic ramifications of empire with references to the surprising scale of national military success during the recently concluded war. After recounting its humiliating 'beginnings', 'from which the timid foreboded national servitude, . . . and even the most sanguine only hoped for a peace that might restore them to former equality', Goldsmith declared that it was in Asia that 'we first learned the art of again conquering the enemy'.[70] 'Asia' here, then, is not the source of temptation and corrupting wealth that it is in anti-nabob discourse, but rather the arena where Britain restored its martial reputation after the war's ignominious early years. Goldsmith added that 'when a nation shines brightest with conquest, it may then like a wasting taper, be only hastening to decay,' and as in his essays on the public celebrations of 1759 he warned against the dangers of being taken in by 'the splendour of victory'.[71] While Goldsmith often argued that colonial expansion hastened domestic corruption and worsened the condition of the poor, though, he presented the unexpectedly far-reaching and comprehensive triumph of 'English' arms in India as something with which it was possible and indeed pleasurable to identify. 'The princes of the country knew the English force, and learned to fear it,' he wrote, and '[s]ince that time nothing considerable has been done against us.'[72]

This appeal to a collective 'us' may be read as the hack-writer Goldsmith giving his audience what he thought they wanted, in the manner described by *The Bee*'s literary warehouseman, but it is nonetheless significant that such a claim appears to channel Patriot bellicosity without immediate qualification. Goldsmith paraphrased 'The Traveller's' account of nabobs 'making slaves at home' in his more substantial *The History of England* (1771), yet when he referred to the pivotal battle of Plassey and its aftermath he again extolled 'the power of the English' over their 'weak and effeminate' opponents; Goldsmith presented 'colonel Clive', for example, as a peerless general rather than the embodiment of avarice that, for many, he had become.[73] Just before concluding his narrative with the death of George II, Goldsmith offered a snapshot of 'the glorious figure the British nation appeared in to the world at this time'. Although the phrase 'at this time' is consistent with Goldsmith's emphasis elsewhere on the transient 'splendour' of victory, here at least his reference to the 'appearance' of glory is unmodified by any note of caution.[74] Goldsmith recognized that much of 'the history of England' during George II's reign in effect happened overseas, and the virtual stalemate in the continental theatre of the Seven Years' War, where either side 'engaged to lose much, and gain little', only threw into relief that away from Europe the nation was enjoying unprecedented military success: 'the efforts of England . . . over every part of the globe were amazing.' The expense of these endeavours was 'greater than had ever been disbursed by any nations before', Goldsmith added, and without referring to the post-war period he hinted at what were to be the larger costs of maintaining the security of Britain's empire – further war, and the eventual loss of America.[75] In his retrospect on 'amazing' efforts and 'glorious' results, however, Goldsmith understood that popular investment in British heroics on the world stage was itself part of the history of the nation from the 'year of victories' through to the end of the conflict. The tale that this later *History* tells is again that of a country trying to adjust to its status as an imperial power, but in contrast with Goldsmith's earlier works it identifies cause for awe as much as for anxiety.

During the war numerous other 'histories of the present' encouraged readers to celebrate the triumphs that now seemed to make Britons, in the un-ironic sense of Goldsmith's phrase, 'lords of human kind'. Where India was concerned, military victory was still given less attention than successes elsewhere, and it was sometimes seen to serve a narrowly sectional EIC interest, as in the writings of James Ridley, which I go on to examine. The anonymous author of *A Complete History of the War in India* (1761), by contrast, asked 'what honest Briton can withhold his tribute of gratitude, when he hears of ... illustrious conquests?' – the phrase 'tribute of gratitude' presenting conquest as something undertaken for and on behalf of Britons.[76] Other works such as *Memoirs of the Revolution in Bengal* (1760) sought to communicate to readers 'what has been effected for their Service at *Bengal*', on the assumption that they would 'accept as kindly the Laurels brought them from *Asia*, as ... from *Afric* or *America*'.[77] This claim that Britons might know less about India than other theatres of military engagement, yet want to know more, was echoed by Richard Owen Cambridge in *An Account of the War in India* (1761). Cambridge based his work on materials provided by men recently returned from India, incorporating information about geography as well as customs and manners, because without 'previous explanations', he stated, readers would be unable to apprehend how 'a handful of Europeans' defeated 'a multitude of Asiatics'.[78] As argued earlier, one of the striking things about Cambridge's work is the way that it draws attention to the newness – for Britons – of the Eastern domain that it describes, markedly different from the 'ideal' realm with which they may previously have been acquainted through their reading of Oriental tales. In the remainder of this chapter I explore the relationship between these registers in fictions of the 1760s, considering the way in which a range of texts directly and indirectly responded to the global expansion of British interests, then concluding with a discussion of works by James Ridley as possibly the first imaginative writer to respond to recent developments in India.

'Wealth Is Their Alla'

In the aftermath of the Seven Years' War, metropolitan conceptions of 'the East' were vague enough for 'Igluka and Sibbersik', billed as 'A Greenland Tale', to be included in a collection titled *The Orientalist* (1764). It was widely acknowledged that works such as *Rasselas* and *The Citizen of the World* conceived of their Eastern-ness in notional terms; Owen Ruffhead, in the *Monthly Review* cited earlier, observed that the insights acquired by Johnson's characters might have been provided without 'going to Ethiopia', which appeared to be a backdrop rather than an object of any interest in itself.[79] One of many Oriental tales to take its point of departure from *Rasselas*, John Langhorne's *Solyman and Almena* (1762) presents a protagonist who leaves the 'pleasant' Mesopotamian valley of his birth, driven by a thirst for knowledge of the world, and it does little to substantiate its Eastern setting. Solyman visits 'the capital of the Mogul's empire' and learns about the 'infernal custom' of widow burning while in Delhi, but the work's otherwise perfunctory treatment of Indian specifics is demonstrated by the fact that when in India he also gets caught up in a war between the rulers of seemingly fictional kingdoms.[80] For the *Monthly* again, *Solyman and Almena* was typical of its genre, demonstrating so little 'invention or originality' that 'a reader, who is but moderately acquainted with this modish kind of literature, may anticipate most of the incidents'; 'in truth,' the reviewer added, 'few of the Oriental Novels differ from each other.'[81]

Even as many works evoked composite Easts in such a predictable and apparently formulaic manner, however, this limited lexicon of Eastern effects also served a variety of political agendas. John Hawkesworth situated his *Almoran and Hamet* (1761), dedicated to George III, in the longstanding tradition of the 'mirror for princes', while numerous other works addressed the predicament of simultaneously outward-looking and porous societies whose condition – more overtly than in *Solyman and Almena* – offered parallels with contemporary Britain. The brief 'Concluding Tale' in *The Orientalist* (1764), for example, depicts the Egyptian province of 'Gojam' (a variant on the Wilkeite Charles Churchill's 'Gotham'), and describes what happened to its inhabitants, 'descended from the ancient Mamalukes of Egypt', after 'their convenient situation for traffick pointed them out to strangers', who 'with commerce, introduced luxury and the sword'. While centuries passed in a 'union of martial and commercial honours', 'Gojam's active sons' began to import the vices of other climes, and 'from the servile race of SELIM ... imported the meaner arts of government'. Takeover by an alien monarchical despotism – loosely associated with the Ottoman empire – signals the irremediable corruption of Gojam, and the tale concludes with a warning to its readers about the 'calamity [that] awaiteth too servile a compliance with the king's pleasure'.[82]

Other, more substantial allegorical works instead considered Crown authority from a Tory perspective, and with reference to still more distant Eastern domains. John Shebbeare's *The History of the Excellence and Decline of the Constitution, Religion, Laws, Manners and Genius of the Sumatrans* (1760) concludes, as its subtitle declares, with 'the Restoration thereof in the Reign of Amurath the Third' – in other words, with the safeguarding of British liberty on George III's accession.[83] Tobias Smollett's shorter but denser *The History and Adventures of an Atom* (1769) tells of events in ancient Japan as they are imparted to Nathaniel Peacock, a London haberdasher, by an omniscient 'atom' that lived in the bodies of the key political actors of the time. In contrast to Shebbeare's *History*, there is no optimistic conclusion to Smollett's work, which presents the position of the Japanese emperor, dominated by his shoguns, as comparable to that of the British monarch, subordinated to minsters acting in their own party or personal interest.

Aravamudan argues that the creativity of Smollett's allegory exceeds any merely transitive function, since it playfully explores the 'amazing translingual parallels between Japanese imperial history and eighteenth-century British politics': 'perhaps his best pun,' he writes, 'is his naming of George II "Got-Hama-Baba" – suggesting Japanese emperor Go-Taba but also the founder of Buddhism, Gautama Buddha, and also "Gotham baby" (England's sovereign).'[84] It is important to recognize both the generic hybridity of a work such as Smollett's and the fact that 'Eastern' fiction of the 1760s encompassed not only the various fables and 'histories' considered earlier, but also less overtly politicized works in the romance mode such as Frances Sheridan's *The History of Nourjahad* (1767), an intricate *Arabian Nights*–style tale of shape-shifting and disguise. Here, though, I want to emphasize again that Orientalist fictions of this period, however topical their focus, demonstrated little direct engagement with the contemporaneous transformation of Britain's position in India. *Adventures of an Atom* briefly refers to 'a factor called Ka-liff, [who] obtained a considerable victory at Fla-sao, in the farther extremity of Tartary, where a trading company of Meaco possessed a commercial settlement', thereby alluding to Clive's triumph at Plassey, and by the rendering of his name, with its verbal echo of 'Caliph', suggesting his princely if not despotic status.[85] It seems fair to say nonetheless that India was still of relatively minor importance in Britons' imagination of empire. Other fictions of the 1760s largely eschewed any mention of recent events in India, even if like Smollett's work they reckoned with the way in which debate about the Seven Years' War and its consequences was bound up with struggles for political power in Britain. Charles Johnstone's pro-Pitt *Chrysal, or The Adventures of a Guinea* (1760) was 'written to appeal to a public avidly engrossed in news of the war', as Kevin Bourque states, but it traces its object narrator's travels only through Europe and America.[86]

James Ridley's *Tales of the Genii* (1764) provides a fascinating counter-example here, and deserves attention for that reason, because while it brings together fantastic and ostensibly apolitical fictions, 'the Delightful Lessons of Horam, the Son of Asmar', it prefaces them with a narrative placing their transmission in the larger context of relations between Britain and India. Ridley held an EIC chaplaincy sometime in the 1750s, although he did not go to India, instead joining a regiment on the 1761 expedition against Belle-Île. His introduction to *Tales of the Genii* takes the form of 'The Life of Horam', written by the likewise fictional figure of 'Sir Charles Morell', referred to on the work's title page as a former 'Ambassador from the British Settlements in India to the Great Mogul'. Morell describes meeting the enlightened Muslim Horam in Madras, where he was 'esteemed as a Saint by all Denominations', and he records a debate with Horam in which his friend expressed his incredulity at the disjunction between Christian teachings and the actual conduct of European merchants in India.[87] Horam's sense of this gulf, and his account of his own earlier time in England (after the death of the English merchant who had bought his services at Aleppo), may have provided Elizabeth Hamilton with the basis for her depiction of Zaarmilla and others in *Letters of a Hindoo Rajah* (1796). Horam's story also alludes to the prior example of Goldsmith's Altangi, since despite recognizing – following his unhappy encounter with the English merchant's brother – that 'Traffic is the prophet of the Europeans, and Wealth is their *Alla*' (1:xxii), he retained his ambition to educate himself in the arts and sciences of Europe, so as to implant 'in Asia the Seeds of that Learning which I had gathered' (1:xxiii). As is similarly the case with Goldsmith's depiction of Altangi, though, Morell's narrative has Horam offer ambivalent reflections on English national character, so that if the achievements of the 'Heaven-taught' Sir Isaac Newton indeed represent the pinnacle of human endeavour, for Horam, the English in general 'behave as though they were wiser than the God they pretend to worship' (1:xvii).

Ridley's nine purportedly 'Persian' tales are stylistically derivative, and only one of them uses an Indian setting, although that tale, 'The Inchanters', is also the longest in the collection. Briefly summarized, it stages the contest between Sultan Misnar, aided by his vizier (also named Horam) and the female genius Macona, and the seven evil genii in the service of Misnar's scheming younger brother, Ahubal. Ros Ballaster demonstrates 'The Inchanters'' indebtedness to the *Arabian Nights* and to previous collections of 'Indian' tales as well as to Spenserian narratives of temptation and trial.[88] While it presents itself as a fable offering generally applicable counsel as to 'the importance of sceptical reading' (in Ballaster's words), however, the tale also incorporates obliquely topical reference to European involvement in the conflict that it describes, as the rebellious Ahubal's armies receive external assistance via Ollomand, one of the genii set against Misnar.[89] Ollomand tells Ahubal about the potency of 'the Arms of *Europe*, a Part of the Earth filled with industrious Robbers, whose Minds are hourly on the Stretch to invent new Plagues to torment each other', and he claims to be able to manipulate these men 'through the Instigations of that God which they worship' (1:329). In an echo of Horam's claim that 'Traffic is the prophet of the Europeans, and Wealth is their *Alla*,' Ollomand states that 'Gold . . . is their God, for whose Sake they will undertake the most daring Enterprizes, and forsake the best of Friends' (1:330). Although he initially makes no distinction between the different Europeans 'settled on the Sea Coasts of our southern Provinces' (1:329), the reader is later told of 'Two hundred *French* Engineers', who were 'invited by large Rewards' (1:332) to join Ahubal's forces. This admittedly minimal point of detail adds further resonance to the tale's staging of conflict between the forces of good and evil, briefly suggesting the possibility that 'The Inchanters' might be read as an allegorization of the recent war in India between Britain and France – an idea that is plausible given that this was a war largely fought by native proxies.

There are aspects of 'The Inchanters' that such an interpretation cannot accommodate. Ridley's tale incorporates much non-specific 'Indian' nomenclature, while Misnar's status as the 'Sultan' of India calls up the Delhi Sultanate of the pre-Mughal historical period as well as the power relations of the present. The subsequent reception of *Tales of the Genii* – translated into French and German, and, later, an influence on Coleridge and Dickens – suggests too that, for many, the collection provided imaginative transport rather than topical allegory; the *Monthly Review* was hostile to the tales' fantastic content, but in stating that they contained 'inflated, jejune bombast', it identified this copiousness as their essential core.[90] Even as a tale such as 'The Inchanters' may have been widely received as an example of intransitive textuality (in Aravamudan's terms), however, it also distinguished itself from other near-contemporary Eastern fictions by situating the very idea of enchantment in the context of larger colonial realities.[91] Although Ballaster does not discuss the obtrusive appearance of '*French* Engineers' in 'The Inchanters', she reads *Tales of the Genii* as a whole as proleptic of the transfer of sovereignty that would be confirmed by the EIC's acquisition of revenue administration rights in Bengal. This transfer appears to be figured decisively at the end of the final tale, when Ridley's narrator directly addresses the reader, declaring that 'the *Genii* are no more, and Horam but the Phantom of my Mind, speaks not again' (2:401), before invoking a vision of Christ and announcing 'a happy Exchange from Pagan Blindness to Christian Verities' (2:403). While a tale such as 'The Inchanters' re-establishes legitimate and virtuous Muslim rule, Ridley's conclusion to the collection, as Ballaster argues, seemingly allegorizes how that sense of order was to be at once subsumed and superseded by an external, 'Christian' source of authority.

This conclusion may not be as clear-cut as Ballaster suggests, however. The closing renunciation of the 'gaudy Trappings of the *East*' (2:401) by Ridley's narratorial persona appears less assured when one considers the space that *Tales of the Genii* actually gives over to such enticing fictional adornment, and the extent to which readers may have been absorbed by it; the narrator concedes that using 'wild romantick Monsters . . . to serve the Cause of moral Truth' is to employ them 'far above their usual sphere'. The visionary account of the crucifixion and resurrection of Christ which follows moreover itself appears to be a product of the potentially delusive realm of 'Phantom and Imagination' against which the narrator cautions (2:402). Further to this, Ridley's frame tale offers an interrogative account of the EIC's authority and – at this time – resolutely commercial sense of purpose.[92] The narrator's declaration that, having exchanged Pagan error for Christian truth, 'We then may . . . look upon ourselves as Creatures dignified with Heaven's peculiar Grace' (2:403), for example, calls up the rather different perspectives on English exceptionalism that are voiced in the preliminary 'Life of Horam'. Here, as already noted, Morell records his friend's observations that 'the English behave as though . . . wiser than the God they pretend to worship' (1:xvii), and that their true God is money.

If his reference to 'Creatures dignified with Heaven's peculiar Grace' is not as obviously double-edged as Goldsmith's phrase 'the lords of human kind', the narrator's final appeal to this idea of conscious rectitude nonetheless fails to close off Horam's claims about the misplaced self-confidence of English Christians, and the atypicality of Morell.

Ridley's incorporation of such a critically detached account of how 'the English behave' is further illuminated by considering *Tales of the Genii* alongside the essays that he published in the *London Chronicle* between 1760 and 1762, collected as *The Schemer* (1763). While indebted to the *Spectator*'s depiction of a coffeehouse milieu, *The Schemer* also adopts a Sterne-like reflexivity: 'I object to all nonsense,' Ridley's narrator states at one point, 'and therefore I object to my own performance.'[93] Ridley's collection of papers purports to be the work of one 'Helter Van Scelter', and this self-positioning – connoting ideas of haste and disorder – is in keeping with the narrator's sense of the difficulty of 'being ... conversant about present objects', as well as of the impressionability of his audience. Where the current war is concerned, he states, his readers are 'a pack of wavering, unsteady, thoughtless, unprincipled blockheads', who have their 'weather-cock opinions' altered by 'Every wind' – every piece of news relating to the progress of the conflict.[94]

Ridley, like Goldsmith, often sought to distance himself from 'the pack', and to explore the workings of such popular curiosity. In a *Schemer* paper of November 1760, for example, the narrator describes meeting three 'very pretty ladies' asking about the destination of an imminent naval expedition, and 'desirous of engaging me in [their] conversation, which ran chiefly upon politics and war'.[95] 'I assured my fair inquisitors,' he writes, that:

> the fleet was to sail to destroy the colony of the *Anamacambites*, on the river *Allassapalata*: that *Nininipotrum*, the *Calapin*, which I told them was the same as *Nabob* in India, was to swear allegiance to his Majesty King *George*, and bring over, by treaty, the illustrious and far-renown'd *Nanpaliqualibamfamila-tapanaskpiniqudumpumpoinpoloneshebetemefuribusopotomares*, who were to come down in little boats, ... and so bring under subjection the whole country.[96]

The paper from which this passage is drawn is especially interesting because, like Swift's *Gulliver's Travels* (1724), it functions as a context-specific satire even as it enjoys its 'irresponsibility towards the cultural referent'.[97] Ridley stated in a footnote that the paper was 'written to laugh at ... the curiosity of the public' during the preparation of the expedition to Belle-Île on which he served, and his narrator fashions himself as a possessor of privileged information whose description of the ladies' 'relish for state matters' identifies them as unthinking devourers of news-mongering gossip. Initially, therefore, the 'inquisitors' represented here appear to demonstrate a debased appetite for novelty, akin to that of Goldsmith's 'ladies of distinction'. Any such satire of inappropriate curi-osity is complicated, however, not only because the women are said to have simply 'stared' in incredulity at the aforementioned recital, but also because the speaker goes on to add that 'I defy any politician in London to give a better,' assuring his audience that 'what I have told you is all that Mr. *Pitt* ever said to me upon the subject.'[98] As absurd as this account of distant actions seems to be, the scenario conjured up perhaps captures something of the difficulty of apprehending, and making sense of, the global conflict in which the nation had become embroiled – for an audience for whom the term 'Calapin' may indeed have been little stranger than 'Nabob'.

While exploring popular curiosity regarding apparently momentous events elsewhere in the world Ridley also emphasized how overseas conflict threw into relief the difficulty of conceiving of Britain as a unified nation. A later *Schemer* essay, published in July 1762, follows the example of Goldsmith's essay 'On Public Rejoicings for Victory', ventriloquizing multiple perspectives while framing these opinions as animated by an irrationality that the narrator himself seeks to transcend: 'On no one Party shall my censure fall,' runs one of the essay's epigraphs, 'All sides are mad, and I shall censure them all.'[99] The essay begins with panegyrics to Bute and Pitt (by 'The Dauber' and 'The Complimenter', respectively), and it rehearses the views of 'The Growler', for whom the loss of Minorca in 1756 still rankles, and of 'The Puffer', who thinks that 'while neither the fleets of *France* or *Spain* dare appear, what has *England* to do but to conquer the whole universe.' 'The Maligner' then claims to offer 'an impartial view' of the war, asking 'what reason [our countrymen] have to rejoice'.[100] His final suggestion that 'perhaps our progeny may say, – *We cannot discover, by the actions of our ancestors in the last century, whether they were wise or foolish*' recalls the provisionality that is often evident in Johnson and Goldsmith's political commentary, and is the closest that the essay gets to offering any position above the fray of the competing voices that it records.[101] Subsequently, though, the essay incorporates the unam-biguously parochial attitudes of 'The Taffy', 'The Teague', and 'The Sawney', followed by expressions of sectional economic interest from 'The Planter', 'The India-Man', and 'The Farmer'. What is especially significant about the latter is that the figures in question are both clamorous in support of their own agendas and resentful of any alternative distribution of national resources. 'Why was that dirty island *Belle-Isle* attempted last year,' the 'India-Man' asks, 'when *Mauritius* isles had otherwise been our own.' An EIC director, the 'India-Man' complains that '[Clive] has conquered for us' but made too much money in the process: 'we do not want to enrich our soldiery,' he declares, 'we want to enrich ourselves.'[102]

This account of a Britain riven by different and competing interest groups substantiates Horam's claim in *Tales of the Genii* that 'Wealth' is the god of Europeans. In a *Schemer* paper published in December 1762, Ridley composed an animal fable regarding the recently concluded Treaty of Paris, presenting a Lion who resolved to listen to his 'true and ancient subjects The Sheep' rather than to continue the conflict 'for the sport and entertainment of ravenous Tygers and Hyenas' or 'indolent and luxurious Hares' (respectively the army and London merchants, a footnote explains).[103] In his writings of the early 1760s Ridley was more emphatic than either Johnson or Goldsmith that the British conduct of the war was driven by a spirit of commercial adventurism and thus symptomatic of a hollowed-out public realm; the manner in which Ridley expressed 'the real interest of England' in his fable suggests that he felt this interest received little other articulation. Like Johnson and Goldsmith, however, Ridley also understood this state of affairs not just in terms of factional struggles for power and influence, but also as in some sense a product of the national character that he anatomized in a comparably ambivalent manner. Even as this trio of writers conceived of the nation's new openness to the world as potentially perilous, therefore, they all in different ways suggested that Britons were possessed of a restless energy that drove them on regardless.

Notes

1. Wilson, *Sense of the People*, 195.
2. Watts, *Cultural Work*.
3. Colley, *Britons*, 105.
4. Wilson, *Sense of the People*, 164.
5. Cited in introduction to De Bruyn and Regan, eds., *Seven Years' War*, 10 and 13.
6. Goldsmith, *Collected Works*, 3:86.
7. Ibid., 4:263.
8. Ridley, *Schemer*, 199.

9. Goldsmith, *Collected Works*, 2:27.
10. Johnson, *Works*, 6:91–2.
11. Johnson, *Works*, 5:296, 297, 300, and 305.
12. Though see Belcher, *Abyssinia's Johnson*, 212–43.
13. Barrell, *Equal, Wide Survey*, 40–5.
14. Johnson, *Works*, 16:17. Further references appear as parenthetical citations in the text.
15. Johnson, *Works*, 3:19.
16. *Monthly Review*, 20 (1759), 429.
17. Hawes, 'Johnson', 116.
18. Macaulay, *Poetry and Prose*, 564.
19. Belcher, *Abyssinia's Johnson*.
20. Hawes, 'Johnson', 115; Hudson, *Johnson*, 183.
21. Johnson, *Works*, 10:130.
22. Ibid., 188.
23. Voltaire, *Candide*, 73.
24. Johnson, *Works*, 2:95.
25. Johnson, *Works*, 10:149.
26. Hudson, *Johnson*, 183.
27. Johnson, *Works*, 2:253.
28. Goldsmith, *Collected Works*, 2:73.
29. Johnson, *Works*, 2:253.
30. Hudson, *Johnson*, 208.
31. Johnson, *World Displayed*, 1:xvi.
32. Neill, *Discovery Literature*, 139–42.
33. Johnson, *Works*, 2:386.
34. Neill, *Discovery Literature*, 144.
35. *Annual Register*, 54.
36. Johnson, *World Displayed*, 1:xvi; Neill, *Discovery Literature*, 143.
37. Voltaire, *Candide*, 99.
38. Scherwatzky, 'Politics of Empire', 110.
39. Watts, *Cultural Work*, 45.
40. Johnson, *Plan*, 33; Barrell, *Equal, Wide Survey*, 148–9.
41. Watts, *Cultural Work*, 49.
42. *Monthly Review*, n.s., 8 (1792), 106.
43. Scott, *Lives*, 161.
44. Goldsmith, *Collected Works*, 1:439.
45. Ibid., 1:370.
46. Ibid., 2:17. Further references appear as parenthetical citations in the text.
47. Ibid., 1:316.
48. Ibid., 1:439.
49. Porter, *Ideographia*, 139.
50. Aravamudan, *Enlightenment Orientalism*, 100.
51. Goldsmith, *Collected Works*, 3:17.
52. Watts, *Cultural Work*, 156; Goldsmith, *Collected Works*, 3:19.

53. Goldsmith, *Collected Works*, 3:19.
54. Ibid., 3:21.
55. Ibid., 3:32.
56. Ibid., 1:355.
57. Ibid., 1:418.
58. Ibid., 3:67–8.
59. Ibid., 3:85.
60. Ibid., 3:86.
61. Ibid., 4:249 and 250.
62. Ibid., 4:251.
63. Ibid., 4:263.
64. Ibid., 4:263.
65. Wilson, *Sense of the People*, 198–205.
66. Goldsmith, *Collected Works*, 4:263.
67. Ibid., 4:267.
68. Ibid., 4:266.
69. Ibid., 4:266.
70. Goldsmith, *An History of England*, 2:222.
71. Ibid., 2:234 and 241.
72. Ibid., 234.
73. Goldsmith, *The History of England*, 4:378 and 380.
74. Ibid., 4:409.
75. Ibid., 4:408.
76. *Complete History*, n.p.
77. Memoirs, vi.
78. Cambridge, *Account of the War*, iv.
79. *Monthly Review*, 20 (1759), 429.
80. Langhorne, *Solyman*, 73 and 78.
81. *Monthly Review*, 26 (1762), 254.
82. *The Orientalist*, 277, 279, and 280.
83. Shebbeare, *Sumatrans*.
84. Aravamudan, *Enlightenment Orientalism*, 242.
85. Smollett, *Atom*, 69.
86. Bourque, introduction to Johnstone, *Chrysal*, xvi.
87. Ridley, *Tales*, 1:x. Further references appear as parenthetical citations in the text.
88. Ballaster, *Fabulous Orients*, 309–25.
89. Ibid., 318.
90. *Monthly Review*, 31 (1764), 479.
91. Aravamudan, *Enlightenment Orientalism*, 56.
92. Ballaster, *Fabulous Orients*, 309.
93. Ridley, *Schemer*, 195.
94. Ibid., 134.
95. Ibid., 126.
96. Ibid., 128.

97. Aravamudan, *Enlightenment Orientalism*, 100.
98. Ridley, *Schemer*, 128.
99. Ibid., 190.
100. Ibid., 198.
101. Ibid., 199.
102. Ibid., 202.
103. Ibid., 238.

CHAPTER 2

'Indian Details'
Fictions of British India, 1774–1789

Like *Rasselas* and other works of the previous decades, the Irish novelist Charles Johnstone's *The History of Arsaces, Prince of Betlis* (1774) uses a minimally substantiated 'Eastern' setting with an allegorical function. Its main narrative describes the predicament of the 'Byrsans', who had founded colonies which 'drained their own country of its most useful inhabitants', and which over time 'felt their own strength' and asserted their independence, ever after 'carr[ying] themselves like states allied upon equal terms, rather than subjects'.[1] As he wrote in the preface to his tale, Johnstone assumed that readers would not expect to find closer description of 'the manners of the times and countries, in which the various scenes of the work are laid', since he drew 'the universal manners of Nature, which suit all climes and ages', and it 'would only have been pedantry' to do otherwise.[2] In his next work, *The Pilgrim: Or, A Picture of Life* (1775), by contrast, Johnstone followed Goldsmith's example instead, introducing the figure of a Chinese philosopher writing to a fellow countryman about his experiences in Britain. *The Pilgrim* addresses the state of the nation (including Britain's relationship with its American colonies) in a similar fashion to *Arsaces*, but its adaptation of the genre of informant narrative means that its attention to contemporary detail is very different. Albeit that it names India as 'Mogulstan', *The Pilgrim* refers to a more specific milieu than Johnstone's previous work, as is demonstrated by the fact that its protagonist, on the sea voyage from China, encounters a number of Britons returning home from the subcontinent.[3]

Juxtaposing these works captures the way in which, over the course of the 1770s and 1780s, prose fiction increasingly registered and in turn disseminated new kinds of awareness of the East. Johnstone remains a little-discussed writer, and he does not appear in Emma Rothschild's 'microhistory' of the global lives of the Johnstones of Dumfriesshire. Rothschild's account of the 'empire of economic opportunity' which was imagined by, and which drove, the Johnstone family before and

after the Seven Years' War does, though, help us to think about the
kind of movement that is represented not just by *The Pilgrim* but also
by numerous other fictions of India written as the EIC established
itself in Bengal.[4] This chapter takes as its point of departure the
intriguingly diverse stories of colonial return included in *The Pilgrim*,
and after considering the most widespread and influential means of
understanding Britain's relationship with India in this period – the
figure of the nabob – it then explores a range of other novels which in
different ways evoke culturally particular settings as they acknowledge
the interconnection of Britain and Bengal. Fictions such as *Memoirs of
a Gentleman, Who Resided Several Years in the East Indies* (1774) and
Helenus Scott's *Adventures of a Rupee* (1782) remain generically uneven
because even as they describe a commercial empire of freely moving
people and things, they additionally sometimes offer dissonant perspectives from outside of this network. Nonetheless, these fictions respond
to the scandal surrounding nabobs not only by countering the idea that
a Britain more connected to India might be dangerously open to the
East but also by circulating alternative reference points, such as the
Black Hole of Calcutta, to substantiate their claims about Indian
(rather than EIC) despotism. As I show in what follows, this emphasis
on an essentially 'Oriental' Indian despotism further provided a way of
asserting that an obverse notion of British liberty was uncompromised
by war – and defeat – in America.

Critics of the EIC, notably Edmund Burke, in turn addressed the
question of what, and especially how little, Britons knew about India.
Burke claimed that the metropolitan public was insufficiently acquainted
with 'Indian details' but that their sympathies might nonetheless be
extended so as to promote more enlightened and responsible colonial
rule.[5] After briefly considering Burke's much-discussed attempts to address
the imaginative challenges of spatial distance and cultural difference,
I examine what might be thought of as the problems of representation –
of bringing home 'Indian details' – in works with Indian settings that
differently engaged with the trial of Warren Hastings and the EIC's recent
record. I conclude by focusing on a text seen by contemporaries as
providing a closely realized and thus in some respects 'successful' picture
of Anglo-Indian society in the foremost EIC settlement, Phebe Gibbes's
Hartly House, Calcutta (1789). Rather than present Gibbes's novel as
heralding a new level of metropolitan awareness of British India through
its filling of the vacancy of Johnstone's 'Mogulstan', however, I think about
its suggestive staging of its narrator's withdrawal from the milieu in which

she initially immerses herself, and about the rape episode at the close which interrogates its readers' knowledge of India and Indian empire.

Stories of Colonial Return

Johnstone's *The Pilgrim* presents itself as a series of letters written by a Chinese philosopher to a friend at home. Like Goldsmith's Altangi, Johnstone's Choang upholds the ideal of 'philosophical' travel, seeking an unprejudiced insight into the 'genius and manners' (1:52) of Britons. Although his first letter is addressed to 'Chang-Ti Supreme Mandarin' (1:1), however, his correspondence thereafter discards this apparatus, and there is no epistolary exchange. Johnstone describes Choang's voyage to Britain in greater detail than Goldsmith, and additionally has him come into contact with various people, on the way home from India, who help reconcile him to their customs. This gradual process of acclimatization means that, compared with previous fictional travellers, he is seldom open to ridicule for misrecognizing what he sees. Johnstone's work is also less interested than Goldsmith's in the metropolitan misrecognition of things Chinese. Even as it rehearses the conventions of informant narrative (often borrowing from *The Citizen of the World*), *The Pilgrim* uses its Chinese philosopher as a means of providing a less mediated national survey, so that, for example, after noting the dreadful 'magnificence' of British preparations for naval warfare, Choang goes on to consider the no less 'magnificent' Royal Naval Hospital at Greenwich. Rewriting Altangi's account of how the poor carry the burden of Britain's military engagements overseas, Choang observes that 'marine veterans ... enjoy the evening of life in peace and plenty.' 'No wonder,' he adds, 'that soldiers should be invincible, who have such a reward in view' (1:147).

As in this reference to the invincibility of British armed forces, Johnstone's narrator is often less equivocal than Goldsmith's Altangi in celebrating the exceptionalist idea of national character that for some explained Britain's boasted supremacy in the arts of trade and war. After expressing his 'astonishment' at the extent of commercial activity on the Thames, and wondering how the people of 'this little island' (1:149) could possibly consume all the different kinds of merchandise that he sees, Choang is made to understand that Britain's geographical situation enables its inhabitants to preside over 'the universal mart' as 'the merchants, or rather the factors, of all other nations' (1:150). He displays a similar fascination with the feats performed by 'these islanders' earlier on when, after describing his own experience of seasickness, he marvels at the hardiness of the mariners who conduct the vessel in which he sails, speculating that they might be 'endowed by nature with a greater contempt of [danger] . . . than all the rest of mankind' (1:22).

On his arrival in Britain Johnstone's awestruck narrator states that '[t]his people are far more powerful than we could think, even from their own accounts' (1:78). Unlike Altangi, Choang provides his addressee with an admiring description of Britain's global reach, referring to Bengal as 'a town built by those sons of industry . . . for the purpose of carrying on their commerce' (1:7). In imagining Bengal in such a way he ignores the vast hinterland of the EIC's coastal trading factory and evades questions about sovereign power in the province as a whole, thus perpetuating the fiction that Britain's empire remained essentially commercial. *The Pilgrim*, like *Arsaces*, registers that this ideology of virtuous empire faced a radical challenge as a result of Britain's ongoing dispute, about to escalate into conflict, with its American colonies: 'the delicate situation' over the taxation of the colonies, a kindly member of the nobility tells Choang, places the government in a double bind, whereby 'To support our authority may too probably plung[e] us into all the horrors of a civil war! To give it up, will be to [give] up an empire, to establish which we have exhausted ourselves' (1:216). If the choice is presented as a 'dreadful' one, however, *The Pilgrim* combines this anticipation of a protracted struggle in America with a sense of the rich, though minimally specified, possibilities afforded to Britons by 'Mogulstan', which clearly stands for India but is named with the inattention to detail of the fictions discussed in the previous chapter. Among the characters that Choang encounters on his voyage from Bengal are men going home after making their fortunes (through 'lucrative employment' [1:62] or 'unwearied industry' [1:63]), as well as a woman, Emily Courtley, carrying with her 'a casket filled with jewels' (1:43), a gift from a native 'Commander' (1:34). Emily tells of how this man had raped her (after the death of her husband left her wandering unprotected), but then went on to become a 'generous benefactor' (1:41), on finding out that her late husband was a man who had once saved the lives of himself and his father.

Although *The Pilgrim*'s matter-of-fact account of Emily's violation is less symbolically charged than the numerous references to rape in other late eighteenth-century writings about India, the seemingly bizarre conjunction of events that Emily narrates is characteristic of the fictions with Indian plots or episodes that were published in the late 1770s and 1780s, as I go on to show. A further measure of *The Pilgrim*'s unevenness is that after describing Emily's return home to enjoy 'the fruits of . . . difficulties and dangers' (1:43), it tells of Choang's visit to another figure just back from the East whose efforts at architectural improvement and art collecting show that his retirement is far less peaceful, such that he 'could not bear to look a second time at any thing he showed us' (1:117). Whereas one of Goldsmith's overbearing 'ladies of distinction' expresses her surprise that Altangi is unable to appreciate true Chinese taste, Choang's unnamed host instead seeks advice on how to imitate 'the style of your country' (1:119) so as to distinguish himself from his peers. *The Pilgrim* departs from Goldsmith's example again here in that Choang's host is identifiable as a specific individual, Robert Clive, associated with 'military exploits [which] rendered his name famous through all the regions of the east'. His residence is 'one of his country seats not far from [London]' (1:116), an allusion to Claremont in Surrey, which Clive commissioned Capability Brown to rebuild in 1772, after ordering the original Vanbrugh-designed house to be pulled down. Johnstone's presentation of Clive appeals to the popular fantasy that the latter felt guilty about having 'ground the faces of the unhappy natives of Mogulstan' (1:121). He is described as 'the most unhappy of human kind' (1:120), and the novel's brief character sketch emphasizes the feverish self-hatred that was widely supposed to have gripped Clive before his probable suicide.

This unflattering portrait may in part be attributed to its author's probable connection with George and William Johnstone (from the family's Dumfriesshire branch), who were both involved in the anti-Clive campaign in the lead-up to the parliamentary inquiry into EIC affairs in 1772–3. *The Pilgrim* does not simply scapegoat Clive, however, since it acknowledges that all high-profile returnees from India are liable to be 'held in abhorrence by the very people who profit of the fruits of their iniquity, and flatter them to their faces' (1:121). While Choang invokes a common knowledge of predatory EIC practices, it is significant too that the novel elsewhere refers to British victims of native barbarity, since Emily's husband is said to have suffocated to death in a 'dungeon' from the contemplation of which 'imagination starts back affrighted' (1:25) – an allusion to the notorious Black Hole of Calcutta. Choang's obtrusive reference to 'Mogulstan' in the passage discussed earlier in this chapter additionally reminds us of his earlier encounter with the Britons sailing home from Bengal on the same ship. If Emily's gift from a native prince ironically alludes to the 'presents' that Clive himself received, one man on this voyage is said to have become rich 'not without ... publick merit' (1:63), while another acquired a fortune from 'imitating the crimes as well as the follies of his superiors' (1:62).

Novels before *The Pilgrim* incorporated equally resonant episodes of 'colonial return': Henry Mackenzie's *The Man of Feeling* (1771) includes the pathos-laden story of the pressganged soldier 'Old Edwards', whose sympathy for suffering Indians prompts the sentimental hero Harley to lament that there are so few others like him.[6] *The Pilgrim* is especially interesting for my purposes, however, not just because of its revision of Goldsmith's work, but since the stories that it tells of newly rich Britons coming home from India are so different from one another, and thus appear to offer competing and seemingly irreconcilable perspectives on the politics of empire in this period. In a work that incorporates, as its subtitle declares, 'curious and interesting anecdotes, and characters drawn from real life', these episodes acknowledge the contentious origins of the wealth flowing to Britain from India, but variously present it as the product of benefaction, industry, and plunder – respectively gifted, earned, and looted. I now further explore the provisionality as well as complexity of Britons' reckoning with their new Eastern empire – in particular its domestic effects – with reference to the ubiquitous figure of the nabob.

Laughing at Nabobs

The EIC's acquisition of revenue administration rights in Bengal in 1765 confirmed the decisive shift in its status from trader to sovereign, bringing into greater focus questions concerning its constitutional position, the desirability of territorial dominion in Asia, and the impact of Indian wealth on Britain's social and political life. By the early 1770s, in the aftermath of the terrible Bengal famine, 'Considerations on Indian Affairs' (the title of William Bolts's influential exposé of EIC corruption) additionally encompassed the conduct of EIC servants, widely accused of exploiting the people of India in the course of amassing their private fortunes. It was the 'scandal of empire' which helped to circulate greater awareness of the subcontinent for Britons in this period, and the stereotype of the 'nabob', embodied by Clive, assumed an especially prominent cultural significance throughout the 1770s and beyond, as has been widely discussed.[7] While the actual influence of returning East Indians has been disputed, the number of textual and visual representations of such men (and occasionally women) indicates that the idea of the nabob provided one of the primary means by which late eighteenth-century Britons conceived of the relationship between metropole and colony.

Samuel Foote's play *The Nabob* (1772) is an important work to consider in this context because of the way in which it stages the connection between colonial wealth and domestic social transformation. The title character, Sir Matthew Mite, attempts to use his riches to gain the hand of a baronet's daughter and to buy his way into Parliament, and the mixture of social ambition, conspicuous consumption, and Orientalized manners that he displays identifies him as a composite portrait of Clive and other prominent contemporaries. *The Nabob* satirizes Mite's efforts to pass as a gentleman and to legitimize his new wealth, as in the scene where he is instructed how to throw dice more gracefully, or where he submits 'relics', including a chamber pot, for the approval of 'the Antiquarian Society', after which he is pronounced 'equally skilled in arts as well as in arms'.[8] Mite is in many ways an absurd figure, then, and ostensibly at least his purpose is to provide audiences with the enjoyable spectacle of his defeat, reassuring them that the essential character of 'home' remains unchanged. After Mite names Sophy Oldham as his price for not calling in her father, Sir John's, debts to him, the merchant Thomas Oldham steps in to discharge his brother's financial obligations, in return for which he secures his son's marriage to Sophy. The strategic class alliance thus forged at the end of the play seems at once to exclude the designing outsider and to protect the position of the landed family on whose vulnerability he had sought to prey.[9]

Foote's play further suggests, however, both that the Oldhams would have been ruined without Thomas's intervention and that the funds with which he saves their daughter and their estate from falling into the clutches of a nabob may themselves have Eastern origins. While Mite is caricatured as a brashly exhibitionist parvenu he is nonetheless given some telling lines, as when he cannily responds to Thomas's fantasy about the 'retribution' that he will one day meet: 'This is not Sparta, nor are these the chaste times of the Roman republic,' he defiantly states, for '[n]owadays, riches possess at least one magical power, that, being rightly dispensed, they closely conceal the source from whence they proceeded' (111). Mite's reference to the 'magical' process of money laundering draws attention to the fact that the source of Thomas's trading fortune itself remains unclear. Thomas earlier declares that 'there are men from the Indies, . . . who dispense nobly and with hospitality here, what they have acquired with honour and credit elsewhere' (88), and the play establishes an opposition between such legitimate activity and the shadowy transactions by which Mite initially gains his hold over Sir John. If Thomas Oldham is contrasted with Mite here, though, in other respects he resembles him, as when he uses the influence provided by his wealth in order to negotiate, on his son's behalf, for the hand of Sophy Oldham. While *The Nabob* portrays Thomas's defeat of Mite as a victory for the commercial classes that confirms their growing social sway, it additionally implies that Mite only represents a particularly flagrant example of the impact of remotely acquired, and largely invisible, riches on the nation.[10]

Thomas responds to Lady Oldham's jeremiad about the corrupting agency of the 'horrid crew' of nabobs by stating that 'a general conclusion from a single instance is but indifferent logic' (88), inviting us to recognize that, for the author and his contemporaries, 'nabob' served as an adaptable term of abuse without a precise definition. Just as *The Pilgrim* reflects on the shaming of individuals such as Clive, so Foote's play shows its awareness of the process by which Mite or any other analogous figure could be regarded as atypical, as an object onto which playgoers were able to project their disquiet while avoiding any deeper scrutiny of Britain's relations with India. Thomas differentiates Mite from 'men from the Indies' who have 'added virtues' as well as 'dominions and wealth' to their country, and he thus provides the mercantile constituency of the play's audience with what the *General Evening Post* identified as 'a very elegant compliment'.[11] He also mystifies the origins of EIC authority in Bengal, referring to 'the caprice of fortune, and ... strange chain of events' that gave Britons 'uncontrolled power abroad' (90).

The Nabob is at its most reflexive in a passage of dialogue between the Mayor of Bribe'em and Touchit, members of the 'Christian Club' seeking to sell the borough of Bribe'em's parliamentary seats. Addressing Mite's wealth and the connection between Britain and India in very basic terms, it begins with the Mayor asking, since he has 'never been beyond sea', how men such as Mite first acquired their riches. Touchit replies 'from our settlements and possessions abroad', and in answer to his friend's question about 'what sort of things them there settlements are', he justifies the EIC's gradual encroachment on the natives with whom it initially established a 'beneficial commerce' by declaring that '[t]hese people are but a little better than Tartars or Turks.' When the Mayor contradicts him to say that instead 'it is they have caught the Tartar in us', Touchit's response is simply to exclaim: 'Ha, ha, ha! Well said, Mr Mayor' (99). Touchit is affiliated to Mite as his election agent, and his laughter could be read as self-incriminating. This laughter nonetheless closes off, without resolving, the preceding debate about the circumstances of the EIC's ascendancy, and – importantly – the play's audience is invited to participate in it. While the idea that Britons might themselves be 'little better than Turks' offers the disturbing reminder of a residual despotism in the British state, as Ahmed argues, Touchit's insouciance ('Well said, Mr Mayor') suggests how readily he is able to accommodate any such claim.[12] As much as the play is generally viewed as a 'satire' of nabobs, dialogue such as this shows how Foote's text sometimes undercuts its attack on Mite and what he represents. Foote himself at first performed the role of the villainous nabob that he created, and his renowned talents as a comic actor may have similarly complicated the meanings of the play, by giving the part of Mite a life of its own in excess of, even divergence from, the agenda that it has most often been seen to serve.

'The Nabob, or Asiatic Plunderers' (1773) demonstrates that at least some contemporaries saw the comedy of Foote's drama as compromising any critical stance on nabobery that it offered. This anonymous poem directly pits gravity against levity, assuming a position of 'honest Indignation' towards nabobs and repudiating a *Beggar's Opera*-style '*laughing* Satyr': 'The Muse must be serious,' the preface declares, 'or the Impression will be lost.'[13] The work takes the form of a dialogue between an 'Author' and his 'Friend', and it makes the latter a devil's advocate who challenges his companion to explain his interest in the affairs of a far-off country. The poem is no more rhetorically consistent than the play, however, because while the Author repeatedly declares that an innate moral sense makes everyone concerned for their fellow human beings, his companion's questioning causes him to lose confidence in this conviction. The Author's Friend is in turn vindicated, since if his claims sometimes partake of Mite's worldly cynicism (his jibe that the Author is '[a] century too late' [28] echoes Mite's 'This is not Sparta'), he also substantiates his assertion that '[c]onscience in some ... is dead' (26), taking Bolts's *Considerations* as evidence. The Author thereafter continues to suggest that nabobs may 'dread ... spectres of the famish'd dead' (31), but at the same time he calls for the public hanging of such 'odious murderers', in case their crimes 'should be too soon forgot' (32), and so as to strike fear into those who would otherwise be tempted to imitate them. In the very process of attempting to 'hand down the Memory of the Oppressors to the latest Posterity' (as the preface puts it), then, the Author acknowledges the possibility, even likelihood, of Britons developing an amnesia regarding the evils perpetrated by 'Asiatic Plunderers', if they were aware of them in the first place. Though the Author initially strives to bring home what his Friend represents as distant ills, his righteous vision of the spectacular punishment of 'guilty Greatness' (32) proclaims the failure of his efforts to establish ties of feeling between Britons and the nameless, voiceless victims of the recent famine in Bengal.

India remains distant in part because, like Foote's Lady Oldham, the Author conceives of 'Asia' more generally as a source of contagion, capable of corrupting others even as it is plundered by them: 'In *Asia*'s realms let slavery be bound,/ Let not her foot defile this sacred ground' (38), he states. 'The Nabob' combines this appeal to Asiatic despotism not only with its sentimental portrayal of Indian victims of British cruelty but also with a footnote reference to slavery in the West Indies, represented – like the irreligion of 'our traders' in India – as 'the fruit of commerce', which 'refines ... manners, but ... corrupts morals' (42). Up until the impeachment of Hastings, numerous other late eighteenth-century works similarly paralleled EIC activities with those of slave owners and traders; 'the nation on trial' was a popular rhetorical trope before the trial of Hastings himself. What is especially interesting about 'The Nabob', however, is that while the Author begins by denouncing Britain's role in the world beyond its shores, in the name of sympathy with the suffering of distant others, he finally concedes the futility of moral critique. The Author closes the poem with an anecdote about an aged parent addressing his son prior to the latter's departure for India, but the familiar scenario set up here is subverted when the wisdom imparted turns out simply to be that 'man's a cypher, if not crown'd with wealth.' After repeatedly telling his Friend that his own fellow-feeling knows no bounds, the Author rehearses what he takes to be the 'maxims of the world's school': 'Friendship's a name; be first thy own dear friend,/ Let friendship here begin, here let it end' (40).

Fictions of Commercial Empire

By presenting his capacity for sympathy as exceptional rather than universal, the Author in 'The Nabob' alludes to a problem identified by many others, that spatial distance and cultural difference made it difficult if not impossible for Britons imaginatively to 'connect' with India.[14] I later consider Burke's efforts to expand Britons' imaginative horizons so as to afford them greater awareness of their subject peoples, and in Chapter 4 I explore Sir William Jones's contemporary project to assimilate Indian otherness for a metropolitan audience. Here, though, I want to examine the way in which new forms of fiction negotiated the 'problem of distance' that was broached by 'The Nabob', while at the same time recuperating the selfish instinct referred to by the figure of the Author, and thereby contesting his emphasis on the scandalous conduct of 'Asiatic Plunderers'.[15] The two works that I focus on, the anonymous *Memoirs of a Gentleman* (1774) and Helenus Scott's *Adventures of a Rupee* (1782), pay more attention to colonial adventure than to colonial return, and in doing so they represent a harnessing of the restlessness that had so fascinated Johnson, Goldsmith, and Ridley a decade or so earlier. Even the first of these works, which suggests its author's direct experience of the subcontinent, does not portray a significantly 'thicker' or more fully realized India than previously published fictions. Both works nonetheless associate Britain's openness to the East with economic opportunity, and they conceive of an interconnection between Britain and India, at least insofar as they depict this relationship as the function of a 'natural' circulation of people and things. The title of this section alludes to the distinction drawn by Adam Smith, in *Wealth of Nations* (1776), between the equalizing potential of global commerce and the EIC's actual record as a trading corporation with monopoly power.[16] The narratives of British India that I now discuss appeal to the fantasy of a commercial empire from which Britain and India might mutually benefit, and they identify the EIC as a guarantor of this state of affairs even as they acknowledge criticism of its operations.

Memoirs of a Gentleman presents itself as the 'back-story' of a nabob prior to his return home, and its narrator is a fortune-seeking German surgeon who sails for Bengal after failing to get ahead in Dutch Batavia. Finding employment with a 'Rajah', he rescues the widow of the Rajah's brother from immolation on his funeral pyre.[17] Rather than dwell on this practice as a marker of 'Indian' difference, however, the narrator emphasizes how the 'Gentoo lady' (105) in question becomes attached to him and jealous of the other women whom he encounters. Across the work as a whole, the narrator styles himself as a libertine rather than a liberator, describing at one point how he and a Danish doctor together enjoyed 'as many black women as we could find' (143). *Memoirs of a Gentleman* concludes with a brief account of its protagonist's infatuation with a Frenchwoman of English descent who in turn takes him for 'an English gentleman' (230), and this resolution seems to prepare the way for his return to respectable society. At the end of the preceding chapter, nonetheless, the narrator unequivocally celebrates his sexual adventurism, stating that 'I was never so happy . . . as when in company with the fair sex, who were always very obliging to me' (221).

When reissued under the title of *The Indian Adventurer* (1780), the work was condemned by the *Monthly Review* as 'vulgar' and 'insufferably coarse and indelicate'.[18] If *Memoirs of a Gentleman* may have been read as a story of individual depravity bearing out popular stereotypes about nabobs in India, however, its account of the EIC's establishment of its sovereignty nonetheless bypasses any notion of the scandal of empire. The vicissitudes of the narrator's life make him a spectator on what the work's subtitle terms 'the late revolutions ... in that part of the world', so that, for example, after fleeing with the Indian widow that he rescues, he and his new companion are apprehended by 'English Seapoys' (113) and held as prisoners in Calcutta. This experience of captivity prompts reference to the horrors of the Black Hole, to Clive's defeat of Siraj ud-Daula, and to the rapid succession of native rulers who followed thereafter. In his 1783 'Speech on Fox's India Bill', Burke presented the EIC's Indian clients as pawns in the hands of a power that had broken every treaty into which it had entered: 'Seraja Dowla was sold to Mir Jaffier; Mir Jaffier was sold to Mir Cossim; and Mir Cossim was sold to Mir Jaffier again.'[19] *Memoirs of a Gentleman*, by contrast, presents the figure of 'Meer Cossim' as a scheming despot, who, having plotted against his father-in-law, and 'exacted ... exorbitant taxes from the people' (119) once in power, then attempts to involve the narrator in soliciting the Dutch to ally with him against the British. The narrator personally testifies to Meer Cossim's untrustworthiness, and this characterization of him is followed by an account of his attack on the garrison in Patna, and his subsequent defeat at the battle of Buxar, which secured EIC authority in Bengal, and paved the way for its assumption of revenue collection rights in 1765.

It is significant that the author of *Memoirs of a Gentleman* opted to rehearse this decade-old story at a time when, because of more recent controversy, the EIC's reputation was at a nadir. While attempting to 'set ... in the clearest light' Siraj-ud-Daula's nefarious 'exploits' (115), the narrator also counters the charge that EIC servants were ruthlessly concerned with their own gain: he presents himself as scrupulously honest in all his dealings, such that in the opinion of one native merchant community, he claims, he was among 'the most humane Europeans they had ever met with' (177). By thus introducing a protagonist who is alive to commercial as well as sexual opportunity, the work at once rehearses and contains the popular critique of men with Indian fortunes, acknowledging their libidinal energies but additionally presenting such energies as to some extent channelled into more honourable pursuits. The narrator's account of his private trading activity does not simply demonstrate his honesty, however, since his mobility conveys an ideologically powerful impression of the state of flux pertaining, until recently, 'in that part of the world'. The 'late revolutions' of the *Memoirs'* subtitle are presented as internally generated as much as they are the product of any external agency, and the work can thus be seen as helping to circulate the enduring story of Mughal implosion that, according to many later histories of empire, served to clear a space for, and to legitimize, British intervention.

The object narrator at the beginning of *Adventures of a Rupee* establishes the idea of Indian lawlessness in a similar fashion to *Memoirs of a Gentleman*, by initially describing its time in the hands of a corrupt fakir, then imagining a different life in England on the basis of the reputation enjoyed by 'that great East India Company' in Bengal.[20] In stating that the EIC 'keep[s] black men in such good order at so great a distance' (13), the rupee both acknowledges and diminishes the 'problem of distance' referred to earlier, albeit that in this instance the problem relates to the feasibility of remotely exercised authority rather than imaginative sympathy. Shortly afterwards, the work incorporates the 'History of Miss Melvil', whose account of her father's final words to his Eastbound son revises the scene of paternal advice at the end of 'The Nabob': 'Your particular province is to protect the trade of your country, against the insults of European powers, or of the Indian nations, who ignorant of the blessings that commerce diffuses, even to themselves, are often disposed to interrupt its equitable course' (59). Whereas Burke complained that '[e]very rupee of profit made by an Englishman is lost forever to India,' Scott here rebuts any such claims about EIC extraction of Indian wealth, suggesting that the equality of commerce imagined as an ideal by Smith might already prevail.[21]

This opposition between the state of anarchy in which the fakir's band flourishes and the conditions of stability provided elsewhere by the EIC is complicated by the initial presentation of Hyder Ali, Sultan of Mysore, as an additional lawgiving force. This seemingly positive depiction of Hyder is especially noteworthy since at the time of publication, as Scott records, the state of Mysore, in alliance with France, had been at war with EIC forces for nearly two years. Hyder is described as a distinguished general who instils a European-style military discipline among his troops, and he is further presented as capable of humane feeling, since he acts as the protector of Miss Melvil, whom his forces had captured at Arcot shortly after she joined her enlisted lover, and her brother. Maria Melvil refers to her temporary guardian as 'illustrious Hyder' and speaks warmly of the 'fatherly affection' (87) she receives in his custody before she is finally returned to her betrothed 'in her native innocence' (91). Contemporary critics of the EIC often invoked Hyder Ali's potency against the military expansionism that they associated with Warren Hastings, Governor-General of Bengal.[22] The scene of parental counsel referred to earlier similarly engages with contemporary debates about the EIC's remit, because while Mr Melvil tells his son that the protection of commerce constitutes a 'glorious' calling, by which unspecified past 'abuses' may be rectified, he acknowledges that others have with justification 'cursed our rapacity' (60). This sense of a general unscrupulousness among EIC servants is signalled by the title of the chapter in question, 'A father's advice to his son on going to India, I am afraid, somewhat unlike that of every modern one' (47).

Subsequently, however, *Adventures of a Rupee* moves away from any such implicit criticism of the EIC, and after recounting Maria Melvil's story shifts its focus back to Britain, as the rupee narrator comes into the possession of 'an English common sailor' (93), and is thus finally granted its wish to travel to England. Among the rupee's later owners is a soldier named Bob, who finds the coin in St James's Park. The soldier's story is pathos laden, since his preparation to serve his country abroad separates him from his sweetheart, but it also enables Scott to reflect on the EIC's 'great success', which Bob attributes to the meritocratic means by which 'their officers attain a high command': 'It is not because a man is of a noble family, or has a weighty purse,' the narrator states, channelling Bob's thoughts, 'it is known abilities and former services that entitle him to a distinguished rank' (244). If this idealized image of the EIC might be read as a function of its author's quest for professional advancement – Scott was about to be commissioned as an assistant surgeon when he wrote the work – it significantly circumvents the history of scandal that Mr Melvil had earlier invoked. As in *Memoirs of a Gentleman*, the critique of EIC rapacity is therefore countered by the claim that Britain's Indian empire remains benignly commercial in character. Mr Melvil in his advice to his son insists on the mutual interdependence generated by commerce, and the potential for harmonious and sociable relations between people of different 'kingdoms' is signalled again, in a domestic context, at the conclusion, when Bob refers to his Jewish friend Moses, renowned for his 'extreme application to business' (248).

Bob states that the 'similarity of sentiment' which unites the two men overrides and renders irrelevant 'distinctions, which neither of us can help' (246). It is important, though, that if Bob and Moses are presented as belonging to different kingdoms, their friendship is established in Britain. While the 'it-narrative' genre was especially hospitable to the staging of circulation and the enacting of relations between peoples and places, *Adventures of a Rupee* – unsurprisingly – does not depict any diffusion of the blessings of commerce taking place in India. Instead, the rupee narrator spends most of its time in Britain, where it is 'a kind of curiosity' (103), but where, since it is not legal tender, it is also out of circulation, and outside of the network of commercial empire. The rupee's distance from actual processes of exchange is emphasized again at the close, when it speaks of being 'laid up in the storehouse of a company of antiquarians, ... with medals, busts, inscriptions, and others of my learned brethren' (260). Here, the rupee tells of how 'Cato gave us a long oration ... against the vices of the age,' speaking 'with much severity against corruption, from which he naturally passed to censure the British parliament' (263). This brief allusion to parliamentary corruption is striking in view of the work's praise elsewhere of George III, who was so often accused at this time of encroaching upon the powers of Parliament. That the figure of 'Cato' more or less has the final word in *Adventures of a Rupee* is especially interesting when the work's engagement with the politics of empire is considered, however, since *Cato's Letters* (1720–3) was widely cited in this period in support of a policy of conciliation towards America.[23] This final scene draws attention to the larger 'crisis of liberty' generated by Britain's war with its American colonies, and with this in view I now examine how in Robert Bage's *Mount Henneth* (1782) as well as in Scott's novel an 'Indian' plot provides a means of negotiating the ideological fall-out of conflict in another part of the world.[24]

'It Might Compensate Many of Our Losses'

According to the anonymous 'Memoirs of the Author' prefacing the second edition of *Adventures of a Rupee*, Scott's 'passionate admiration of liberty ... called his notice to America', inspiring him 'to make ... the offer of his sword' to George Washington; 'from this youthful sally, in which he consulted chiefly the vivacity of his temper,' however, 'he was diverted by the prudence of his friends,' who were able to obtain him a cadetship in India.[25] Scott's apparent support for the revolutionary cause, represented here as quixotic enthusiasm, makes his novel's lack of reference to America all the more intriguing. The work's engagement with the consequences of this conflict is nonetheless evident when the English sailor who gains possession of the rupee deposits his Indian souvenir with a pawnbroker, and the rupee then inspects the different customers who come into the pawnbroker's shop. Shortly after describing a military veteran who 'left his legs in Germany' (143) during the Seven Years' War and now exchanges his sword for cash to enable him to carry on drinking the King's health, the narrator observes the entrance of a 'powdered and scented' gentleman officer, 'with a belly somewhat prominent, a certain sign of ease'. This man comes to purchase rather than to pledge, acquiring 'a breast-pin set with diamonds' (163), which he fixes to his shirt before admiring himself in a mirror and strutting out. The novel later describes the same figure as typical of 'many of our military youths', 'with no knowledge of war, and with no predilection for the army that reason can justify' (243), and it becomes clear here that it participates in the denunciation of an effeminate and ineffectual officer caste. Scott employs a form of class critique which sometimes overlapped with the censure of an 'aristocratic' nabobery but which in this episode alludes especially to the incompetence of those associated with Britain's defeat in America.

The novel's remedial response to such corruption is most evident when it introduces Signor Antonio, a political refugee from Venice who in a chance encounter meets his old friend Signor Tedeschi, now contentedly settled in Britain. Just as Scott's work uses 'the most objective of sources: the object itself' (in Lynn Festa's words) to praise the effectiveness of EIC rule, so it uses Tedeschi to remind Britons of their own privileged birthright: 'This happy land shall shine for ever in the historian's page, a glorious instance of the blessings that freedom bestows' (197).[26] Antonio for his part hails this '[b]lest country' as 'the refuge of mortals from oppression', adding that '[s]urely Britons cannot know the extent of their own happiness, which experience enables me to see from comparison in its strongest colours!' (198).

In claiming that a native spirit of British liberty remains uncompromised (and will indeed 'shine for ever' [197]), Scott's Venetians sidestep the fact that American revolutionaries had appealed to the very same heritage in their resistance to British colonial rule. That Scott sought to pass over his own earlier support for that cause is suggested by a subsequent episode, in which the rupee comes into the hands of a nurse taking care of the King's children. Scott's work appears to absolve the monarchy of any responsibility for the American debacle, while at the same time distancing itself from the Whig campaign against the EIC (which, especially after the fall of the Fox-North coalition in late 1783, presented George III as a despotic figure). The favourability of the immediate impression created by the King – exalted above his subjects in 'merit' as well as in 'dignity' – is heightened by the fact that, as the narrator explains, 'Hyder Alli was the only potentate I had before visited.' Invoking an ability to read people's thoughts, the rupee now tempers its earlier account of the Sultan, presenting him as a man whose mind was 'perpetually . . . forming dark designs to accomplish his bloody purposes'. Whereas Hyder dreams of avenging himself on 'these white men that infest our country', King George 'hold[s] in his hands the scales in which mighty Kingdoms were weighed', remaining the embodiment of justice in defiance of the nations, France and Spain, that had recently 'taken up arms against his sea surrounded land' – additional but also reassuringly familiar adversaries. The narrator goes on to assert that the 'impotent efforts' of these nations 'will expose them to contempt, while Britain shall remain the admiration of future times', and the rupee prophesies that George III's 'free born subjects' (231), wherever they subsequently go, will 'carry in their hands both victory and law!' (232).

The idea implicit here, that India might provide Britons with a way of forgetting about America, is more clearly evident in Thomas Day's *Reflections upon the Present State of England, and the Independence of America* (1783). As if to indicate that he had himself already adjusted to the nation's reduced status in the world, Day ridiculed the idea that America needed to maintain any connection with 'a small damp island, placed at the distance of many thousand miles, in order to enable it to subsist'.[27] While Day thus mocked the nation's 'conviction of its ... greatness', however, he also argued that American independence might in fact be beneficial to Britain.[28] A peace settlement with the colonists, he declared, 'would enable us to turn our attention at leisure to the immense territories we possess in India; a territory so vast, so fertile, so well peopled, that it might compensate many of our losses, could we be convinced of the need of regulating it by wholesome laws ... instead of making it the theatre where European plunderers contend for pillage'. Day referred to India only once, in a passage which tempers this sense of Eastern promise by acknowledging the EIC's inglorious recent history.[29] Like many writers and politicians of the early 1780s, nonetheless, Day suggested that the project of colonial integration which had failed in the West might still be successful in the East, and indeed might help to offset that earlier failure.

Even more directly than *Adventures of a Rupee* and Day's *Reflections*, Robert Bage's epistolary novel *Mount Henneth* addresses, in the words of the character Tom Sutton, 'the wound given to this country, by its breach with the colonies'.[30] A story related by another, John Cheslyn, tells of Carthage's failed attempt to tax 'the Hesperides' (1:60) 2,000 years previously, and in similarly suggestive terms, the American Camitha Melton asserts 'her claim to independency' (1:75) when she is confined 'under a general warrant' (1:131) by a London brothel keeper, following the capture by a privateer of the ship on which she was sailing to Europe. Miss Melton's allegorical function is complicated by the fact that she turns out to be half Native American; furthermore, the reader is informed that her father left America a disillusioned man, 'thinking himself not well used by some of his own party' (1:26). If Bage's work provides little overt commentary on the ideological repercussions of the conflict in America, however, numerous characters express their opposition to the war because of its impact upon their stakes in transatlantic commerce. Like many of Bage's later novels, *Mount Henneth* also sets up a contrast between the strife that rages elsewhere and an alternative, small-scale model of virtuous community, centred on the Henneth estate itself, 'a neighbourhood, of the worthy and the good' (1:68).

Before he becomes a steward to James Foston (the estate's new owner), Tom Sutton is tempted by the prospect of an EIC commission, prompting his sister Nancy to caution that his quest for an Indian fortune will take him to 'tainted regions, where war and desolation reign; to become an adept in the murder of mankind!' (1:57). Bage's novel rehearses the terms of anti-EIC rhetoric on other occasions, coupling America and India and referring to the 'mercantile or military oppression, for which our generous countrymen are at present famous' (1:29). When John Cheslyn contemplates what lies ahead for Sutton, however, he expresses a wish that Sutton follow the early career of his future employer, who, we are told, 'went out a writer . . ., but was a lieutenant under Col. Clive, when [a] chapter of accidents, and the exercise of all the virtues of humanity, gave him possession of a fortune, that exceeded his wishes, almost as much as it exceeded his hopes'. Cheslyn goes on to present Foston as an exception to the rule of 'metropolitan nabobs' (1:34), and the story of Foston rewrites the EIC's recent history by eliding the 'chapter of accidents' by which he attained his fortune with an account of how Britain acquired its empire. Such an interpretation is plausible because Foston represents himself, at the outset of his narrative, as an unreconstructed figure, who – like *Memoirs of a Gentleman*'s narrator – initially exploits every possible opportunity both for sexual conquest and for self-enrichment: 'not to grow rich,' he confesses, was 'beyond the power of human virtue' (1:202). As Foston relates, the first stage of his career in India culminates in him drunkenly spitting at and then striking a 'wooden deity' attached to a village temple, following which he is seized and 'fairly and speedily plumpt' in the Ganges, for 'the river god, to drown, or purify . . . as he thought fit' (1:206).

Bage's novel does not press the symbolism of this moment of cleansing, nor does it dwell upon Foston's encounter with 'the venerable old priest' (1:208) who had witnessed the whole sequence of events. Foston's contact with this 'priest' nonetheless assumes a pivotal status within his narrative, since it helps him to get rid of his 'coxcombry', and also to begin to acquire 'a more liberal cast of mind' (1:213). The process of purification that Foston undergoes makes him right-eously eager to avenge 'the well-known horrible catastrophe of the black hole' (1:215) (in which one of his friends had perished), and to hunt down Siraj ud-Daula after the defeat of his forces at Plassey. As this appeal to the mythology of the Black Hole shows, Bage's representation of Foston's redemption establishes some different 'Indian' reference points from those – such as the Bengal famine – invoked by the anti-EIC polemic that the novel earlier rehearses. In a characteristically oblique engagement with this rhetoric, the novel presents the second stage of Foston's Indian career culminating in his summary execution of two of Siraj's soldiers, after catching them in the act of raping the daughter of a Persian merchant. The predation of 'Asiatic plunderers' was frequently figured in terms of sexual violation, most notably in Burke's speeches at the trial of Hastings, but what is notable here is that the perpetrators of rape are themselves Indian, their crime allowing Foston to a perform a new sense of moral agency. With a neat metafic-tional touch, Bage has the victim, Caralia, declare that '[n]o author has yet been so bold as to permit a lady to live and marry, and be a woman, after this stain' (1:233). Ignoring these protestations, Caralia's father, Duverda, subsequently pledges her hand, along with 'all his effects in all the formalities of the Hindostan law' (1:257), to their joint rescuer.

As Betty Joseph suggests, Caralia's minimal role in Foston's story draws attention to her narrative function, which is to prove that Foston's redemption is genuine and then reward him for it, by setting in motion the 'laundering' of colonial wealth by which her father's fortune is used to purchase a landed retreat in rural Wales.[31] Further to this, though, the description of Foston's encounter with Caralia and Duverda also strives for a more secure meaning for the idea of British liberty, which for supporters of the American cause such as Bage had been radically called into question by Britain's treatment of its American colonies. When Duverda tells Foston of how he made his money from trading with 'European factories', for example, he details the peculiar 'sense, knowledge and virtue' of the English merchants that he had dealt with, presenting their conduct as the obverse of the despotism, lust, and violence which Siraj ud-Daula embo-dies, and which are said to reign '[a]ll over the East' (1:239). Pledging that his daughter will never find a partner among 'sons of slavery or rapine', Duverda entreats Foston to carry Caralia to Britain so as to 'shew her the blessings of freedom' (1:256). In a similar way to both *Memoirs of a Gentleman* and *Adventures of a Rupee*, *Mount Henneth* here presents a seemingly objective 'external' view of virtuous commerce and the British liberty of which it is apparently a manifestation.

The episodes featuring Foston and the 'priest' and Foston and Duverda rework the scene of cross-cultural encounter narrated by 'Old Edwards' in Mackenzie's *The Man of Feeling*, and their brevity, coupled with their lack of interest in the specificity of 'Indian' detail, serves to solicit critical attention as to their significance within the novel as a whole.[32] If Bage's 'India plot' allegorizes the wealth of Bengal as gifted to – rather than expropriated by – the British, its function seems to have at least as much to do with closing off the novel's more complicated and extensive 'America plot' as with attempting any larger vindication of the EIC and its servants. In other words, if *Mount Henneth*'s account of conflict in Bengal in the 1750s may have encouraged readers to support military campaigns elsewhere in India in the early 1780s, the novel nonetheless makes no mention of the ongoing war with Mysore, and its reference to a generalized Oriental despotism, as the antithesis of British freedom, most immediately responds to the 'crisis of liberty' consequent upon the break with America. Like *Adventures of a Rupee*, *Mount Henneth* demonstrates the difficulty, or implausibility, of representing 'the blessings that commerce diffuses' in an Indian setting. At the same time, though, Bage's vision of virtuous community in Britain, centred on the Henneth estate, is more parochial than that of Scott, for whom the King's 'free born subjects' may still carry 'victory and law' beyond the nation's shores.[33] If we read *Mount Henneth* as a work that, like *The Nabob*, stages the transformation of Britain's economy, then it bears out Mite's point about the 'magical power' of riches to conceal their origins even as it acknowledges the domestic impact of colonial wealth. Bage's India provides a source of both economic and ideological 'compensation', to recall Thomas Day's resonant term, yet its presence in the novel remains tellingly marginal.

Empire and Sympathy

One way of substantiating this point about Bage's lack of interest in India is to consider his description of Foston's decisive encounter with the native 'priest' in relation to the detailed scholarly engagement with Hindu culture in the work of Sir William Jones, who sailed for India in 1783. Bage's 'priest' and the 'pagoda' that he occupies are generically Eastern, while his mention of the 'river god' of the Ganges only gestures towards a nonspecific polytheism. Jones's 'Hymn to Ganga' by contrast directly addresses the presiding deity of the Ganges, in the voice of a Brahmin devotee.

I return to the work of Jones in Chapter 4, but here I want to register the broader point that even as 'India' could provide an ideological function for a writer such as Bage, metropolitan Britons also grappled with the imaginative 'challenges and opportunities' (in Andrew Rudd's phrase) which the nation's greater openness to India presented.[34] In his 1783 'Speech on Fox's India Bill', in which he called for the EIC to be made accountable to Parliament, Burke acknowledged that the 'challenge' of Indian empire would be ignored or even rejected by some: because 'even the very names' of those suffering from the effects of EIC policy were 'so uncouth and strange to our ears', he conceded, it was very difficult for Britons to find objects to which they could attach their sympathies.[35] Since Burke attributed this state of affairs to people being 'so little acquainted with Indian details' (404), however, he suggested that, with greater effort, the problem might be rectified. The loss of America raised troubling questions about the status of the nation, as the writers previously discussed all recognized, but it additionally helped to bring into sharper focus the reality that Britain still possessed, in Day's words, 'immense territories' in India.[36] For Burke in particular too, the problems of the present generated a heightened consciousness of imperial responsibility.

Burke understood that defeat in America and the recent history of scandal in India jeopardized Britain's reputation, and at the beginning of the speech cited earlier he stressed that the contemporary moment represented a political crossroads, to be followed either by 'great disgrace or great glory to the whole British nation' (381). Indian empire was redeemable for Burke because while he knew that the EIC's record was shameful, he thought that there was no essential 'incompatibility of interests' (383) between Britain and India of the kind that had developed between Britain and America. It was possible to reform British rule in India, Burke argued, provided that the EIC was made accountable to Parliament, that Britons recognized the 'quality' as well as the antiquity of Indian civilization, and that they in turn extended to Indians both their moral and legal standards. Hitherto, he stated in a famous passage, Indians in EIC-administered territories had been governed by young men who appeared to them only as 'birds of prey, with appetites continually renewing for a food that is continually wasting' (404). Burke identified the EIC's role as an extractor of wealth with this arresting metaphor, and – as if acknowledging the debate between Foote's Mayor and Touchit – he stated that Britons had shown themselves to be far worse than their 'ferocious, bloody, and wasteful' predecessors in India, 'Arabs, Tartars, and Persians' (403). In a similar way to his claim about Britons' minimal acquaintance with 'Indian details', however, Burke's account of the EIC's record also enabled him here to imagine an alternative to the situation that he decried. In declaring that, thus far in Bengal, 'England' had 'erected no churches, no hospitals, no palaces, no schools ... built no bridges, made no high roads, cut no navigations, dug out no reservoirs' (404), Burke defined, albeit in negative terms, the agenda for a new, self-consciously 'improving' kind of imperial rule.

Burke in this speech laid many of the charges against Hastings that he would substantiate in greater detail in the impeachment proceedings which were to begin early in 1788. He denounced him for presiding over 'the most despotic power ever known in India' (434), which had extorted ruinous levels of tribute from the native princes placing their trust in it, and set up 'the whole landed interest' for sale to 'the highest bidder' (426). This reference to the fate of Bengal's 'landed interest' is characteristic of the way in which Burke frequently presented the EIC as undermining the customary foundations of Indian society. Burke saw 'the reverence paid to the female sex' as one of the 'prejudices not less regarded in the east than those of religion' (417), and seeking to provide his audience with objects on whom they could 'fix' their sympathies, he introduced case studies exhibiting the lack of respect for this cultural norm; even as he invoked a generalized 'East', Burke eschewed any mention of the sexual despotism with which this imaginary domain was often associated by contemporaries. What would become the most famous of these examples related to the Begums of Oudh (mother and grandmother of the Wazir of Oudh), who two years previously had had their property and effects seized by the EIC – acting on the pretext of putting down a rebellion – when they were unable to meet the payments demanded of them. Burke returned more dramatically to the 'barbarous usage' experienced by these 'unfortunate princesses' (465) in his 'Speech on Almas Ali Khan' (1784), following the passage of Pitt's India Act. The so-called Begums charge was the main focus of Richard Brinsley Sheridan's 1787 speech to the House of Commons which ensured that Hastings's impeachment would go ahead, and it was central to speeches by both Burke and Sheridan during the early stages of the trial itself.

Much has now been written about the adversarial 'theatre' of Hastings's impeachment, and recent work has emphasized not only Burke's efforts to narrativize and so render more vivid the plight of the EIC's subject peoples, but also his awareness of the difficulty of this endeavour, and the often jocular and unsympathetic responses that it generated.[37] Historians and literary scholars have focused in particular on the way in which Burke's language 'burgeoned out of control into voyeurism and inadvertent titillation'.[38] The excess of Burke's language is most famously evident in his attempt to substantiate Sheridan's claim, intended to stress the scale of the offence against the Begums, that 'nothing could be more sacred than the character of a woman, nor more venerable than that of a mother, in India.' Burke illustrated this point by citing a passage from Prince Demetrius Cantemir's *History of the Turks* that referred to the 'Sultan-mother's' authority over the seraglio, and her procurement of beautiful virgins 'for her son's use'.[39] He thus played to long-standing fantasies about the sexualization of 'Eastern' domestic space, in the process providing rich material for graphic satirists and compromising the prosecution's argument about the sanctity of the Begums' zenana.[40] There is much more to say about Burke's rhetoric and contemporary reactions to it, as well as about the fact that Hastings no less than Burke sought to create ties of sympathy between Britons and their colonial subjects. One good example of Hastings's appeal to the language of sympathy appears in his preface to Charles Wilkins's translation of *The Bhagvat-Geeta* (1785), in which he argued that projects such as Wilkins's helped to reconcile Britons to their colonial subjects, and 'lessen[ed] the weight of the chain' by which Indians experienced their subjection: while they could thus be disarmingly candid about the power relations of empire, Hastings and the scholars under his patronage conceived of the EIC as 'protecting' its Hindu subjects from Muslim despotism, and thereby as exemplifying an already enlightened form of colonial administration.[41]

I go on to discuss the scholarly Orientalism of the 1780s in Chapter 4, which focuses on the centrality of Sir William Jones to an ambitious collective project of cultural translation. In the context of Burke's attempt to negotiate the 'problem of distance' (and of this chapter's overall emphasis on metropolitan understandings of the relationship between Britain and India), however, I want now to consider two works of 1788, Hugh Mulligan's poem 'The Virgins' and Mariana Starke's play *The Sword of Peace*. While both written against Hastings, these works can be seen in very different ways to engage with the rhetoric of the trial and with contemporary debate about Indian empire, providing particular kinds of 'Indian details' as they respectively describe EIC rapacity and the reform of its governance. What makes them especially interesting, I argue, is that, whether attempting to convey the reality of native suffering or the transition to a new colonial order, they both exemplify significant problems of representation that jeopardize their ostensible objectives.

Mulligan's 'Asiatic Eclogue' registers the impact of Burke's commentary on Indian affairs, most obviously because its title alludes to the latter's testimony during the opening stages of the impeachment about the means by which taxes were collected from the peasants of Rangpur in northern Bengal: during his evidence Burke referred to how '[v]irgins whose fathers kept them from the sight of sin' were 'dragged into the public Court', where 'their shrieks were mingled with the cries and groans of an indignant people', and they were 'violated by the basest and wickedest of mankind'.[42] One of a collection of *Poems Chiefly on Slavery and Oppression* – appearing after 'The Slave' and before 'The Herdsmen' – 'The Virgins' parallels EIC operations with forms of tyranny elsewhere in the world. It follows Burke not only in its focus on the sexual danger facing the 'princely Shawna' and 'gentle Alvia' as they flee 'the conqueror's sword' but also in its reference to other episodes of colonial scandal that Burke had helped to publicize, among them the execution of Rajah Nandakumar, hanged on a charge of forgery after he had accused Hastings of corruption.[43]

'The Virgins' can additionally be seen to demonstrate a representational problem, however, as suggested earlier, because in setting its 'Asiatic' scene it combines the composite Orientalism of 'spicy grove[s]' and 'spreading Banians' with obtrusively inaccurate detail.[44] *European Magazine* observed that '[o]ne of the young ladies['] names is Shawna, which strikes on our ear as right Hibernian,' and for the (unsympathetic) reviewer in question this moment of bathos provided an opportunity to deflect attention from the poem's use of the rape metaphor to symbolize EIC rule.[45] Mulligan's deployment of the rhetoric of sexual violation is itself unstable, since after Alvia calls upon Shawna to join her in hiding, the poem's narrator describes how the 'hungry vultures' of conquest 'eye their destin'd prey', as if lining up the two native women in their sights. The poem tails off with its final couplet: 'Fast by that grot the females breathless lay,/ While rape and murder mark'd the Victor's way.'[46] This account of a female defenceless-ness that is at the same time erotically alluring – 'breathless' – exemplifies a similar kind of 'inadvertent titillation' (in Anna Clark's phrase) to that which is evident in Burke's testimony regarding the 'virgins' of Rangpur or the Begums of Oudh.[47] Mulligan's poem therefore illustrates the difficulty both of bringing home 'Indian details' and of ensuring that readers focus on the right ones.

While 'The Virgins' demonstrates that the objectification of Indian female victimhood could have unintended consequences, *The Sword of Peace* illustrates the different problem of how to represent in a plausible manner the idea that British rule in India was now being conducted on a more just basis. In comparison with Foote's *The Nabob*, to which it bears some similarities, Starke's work is rhetorically straightforward. Subtitled 'A Voyage of Love', it begins by introducing Eliza and Louisa Moreton 'on the coast of Coromandel', where each has a personal quest to undertake, Eliza in pursuit of her lover, Edwards, and Louisa to recover and to bring home the sword of 'the generous Clairville', who had met his death while trying to make the fortune denied him by his father.[48] The play sets up a distinction between the two sisters – 'Virtuous and mild, like all our British fair!', the prologue puts it – and their sofa-bound 'lady hostess' Madam Tartar, an Orientalized caricature. Starke's work also personifies colonial corruption in 'the Resident', a figuring of Hastings mediated via Sir Matthew Mite. Unlike Foote's play or any of the other texts considered thus far, however, *The Sword of Peace* enacts the purging of corruption, via the replacement of the Resident (to some extent a victim of his 'secretary' Supple) with David Northcote, usually regarded as standing for Hastings's successor, Lord Cornwallis. In setting up a schematic opposition between Anglo-Indian vice and 'English' virtue, the play repudiates the cross-cultural exchange that characterized the Hastings era and at the same time revises older, aristocratic codes of honour. The sword of the play's title is kept in the possession of Lieutenant Dormer, who chivalrously pronounces it ever ready to combat 'oppression, wrong, or robbery' (26), and refuses to take the money that Louisa initially offers for the weapon, instead transmitting it to her in an encounter which heralds their later marriage. Starke's depiction of Northcote serves in a similar manner to refashion aristocratic masculinity, as Daniel O'Quinn argues, 'erasing' the actual status of the figure that he seems most to resemble, and casting him as 'a new kind of imperial hero'.[49]

As this plot summary indicates, *The Sword of Peace* offers intertextual reference to many of the other works discussed so far, notably in its use of the 'voyage of love' plot (from *Adventures of a Rupee*) and in its inclusion of a character named 'Mrs Tartar' (a nod to Burke, and to Mayor and Touchit's debate in *The Nabob*). This allusiveness draws attention to the process of rewriting by which the play at once redeems the idea of colonial adventure and exorcizes the idea of colonial corruption, as it anticipates the ascendancy of a reforming administration. *The Sword of Peace* indeed brings together different reform agendas, because its allegorization of regime change incorporates a subplot concerning the liberation of Mrs Tartar's black slave, Caesar. While this subplot in proximate terms refers to the campaign to abolish the slave trade that went through Calcutta, it more broadly participates in the campaign against the transatlantic slave trade that, after defeat in America, was so central to many Britons' understand-ings of how to redeem the nation's reputation. The play additionally alludes to the colonial market for newly arrived women, as memorably depicted in James Gillray's 1786 etching 'A Sale of English Beauties, in the East Indies'.[50] Drawing what would become a common analogy in feminist discourse, Eliza early on declares her hope that the 'traffic' of women be abolished, because it is 'still *more disgraceful* to our sex than that of the poor slaves to a nation' (5).

In thus invoking these different notions of slavery, *The Sword of Peace* helps us to think about the terms on which Britons could imagine them-selves as possessed of free will and agency. It is instructive, however, that the play's abolitionist subplot should take up so much space, and that the crudely depicted figure of Caesar should have a much bigger part than that of the sole Indian character, the merchant Mazinghi Dowza (who, like Caesar, speaks the generic 'slave' dialect ubiquitous in abolitionist litera-ture). On one level the focus of *The Sword of Peace* is both topical and specific, because the play refers to Tipu Sultan and the ongoing Third Mysore War as well as to the recent arrival of Cornwallis. At the same time, though, Starke's nominally 'Indian' setting serves as a vehicle for metro-politan self-examination – in particular for demonstrating that the national character remains unaffected by empire and the encounters with Eastern otherness that it generated. This concern is especially evident when Caesar's liberator, Jeffreys, glosses Britons' privileged understanding of the meaning of liberty, which he construes as the absence of restraint: 'An Englishman . . . lives as he likes – lives *where* he likes – *goes* where he likes – *stays* where he likes – *works* if he likes – lets it *alone* if he likes – starves, if he likes . . . ' (31–2).

Jeffreys's celebration of the freedom to starve harks back to the false consciousness of Goldsmith's disabled veteran, who experiences his own subjection as superiority over the French. Jeffreys also invites audiences to identify with him, however, as when he elsewhere stumbles over the name of the settlement in which the play's action takes place, 'Mazag-ha-ga-gaga', before calling it simply 'this place here with its hard name' (20). Although he provides a reminder of Burke's point about the way in which the 'uncouth and strange' sound of Indian proper names militates against cross-cultural sympathy, Jeffreys's ignorance is presented as pardonable. The bluff Englishman's absence of curiosity about India in turn empha-sizes that the function of local detail in the play (primarily relating to costume, furnishings, and so on) is to evoke the corrupt milieu of the Resident and his circle. Starke's lack of interest in the specificity of nomenclature, or customs and manners, bears out O'Quinn's persuasive argument about the work's embeddedness in overlapping reformist discourses of 'regulation'.[51] It may also, though, exemplify a representational problem – or, in other words, reflect on what the play is unable to represent – because even as *The Sword of Peace* stages the end of the Hastings era, it can only emphasize the difference of the scandal-cleansing new regime by ignoring Indian society and the effects of EIC rule almost completely.

'I Now Rejoice ... That I Am about to Leave'

The inward-looking 'reputational' focus of Starke's play is encapsulated by Edwards's final statement that Northcote's action against the late Resident's influence serves to guarantee 'our prosperity, glory, and applause as a nation' (61). *Hartly House, Calcutta* more fully and directly engages with debates about the character of EIC rule, actually naming, if only minimally depicting, Hastings and Cornwallis, along with other historical figures. Like Eliza and Louisa Moreton, the novel's narrator, Sophia Goldborne, writing home to her friend Arabella, is concerned to emphasize that, contrary to what her name suggests, she is not an adventuress seeking a husband. Whereas the Moretons immediately repudiate the grotesquely 'Indianized' Mrs Tartar, however, Sophia's first experiences of Calcutta, after arriving with her father, prompt her rather flightily to declare herself '*orientalised*', and she later claims to 'adore the customs of the East'.[52] *Hartly House* also differs from *The Sword of Peace* and the fictions of British India discussed so far because it attempts realistically to evoke life on the ground for 'Calcuttonians' (28), and the thickness of the Indian milieu it describes ostensibly testifies to a sense of India's increasing imaginative proximity for metropolitan readers. Praised by contemporaries for the apparently authentic 'information' it provided (Gibbes may have drawn upon letters which her son sent her from Calcutta), the novel is in some ways a literary analogue of William Hodges's earlier 'Views' of the city, likewise portraying an established colonial community.[53] As if in response to Burke's charge that 'England has erected no churches, no hospitals, no palaces, no schools,' Sophia's account of Calcutta frequently suggests that the EIC's presence in Bengal has helped to create a flourishing civil society where none existed before. *Hartly House* refers to the infrastructure that 'originates from commerce and owes its support ... to commerce', as symbolized by a hospital 'erected for the reception of *all* indisposed persons', the

sight of which leads Sophia to quote from Pope's 'Epistle to Burlington':
'These are imperial works, and worthy kings' (43).

Both 'extolling the country I now reside in' and 'sighing for the disgraces
of the country I have quitted', Sophia at times presents British India as
a reproach to Britain itself, just as Elizabeth Hamilton would do in *Letters
of a Hindoo Rajah* (1796); in a playful allusion to the Hastings trial, Sophia
indeed describes 'the utility and the benevolence' of the Calcutta hospital
as 'an impeachment of the customs ... in my native country' (44). That
Gibbes was concerned to vindicate Hastings is also implied by Sophia's
sympathetic account of 'the fiery ordeal of virtue' undergone by EIC
servants, so frequently tempted by 'eastern bribes' that it is 'almost
a miracle' (82) for them to escape unaffected. When Sophia later refers to
Hastings's recall, she reports the popular reaction that his departure will
deprive the EIC of 'a faithful and able servant; the poor, of a compassionate
friend; the genteel circles, of their best ornament; and Hartly House of
a revered guest'.

If this letter constitutes Sophia's clearest identification with what she
refers to as 'the British interest' (106) in India, the novel invites the reader
on other occasions to draw a moral from the gulf between the apparent
stability of the present and the disorder of the recent past. Sophia's account
of 'the Trees of Destruction' (53) beneath which duels had been fought
alludes to the combat that took place between Hastings and his arch-critic
Philip Francis in 1780, offering a reminder of the precariousness of
Hastings-era civility. Where the recent past is concerned, Sophia's visit
to the ruined site of the Black Hole of Calcutta is especially significant,
however, because it invokes an originary moment of native violence that, as
in Bage's *Mount Henneth*, at once legitimizes and helps to submerge the
ongoing violence of EIC consolidation and expansion.[54] Sophia follows her
memorial of the 'melancholy catastrophe' (35) that took place thirty years
earlier with a reference to the way in which the 'seasonable arrival' (36) on
the scene of forces led by Clive – for Gibbes, as for Bage, a military man not
a nabob – helped to re-establish British control of the city. She thereafter
telescopes subsequent historical events into a single, long sentence which
concludes with the statement that Calcutta, after the decisive battle of
Plassey, began to become 'what we find it at this day'.

Hartly House is much more than an attempt to defend Hastings and the
EIC, however, because it additionally sets up an implicit parallel between
the Orientalist research that Hastings sponsored and Sophia's sentimental
encounter with Hinduism, as embodied by the figure of a young Brahmin,
the nephew of her father's chief servant. The novel clearly circumscribes

the terms on which Sophia is able to indulge her cultural curiosity: in keeping with the norms of 'colonial romance', it kills off the love object of its protagonist, and the Brahmin is not individuated or even named, remaining an idealized creation throughout.[55] Gibbes's account of Sophia and the man that she refers to throughout as 'my Bramin' (94) is nonetheless more developed than any comparable representation of cross-cultural encounter in late eighteenth-century fictions of British India. Even as Sophia rehearses the larger political rationale of scholarly Orientalism (for example, when she states that Persian is 'key to the knowledge of all that ... can truly advance the British interest' [106]), her letters demonstrate the Brahmin's formative role as her personal mentor. While Sophia conceives of the Brahmin as if he were an imaginary observer like Goldsmith's Altangi, asking how 'we Europeans' (58) must appear in 'Gentoo' eyes, she also invites his scrutiny of her own behaviour: 'to please a Bramin I must have perfections of the mental sort' (51), she writes. Sophia's fascination with the Brahmin and his religion has her declare herself 'a convert to the Gentoo faith' (111), and her exploration of this identity through her contact with her preceptor may be interpreted as carrying a transgressive sexual charge. Certainly, Sophia thinks of India as a space of relative freedom from the constraints and expectations that apply at home, and even after she recognizes that she is destined to marry the honourable but unexciting Edmund Doyly, she imagines herself being carried off by the Nawab of Bengal, Mubarak ud-Daula, whose gaze prompts 'ambitious throbs' in her heart. The prince's potency is to some extent contained by his 'astonishment' (154) at a display of British fire-power, but Sophia goes on to note the jealousy of 'Poor Doyly', and the strength of her illicit fantasy is such that she has to invoke the memory of 'my Bramin' (155) to regulate her feelings.

Sophia's next, and penultimate, letter even more clearly discloses the novel's political complexity. After describing herself as 'undone' (153) by her exchange of glances with the Nawab, then suggesting that the spectacle of 'martial manoeuvrings' (154) by EIC forces put the prince in his place, she now recounts the story of an army officer's rape of an Indian woman and murder of her father. While this episode emphasizes again the ubiquity of representations of rape in contemporary writing about British India, it is particularly striking because it appears to channel Burkean rhetoric after the work had previously done so much to defend Hastings. *Hartly House* activates the idea of native violence with its allusion to the Black Hole, in a similar fashion to nearly all of the fictions discussed earlier, but its concluding episode obviously departs from the example of *The Pilgrim* and *Mount Henneth* in referring to an Indian victim and an apparently British rapist. Sophia's account of the offender's likely capital punishment might be seen to offer a reassuring display of even-handedness: 'Lord C[ornwallis] will not ... stain his noble deeds,' she states, 'by suffering such a villain to escape.' Even as we are told that the 'guilty wretch' is set to be appropriately punished, however, Sophia qualifies any idea of self-regulation by claiming that in India, 'fiend-like acts are ... much oftener perpetrated than detected' (158). If Sophia's relationship with the Brahmin is a product of the 'intellectual sympathy and racial tolerance' of the Hastings era, as Michael J. Franklin argues, then this final episode registers the prevalence of such examples of quotidian violence as well, as if in anticipatory critique of the elegizing of a lost openness to the East in some treatments of the 'Orientalist' phase of EIC rule.[56] For all that the novel is built around the possibility of forms of cross-cultural dialogue, Sophia declares at the close that India is 'the scene of tragedies that dishonour mankind' (157), and she eagerly looks forward to her departure for England.

I want in conclusion to consider Sophia's relief at the prospect of returning home, in the broader context of my focus on Britons' understanding of their connection with India across the 1770s and 1780s. The contrast between the non-specific 'Mogulstan' and the much more precisely realized Bengal in *Hartly House* may suggest a kind of progress towards a better and fuller metropolitan knowledge of British India, as recognized by William Hodges at the outset of his *Travels in India* (1794): 'The intimate connexion which has so long subsisted between this country and the continent of India naturally renders every Englishman deeply interested in all that relates to a quarter of the globe which has been the theatre of scenes highly important to his country.'[57] Tellingly, however, *Hartly House* locates the curiosity of its narrator in the past, and Sophia seems to understand her imminent return home not just as a departure but as a disengagement from India: 'I now rejoice ... that I am about to leave' (158), she declares. Rudd notes that Sophia is 'purged of her sympathetic immersion in the East', and this claim points to the larger significance of the novel's trajectory, as its narrator moves from a state of feeling 'orientalised' to, in her final letter, welcoming the familiarity of Guildford.[58] Whereas Burke argued that better acquaintance with 'Indian details' would help Britons to negotiate both spatial and cultural distance, Gibbes's protagonist finally takes comfort in the idea of such distance.

I want to finish, however, by emphasizing that the narrowing of imaginative horizons that is seemingly willed by Sophia in no way closes off the disquieting resonance of the rape episode at the work's close. As much as Sophia herself embraces the idea of 'retreat' from India at the end of *Hartly House*, her desire for distance from the subcontinent does not straightforwardly entail her or the novel's forgetting of the recent history of British India. In another instance of the disjointedness that I have argued is characteristic of fictions of the period, Sophia's penultimate letter alludes to the possibility of a very different kind of text, since it states that the violated Indian woman survives to shame her attacker by her 'melancholy testimony' (158). This text remains unwritten – the story of the woman remains untold – because the novel abruptly ends, but the very invocation of 'testimony' nonetheless provides a reminder of its centrality to contemporary controversy about the scandal of empire.[59] By alluding to the idea of native testimony, and the importance of crediting it, without then ventriloquizing any such act, Gibbes may have signalled her awareness of the problems of representation discussed earlier, in particular the ethical difficulty attendant upon attempting to do proper justice to the suffering of others. The narrator's reference to the 'scene of tragedies' (157) here recalls her account of the 'tragical' (35) events of the Black Hole which in a similar way she declared herself both 'unequal to paint' (36) and 'unable to forget' (126).[60] This implicit relativization of acts of violence and experiences of victimhood short-circuits the novel's earlier indication that memory of the outrage of the Black Hole might function as an always available *casus belli*, as it does in some of the other works discussed earlier. It also undercuts the allegory of rape that produced the figure of the vulnerable white woman in such a way as to legitimize any violence apparently done for her protection, since in its reference to the rape of an Indian woman the novel offers its readers, as Joseph argues, 'forms of identification with other victims, victims who shared with English women their common oppression by English men'.[61] My next chapter throws the interrogative nature of Gibbes's conclusion into relief, because it focuses in particular on the representation of sexual despotism as a primarily if not exclusively 'Eastern' phenomenon.

Notes

1. Johnstone, *Arsaces*, 1:139–40.
2. Ibid., 1:viii.
3. Johnstone, *Pilgrim*, 1:7. Further references appear as parenthetical citations in the text.

4. Rothschild, *Inner Life*, 3.
5. Burke, *Writings and Speeches*, 5:404.
6. Mackenzie, *Man of Feeling*, 77.
7. Dirks, *Scandal*.
8. *Plays by Foote*, 106. Further references appear as parenthetical citations in the text.
9. O'Quinn, *Staging Governance*, 66.
10. Kaul, *Eighteenth-Century British Literature*, 159.
11. *General Evening Post*, 27 June 1772.
12. Ahmed, *Stillbirth*, 97.
13. 'The Nabob', iii and v. Further references appear as parenthetical citations in the text.
14. Rudd, *Sympathy*, 1–25.
15. Ibid., 17.
16. Ahmed, *Stillbirth*, 117.
17. *Memoirs of a Gentleman*, 95. Further references appear as parenthetical citations in the text.
18. *Monthly Review*, 63 (1780), 233.
19. Burke, *Writings and Speeches*, 5:394 and 393.
20. Scott, *Rupee*, 13. Further references appear as parenthetical citations in the text.
21. Burke, *Writings and Speeches*, 5:402.
22. Ibid., 5:401.
23. Day, *Reflections*, 50–2.
24. Brown, *Moral Capital*, 27.
25. Scott, *Rupee*, second edition, iii.
26. Festa, *Sentimental Empire*, 122.
27. Day, *Reflections*, 26.
28. Ibid., 22.
29. Ibid., 64–5.
30. Bage, *Mount Henneth*, 1:13. Further references appear as parenthetical citations in the text.
31. Joseph, *Reading the EIC*, 74.
32. Festa, *Sentimental Empire*, 62–4.
33. Scott, *Rupee*, 232.
34. Rudd, *Sympathy*, 30.
35. Burke, *Writings and Speeches*, 5:404. Further references appear as parenthetical citations in the text.
36. Day, *Reflections*, 64.
37. O'Quinn, *Staging Governance*, 164–221.
38. Clark, *Scandal*, 110.
39. Sheridan and Burke cited in O'Quinn, *Staging Governance*, 213.
40. Garcia, *Islam*, 110–25.
41. *Bhagvat-Geeta*, 13.
42. Burke, *Writings and Speeches*, 6:420.

43. Mulligan, *Poems*, 8; Burke, *Writings and Speeches*, 5:435–6.
44. Mulligan, *Poems*, 8.
45. *European Magazine*, 13 (1788), 415.
46. Mulligan, *Poems*, 15.
47. Clark, *Scandal*, 110.
48. Starke, *Sword of Peace*, 3. Further references appear as parenthetical citations in the text.
49. O'Quinn, *Staging Governance*, 273.
50. Ibid., 290–2.
51. Ibid., 266–98.
52. Gibbes, *Hartly House*, 8 and 33. Further references appear as parenthetical references in the text.
53. Franklin, introduction, ibid., xx.
54. Joseph, *Reading the EIC*, 85.
55. Teltscher, *India*, 137.
56. Introduction to *Hartly House*, xxiii.
57. Hodges, *Travels*, preface.
58. Rudd, *Sympathy*, 105.
59. Burke, *Writings and Speeches*, 5:436.
60. Joseph, *Reading the EIC*, 87.
61. Ibid., 88.

CHAPTER 3

'All Asia Is Covered in Prisons'
Oriental Despotism and British Liberty in an Age of Revolutions

The conclusion to *Hartly House, Calcutta* invites readers to recognize the plight of those who 'shared with English women their common oppression by English men'.[1] During the impeachment of Hastings, Burke-inspired works such as Hugh Mulligan's poem 'The Virgins' similarly made use of the rape metaphor in order to symbolize the effects of EIC rule. Other fictions of the 1770s and 1780s depicted English and Indian women who were victims of Indian men, however, and in doing so drew on and further circulated an already well-established sense of sexual despotism as a specifically 'Eastern' phenomenon. Where India is concerned, much recent criticism has emphasized the intellectual and creative cross-fertilization that took place under the EIC's aegis during the Hastings era. There is a parallel story to tell about British metropolitan imaginings of 'the East' in the late eighteenth century, though, and it concerns the ossification of unexamined claims about the benighted condition of ser-aglio-bound women across 'Asia' as a whole – the seeming inescapability of this notion an index of its ideological usefulness. In schematic terms, it might therefore be said that if a 'Burkean' or 'Jonesian' Orientalism sought to identify forms of affinity and resemblance between peoples and cultures, this account of a generalized state of Oriental despotism in which men tyrannized over women in turn eschewed any such imaginative openness to the East.

This chapter focuses on a received idea regarding the bondage of Eastern women – its cultural origins predating the Seven Years' War and the EIC's acquisition of sovereign authority in Bengal, around which my previous chapters were organized. I begin by rehearsing a now well-known story about the way in which this idea often provided a rhetorical foil for celebration of the mixed sociability that was seen as a defining feature of life in Britain. Developing my introductory claim about how familiar fictions were adapted, reworked, and reacted against across our period, I then go on to show that even as readers continued to be drawn to 'fabulous Orients', assumptions

90

about the comparative condition of women began to provide a lens through which tales of the East might be packaged and understood. While a collection such as the *Arabian Nights* was 'internalized' in British culture as a familiar source of delight, its frame tale scenario of Schahriar and Scheherazade was widely revised, notably by dramatists depicting the encounter between Sultans and their free-speaking English captives. Across all genres of writing, I argue, one function of seraglio discourse in the 1770s and 1780s was to help to stabilize the meaning of British liberty during and after the war in America, and to suggest that Britain was essentially unmarked by its experience of defeat. Reflection on domestic relations of gender and class was also (at least) implicit in any representation of the seraglio, however, and this domestic resonance became much more overtly politicized in the 1790s, as the pleasures of the seraglio came to be identified by many radicals with the corruption of the old regime.

The figure of the Eastern despot and the institution of the seraglio were key tropes in the 'radical Orientalist' rhetoric of the 1810s and 1820s as well, and there is much to say both about the enduring purchase of this lexicon and forms of contemporary reflection on its usage: Byron's *Don Juan* (1819–24), for example, appears to map slavery onto the East when its protagonist resists Sultana Gulbeyaz's overtures by telling her that 'Love is for the free!', yet in the same canto it undercuts any obverse notion of 'English' liberty by depicting Juan's companion John Johnson as most concerned with his next meal ('I'm hungry and just now would take,/ Like Esau, for my birthright a beefsteak').[2] The poem's narrator at times indulges in the fantasy of 'playing the sultan' too ('By solitude I mean a sultan's', he states, 'not/ A hermit's, with a haram for a grot'), and I later discuss the way in which Byron's friend Thomas Moore, in *Lalla Rookh* (1817), effected a partial 're-enchantment' of the seraglio.[3] This chapter remains focused on the final decades of the eighteenth century, however, and it examines both the ubiquity and the increasing political contestation of seraglio discourse across the period. It concludes by looking at the work of a writer who may have identified with the idea of the 'moral north' satirized by Byron's narrator in *Don Juan*'s first canto.[4] As its title suggests, Elizabeth Hamilton's *Translation of Letters of a Hindoo Rajah* (1796) often refers to a more specific East than other works considered in this chapter, but it additionally explores ideas of a generically 'Oriental' sexual despotism and an 'exceptional' British liberty, and the relationship between them. Hamilton's work provides a fitting end point for this chapter because it reflexively addresses the functioning of these mutually imbricated mythologies in the national imaginary, in turn interrogating the modernity of an imperial Britain ambivalent about its openness to the world.

'Beauty in Bondage'

The Seven Years' War brought about a major shift in Britain's position in the world, as I have already discussed, and this in turn provided the impetus for a variety of historical investigations which sought to identify a heritage of freedom that remained uncompromised by empire and territorial expansion.[5] In the 1760s and after claims about this distinctive character were often substantiated with reference to the esteem in which women were held, and to the mutually beneficial social intercourse between the sexes that, it was alleged, had long taken place among Britons. For writers such as Richard Hurd and Thomas Percy, for example, this exceptional state of affairs was the product of an enduring 'Gothic' legacy. In *Letters on Chivalry and Romance* (1762), Hurd traced the continuity between Gothic antiquity, the Middle Ages, and the present, in the form of the 'refined gallantry' that originated in 'the antient manners of the German nations'.[6] In an essay appended to his *Reliques of Ancient Poetry* (1765), Percy similarly associated 'respect for the fair sex' with 'the Gothic nations of the north', while contrasting this feature of 'northern' life with 'the manners of Mahometan nations'.[7]

While Scottish Enlightenment historians such as William Robertson and John Millar agreed that the institution of chivalry had progressive effects, they assumed that in ages more 'remote from improvement', as Millar put it, women across the world were 'degraded' and 'reduced under that authority which the strong acquire over the weak'.[8] Another Scot, Gilbert Stuart, however, disputed this influential claim, arguing in *A View of Society in Europe* (1778) that the ancient Germans' case defied the 'stadial' logic of conjectural history. For Stuart, the absence of individual property ownership and the related 'meannesses' of commerce and divided labour in Germanic society underwrote the equality of women in marriage and their involvement in public life; what many previous writers had assumed to result from chivalric 'ceremonies and ... usages', he argued, in fact preceded the culture of chivalry by several centuries, and actually came under threat during the Middle Ages, as 'refinement and property' opened up 'the selfishness of mankind'.[9] By thus conjoining 'refinement' and 'selfishness' Stuart challenged narratives of societal progress, questioning the compatibility of wealth and virtue more fundamentally than most other contemporaries. Stuart's reading of the Gothic past nonetheless eventually generated (in Jane Rendall's phrase) a 'Whig compromise' on ancient German customs and manners, a more or less consensual position which accommodated much of what Stuart had to say and which acknowledged the civilizing processes already in effect in Anglo-Saxon England.[10]

I return to the idea of the trade-off between wealth and virtue in my discussion of Hamilton's *Hindoo Rajah*, but the key point I want to emphasize now is the familiar one that those writers who circulated shorthand accounts of this inheritance of mixed sociability often defined it, as Percy did, against an unexamined sense of 'Mahometan', or more broadly Oriental or Asiatic, sexual despotism; in many of the works that I go on to cite there is a slippage between reference to Islam and to 'the East' in general. In *The Character and Conduct of the Female Sex* (1776), for example, Church of Scotland minister James Fordyce took it as a given that 'the Ladies of ancient days' frequently exercised a 'wonderful influence' over men, and he cited this precedent as the foundation for what he described as 'the benefit to be derived by young men from the society of virtuous women'.[11] Fordyce distinguished between such a happy if precarious state of affairs and the sad reality of relations between the sexes in the East, which he presented to his readers in the form of a vast tableau comprising 'swarms of effeminate and voluptuous men' and 'ignorant, idle, luxurious women, whose highest destination is to gratify the intemperate desires, or humour the proud caprices, of their masters'.[12]

While Millar was also, after Montesquieu, interested in the potentially determining impact of climate on human behaviour, Fordyce and others circulated claims about the effects of climate in a much more accessible idiom than that of the conjectural history they popularized. The notion of 'intemperate' sexual desire referred to by Fordyce is common in the writing of this period in a range of genres, and it served to consolidate the imagined difference of a 'monogamous' Britain from the 'torrid zones' of the East where, it was assumed, polygamy universally prevailed.[13] Another example of this appeal to climate is provided by the Aberdeen poet and philosopher James Beattie's 1783 essay 'On Fable and Romance', ostensibly a work of literary criticism in the tradition of Hurd's *Letters*. Beattie like Hurd and others explored the broadly 'cultural' (rather than political or constitutional) ramifications of Britain's Gothic past, and in doing so he mapped the distinction between companionate marriage and harem excess onto the climactic difference between 'Gothick nations' and those 'warm and fruitful countries, [which] by promoting indolence and luxury, are favourable to the views of tyrannical princes'.[14]

The idea of the relationship between climate, 'character', and government that Montesquieu influentially circulated in *The Spirit of the Laws*
(translated in 1750) goes back as far as classical antiquity. Discussions of the
comparative condition of women also predate the period in question here,
as is illustrated by George Lyttelton's *Letters from a Persian in England*
(1735), whose narrator observes that while Persian women live in confinement, their English counterparts have 'a familiar and constant Share in
every active Scene of Life'.[15] It is fair to say nonetheless that as the rhetoric
of sexual despotism became increasingly serviceable in defining a politically
moderate idea of the 'spirit of liberty', for reasons to which I return, it was
also invoked in a newly assertive fashion.[16] An escalation in this rhetoric is
evident in William Russell's *Essay on the Character, Manners, and Genius of
Women* (1773), a translation from the French of Antoine Leonard Thomas.
Russell cited Adam Ferguson's Montesquieu-inflected claim regarding the
'burning ardours and torturing jealousies of the seraglio and harem', and he
offered an expansive account of the geographical reach of this state of
female slavery: 'In Turky, in Persia, in India, in Japan, and over the vast
empire of China, one half of the human species is oppressed by the other.'
Further to this, he dramatized his portrayal of such oppression by hyperbolically declaring that '[a]ll Asia is covered with prisons, where beauty in
bondage awaits the caprices of a master.'[17] John Logan's *A Dissertation on
the Governments, Manners, and Spirit of Asia* (1787) similarly reduces
'Asia's' history to a single essential fact, substantiating its appeal to a proto-
Hegelian 'spirit' by stating that '[o]ne form of government hath prevailed
in Asia from the earliest records . . . to the present time. A despot, under the
name of the Great King, or King of Kings, possessed supreme and unlim-
ited power. His will is the law.'[18]

For Burke, as noted earlier, 'reverence . . . to the female sex' was one of
the features of the Mughal customary society being uprooted by EIC
despotism.[19] For the most part, however, accounts of the state of 'Asia'
such as those referred to here paid little attention either to the recent
history of British India or to Orientalist scholarship. (Stuart's work is
unusual again in this respect because it cites Nathaniel Halhed's *Code of
Gentoo Laws* [1776] in order to argue for the resemblances between
'Hindoo' and ancient German women.) Those with experience of travel
sometimes disputed generalizing claims about the sway of despotism and
the predicament of women, and a work such as the diplomat Sir James
Porter's *Observations on the Turks* (1768) is significant in this context
because it cites George Sale's translation of the Koran against
Montesquieu: for Porter, 'the single chapter in the Koran intitled *Women*

would have shewn [Montesquieu] how successions in families ... are fixed and regulated by the prophet; and consequently, how far private property is secured by law beyond the reach, and out of the power, of the sultan.'[20] It is broadly true nonetheless that, however variously it would go on to be mobilized, the seraglio-fixated idea of Oriental sexual despotism itself remained beyond interrogation. This idea proved especially useful in attempts to recover the meaning of British liberty during and after the American war. It also provided the lens through which different kinds of fictional narrative could sometimes be viewed either as generating false impressions of, or – by a circular logic – illustrating an already established truth about, the East.

'When an Eastern Prince Happens to Be Idle'

Like writings by Fordyce and others, William Alexander's *The History of Women* (1779) popularizes the contemporary debate about the link between the condition of women and the progress of society. Alexander's work adopts the 'stadial' position that 'the rank ... in which we find women in any country, mark[s] out ... the exact point in the scale of civil society, to which the people of such [a] country have arrived,' but it also sometimes endorses Stuart's argument that 'the greatest purity of manners' might be found away from 'states of cultivation and refinement'.[21] *The History of Women*'s different intellectual debts are apparent in the way in which it shifts between rehearsing a narrative of progress according to which exemption from labour has secured for women their proper role as civilizers of men, and suggesting that in modern commercial society this exemption actually makes women particularly susceptible to corruption. When considering present-day Britain, Alexander's work often assumes that the nation's Gothic inheritance underpins an enlightened system of mutually respectful gender relations. It intermittently contends too, though, that female virtue is becoming ever more scarce, as the feminine qualities of care and concern for others 'diminish gradually, in proportion as women advance more toward that perfection, or rather imperfection of politeness' (1:92).[22]

While *The History of Women* is contradictory in its estimation of the modern age, however, it is consistent in its frequent reference to women in 'the East', said to be released from labour 'not because they are esteemed', as in Britain, but because productive work would 'render them less delicate instruments of voluptuous pleasure'. According to Alexander, such women are 'confined to seraglios and harams', where 'their time is ... slumbered away in that soft indolence and relaxation of mind, which the inhabitants of the banks of the Ganges reckon the highest felicity that can be attained in this world' (1:60). If this reference to the Ganges gestures towards the British presence in India, it is integrated into a composite notion of an undifferentiated, though implicitly Muslim, East. Alexander's work elsewhere combines claims about how polygamy and the confinement of the female sex accompanied the spread of Islam with a story of how the nascent 'spirit of chivalry' in Europe elevated women and the men who protected them. In doing so it identifies a 'great divergence' of gender relations that began around a millennium earlier, resulting in women 'gradually rising into consequence in one part of the Globe, [and] losing it altogether in another' (1:156).

Comparable accounts of 'seraglios and harams' are to be found in numerous other contemporary works, needless to say, but *The History of Women* is especially interesting here because of its suggestion that 'eastern tales and romances' had provided readers with a misleadingly benign impression of interaction between the sexes in the East. '[I]f not contradicted by facts,' Alexander argued, such narratives 'would impose upon us a belief, that the women were the most beautiful, and the most happy beings in the creation; because the men constantly approach them in the most submissive manner, while every flowery epithet . . . hangs upon their tongue; and every promise they make, is to last for life, or to eternity.' '[T]he reverse of the picture' is true, though, he went on, since Eastern men subject 'the beings they seem to adore, and while they appear to humble themselves at their feet, are actually the jailors who confine, and the tyrants who enslave them' (1:194–5). Alexander did not specify which fictions that he thought had helped to create this illusion, but if we assume that the *Arabian Nights* was one of his reference points, his claims about the subjection of Eastern women can be seen to reimagine its portrayal of Sultan Schahriar and Scheherazade. Read in this manner, the extract cited earlier takes its incarnation of Schahriar – whose plan of vengeance on his wives is the ultimate expression of sexual despotism – as a culturally representative figure. At the same time it ignores the way in which Scheherazade's story-telling constitutes an act of resistance as well as self-preservation which contributes, as the *Nights* concludes, 'towards removing the sultan's fatal prejudice'.[23]

While in Galland's edition of the *Nights* Scheherazade is finally credited with having used her 'courage, wit, and penetration' to 'sweeten' Schahriar's temper, in Alexander's *History* and other contemporary works, such refining agency is often attributed to British women instead, and defined against an 'Eastern' passivity.[24] Beattie's essay 'On Fable and Romance' still more clearly exemplifies what might be regarded as a transfer of female agency from East to West. In the process of (like Hurd) considering the culture of chivalry from which romance arose, Beattie approvingly noted the way in which men and women in the present 'mutually improve and polish one another'.[25] He cited this state of affairs as the product of an ethnic inheritance, defining mixed sociability and the civilizing influence of women against both classical republican ideas of female patriotism and the unchanging plight of women in the East: 'With us, the two sexes associate together . . . but in Rome and Greece they lived separate; and the condition of the female was little better than slavery; as it still is, and has been from very early times, in many parts of Asia, and in European and African Turkey' (525–6).

One striking feature of Beattie's essay is that it incorporates a sociological account of story-telling in the East in order to provide a foundation for this claim. Just as it presents Gothic romance as a product of chivalry, so it traces Oriental fictions back to their originary context:

> The indolence . . . of Asia, and the luxurious life which the kings and other great men . . . live in their seraglios, have made them seek for this sort of amusement, and set a high value upon it. When an Eastern prince happens to be idle . . . and at a loss for expedients to kill the time, he commands his Grand Visir, or his favourite, to tell him stories. Being ignorant, and consequently credulous; having no passion for moral improvement, and little knowledge of nature; he does not desire, that they should be probable, or of an instructive tendency: it is enough if they be astonishing. And hence it is no doubt that those oriental tales are so extravagant. (508–9)

Whereas the Gothic supernatural was for Hurd one component of an irregular national genius, 'inchantment and prodigy' (509) in Eastern narrative, for Beattie, serve only to awaken 'great men' from their lethargy. If we consider this brief scenario in relation to the *Arabian Nights'* frame tale, it can be seen to deny both the invention of Scheherazade and her surrogates and the famed inexhaustibility of the collection as a whole, since it contains the king and his entertainer within a repetitive, rather than dialogic or transactional, cycle of narration.

The teller of stories in the quotation just cited is male, and Beattie's engagement with the idea of sexual despotism is both minimal and decorous. Beattie's reference to seraglio pleasures serves not to arouse his readers, therefore, but rather to produce a stable and consensual – because sufficiently generalized – understanding of the British liberty that is the obverse of Eastern sexual despotism. In contrast to idle, pleasure-seeking

Orientals, the 'natives of the north' are 'active and valiant', and animated by an 'invincible spirit' (527) of freedom that is already within them as much as imprinted upon them from without. Beattie's claim that 'the two sexes associate together' (525) in Britain constitutes a seemingly uncontroversial statement of national distinctiveness, and just as importantly hails a system of customs and manners that has been continuous over time. Although this argument could have been made at any time in the second half of the century, in response to the specific ideological challenges of the 1780s it offered an especially useful rhetorical resource. Beattie attempted to salvage a sense of national honour from the humiliation of the American war by emphasizing that, irrespective of past crisis, British liberty was still secured by historical ballast. Defining an exceptional 'Gothic' inheritance against Oriental despotism enabled him to conceive of this liberty as untarnished by a conflict with adversaries who in their rebellion against colonial authority had themselves invoked the language of freedom.

Beattie still displayed his habituated knowledge of collections such as the *Nights*, and when he expanded on how the action in Oriental tales is advanced 'by fairies, genii, and demons, and wooden horses, which, on turning a peg, fly through the air with inconceivable swiftness' (509), he hinted at a less guarded response to the pleasures of fiction, betraying a residual fondness for fabulous narrative. Elsewhere, however, he soberly declared a preference for 'fables ... of a moral tendency' (511) notably Johnson's *Rasselas*, dismissing the *Nights* as a work for 'young people' containing 'nothing that elevates the mind or touches the heart'. The 'two things ... which deserve commendation, and may entitle [the *Nights*] to one perusal', he stated, are that it discloses 'the customs of ... eastern nations', and that 'there is somewhere in it a story of a barber and his six brothers, that contains many good strokes of satire and comick description'. Unlike Alexander, who claimed that 'tales and romances' in effect delude readers about the East, Beattie here presented the *Nights'* evidential value as its primary source of interest, elevating this function above any notion of readerly delight. The tale that Beattie names (part of 'The Story of the Little Hunch-Back') significantly includes none of the supernatural phenomena that for many helped to provide the *Nights* with its enduring aura, and Beattie's concern to present himself as un-enchanted by this spell is manifest in his claim about his 'one perusal' of the collection, as well as in his vague reference to finding memorable content 'somewhere in it' (510).

It might be objected that I have given too much weight to this example of an author distancing himself from the *Nights*, not least since Beattie was wary of fiction of all kinds. A similar display of distance is apparent, however, even in the preface to a collection of *Arabian Tales* (1792), newly translated from French, and advertising itself as 'A Continuation of the Arabian Nights Entertainments'. Written by Robert Heron, this preface recognizes that the novel '*machinery*' of the *Nights* distinguished it from other forms of fiction earlier in the century: 'Magicians, Genies, Fairies, Lamps, Rings, and . . . Talismans, dance in such profusion through these volumes, as could not but make the reader wonder and stare.'[26] A contrary impulse is also evident here, though, as Heron recalls that the 'anomalous character' of the supernatural agents that 'operate[d] so power-fully' on readers produced a '*gawky* admiration and curiosity' that a present-day audience would be too sophisticated to share.[27] Heron's preface moreover demonstrates the continuing circulation of claims advanced in non-fictional writings about the condition of Eastern women, since its initial account of the 'strange and singular' customs and manners exhibited in the tales themselves sketches a representative tableau reminiscent of Beattie's. It unsurprisingly includes 'Beauties, cooped up together by scores, or perhaps hundreds, in a Haram, all for the amusement of one man', albeit that the 'sprightly gaieties of the fair sex' provide no satisfaction for him, since he is 'indifferent, feeble, old, and fitter to repose in the grave or the hospital, than to riot on the nuptial couch'.[28]

It is impossible to recover how contemporaries would have responded to this preface, if they took any notice of it at all, and I do not want to downplay the great and well-documented popularity of collections such as the *Nights*. Even as Beattie and Heron reduced the process of story-telling and the content of stories themselves to an already familiar 'knowledge' of the East, readers continued to be drawn to the *Nights*, especially, for its matter-of-fact depiction of the strange and unexpected – whether at the level of magical phenomena such as flying carpets and speaking fishes, or of capricious turns of fate such as that experienced by the merchant con-demned to death for killing the son of a genie with a discarded date shell. Coleridge referred to this story of 'The Merchant and the Genie' as an example of 'pure imagination' because no moral or ethical considerations 'obtrude' on its development, and other writers similarly understood the *Nights* as a source of creative stimulus, demonstrating a deep knowledge of the collection by their ease of reference to particular episodes or scenarios.[29] They also associated the *Nights* with a domain of 'fabulous' narrative which was detached from social reality, and which for that reason provided those who entered it with a pleasurable release from responsibility. In his intro-duction to *Tales of the East* (1812), Henry Weber presented this experience of enchantment as a shared memory, stating: 'There are few who do not recollect with pleasure the emotions they felt when the . . . Nights were first put into their hands.'[30] Weber's commentary endorses Beattie's sense of the *Nights* as a collection containing stories for 'young people', but it associates childhood reading with a never-to-be-forgotten realm of wonder.

Some critics now emphasize the larger significance of the 'transport' that took place when readers thus immersed themselves in fictions of the East. For Ros Ballaster, rather than offering 'identification and recognition of "selfhood"', such narratives provided their readers with a licensed space in which they could willingly relinquish self-sovereignty and open themselves to other worlds.[31] Marina Warner argues in a similar vein that from the early eighteenth century to the present, the reception of the *Nights* and its offshoots has taken the form of an under-the-radar process of cultural dialogue and exchange, since '*Homo narrans* observes no ethnic divisions.'[32] Warner's concept of 'stranger magic' alludes both to the prominence of the figure of the stranger, especially the enigmatic 'dark magician', in the *Nights* and elsewhere, and to the productively estranging effects of readerly absorption in tales of wonder that do not 'report on real life, but clear the way to changing the experience of living it'.[33] For both Ballaster and Warner, such absorption is to be differentiated from a narrower notion of 'escapism', because of its potential to challenge or even to confound the racialized distinctions insisted upon by critics such as Beattie. There is something utopian about this account of free-floating readers displaying an unconditional hospitality to the other and being transformed in the process. The idea that the space of reading might be regarded as a virtual contact zone remains a productive one, nonetheless, and I return to it in a later discussion of Romantic Orientalist poems such as Southey's *Thalaba the Destroyer* (1801), in part inspired by the *Arabian Tales*' story of 'Maugraby the Magician'.

Here, however, I want to emphasize that, even if forms of critical or editorial 'containment' failed to interrupt self-consciously captivated readers, the fact that a collection such as *Arabian Tales* could be prefaced with demystifying commentary in itself solicits critical attention. In view of the concerns of this chapter as a whole, it is significant that Heron's introduction is not only more detailed in its reference to the 'strange and singular' cultural context of fictions of the East than any previous such preface, but that – like Beattie's essay – in imagining the scene of story-telling it writes out Scheherazade and focuses instead solely on an aged surrogate of Schahriar. The EIC scholar Jonathan

Scott's translation of the Persian romance *Bahar-Danush; Or, Garden of Knowledge* (1799) offers another good example of such a preface, which at the same time indicates that received opinion about 'the East' could provide a way of mediating first-hand experiences: Scott contrasted the collection's display of 'the cruel tyranny of the haram, and the shameful ignorance in which women are kept in Asia' with 'the superiority which liberty, education, and well merited confidence give to the fair sex of this happy island and other unrevolutionized parts of Europe'.[34] I go on to say more about the post–French Revolution politics of the seraglio, but I turn now to a trio of late-century plays that, while they testify to the internalization of the *Nights* in British culture, can also be seen to adapt, or significantly to revise, well-known stories, including that of Scheherazade and Schahriar.

Sultans and Slaves

It is useful now to shift attention to the stage, since doing so allows us to think a little less speculatively about the formative impact of cultural representation. The theatre was 'crucial in socializing ... people into recognizing difference', in Kathleen Wilson's words, and dozens of productions in this period portrayed Britons' engagement with the wider world, and their invariably comic encounter with alien customs and manners.[35] The plays that I discuss here are especially interesting not simply because of their Eastern (specifically, Ottoman) settings, but because they incorporate free-speaking characters, English in fact or by proxy, whose experience of the East only makes them perform their sense of selfhood in a more assertive and uncompromising fashion. The way in which these works treat this encounter is sometimes less clear-cut than at first seems to be the case, as they also attend to class-related tensions of a kind that I explore in greater detail later in the chapter. At the same time, though, there are significant continuities between the plays in question, not least since they all conjoin, and address the relationship between, ideas of 'English' liberty and Oriental despotism; while the overarching term 'British' is most apposite for this chapter as a whole, in relation to the revolutionary contexts addressed, the plays under discussion here often invoke 'Englishness' as a specific ethnic identity.

The 'internalization' of the *Arabian Nights* referred to earlier is exemplified by the career of London Irishman John O'Keeffe, a prolific dramatist who produced plays including *The Dead Alive* (1780), which draws on 'The Story of the Sleeper Awakened', and *Aladdin* (1788); the 'orphan stories' of Aladdin, Ali Baba, and Sindbad were especially popular in this period, as Bridget Orr suggests, because they addressed a topic that resonated with their audiences – namely 'the fantastic material and social transformations in the lives of plebeian or middle-class characters who begin life oppressed by power or poverty'.[36] O'Keeffe's farce *The Little Hunch-Back; or, a Frolic in Bagdad* (1789) closely follows its source in the *Nights'* story of the same title, presenting the bizarre events that result when the Bassa's jester Crumpy chokes on a fishbone while having dinner at the house of Timothy Cross-Leg, a Christian tailor. Presuming their guest dead, Cross-Leg and his wife leave Crumpy outside in the street, from where he is taken in by the French doctor Quinquina, who hopes that he will be able to make money from curing him. In turn thinking that he has killed the Bassa's favourite, Quinquina lowers the supposed corpse down the chimney of the house of the Bassa's Jewish purveyor Zebede, who takes Crumpy for an intruder and thief, and lambasts his person. The English sailor Crank then strikes Crumpy down for the final time, imagining that he has been affronted by the taciturn Turk when he encounters him outside of Zebede's house.

Even as O'Keeffe's farce is indebted to a story in the *Nights*, however, it offers some notable reworkings of its source. Not only does it present (in the figure of Crank) a recognizable stereotype of English masculinity, but it also describes its action taking place against the backdrop of a proclamation from Constantinople that 'any Christian who offends a Mussulman shall receive the bastinado; and death if he kills one, even by chance.'[37] This climate of persecution provides the context for a subplot in which Zebede's nephew Absolom and Quinquina's stepdaughter Dora plan to elope to Europe and thereby, in Orr's words, to 'escape from the Islamic world'.[38] That sexual despotism makes companionate marriage impossible is not the play's key concern, though, and O'Keeffe's main innovation is to portray the 'English' honesty of Crank as differentiating him from the other characters involved in the handling of Crumpy's lifeless body. Whereas they all claim responsibility for the jester's apparent death as soon as the Bassa offers to reward rather than to punish his killer, Crank refuses any such recompense: having confessed that he gave Crumpy 'a dowse' because 'he wou'dn't drink with me' (33), Crank states that 'If I've kill'd a man I cou'd weep for it; but the price of blood shall never stain this hand' (34). The play's climax sees the return to consciousness of Crumpy, who demands among other things that his master 'repeal the law against the Christians' and give a purse to 'the generous Englishman, to give to me when I refuse next to drink with him' (35). While the play makes a joke of

Crank's drinking, it additionally associates sharing a drink with sociable interaction on more or less equal terms, as is the case when, after complaining that 'I can't get one honest fellow to take a bottle with me!', Crank declares that 'the Grand Turk himself needn't be asham'd to talk to a Briton' (32–3). I return to the connection between liberty and free speech in seraglio discourse, but here it is worth emphasizing the importance of O'Keeffe's insertion of an English character into the familiar – because *Arabian Nights*–derived – world of the play. Crank's albeit unwittingly decisive role at the end of *The Little Hunch-Back* shows the loosely Eastern milieu of the play to be, as Orr argues, 'a place existing in relation to, and acted upon by, British subjects, rather than a parallel universe in which Europeans, if they appeared, were marginal'.[39]

Isaac Bickerstaff's farce *The Sultan, or A Peep into the Seraglio* (first performed in 1775) provides another rich example of a work which presents the East being 'acted upon' by a British protagonist. In this case despotic authority is more overtly defined in sexual terms, and the play exemplifies a transfer of agency from East to West, since its unnamed Sultan is converted to a new understanding of marriage by an English harem slave named Roxolana, after she overcomes his Eastern 'prejudices' with the force of her 'reason'.[40] This reference to 'prejudice' calls up Sultan Schahriar's 'fatal prejudice against all women', and Bickerstaff's English heroine takes on a role in some ways akin to that of Scheherazade (who in the *Nights*' frame tale succeeds in 'convincing [Schahriar] of her merit and great wisdom').[41] The play at the same time alludes to other sultans and other female slaves, and it thus offers a reminder of the multiplicity of French as well as British sources that were drawn upon by the literary Orientalisms of the late eighteenth century.

Bickerstaff borrowed from Charles-Simon Favart's *Les Trois Sultanes* (1761) (itself an adaptation of Marmontel's 'Soliman the Second'), and the play's composite identity means that its representation of Roxolana's 'improving' influence is not straightforward. In keeping the name of Roxolana for its heroine, *The Sultan* acknowledges the long tradition of literary Roxanas modelled on the slave-turned-wife of Ottoman emperor Suleiman I ('the Magnificent'), and distinguished from Scheherazade's descendants by their more overtly sexualized self-fashioning.[42] While Roxolana reforms the Sultan, then, she does so not with inventive story-telling but with a coquettish performance of the kind associated with her namesakes, making the Sultan marvel at the effect of 'her little nose, cock'd in the air, her laughing eyes, and the play of her features' (11). This is therefore an account of feminine agency very different from that of contemporary historians of the progress of society. Bickerstaff's subtitle appeals to an audience familiar with prior portrayals of harem intrigue, and for all that the play does not quite live up to such expectations it depicts Roxolana as a worldly figure who, in declining an invitation to 'sup with' the Sultan, knowingly states that 'suppers here tend to certain – things . . .' (13). The *Middlesex Journal*'s reviewer perhaps had this moment in mind when objecting to the play's 'obvious incorrectness of . . . language, which was occasionally remarkably coarse'.

The same reviewer stated that Frances Abington's 'uncommon merit' in the role of Bickerstaff's heroine 'surmounted every obstacle to the success of the piece' (*The Sultan* was written for Abington, and she apparently pressured David Garrick into staging it).[43] Roxolana commands attention at the expense of her fellow harem slaves, and it is significant too that Bickerstaff makes the figure of Elmira Circassian rather than Spanish – therefore more clearly 'Oriental' than she is in Favart's version of the story.[44] Elmira has less involvement in *The Sultan* than in the play's source texts, and by declaring herself to be 'reconcil'd' (6) to her sexual servitude by the love she imagines the Sultan has shown her, she throws into relief Roxolana's refusal to be governed by her nominal master. Bickerstaff's revision of his sources additionally means that the Sultan declares his weariness with seraglio pleasures at an early stage, thereby signalling his readiness for the reforming influence of Roxolana, who educates him as to the difference between 'Turkish gallantry' (9) and her own instinctive sense of 'English' liberty. If, as the *Middlesex Journal* stated, Roxolana's account of this distinction 'would have had a better effect, had the author given her an English name' (the idea of an *English* Roxolana remained problematic for some), Bickerstaff's heroine nonetheless offers a crowd-pleasing sense of herself as a 'free-born woman, prouder of that than all the pomp and splendour eastern monarchs can bestow' (13); absent from the play's sources, but endorsed by the Sultan's reference to her 'national vivacity' (12), this claim at once establishes Roxolana's individuality of character and the connection between liberty and free speech.[45] One further slight but significant detail in Bickerstaff's reworking of Marmontel and Favart is that even as his play accentuates Roxolana's outspokenness it also makes her a more modest figure than her predecessors, depriving her of the sexual experience that they had demonstrated.[46]

When situated in its initial performance context, *The Sultan* may be read as wishfully allegorizing George III's rejection of his ministers and his eventual conversion to the cause of the liberty then being championed by American colonists.[47] *The Sultan* continued to be widely performed well after the American war, however, and it may thus have gone on to be understood in more binary terms than this, with Oriental sexual despotism a foil for Roxolana's agency rather than an analogue for British tyranny. Having said that, to return to my earlier point about the rhetorical complexity of much contemporary drama, it is important to keep in mind the dialogism of a work such as this too, its 'activation' of the harem scenario that in the writing of Beattie or Heron is simply a static tableau. Even as *The Sultan* – like other plays of the period – invokes the idea of Oriental despotism as a way of thinking about the meaning of British liberty, it also suggests that there may be something overbearing if not indeed despotic about its heroine's understanding of the freedom of the individual: anticipating Crank's attempt to make Crumpy 'take a bottle' with him, Roxolana demands that the Sultan and his eunuch Osmyn drink wine with her, despite their reluctance to do so, and she mimics the Sultan in telling Osmyn that '[i]f you neglect obeying my orders, your head shall answer for it' (15). Another point to emphasize here is that whereas Beattie's 'On Fable and Romance' defines a 'cultural' Gothicism against Asiatic slavery in terms of a broad-based consensus ('*With us*, the two sexes associate together'), *The Sultan*, like *The Little Hunch-Back*, appears more specifically to hail the constituency of the middle and lower-middle orders. I say more about the exposure of a class-based fault line in Britons' Eastern imaginary in the 1780s and after, but before doing so I briefly discuss a longer play that both demonstrates how a seraglio setting might allegorize domestic social relations and testifies to the passing of 'Scheherazadean' agency from Oriental to European women.

The title of Hannah Cowley's comedy *A Day in Turkey; Or, The Russian Slaves* (1792) ostensibly distinguishes it from the farces considered earlier, but it is indebted to Bickerstaff's treatment of the sultan/slave scenario, and its non-aristocratic Russian characters, because they perform already familiar roles, appear to possess identifiably 'English' qualities. The play begins with Paulina and her family, along with Count Orloff and his French attendant, being captured by marauding Turks. Paulina, modelled on Roxolana, serves as a counterpoint to the high-born Russian slave (and Orloff's new wife) Alexina, for whereas the latter plays the part of a victim (down to her reference to the 'bodkin' that represents her final defence against violation), Paulina is a loquacious heroine who succeeds in charming the Turkish Bassa Ibrahim.[48] Ibrahim, like Bickerstaff's Sultan, declares his tiredness with 'the dull acquiescence of our eastern slaves' (20), and he hopes to 'astonish' (14) the proud Alexina into love, but before he sees her he is captivated by Paulina, thinking that she is the woman about whom he has heard so much. The harem paradoxically becomes an equalizing space in the play as Ibrahim abases himself before Paulina as her 'humble slave' (43), and she in turn performs the elevated status attributed to her, while attempting to conceal her own attraction to the Bassa: 'How hard it is,' she complains, 'when one sees a great gentleman, and so handsome withal, ready to die at one's feet, to be forced to be snappish and ill-natur'd' (61). Paulina confesses her love to Ibrahim when she realizes that he has mistaken her for Alexina (and that he therefore thinks she is already betrothed), and, having been taught to love by Paulina, his heart 'engrossed' (83) by her, Ibrahim finally declares liberty for all.

Cowley's post-revolutionary drama is teasingly reflexive about its topical resonance, as is suggested by its initial show of repudiating politics ('will Miss Wollstonecraft forgive me … ?' [i]), its treatment of the Frenchman À La Greque, and its focus on 'Russian slaves' in a Turkish setting, not long after Pitt had broached the idea of an alliance with the Ottoman empire against Russia. What I want to emphasize here, however, is the way in which *A Day in Turkey* displays underlying structural similarities with the other works discussed in this section, not just because – like *The Sultan* – it stages a transfer of agency (as a lower-class European woman comes to exert a kind of 'Scheherazadean' influence), but because it plays the idea of despotic authority for laughs. The spectacle of Oriental despotism, often sexual in character, is offered for entertainment in all of the productions considered earlier, and the manner of its representation may have been congenial to audiences of these popular plays since it provided them with an appealing way of thinking about themselves. The nominal foreignness of 'Turkish' interlocutors helps English and other European characters to imagine a 'horizontal' relationship with those of a more elevated social status, and laughter is possible here precisely of the way in which these self-possessed figures assert their equality with the various Sultans and Bassas that they encounter, thus bringing about the collapse of despotic rule. It is open to debate as to whether the foreignness of their interlocutors to some extent contains the assertiveness of free-speaking Britons (and others) in these plays, and I go on to say more about the political functioning of seraglio discourse in non-fictional prose of the 1790s. I turn now, though, to a comic novel, Robert Bage's *The Fair Syrian* (1787), which rehearses the well-established mythology of sexual despotism considered earlier, but also offers a more comparative perspective on elite male gallantry.

Bage's Laughing Heroines

Before discussing *The Fair Syrian*, it is useful briefly to acknowledge the diverse possibilities of late eighteenth-century plays with Eastern settings which engage with the politics of empire in India as well as in America. Elizabeth Inchbald's *The Mogul Tale* (first performed in 1784), for example, is another seraglio farce, but it allegorizes the overlap of domestic and imperial politics, conceiving of despotic authority in relativizing terms: the Indian prince of the title knowingly performs the role of a tyrant so as to 'aggravate [the] fears' of the motley English trio whose balloon has strayed off course and descended in the gardens of his palace, and having made his captives anticipate a horrible death as punishment for their trespass, he finally tells them that their 'countrymen's cruelty to the poor Gentoos has shewn ... tyranny in so foul a light' that he is determined to be 'mild, just and merciful' with them.[49] The title of Samuel Jackson Pratt's *The Fair Circassian* (1781) sounds like that of a harem comedy, but the play is actually an adaptation of John Hawkesworth's prose tale *Almoran and Hamet* (1761) and, like its source, it makes shape-shifting integral to its action. Pratt's work begins by outlining the recent division of the Persian throne between the brothers Almoran and Hamet after the death of their father, and in thus alluding to the ongoing American war the play conceives of Persia as a 'parallel universe' rather than as a place to be 'acted upon' by Europeans.[50] After the schemes of Almoran are finally thwarted and he commits suicide, *The Fair Circassian* concludes with Hamet's marriage to Almeida, the heroine of the title, and thereby looks ahead to the future revival of Persian fortunes.

The allegorical plot of Pratt's play serves to highlight the distinctiveness of Bage's similarly titled text. While it often refers to the 'king's' seraglio, it does not use its Persian setting as a means of generalizing about 'the East' more broadly. *The Fair Syrian*, by contrast, is clearly embedded in the discourses of despotism discussed so far, while at the same time – unlike the plays examined earlier – introducing European characters who sometimes themselves perform 'Eastern' manners. In a comparable way to Bage's *Mount Henneth*, *The Fair Syrian* incorporates both an 'Eastern' and a 'Western' plot, where the former enables a negotiation of the problems generated by the latter, which begins with the American war – a source of such ideological confusion because, as in Pratt's play, it was so often regarded as a familial conflict. The English Captain Sir John Amington and the French Marquis de St. Claur first meet in America (where they are caught up in the war against their better judgement), and they encounter

Honoria Warren, 'the Fair Syrian', during their subsequent travels in Ireland, where she is on trial for murder, charged with poisoning her guardian. Honoria is acquitted when her accusers' perjury is established, and she later gives an account of her life to Sir John's sister Lady Bembridge, describing how she was born in Syria – hence her sobriquet – after her merchant father had settled there, but came to be separated from him when the two of them were seized by Saif Ebn Abu, the son of her father's business associate. Honoria's narrative appeals to a common knowledge of 'how fruitful the east is in insurrections and rebellions', presenting such events as 'the things of every day, for avarice and despotism, their productive causes, are never wanting'.[51] This notion of an unchanging, 'everyday' despotism helps to frame Britain's attempt to enforce its sovereignty over its American colonies as an aberrant, misguided, and now best forgotten venture which, as Sir John puts it, generated a 'natural' spirit of resistance that saved Britain from the consequences of its own actions: 'Fatal to half the world would have been the hour in which we had enslaved America. – Most fatal to ourselves' (1:23).

Unlike Pratt's Fair Circassian, Bage's Fair Syrian is presented as a onetime victim of sexual despotism. Honoria recalls Saif's 'free stare of irregular desire' (2:43), and describing the threat that he posed to her during her captivity, she recounts that she carried a knife with which to ensure 'his death or my own', adding that 'never, whilst I stayed in Asia, did I part with it from my person' (2:70). Honoria once more invokes this sense of a monolithic 'Asia', again primarily defined by the condition of women, when she tells of how she was taken from Saif by a gang of banditti, then sold to a new master whose attention to her likewise exhibited 'the idea of property . . . that is visible in the regards of [all] the Orientals', an idea which she contrasts with the 'polite attention' that is paid to women by 'the gentlemen of Europe' (2:85). As Honoria tells Lady Bembridge, she managed to retain her chastity by stabbing herself with the knife she carried when the time came for her to be taken to her master's bed. Subsequently put up for sale again, after her master took an overdose of 'provocatives' in preparation for the arrival of a new recruit to his harem, Honoria then describes how she was eventually united with her guardian.

While this short summary of Honoria's narrative suggests her similarity to Cowley's Alexina, especially in her consciousness of sexual danger, Honoria's retrospect on her captivity also displays an irreverent humour characteristic of lower-born figures such as Bickerstaff's Roxolana and Cowley's Paulina. *The Fair Syrian* accentuates the comedy of *The Sultan*, so that at a number of points in her narrative Honoria interjects with wryly detached observations on the predicament of Eastern women, referring for example to the 'lock-up houses' established in the era of 'that horrid bear, Mahomet' (2:36). She additionally recalls her encounter with the remarkable Georgian slave Amina, a fellow captive who combines Roxolana's instinct for free speech with a far greater degree of sexual candour. The case of Amina helps to clarify a larger contemporary shift in the representation of Eastern women precisely because Bage's portrayal of her is so exceptional. Without self-pity or sensation, Amina tells of how she spent nine years adorning the 'splendid harams' (2:78) of eleven different owners, most of whom beat her because she 'disturbed their ... gravity with laughing' (2:79). Honoria describes how 'this wild, untutored, sensible mad-cap' in turn laughed at her, and 'the most serious arguments' she could use, collapsing in 'an extravagant fit' at her principled assertion that she would 'prefer death a thousand times' to the kind of experiences that her companion blithely narrates (2:81). Always gaining the upper hand in such exchanges, Amina might be regarded as a re-Orientalized Roxolana. It is significant that Amina has only a cameo role in the novel, though, and that while she retains a wittily dissenting pose her contrariness appears simply to shock or – as with her previous masters – to offend rather than 'act upon' her interlocutors. Amina is detached from any kind of 'Scheherazadean' plot, therefore, and her story is contained as an episode within the title character's life: 'What became of her, I never heard' (2:90), Honoria states after their separation.

While it draws on the sultan/slave plot of contemporary drama, then, Bage's novel offers a more idiosyncratic exploration of sexual politics than *The Sultan* or *A Day in Turkey*. Another way of illustrating this is to consider the novel's playful treatment of the male 'gallantry' that, according to the neo-chivalric ideology of writers such as Hurd, Fordyce, and Beattie, helped to elevate women in Britain above their counterparts elsewhere. Bage's representation of Sir John and the Marquis ostensibly upholds a distinction between British and French understandings of gallantry, where the latter is exemplified by the Marquis's fond recollection of buying and selling 'Mingrelian girls' (2:282) while on a pleasure trip to Constantinople. The novel to some extent licenses the conduct of the Marquis, however, because it differentiates his understanding of 'the liberty of love' (1:45) from the more problematically 'French' notion of despotic authority embodied by his mother. It moreover aligns his idea of personal freedom – the 'natural disposition to do what [one] likes', as he puts it – with a deep sense of 'transatlantic' liberty that endures irrespective of the breach between Britain and America: 'my egregious failings, my rebellious principles, my scanty pittance of filial piety,' he tells Sir John, 'were picked up in the thirteen provinces, and amongst your licentious Americo-Angles of the old world' (2:316).

The suggestion that the Marquis gains sexual pleasure from the 'sprightly' (2:282) women he buys separates him both from the Turk who buys Honoria, a man whose impotence is signalled by his need for 'provocatives' (2:89), and from the unworldly Sir John, whom the Marquis teases as an 'intellectual eunuch' (1:141). Bage's satire seems to be directed at Sir John more than at the Marquis, because as the novel ridicules the attempt of the former to imitate his friend, it implies that 'English' gallantry may really be no more than a façade to disguise baser instincts that others are more ready to avow. When Sir John drunkenly attempts to seduce Honoria, she mockingly asks him to translate his raptures into a more comprehensible language, at which point he ventriloquizes an 'Eastern' style of address, declaring his desire to 'improve felicity, and create a paradise for man'. After responding that this paradise would be 'a purgatory for women', Honoria criticizes the 'cold and lifeless' style rather than the substance of Sir John's approach. She subsequently offers her own version of how to praise the beauty of an imaginary woman in a properly Eastern idiom: '"Her eyes were large and black, like the eyes of the heifer of Yerak – their lustre surpassed the gems of Golconda – Her cheeks were the full blown rose of Damascus – Her teeth, the cypresses of Diarbekir – Her hair was black as the raven's plumes . . . "' (2:248). Honoria's riposte to Sir John conveys what appears to be an enjoyment of Orientalist flights of fancy, predicated on her sophisticated awareness of the gulf between fantasy and reality. Here, however, I want in particular to emphasize Honoria's critique of Sir John's performance rather than the playfulness of her alternative to it. Bage's depiction of Sir John's gallantry acknowledges the theatrical tradition of harem comedy, and in his clumsy approach to Honoria, he might be seen as trying but failing to play the part of an unreconstructed sultan. As I now show in what follows, Bage's satire of Sir John's gallantry also converges with other works of the late 1780s and 1790s that provided less comic accounts of the ways in which women were subordinated – and 'Eastern manners' established – in Britain.

'Eastern Manners without Going to the East'

In *Letters from Barbary* (1788), the army officer Alexander Jardine denounced the 'nonsense of modern gallantry' by which men were able to 'act the tyrants over the female part of society' by pretending that they were subservient to it.[52] Jardine travelled to Morocco in the early 1770s as part of an embassy from Gibraltar, and he cited the condition of women as one aspect of the 'total difference' (12) of the customs and manners that he witnessed. Arguing in familiar terms that where women are 'considered only as domestic slaves . . ., they can have no weight or polish in society, which therefore can hardly be polished or improved', Jardine presented the appearance of Moroccan women, 'covered up to the eyes' (108–9), as evidence of an unnatural curbing of humankind's instinct for improving social intercourse. While he initially argued that it was in North Africa that one could apprehend 'Eastern manners . . . without going to the East' (15), however, Jardine also asserted that Morocco provided a cautionary tale for Europeans, who might be sensible of the perils facing them 'if they were to come and see their brethren here' (34). Jardine later focused on the state of France, where 'the footsteps of despotism' (272) were already traceable, and in identifying the slow creep or phantom 'spirit' (41) of despotism in this way he suggested that its malign effects might be felt anywhere in the world.

John Barrell's *The Spirit of Despotism* begins with an analysis of how Vicesimus Knox's 1795 work of the same title anatomizes the state of Britain, where war with France and aggressive counter-revolutionary opposition to the cause of political reform had generated further institutional encroachment on individual liberties.[53] Knox stated at the outset that 'Oriental Manners, and the Ideas imbibed in Youth, both in the West and East Indies, [were] favourable to the Spirit of Despotism,' and by the early 1790s, as in the first responses to Burke's *Reflections on the Revolution in France* (1790), it was a rhetorical commonplace to state that Oriental or Eastern manners were evident in modern Britain.[54] While such a claim was not in itself new (as Knox's allusion to nabobs indicates), what is especially notable about a work such as Mary Wollstonecraft's *A Vindication of the Rights of Men* (1790) is that it Orientalizes Burke and the whole culture of 'Gothic gallantry' that it associates with him.[55] In *Reflections* Burke presented the legacy of chivalric manners as helping to differentiate the 'character' of modern Europe from that of Asia; for Percy, Beattie, and others considered earlier, as for Burke, these manners had an explicitly 'Gothic' foundation.[56] Wollstonecraft by contrast aligned Gothic chivalry with Oriental sexual despotism, and thus collapsed the distinction that Burke and others had drawn. She did this in part by accusing Burke of partiality to 'the mussulman's creed', equating Burke's 'Gothic' ideas of femininity with the enduring popular stereotype which held that Islam denied women the possession of souls.[57] Wollstonecraft ridiculed Burke's paean to Marie Antoinette in an innuendo-filled passage describing his rhetorical flights as the product of a 'teeming fancy' that was likely to gush forth 'another Chinese erection, to stare . . . the plain country people in the face, who bluntly call such an airy edifice – a folly!'.[58] As is the case with Bage's Sir John, there is something of the inept libertine about Wollstonecraft's Burke, presented here as a superannuated figure caught in the act of pleasuring himself.

It is well known that Wollstonecraft's *Vindication of the Rights of Woman* (1792) still more frequently refers to the 'Eastern', often 'Mahometan', treatment of women, presenting this as a form of oppression that is reproduced in modern Britain.[59] Saree Makdisi argues that in the writing of Wollstonecraft and her contemporaries, the seraglio functioned as 'the ideal surrogate target for radical critique, an imaginary space on which to project all the supposed faults of the old regime, and then subject them to attack'.[60] It was now widely portrayed simply as a site of male pleasure, without reference to any possibility of 'Scheherazadean' agency, and it was thus, in Makdisi's words, 'the most appropriate synecdoche for the Orient as a locus of despotism, idleness, femininity, and luxury'.[61] While a writer such as Beattie had a decade earlier invoked the figure of an 'idle' Eastern prince as the embodiment of an alien culture and form of governance, Tom Paine (in *Rights of Man* [1791–2]) projected an Orientalized idleness onto members of the British aristocracy, describing them as 'a seraglio of males, who neither collect the honey nor form the hive, but exist only for lazy enjoyment'.[62] A fault line in Britons' Eastern imaginary was exposed in the 1790s, then, because this 'new Orient' served not to define a broadly consensual idea of British liberty (as in Beattie's work), but to constitute a more overtly politicized subjectivity.[63] Makdisi identifies the emergence in this period of a 'bourgeois radicalism' that defined values of sobriety, rationality, and, above all, self-determination against popular enthusiasm as well as aristocratic corruption.[64] He further argues that this new radicalism appealed to a purportedly universal but in fact specifically 'Western' language of individual rights, which in turn provided a new, modernizing paradigm of European imperialism.

This claim that late eighteenth-century radicals helped to make the idea of empire more thinkable requires qualification. Jardine's *Letters* certainly demonstrates that the critique of despotism at home and abroad could provide the intellectual foundation for an ideology of liberal imperialism, since it states that those who live under despotic rule need to be roused to industry: as people are 'not to be *written* into virtue', there is sometimes 'no possibility of getting them up again, but by conquering and colonising their country' (33–4). The most overt and influential interventionist thinking at this time probably came from Clapham Sect evangelicals, however, and many prominent reformers were critics of empire past and present. In 'A Discourse on the Love of our Country' (1790), for example, Richard Price acknowledged both the 'despotism' which kept so much of the world in darkness and the domestically enfeebling effects of any dominion established 'by extending territory, and enslaving surrounding countries'.[65] Tom Paine, in *Rights of Man*, appeared to legitimize quasi-imperial intervention when he wrote of the 'glory, and advantage' accruing to a nation which 'exerts its powers to rescue the world from bondage', but he also referred to 'the horrid scene that is now acting by the English government in the East Indies', its members behaving like 'Goths and Vandals, who, destitute of principles, robbed and tortured the world they were incapable of enjoying'.[66] For all that Paine appears to suggest here that some might be constitutionally unable to appreciate the mutual benefits of social intercourse, he asserted that empire would be inconceivable 'if commerce were permitted to act to the universal extent it is capable'.[67]

Makdisi's account of the connection between the seraglio-fixated 'radical Orientalism' of the 1790s and a new ideology of empire as modernization does, however, draw attention to the ideological mobility of the received idea of sexual despotism which provides this chapter with its focus. In later chapters I explore other aspects of the cultural history of British Orientalisms in the 1790s, in particular the contest over the record of Sir William Jones that began after his death in 1794, and the appeal made by radical poets (notably Coleridge and Southey) to the civic virtue of early Islam, which they largely separated from any idea of Eastern sexual despotism; I also briefly consider the impact of Macartney's 1792–4 embassy to the Chinese imperial court on subsequent imaginings of China. Here, though, I want to acknowledge another – less discussed – dimension of this story, the development of an 'anti-Jacobin Orientalism' that may be understood as signalling an awareness of, and responding to, the newly politicized seraglio discourse of the 1790s.

M. O. Grenby's essay 'Orientalism and Propaganda' examines the revival of the Oriental 'apologue' or moral tale after the French Revolution, arguing that this long-established form came back into favour both as a means of portraying an idealized social cohesion and of providing warnings about the consequences of intellectual presumption. Grenby recovers numerous little-known texts, and in the light of Orr's identification of Aladdin as an exemplar of social mobility, it is striking that one of them, *Massouf; or, the Philosophy of the Day* (1802), includes an upstart character by the name of 'Aladin' who, in Grenby's summary, is 'every inch a Tom Paine'.[68] The counter-revolutionary possibilities of fictionalized Easts are just as evident in Heron's preface to *Arabian Tales*, cited earlier, because while it takes Oriental sexual despotism for granted, it also presents as typical of the composite society it describes the fact that prayers are 'repeated by all ranks, with serious devotion, almost as often in the day as our men of fashion call upon their Maker in contemptuous scorn'.[69] As much as Heron's preface rehearses the rhetoric of sexual despotism that helped Britons to recognize themselves as un-enslaved, then, it also suggests that 'Eastern' manners might in other respects embarrass Britons, by throwing into relief the moral corruption of an advanced commercial society. Heron's contrast between the ritualized devotion of Muslims and the blasphemy of 'our men of fashion' nicely sets up my concluding discussion of Elizabeth Hamilton's sustained reflection on Britons' self-mythology in *Letters of a Hindoo Rajah*.

'Christianity Is Not Yet Entirely Extinct'

Letters of a Hindoo Rajah could have been discussed in the previous chapter alongside *Hartly House, Calcutta*, as a fiction of British India written to vindicate Warren Hastings. It provides a good conclusion to this chapter because it reflects on the mutual constitution of ideas of 'Oriental' despotism and 'British' liberty in a revolutionary era, while also acknowledging the force of contemporary claims about the growing sway of 'Eastern manners' in Britain itself; as such, it might be regarded as offering a critical retrospect on the three decades or so of seraglio discourse explored thus far. In what follows I largely bypass Hamilton's intervention in debates about the politics of empire (and her endorsement of the codification of customary Indian property rights), and instead treat *Letters of a Hindoo Rajah* as a text that above all addresses the condition of modern Britain, which it represents as in some ways determined by empire, or at least global commerce.[70] I focus in particular on Hamilton's sophisticated adaptation of the genre of informant narrative, by which her work registers different kinds of pressure on the notion of a distinctly British moral virtue that it initially establishes.

Unlike most other works discussed earlier, *Letters of a Hindoo Rajah* situates the idea of Oriental despotism within a clearly defined historical and geographical context. Hamilton's 'Preliminary Dissertation' considers the enduring effects of the Mughal yoke in India, describing first how the forces of 'Fanatic zeal' had founded an empire, then how, as its authority waned, 'the power of one despot' gave way to 'the uncontrouled licentiousness of numberless petty tyrants'.[71] This introduction refers specifically to the defeat of the Rohilla Afghans by EIC forces twenty years earlier, but in thus invoking the idea of 'uncontrouled licentiousness' it also clearly draws upon a generalized notion of sexual despotism, here projected onto barbarous Muslims. Hamilton's dissertation contrasts the 'resistless fury' (67) of the initial invaders of northern India with the mildness of the 'aboriginal' population that they conquered. While the federative 'ancient government' of this people was structurally similar to the feudal system, according to Hamilton, the sovereignty of local rulers in the past was more benign than such a comparison allows, because it bore 'the mild aspect of parental authority' (57). This construction of Hindu society's 'familial' harmony is extended in an account of 'the division of the Hindoos into four *Casts*' (58), as a result of which men assuming hereditarily ordained occupations and roles could be understood as 'walking in the steps of [their] fathers' (60). Hamilton's representation of a society where discontent is 'unknown' because people believe their situation to be 'marked out ... by the hand of Providence' (63) is congruent with the emphasis of the anti-Jacobin texts considered earlier, then, although the subsequent interplay between different narrators makes her work resistant to any clear-cut ideological classification.

In the first letter of the main text the Rajah Zaarmilla gives a sentimental description of his encounter with the English officer Captain Percy, recollecting that the latter spoke perfect Persian, and thereby helping the reader to recognize Percy as in part modelled on the author's brother, the Orientalist scholar Charles Hamilton. Zaarmilla learns from Percy that '[i]n Europe man has not always, as in Asia, been degraded by slavery, or corrupted by the possession of despotic power' (82), and he is astounded to hear that, according to 'the Christian Shaster', 'women are considered in the light of rational beings! free agents! In short, as a moiety of the human species' (87). In line with his generalized reference to slavery 'in Asia', Zaarmilla to a large extent elides the distinction between Islam and Hinduism upon which Hamilton's dissertation had insisted. He concedes that if 'the laws of the Mussulmans absolutely exclude women from the participation of happiness in a future state' (87), then 'admission into Paradise' (88) remains in the balance for Hindu women too, even if they immolate themselves on their husbands' funeral pyres. Zaarmilla also appears to invoke a notion of 'Asiatic' polygamy here by contrasting the idea that in Britain 'a wife is the friend of her husband' (88) with the 'disquiet, ... quarrels, jealousies, and strifes' which – he confides to his addressee, Maandaara – 'our wives frequently produce' among themselves.

Zaarmilla's shock at the fact that Percy's sister Charlotte had written an inscription on the Bible that she gave her brother elicits from Percy a brief explanation of how the progress of society improves the status of women. Accordingly, Percy's narrative discriminates on stadial grounds between the situation of 'Hindoo' and 'Afgan' women, since the former live among men more 'advanced in civilization' who have come to value 'the advantages of reason' over brute 'bodily strength'. Percy additionally appeals to the determining influence of Christianity in distinguishing European women from all others: 'had not the powerful mandate of religion snapped their chains', he argues, then man's 'innate love of the exercise of despotic authority must have for ever kept the female sex in a state of subjection' (89).

This narrative of British exceptionalism (and the essential difference between 'Europe' and 'Asia') is complicated almost immediately, however, as when Zaarmilla presents the colonization of America, the cultivation of 'the trans-Atlantic isles', and the 'rescue [of] *our* nation from the hands of the oppressor' as evidence of Britons' 'love of virtue and freedom' – their adherence to 'the fundamental precepts of their Shaster, "to do to others as they would have others do to them"' (84). Hamilton's interjection that her title character wrote his letters 'toward the beginning of 1775' (144) invites us to see Zaarmilla as a naïve figure who is unaware of what readers know about Britain's humiliating loss of its American colonies (and the colonists' competing claim to the language of 'virtue and freedom'). More striking than this is Zaarmilla's bracketing together of the 'trans-Atlantic isles' and '*our* nation' as objects of Britain's 'benevolent' and 'generous' (84) attention. Albeit obliquely, the allusion to plantation slavery here calls into question the nature of the 'rescue' mission in India with which it is coupled, undercutting Hamilton's earlier argument about the EIC's liberating role.

The novel's engagement with the mythology of British liberty gets more complex still when Maandaara alerts Zaarmilla to the recent experience of the Brahmin Sheermaal in Britain; one feature of the text that differentiates it from a precursor such as *The Citizen of the World*, from which it borrows extensively, is that its main narrator in effect follows in the footsteps of a fellow countryman. As is signalled by his reference to visiting 'the remotest corner of the habitable world' (108), Sheermaal is less open to the other than Zaarmilla, his experience of the nation through an 'Oriental' – and sometimes specifically Hindu – lens generating some revealing moments of misrecognition. One rich example of this occurs when Sheermaal encounters a man who had written a work 'more voluminous than the Mahabbarat'

(109), apparently devoted to converting Christians to Islam – most likely an allusion to Edward Gibbon. Sheermaal considers obstacles to the take-up of Islam in Britain, among them that Koranic 'injunctions concerning the treatment of slaves' would be too strict for 'the Christians of England' to bear. He notes, though, that the ideas of polygamy and 'the Mahommedan Paradise' may be 'alluring' to 'men of taste and sentiment' (110) (Bage's Sir John Amington comes to mind here), and he subsequently registers the way in which, recalling Jardine's terms, it might be possible in Britain to see 'Eastern manners, without going to the East'. Sheermaal refers to an English 'Rajah' who, drawn to 'the system of Mahommet', thought that the daughter of a local labourer would be 'no unworthy ornament of his zenana' (117–18). He is made to betray his own prejudice when he adds that social 'inferiors' should not be able to 'defeat the intentions of their Lords' (118), but his reading of English society as a caste system nonetheless accentuates the idea of social stratification that so occupied writers across the political spectrum in the 1790s. In his account of rural Scotland, Sheermaal appeals to anti-nabob discourse as well as to the language of caste/class, since he explains the absence of socially upstart 'people of style' there as resulting from the strength of barriers to '[t]he flood of wealth, which the golden stream of commerce has diffused over the kingdom of England' (123).

The clearest index of Sheermaal's retention of a 'Bramin' identity is provided by his reference to the 'wisdom' of the institution of sati by which, he says, 'creatures, incapable of acting with propriety for themselves, are effectually put out of the way of mischief' (129). By the time that Hamilton wrote *Letters of a Hindoo Rajah*, the idea of sati as a form of sexual despotism had become, like the idea of seraglio slavery, an established counter in discourse on the oppression of Eastern women; in the writings and speeches of Clapham evangelicals such as Charles Grant, moreover, sati had begun to be invoked as an example of Hindu cruelty that justified new forms of imperial intervention. In view of this, what is notable about Sheermaal's own exercise in cultural comparison in the passage cited is that it blocks sati's rhetorical functioning as a 'representative' practice differentiating Asia from Europe. While Sheermaal remains a prejudiced figure who believes that by their 'voluntary sacrifice' Hindu women attain 'glory here, and . . . happiness hereafter!', his observation that people in Britain 'grieve at equivocal and distant evils' but ignore those 'before their eyes' (132) suggests that Britons indulge in a kind of telescopic philanthropy where the condition of women is concerned. Hamilton's novel at no point attempts to appeal to any cross-cultural 'solidarity of gender', but instead, as Nigel Leask argues, refuses readers 'the narcissistic satisfaction of self-reflection in an oriental mirror'.[72]

In response to Sheermaal's narrative, Zaarmilla questions whether someone so close-minded can be 'a proper judge' of what he sees. The main target of Hamilton's irony, however, as Leask suggests, is 'Zaarmilla's naïve exclamation', which inadvertently makes a larger point about 'the act of (mis)representation' that implicates Britons too: 'Ah! What a pattern might Sheermaal have found in the travellers, and the travel-writers of Europe. How many of these does England alone, every year, pour from her maternal bosom? Happy for Sheermaal, if he had followed the laudable example of these sapient youths ... !' (139).[73] After his arrival in what he had imagined as a 'favoured Island' (201), Zaarmilla comes to recognize that he was wrong to have thought Britain a Christian country. Like Sheermaal, he invites the reader to consider the analogy between 'aristocratic' and 'Oriental' manners when he describes his encounter with the 'philosopher' Sir Caprice Ardent, who asks him for 'a plan of a Mosque, a Minaret, or some such thing' (212) with which to adorn an architectural project. Zaarmilla's involvement with Sir Caprice gives him further insight into the luxury of upper-class society that Sheermaal had previously noted, and it also introduces him to the other philosophers who meet at Ardent Hall. Hamilton's representation of 'philosophy' has received particular attention from critics interested in the cultural politics of the 1790s, and the novel's portrayal of Sir Caprice's collaborators as 'worshippers of System' (273) has been taken as evidence of its anti-Jacobin affiliations. Any attempt to classify the politics of the novel on the basis of its later scenes is nonetheless complicated by the fact that in engaging with debates about what the Wollstonecraftian Miss Ardent refers to as 'the perfection of the female understanding' (261), it is clearly embedded within contemporary discourses of feminism.

Where the question of education is concerned, more might be said about Hamilton's interest in redefining the domestic sphere and, with it, the character of the mixed sociability that had been invoked in self-congratulatory terms by writers such as Beattie or Fordyce. To conclude, however, I want to focus on Hamilton's conclusion, and to think especially about its reflection on the strength and purchase of the exceptional 'native' virtue celebrated by Beattie and others. As Zaarmilla moves from Ardent Hall to Violet-dale, following the philosopher Sceptic's suicide, he encounters what is to him a new form of community, centred on the family of Percy's friend Mr Denbeigh. When Charlotte Percy goes to stay at Violet-dale – 'this Temple of domestic bliss' (302), Zaarmilla calls it – she throws off the 'melancholy' with which she had been afflicted after the death of her brother, and she is persuaded by Denbeigh's father to reconcile herself to her situation (303). Mr Denbeigh invites Charlotte Percy to consider 'the exertion of activity' as the most appropriate tribute that she could pay her brother, and in stating that opportunities of 'benefiting a fellow-creature' (302) are always available he emphasizes the gulf between Christian benevolence and 'system'-related theorizing. Significantly too Mr Denbeigh understands authorship as a form of practical endeavour, and a potential means of instructing as well as entertaining others. If we view Captain Percy as a figuring of Charles Hamilton, then it is tempting in turn to see Charlotte Percy as an authorial self-portrait. In the light of this chapter's analysis of the contested representation of female agency, one way of reading *Letters of a Hindoo Rajah*'s conclusion is to see it as affirming both Hamilton's identity as a writer and her readiness to challenge 'histories of women' produced by men.

While Zaarmilla concludes that 'Christianity is not *yet entirely extinct*' in Britain, however, his observation that its adherents are to be found 'in the retired scenes of life' (307) suggests that its influence on the life of the nation as a whole may be limited. Zaarmilla's claim provides a sceptical counterpoint to Captain Percy's notion that the establishment of Christianity constitutes a key index of the difference of 'Europe' from 'Asia'. In many of the works discussed earlier, ideas about 'the East', and especially about Eastern sexual despotism, often seem to have provided a recuperative function for Britons, allowing them better to appreciate their own freedoms. Rather than deploying Zaarmilla and his fellow travellers in such a manner, though, *Letters of a Hindoo Rajah* continually undercuts any self-congratulatory myths of national virtue. Hamilton's work does finally identify a resilient strain of active Christian faith at Violet-dale, but it is uncertain as to whether this indigenous resource is adequate – beyond the provincial community with which it is associated – to withstand the destabilizing effects of the 'flood of wealth' produced by the 'golden stream of commerce' (123). This uncertainty is a function of the fact that, like eighteenth-century 'progress of society' narratives, *Letters of a Hindoo Rajah* is intellectually rooted in a long-standing debate about the relationship, often conceived of in inverse terms, between wealth and virtue. Sheermaal's claim that 'the golden stream of commerce' might produce 'a flood of wealth' comes close to Anna Laetitia Barbauld's near-contemporary claim (in her 'Epistle to Wilberforce' [1791]) that 'British morals' are irrevocably 'chang'd' by 'foreign wealth', and it stages the enduring anxiety (evident in so much commentary on the Seven Years'

War, as we have seen) that Britain's openness to the world beyond its shores served to compromise the integrity of the nation.[74]

Letters of a Hindoo Rajah does minimally acknowledge that the new wealth which has elevated 'people of style' and disrupted social hierarchy has its origins in the network of global commerce established by trading corporations such as the EIC. At the same time, however, the potentially precarious state of 'Christianity, . . . Virtue and Wisdom' (307) in Britain is not (as in Barbauld's poem) directly attributed by Hamilton to the global extension of the nation's interests or the porousness of its boundaries. The novel is strikingly ambivalent about the idea of openness to the East, indeed, because while it indirectly acknowledges the domestically destabilizing effects of empire, it does not criticize empire itself. This is in part because it presents British India as being (thanks to Hastings and others) on a more moral footing than Britain. It is also the case because at its very outset Hamilton's work signals its awareness that the inter-cultural sympathy manifested by the scholarship of Charles Hamilton is inextricable from the 'thirst of conquest and the desire of gain' (55) that attracted European nations to India in the first place. The next chapter focuses in more detail on the late eighteenth-century debate about the ethics of importing 'literary treasure', and it centres on the figure of Sir William Jones.

Notes

1. Joseph, *Reading the EIC*, 88.
2. Cohen-Vrignaud, *Radical Orientalism*; Byron, *CPW*, 5:281; V:1012 and 5:255; V:351–2.
3. Byron, *CPW*, 5:36; I:695–6.
4. Ibid., 5:29; I:505.
5. Wilson, *Island Race*, 5.
6. Hurd, *Letters*, 19.
7. Percy, 'Metrical Romances', *Reliques*, 3:xvi.
8. Millar, *Distinction of Ranks*, 42.
9. Stuart, *View of Society*, 13, 54, and 69.
10. Rendall, 'Tacitus', 69.
11. Fordyce, *Female Sex*, 6 and 2.
12. Ibid., 27.
13. Nussbaum, *Torrid Zones*.
14. Beattie, *Dissertations*, 527.
15. Lyttelton, *Letters*, 157.
16. Beattie, *Dissertations*, 527.
17. Russell, *Essay on Women*, 12 and 7.

18. Logan, *Spirit of Asia*, 10.
19. Burke, 'Speech on Fox's India Bill', *Writings and Speeches*, 5:417.
20. Porter, *Observations*, 54.
21. Alexander, *History*, 1:103 and 1:260. Further references appear as parenthetical citations in the text.
22. Guest, *Small Change*, 236–48.
23. *Arabian Nights*, 892.
24. Ibid., 10.
25. Beattie, *Dissertations*, 522 and 526. Further references appear as parenthetical citations in the text.
26. *Arabian Tales*, 1:ix.
27. Ibid., 1:x and 1:xviii.
28. Ibid., 1:vii.
29. Coleridge, *Table Talk*, 1:272–3.
30. Weber, *Tales of the East*, 1:i.
31. Ballaster, *Fabulous Orients*, 14.
32. Warner, *Stranger Magic*, 8.
33. Ibid., 26–7.
34. Scott, *Bahar-Danush*, 1:v.
35. Wilson, *Island Race*, 63.
36. Orr, 'Popular Orientalism', 126.
37. O'Keeffe, *Hunch-Back*, 15. Further references appear as parenthetical citations in the text.
38. Orr, 'Popular Orientalism', 121.
39. Ibid., 122.
40. Bickerstaff, *Sultan*, 19 and 20. Further references appear as parenthetical citations in the text.
41. *Arabian Nights*, 892.
42. Ballaster, *Fabulous Orients*, 59–70.
43. *Middlesex Journal* (12–14 December 1775), 1.
44. Yeazell, *Harems*, 157.
45. *Middlesex Journal* (12–14 December 1775), 1.
46. Yeazell, *Harems*, 158.
47. O'Quinn, 'Islam', 646–51.
48. Cowley, *Day in Turkey*, 9. Further references appear as parenthetical citations in the text.
49. Inchbald, *Mogul Tale*, 9 and 22; O'Quinn, *Staging Governance*, 15–21.
50. Orr, 'Popular Orientalism', 122.
51. Bage, *Fair Syrian*, 2:44. Further references appear as parenthetical citations in the text.
52. Jardine, *Letters*, 323. Further references appear as parenthetical citations in the text.
53. Barrell, *Spirit of Despotism*, 4–7.
54. Knox, *Spirit of Despotism*, 13.
55. Wollstonecraft, *Works*, 5:37.

56. Pocock, *Virtue*, 197–8.
57. Wollstonecraft, *Works*, 5:45.
58. Ibid., 5:9.
59. Nussbaum, *Torrid Zones*, 92–3 and 192–3.
60. Makdisi, *Blake*, 206.
61. Ibid., 215.
62. Paine, *Rights*, 227.
63. Makdisi, *Blake*, 219.
64. Ibid., 205.
65. Price, *Political Writings*, 179.
66. Paine, *Rights*, 267.
67. Ibid., 212.
68. Grenby, 'Orientalism', 226.
69. *Arabian Tales*, 1:viii.
70. Ahmed, *Stillbirth*, 181–4.
71. Hamilton, *Hindoo Rajah*, 69. Further references appear as parenthetical citations in the text.
72. Leask, 'Hamilton's *Hindoo Rajah*', 188.
73. Ibid., 190.
74. Barbauld, *Poetry and Prose*, 126.

CHAPTER 4

'In Love with the Gopia'
Sir William Jones and His Contemporaries

In the previous chapter I discussed how in his essay 'On Fable and Romance' James Beattie presented 'oriental tales' as bearing the indelible imprint of Eastern despotism. In correspondence with Elizabeth Montagu in 1772, Beattie claimed that the works collected in Sir William Jones's *Poems Consisting Chiefly of Translations from the Asiatick Languages* were just as revelatory about 'the minds and manners of the people among whom they [were] produced'. One explanation for the 'glaring images, exaggerated metaphors, and gigantic descriptions' of the poetry of 'eastern nations', he suggested, was that Eastern peoples were 'unfriendly to liberty' – their 'ignorance and indolence' disposing them 'to regard their governors as of supernatural dignity, and to decorate them with ... high-sounding titles', so as to 'infect their whole conversation with bombast'.[1] In the letter to which Beattie responded, however, Montagu – who, unlike Beattie, had read the works in question – praised the mastery of 'oriental languages' and versification that they displayed: 'there is a gaiety and splendour in the poems,' she stated, 'which is naturally derived from the happy soil and climate of the poets, and they breathe Asiatic luxury.' While Montagu signalled her awareness that Jones's poems were 'imitations of Asiatic poetry', she nonetheless confessed to her absorption in their literary novelty: 'the descriptions are so fine, and all the objects so brilliant, *that the sense akes at them*, and I wished that Ossian's poems had been laying by me, that I might sometimes have turned my eyes, from the dazzling splendour of the eastern noonday, to the moonlight picture of a bleak mountain.'[2] Montagu was much more enthusiastic than Beattie about the possibility of an 'Oriental' poetry, then, and she invoked 'northern' climes as a relief from sensory overload, rather than, as Beattie did in *The Minstrel* (1771–4), the locus of a vitalizing 'freedom' or a 'boundless store/ Of charms' requiring no external supplement.[3]

This exchange provides a useful point of departure for the present chapter and the next, anticipating positions that would be taken in a long-running, value-laden, and often less cordial debate about the terms on which 'Orientalism', however conceived, might be admitted into British poetry. Sir William Jones, the subject of this correspondence, has lately assumed a prominent status in literary-historical accounts of the origins of Romantic verse, and he has been credited with a central role in a broader European 'rediscovery' of India and the East.[4] This narrative of Jones's role as a cultural translator acknowledges the potentiality of his 1772 *Poems* and appended essays, but accords particular importance to the diverse writings that he produced after arriving in Bengal in 1784. William Hayley lauded 'all-accomplished JONES!' in the elegy that he wrote on Jones's death, and there is a celebratory strain in some recent treatments of Jones too.[5] An authoritative biography of Jones presents him as an exemplary figure who was generously open to the East and in turn broadened the horizons of sympathetically disposed readers from Montagu onwards – even if he also had to face the 'unreconstructed prejudice' of those such as Beattie.[6]

The central chapter of this book focuses primarily on the now well-known figure of Jones both because of the apparent intensity of his responsiveness to the East (he declared himself 'in love with the *Gopia*', Krishna's young female attendants, in a letter of 1784), and because of the strength of critical claims about his importance.[7] It takes this importance as a given, but by situating Jones in relation to his contemporaries, it empha-sizes that his mediation of difference contested the work of other writers and was in turn itself contested. This chapter therefore seeks to complicate both the story of Jones as an apostle of toleration fighting the forces of prejudice and the story of a larger metropolitan cultural awakening partly effected by Jones. It initially does this by demonstrating that while Jones certainly expanded the possibilities of poetry in English, the process by which new source materials were transmitted to Britons was nonetheless much disputed, not least because it was closely bound up with the well-publicized scandal of EIC rule. Jones himself had fewer concerns about the foundations of EIC sovereignty than other poets of the 1770s and 1780s, I argue, and in the case of a work such as 'A Hymn to Ganga' (1785), his respectful construction of Hindu mythology silently rewrote previous attempts to voice native grievance about British culpability for the Bengal famine of 1770.

The commentary on Jones's hymns to Hindu deities is now extensive, and I consider the critical controversy relating to this project as to some extent a product of the play of voices – governmental and devotional – evident in the poems themselves. Attending also to the late eighteenth-century contest over the significance of Jones's Orientalist scholarship,

I argue that it is most productive to suspend biographical speculation as to Jones's character, and instead to acknowledge the plural and different 'Joneses' that were produced by different audiences of his work. After briefly considering the way in which traces of Jones's self-representation as a scholar-hero as well as of 'Jonesian' ideas are evident in canonical Romantic poetry, I conclude by discussing Sydney Owenson's engagement with Jones in *The Missionary* (1811). Owenson's novel pays tribute to, yet also explores the limits of, a humanistic openness to the East, calling into question the purchase of exemplary individual – for some, Jonesian – virtues in the face of prejudice allied to power.

Sparks of Orientalism

In the preface to his *Persian Eclogues* (1742), William Collins celebrated the 'rich and figurative' manner of Arabian and Persian poetry: 'There is an Elegancy and Wildness of Thought which recommends all their Compositions, and our Genius's are as much too cold for the Entertainment of such Sentiments, as our Climate is for their Fruits and Spices.' Collins conflated nomadic and courtly cultures here, and in his pastiche of 'the Works of *Orientals*' he assumed a contractual understanding with his audience that absolved him from having to substantiate Eastern scenes any more specifically; he claimed to have received the poems from 'the Hands of a Merchant', and attributed their authorship to a native of Tauris unimaginatively named 'Mahamed'.[8] Collins later distanced himself from this artifice, stating that the poems had 'not one spark of Orientalism' about them. As formulaic as his eclogues seem to be, however, the 'spark' metaphor indicates that Collins saw 'Orientalism' as a means of revitalizing English poetry, as if to acknowledge that the nation's literary culture needed such stimulation to prevent it from stagnating.

Collins's four eclogues are significant from a literary-historical perspective because while prose fiction in English had already begun to engage with the *Arabian Nights* and other sequences of tales, they may have been the first poems to avow that the 'Works of Orientals' were an inspiration. The temperature metaphor that Collins used to refer to the Eastern 'genius' had long been current, however, especially in accounts of the Psalms or the prophetic books in the Hebrew Bible, which were commonly interpreted as a kind of Oriental literature: in *Spectator* 339 (1712), for example, Joseph Addison praised Milton's *Paradise Lost* for 'duly qualifying those high Strains of Eastern Poetry, ... suited to Readers whose

Imaginations were set to an higher pitch than those of colder Climates'.[9] Whereas Collins conceived of 'Orientalism' simply as a source of literary raw materials, the Biblical scholar Robert Lowth, in his *Lectures on the Sacred Poetry of the Hebrews* (1787), argued that Eastern imagery had to be understood in deeper historical terms, beyond the novelty of associations and ideas that it generated. Lowth called for the reader of Hebrew poetry to 'imagine himself exactly situated as the persons for whom it was written', and he understood figurative language as the product of a society without divided labour, where 'common or domestic life . . . was simple and uniform in the greatest degree.'[10]

Jones's 'Essay on the Poetry of the Eastern Nations', appended to his 1772 *Poems*, follows Lowth in claiming – against Voltairean neoclassicism – that 'every nation has a set of images, and expressions, peculiar to itself, which arise[s] from the difference of its climate, manners, and history.'[11] While steeped in 'Biblical Orientalism', Jones also developed a wider interest in 'the manners of the *Arabs, Persians, Indians*, and *Turks*, the four principal nations . . . that profess the religion of *Mahomet*' (320). He paid particular attention to the way in which differences in manners were exhibited by contrasting styles of composition, outlining the distinction, effaced by Collins, between the milieus of Arabia, the true 'scene' of pastoral poetry, and Persia, an ancient empire in which the effeminacy of the people rendered their poetry 'the softest, as it is one of the richest, in the world' (330). While Jones still asserted the primacy of Greek and Latin literature, he additionally conceived an 'expanded classicism' that treated Arabic and Persian as classical languages.[12] This broadening of the parameters of what might be regarded as 'classical' is especially clear in Jones's other appended 'Essay on the Arts, Commonly Called Imitative', where he stated that '[i]n defining what true poetry *ought to be*, according to our principles, we have described what it really *was* among the *Hebrews*, the *Greeks* and *Romans*, the *Arabs* and *Persians*' (343).

In the often-cited conclusion to his 'Essay on the Poetry of the Eastern Nations', Jones argued that greater openness to 'the principal writings of the Asiaticks' would help to reinvigorate European literary culture, by circulating 'a new set of images and similitudes, and a number of excellent compositions . . . which future scholars might explain, and future poets might imitate' (336). There is ostensibly a paradox here because, as Zak Sitter notes, 'Jones recommends the imitation of Oriental poetry as a cure for Europe's imitativeness.'[13] If Jones regarded this lack of originality as a symptom of modernity, however, he saw imitation as a potential means of access to that distant past when poets such as Homer and Ferdusi 'drew their images from nature herself', demonstrating '*that rich and creative invention, which is the very soul of poetry*' (334). In his essay on imitation, Jones identified poetry's 'originary' moment (and true spirit) in the 'extasy' of a man experiencing the wonders of the natural world and pouring out his praise to the Creator, thus exemplifying a universal passion rather than one that the British 'Genius' might be too cold to entertain.

Jones staked a claim for the regenerative impact of his own self-styled 'translations' and defined his project against the inauthenticity of literary forgery; suggesting that unnamed 'productions, invented in *France*' had perpetrated such 'imposture', he signalled that, even as it was cosmopolitan in its sympathies, his was a *British* Orientalism.[14] As Elizabeth Montagu recognized, Jones was already an innovator more than a decade before his first-hand encounter with Asia began. In the preface to 'Solima, An Arabian Eclogue' (1768), for example, he differentiated himself from Collins by stating that although the poem was 'not a regular translation', the 'sentiments' as well as 'figures' and 'descriptions' in it were 'really taken from the poets of *Arabia*'.[15] While the narrative trajectory of 'The Seven Fountains' (1767) and 'The Palace of Fortune' (1769) would have been familiar to Jones's audience from prose tales such as Addison's 'The Vision of Mirza' (they respectively feature male and female protagonists who learn to distinguish between true and illusory pleasures), Jones in these poems drew upon heterogeneous sources so as to produce new, composite works.

If Jones thus extended the register of poetry in English, however, his early literary works have often been regarded as, in Tim Fulford's words, 'less of a challenge to conventional taste than ... his critical tenets'.[16] I return to Jones's role as a theorist of Romantic poetics, but here I want to mention another contemporary verdict on the poems themselves. Much less impressed than Montagu, Horace Walpole dismissed Jones's poetry as 'very flowery' but 'not at all Eastern', stating that it committed 'a blunder of *oriental* for *ornamental*'.[17] Walpole's identification of the 'ornamental' quality of Jones's writing is especially interesting because it situates literary novelty in a material context, by alluding to networks of trade and commerce. (Collins did this more explicitly when claiming to have received his eclogues from a merchant who dealt in both the 'Silks and Carpets' and the 'Learning' of Persians.)[18] In the next chapter I say more about the conflicted relation to 'ornament' that is evident in Romantic Orientalist poetry, as captured by Byron's self-ironizing description of his Turkish tales, in *Beppo* (1817), as 'samples of the finest Orientalism'.[19] Now, though, I turn to the work of writers in the 1770s and early 1780s whose access to sources of literary novelty was made available by colonial conquest, and for some of whom at least, the idea of new, culturally specific subject matter was inseparable from ongoing controversy about the ethics of empire.

India's 'Mythologic Mine'

In 'The Palace of Fortune' Jones made what was probably his first reference to Hindu mythology, in the form of the celestial carriage drawn by 'starry peacocks' (38) in which the Indian protagonist is conducted to the palace of the title. I have previously discussed how metropolitan readers were introduced to 'new' Easts as a result of the Seven Years' War and the subsequent consolidation of EIC authority, and Jones's source here, Alexander Dow's *Tales of Inatulla* (1768), was a product of this recent history. A Scottish army officer employed by the EIC, Dow claimed that he was drawn to the tales in question because they afforded an opportunity for him to improve his translation skills.[20] He also acknowledged the rich potential of the materials that he helped to circulate, however, beginning his preface by stating that European attempts 'to imitate the eastern manner of writing' had hitherto been performed by 'men totally unacquainted with the literature of Asia'.[21] In his translated *History of Hindostan* (1768), Dow similarly recognized the 'field [which] opened before him' during the course of his project, referring both to the 'minute and authentic history of a great empire' and to the 'Hindoo learning' of which the Mughal elite was allegedly ignorant.[22]

Dow claimed that the Persian author of this work knew little of Hindu antiquity because of his bigoted hostility to 'the Brahmin religion'.[23] He conceded too, though, that Britons themselves had 'never had the curiosity to examine' Hindu culture, since, he asserted, 'literary inquiries' were not a priority for 'our adventurers in Asia'.[24] Dow's reference to 'our adventurers' alludes to Clive (against whom he had campaigned during his time in India), and it emphasizes that the transmission of information in which his *History* participated was closely bound up with the circulation of charges against the EIC. Dow understood the role of Orientalist scholarship in legitimizing EIC authority, and with this in mind he argued that it was time to explore records of 'the affairs of the Hindoos' as well as 'the literary treasures, which lay concealed in the obscurity of the Persian'.[25] This notion of a quest for scholarly gold appears to undercut Dow's effort to differentiate seemingly disinterested 'literary inquiries' from the overt self-interest of 'our adventurers'. As fragile as the distinction may be, however, it is significant that Dow invoked it. His doing so points to the concern that he and some of his contemporaries had to negotiate the tension between their personally enlightening experience of cultural discovery and their troubled awareness of the circumstances in which that discovery was made possible.

As the 'intimate connection' (in Dow's phrase) between Britain and Bengal was increasingly recognized in metropolitan circles, writers who never travelled but nonetheless responded to Jones's call for the 'Asiatic' regeneration of English poetry confronted their own version of the problem that Dow acknowledged.[26] The series of 'Oriental Eclogues' written in the late 1770s by the Quaker John Scott is especially interesting in this respect, because even as his title harks back to Collins's example, Scott's poems display a familiarity both with Jones's work and with anti-EIC polemics. Scott's 'Serim; or the Artificial Famine', for example, is a formally conventional but – in terms of content – topical poem which refers in its notes to the anonymous *A Short History of the English Transactions in the East-Indies* (1776) as well as works by Dow and John Zephanieh Holwell. It uses the *Short History* to substantiate its account of British culpability – hence the 'artificial' of the title – for the scale of the Bengal famine of 1770, and it cites Dow and Holwell as among the then most knowledgeable British authorities on Hinduism. 'From the best accounts we have of India,' one of Scott's notes declares, 'the intelligent part of the natives do not worship "stocks and stones", merely as such; but rather the Supreme Existence, in a variety of attributes or manifestations.'[27] While the poem thus concedes the limits of its book-derived knowledge, it tentatively approaches Hinduism on its own terms rather than as a species of idolatry. It also incorporates Hindu devotion into a ventriloquized story of indigenous opposition to EIC authority that culminates in a scene where the narrator encounters a 'white-rob'd Bramin' (147) grieving for his dead family. After being visited by the divine spirit of 'Birmah' (148), the Brahmin tempers his call for vengeance on his country's oppressors by predicting that 'Europe's cowards' (151) will – like Clive, as rumour had it – take their own lives as their guilty consciences get the better of them.

Scott began his poem 'On the ingenious Mr Jones's Elegant Translations and Imitations of the Eastern Poetry' (1782) by declaring that, in Jones's earlier works, 'The Asian Muse, a Stranger fair!,/ Becomes at length Britannia's care.'[28] In thus invoking British hospitality towards a feminized Eastern other, Scott rehearsed the familiar argument that scholarly Orientalism in its various forms provided an index of EIC protection of its Indian subjects. With 'Serim', by contrast, Scott anticipated the concern that Burke expressed throughout the 1780s, namely that

India might be too remote and strange for Britons to be interested in what happened there. Scott stated in his collection's Advertisement that 'he, who describes what he has not seen, must depend for much on the accounts of others, and supply the rest from his own imagination,' and 'Serim' indeed makes a remarkable effort to register distant suffering.[29] It is also conscious of the limits of this endeavour, however, since the action of the 'British ruffian' who hears the Brahmin's lament and kills him anyway starkly acknowledges the possibility of readerly indifference to any such tale of woe.[30] The manner of the Brahmin's demise – 'headlong plung'd . . . into [a] foaming tide' (152) – is especially interesting here, since it recalls the conclusion to Thomas Gray's poem 'The Bard' (1757). If Gray's account of colonial conquest as a process of cultural subjugation offers no parallel for the activities of the EIC in its 'Orientalist' phase, Scott's adoption of Gray's poem as the foundation for his own dramatically stages the gulf between the intercultural exchange that took place under 'Britannia's care' and the violence by which the EIC established and expanded its authority.

William Hayley's versified *An Essay on Epic Poetry* (1782) likewise reflects on the relationship between intellectual discovery, literary innovation, and colonialism. Towards the end of the fifth epistle, the poet invokes a knightly 'Genius' looking for subject matter, stating that in India, the epic muse 'may . . . his course of honor run,/ And spotless laurels in that field be won'.[31] Hayley's end note glossing the phrase 'spotless laurels' goes on to complicate this scenario of curiosity-driven adventure, however, by arguing that a poet 'desirous of laying the scene of his action in India, would be more embarrassed to find interesting Heroes than proper Divinities'. If 'every reader of imagination may . . . perceive that the Shastah [like "Birmah", a Holwell coinage] might supply a poetical spirit that was as rich a mass of ideal treasure as fancy could wish to work upon,' Hayley wrote, a poem featuring an English protagonist's heroic exploits would be all but impossible to produce: it would stretch credulity too far to suggest that 'justice and generosity inspired and guided that English valour, which has signalized itself on the plains of Indostan.' Hayley offered a way out of such 'embarrassment' by stating that 'had the arms of our country been employed to deliver the native Indians from the oppressive usurpation of the Mahometan powers,' then the epic muse would indeed have 'a subject truly noble'.[32] The lines preceding those quoted earlier also disclose, though, that even the scholarly quest for 'ideal treasure' is inherently compromised: 'India yet holds a Mythologic mine,/ Her strength may open, and her art refine:/ Tho' Asian spoils the realms of Europe fill,/ Those Eastern riches are unrifled still.'[33] Hayley's presentation of the riches of Hindu mythology as 'unrifled still' – yet to be plundered – knowingly or not frames this cultural resource as just another variety of the loot already filling European coffers. The process by which this addition to Britain's literary lexicon would be made is therefore shown here to be inseparable from a more prosaic history of resource extraction, under-cutting Hayley's depiction of a solitary, high-mindedly inquiring 'Genius'.

In the decade following the publication of Jones's *Poems*, then, writers in Britain including Scott and Hayley were secondary participants in the British 'discovery' of Hinduism, alert to the excitement of this process while also sharing in the awareness of pioneering figures such as Dow as to how and why new 'literary treasure' had become accessible in the first place. Diverse other materials from Arabic and Persian continued to be published in the 1770s and 1780s, and in the work of the EIC surgeon John Nott, for example, there is evidence of both a passion for new literatures and regret for how the translation work that circulated them took place in the context of an illegitimate colonial occupation. In the preface to his *Select Odes from the Persian Poet Hafez* (1787), Nott declared that his knowledge of Persian arose from the 'fatal ambition' to 'possess' India which made Britons 'cruel invaders of another's right'.[34] He referred to Persian as his own 'favourite language' but he also recognized its impor-tance as an administrative medium, acknowledging that his experience of intellectual awakening and creative stimulation was tainted by instrumen-tal concerns.[35]

In the work of Jones himself, by contrast, there is little comparable reflection on the ethical basis of EIC sovereignty; as he wrote to Arthur Lee in 1786, for example, Jones generally assumed that subject peoples were 'happier under us' than they would have been under any other regime.[36] Correspondingly, Jones's writing about his intellectual discoveries appears more enthusiastic and less troubled than that of his contemporaries. It is instructive to read Jones's account of his voyage to India alongside the passage in Hayley's *Essay on Epic Poetry* discussed earlier. In his inaugural address to the Asiatic Society of Bengal, Jones identified Sanskrit as one of 'the treasures ... we may now hope to see unlocked' and presented the 'immense mine' of Asiatic learning as one 'in which we might labour with equal delight and advantage'.[37] The ubiquitous formulation of 'delight and advantage' (10) in this context asserts Jones's sense of the compatibility between individual scholarly pleasure and collective EIC gain. Jones invoked the idea of curiosity-driven intellectual adventure in a similar manner to Hayley and others, but provided no modifying perspective on the actual history, glorious or otherwise, of 'English valour' over the previous decades. Instead, Jones styled himself as a scholar-hero, in a dramatization of his encounter with the 'East' about which he had before only read and fantasized:

> When I was at sea last August, on my voyage to this country, which I had long and ardently desired to visit, I found one evening, on inspecting the observations of the day, that *India* lay before us, and *Persia* on our left, whilst a breeze from *Arabia* blew nearly on our stern. A situation so pleasing in itself, and to me so new, could not fail to awaken a train of reflections in a mind, which had early been accustomed to contemplate with delight the eventful histories and agreeable fictions of the eastern world. It gave me inexpressible pleasure to find myself in the midst of so noble an amphitheatre, almost encircled by the vast regions of *Asia*, which has ever been esteemed the nurse of sciences, the inventress of delightful and useful arts. (3–4)

The 'pleasing' nature of the situation recalled by Jones is shadowed by his allusion to *Paradise Lost*: on his approach to the Garden of Eden in Book IV, Satan is described as being 'entertained' with 'odorous sweets' like those 'who sail/ Beyond the Cape of Hope, and now are past/ Mozambic', as 'off at sea northeast winds blow/ Sabean odors from the spicy shore/ Of Araby the Blest'.[38] Whether or not deliberate, this is a resonant allusion, because the background presence of *Paradise Lost* not only calls up a long history of European exploration and commercial ambition, but also – via Milton's association of the spice trade and the wiles of Satan – suggests that Britain's entanglement with India may itself be the product of a fatal attraction. Unlike Nott, however, Jones himself eschewed such reflection, instead narrating a personal voyage of discovery that dwells on the connection between his new experience and his prior reading, the latter making the former all the more vivid. It is worth noting in this respect that the echo of *Spectator* 69 in Jones's 'Discourse' is no less resonant than that of *Paradise Lost*. Jones's account of his 'inexpressible pleasure' at finding himself in the natural 'amphitheatre' constituted by the proximity of Arabia, Persia, and India offers a maritime analogue of Mr Spectator's 'infinite' delight in the company of international 'Ministers of Commerce' at the Royal Exchange.[39] *Spectator* 69's imprint on Jones's address is additionally evident when one considers the way in which he describes himself as 'almost encircled' (4) in this imaginary arena, the important qualifier 'almost' safeguarding a stable position of 'spectatorial' pleasure similar to that enjoyed by Addison's persona.

Jones here sees with 'imperial eyes', but his survey does not simply celebrate its conditions of possibility.[40] Though not completely encircled,

Jones still presents himself as all but surrounded by 'the vast regions of Asia', an immense landmass which, as 'the nurse of sciences, [and] the inventress of . . . arts' (4), is also a point of origin for world civilization. Jones's 'Discourse' thus suggests that even as Britons in India may privilege their own interests, they have to reckon with a new sense of Britain's actual position in the world. Raymond Schwab noted that after Anquetil du Perron's 1771 translation of the Zoroastrian *Zend Avesta*, it became trite to say that Europe was a peninsula of Asia, and Jones's reference to '*Hindostan* as a centre', bordered by other 'important kingdoms' (6), instantiates Schwab's account of the 'Oriental sublime'.[41] Schwab's claim that it was inevitable that 'a civilization believing itself unique would find itself drowned in the sum total of civilizations' is famously exemplified in De Quincey's rewriting of Jones's 'Discourse' in *Confessions of an English Opium-Eater* (1821), when he is involuntarily 'transported into Asiatic scenes'.[42] For Jones, however, the experience of the Oriental sublime represented an expansion of intellectual horizons that generated in him only a greater scholarly resolve. Developing his future-oriented focus on what was yet 'unexplored' and 'unimproved' (4), Jones defined the purview of the Asiatic Society of Bengal as nothing less than 'MAN and NATURE' (8).

Jones wrote to the second Earl Spencer in 1787 that 'it is my ambition to know India better than any other European ever knew it.'[43] This statement of intent demonstrates a strongly competitive impulse on Jones's part, and there is a comparable self-fashioning evident in Dow's comparison of himself and his predecessors, as well as in the Scottish Orientalist John Leyden's later boast that he would surpass Jones 'a hundredfold in Oriental learning'.[44] From a contemporary perspective it is difficult to divorce the desire to know from the knowledge/power nexus that has been so central to the study of colonial discourse since Said's *Orientalism*. Recent criticism has also sought to recover less instrumental forms of engagement with Indian cultural difference in Jones's work, however, and one of his letters to Charles Wilkins in 1784 has been cited as evidence of the way in which Jones could conceive of a 'delight' independent of any calculation of Company 'advantage'. Jones here declared himself enraptured with the Hindu pantheon: 'I am in love with the *Gopia*, charmed with *Crishen*, an enthusiastic admirer of *Rám*, and a devout adorer of *Brimha-bishen-mehais*.'[45] For Michael J. Franklin, Jones expresses himself in 'the impassioned erotic tones of a bhakta (Hindu devotee)', and his openness to the other is such that he has all but 'gone native'.[46]

We should be cautious about treating this statement as direct self-revelation, not least because it is clearly a rhetorical performance: as in his 1784 'Discourse', *Spectator* 69 provides a model for the way in which Jones is able to summon a pleasingly novel spectacle of difference before his mind's eye, with Hindu deities and their attendants taking the place of the '*Armenians*', '*Jews*', and '*Dutch-men*' among whom Mr Spectator moves at the Royal Exchange.[47] The preamble to Jones's rapturous outpouring is written in what he calls a 'facetious vein', and if we re-insert the quotation cited earlier into the letter in which it appears, then Jones's profession of 'love' again begins to look less straightforwardly personal, exemplifying instead the shared language of – sometimes arch and flippant – familiar address that we might expect from scholars' private correspondence.[48] If we can only speculate about Jones's subjectivity, however, the various terms employed in the quotation just referenced do at least help us to think about the different reading positions that Jones's 'hymns' to Hindu deities were to offer their first audiences. While Jones's claim about being 'charmed with *Crishen*' (Krishna) is suggestive of detached curiosity, his enthusiastic admiration of Ram (Rama) and 'devotion' to '*Brimha-bishen-mehais*' (Brahma, Vishnu, and Shiva) invite us to consider the way in which Jones's poetry also staged more involved forms of response to Hindu mythology. Just as Jones's letter to Wilkins shifts between registers, so his Hindu hymns adopt a range of voices offering readers very different kinds of relation to Indian otherness – a feature of the poems that helps to explain their varied reception.

Reading Jones's Hindu Hymns

When Jones's 'Discourse' was published in London in 1784, it appeared together with 'A Hymn to Camdeo', previously circulated by Jones in Calcutta. The first of a series of nine hymns to Hindu deities, this was not (despite its billing) a translation but rather another 'blended' work in the style of his earlier poems. If the opening couplet's 'orient bow'rs'/ 'living flow'rs' (100) rhyme prepares readers for a composite Orientalism, however, Jones's description of Camdeo, god of love, provides culturally specific reference to his 'at least twenty-three' different names (99), and to the 'five flow'rets' with which he tips his darts: 'Strong *Chumpa*, rich in od'rous gold,/ Warm *Amer*, nurs'd in heav'nly mould,/ Dry *Nagkeser* in silver smiling,/ Hot *Kiticum* our sense beguiling,/ And last, to kindle fierce the scorching flame,/ *Loveshaft*, which Gods bright *Bela* name' (102). In a modification of the temperature metaphor used by Collins, the final couplet beseeches Camdeo 'Thy mildest influence to thy bard impart/ To warm, but not consume, his heart.' This restrained conclusion does not, though, contain the enthusiasm that is evident in the line 'Hot *Kiticum* our sense beguiling' (102), where the poet includes himself among those 'entranc'd' by the sensual pleasures that Camdeo represents. At the end of the first stanza, similarly, the poet exclaims 'I feel, I feel thy genial flame divine,/ And hallow thee and kiss thy shrine' (100). While the 'flame divine' is benign rather than blazing, the poem's sexualized idiom here is seemingly at odds with the 'objective' scholarly voice of Jones's preface.

Jones's Argument begins by stating that '[t]he Hindu God, to whom the following poem is addressed is ... the same with the *Grecian* EROS and the *Roman* CUPIDO,' and this assertion is one that he would substantiate in his 'Essay on the Gods of Greece, Italy, and India', delivered to the Asiatic Society in 1785. Numerous scholars have emphasized the magnitude of Jones's claim that different systems of mythology were versions of one another, as well as of his insight (in his 'Third Anniversary Discourse' of 1786) as to the structural affinity between Sanskrit and European languages. This exploration of an essentially familial relationship between peoples and cultures is understandably attractive in the present, not least as an anticipation of 'global history', and some critics have credited Jones's poetry, especially, with a powerful agency in its own historical moment too. Though the idea that Jones initiated 'a kind of colonization-in-reverse' in late eighteenth-century Britain and Europe is problematic, as my introduction argues, the idiom of 'conquest' is evident in a range of accounts of the 'Indian' sway over European imaginations in this period.[49]

The substance of Jones's impact continues to be disputed, however, and one area of debate concerns the mediating role that he played as he assimilated deities such as Camdeo with reference to their classical analogues. It may be reductive to say that critics argue either that Jones minimized the 'cultural dissonance' of the Hindu pantheon (as Kate Teltscher claims), or that he was himself transfixed and transformed by his subject matter even as he sought to make it accessible to others.[50] There is, all the same, an obvious difference of emphasis in recent readings of the larger importance of Jones's translation project, and of the taste for the exotic that it helped to generate. Nigel Leask, for example, argues that Jones's use of the Miltonic or Pindaric ode helped to make new imagery available to British readers in a readily consumable form, which was additionally a kind of 'imperial heraldry' that reflected Britain's 'protection' of its Indian subjects in the most honourable possible light; since this treatment of

Hindu deities in effect fixed Indian culture in terms of a stable, classical ideal, it also (Leask suggests) represented an 'ethnocentric' vision denying the temporal 'coevalness' of India and modern Europe.[51] Franklin by contrast denies that there could be anything ethnocentric about the Hindu hymns, since Jones remained committed to the idea of 'a syncretic East-West synthesis' and a shared human history, to the extent that his example still offers a 'beacon' of enlightenment today.[52] While there is no space for any sustained analysis, I discuss in the rest of this section the critical contest over the immediate and longer-run significance of Jones's poetry, with particular reference to the play of voices considered earlier.

One poem that illustrates Leask's argument about the ideological work done by Jones's construction of the Hindu pantheon is 'A Hymn to Ganga' (1785), addressed to the presiding deity of the Ganges. It begins by celebrating the river's stately course, as it flows from the Himalayas to the Bay of Bengal: 'How sweetly GANGA smiles, and glides/ Luxuriant o'er her broad autumnal bed!/ Her waves perpetual verdure spread,/ Whilst health and plenty deck her golden sides' (127). The prefatory account of the river's 'birth', referring both to Greek and to Indian gods, presents Hindu mythology to the reader as an analogous classicism, but if we attend to the poem in its historical context and if we read Jones alongside John Scott, it is possible to appreciate the political implications of such a respectful rendering of Hindu tradition. As discussed earlier, Scott's 'Serim' depicts a Brahmin on the banks of the Ganges who mourns his family's death from starvation before being drowned by a Briton indifferent to his lament. Jones's poem represents instead the timeless passage of the sacred Ganges, while also recording the libidinal energy of the river and its 'companion', the Brahmaputra, as they are kept apart from each other, before their 'blending' in the penultimate stanza. In its mythopoeic account of 'perpetual verdure' and 'health and plenty' along the 'golden sides' (127) of the Ganges, Jones's poem might be seen to offer a counter-ventriloquization, an implicit response to Scott's Brahmin, who by contrast speaks of 'the plenty to our prayers denied'.[53] By emphasizing such fecundity, 'A Hymn to Ganga' occludes the history of the famine and the suffering that resulted from it, of which Jones must have been aware.[54] Rather than memorialize the famine, Jones's Brahmin, the 'author' of the poem, recognizes 'the toleration and equity of the BRITISH government' and prays '*for its peaceful duration under good laws well administered*'.

'A Hymn to Ganga' adopts Gray's version of the Pindaric ode, but it departs from Gray and Scott's example in the manner in which it incorporates a moment of 'native' prophecy. In its address to Ganga, this prophecy replaces the defiance of Gray's Bard and Scott's Brahmin with a vision of British protection: 'Nor frown, dread Goddess, on a peerless race/ With lib'ral heart and martial grace,/ Wafted from colder isles remote:/ As they preserve our laws, and bid our terror cease,/ So be their darling laws preserv'd in wealth, in joy, in peace!' (132). Even as the oxymoronic notion of 'martial grace' and the ambiguous reference to 'our terror' make for a somewhat unstable conclusion (as James Mulholland argues), the poem here recapitulates its vision of a 'natural' EIC authority: if the Ganges itself has 'fost'ring arms' (127), then the EIC protects a protector.[55] In another moment of prophecy, presented as if from an earlier period, the poet offers the reassurance that while the Mughal emperor Aurangzeb's 'ruthless bandits' may deface Hindu shrines, 'So shall his frantic sons with discord rend his throne,/ And his fair-smiling realms be sway'd by nations yet unknown' (130). If we once more read Jones's poem as a response to Scott's, Aurangzeb takes the place of the unnamed 'British ruffian' as the work's primary agent of violence; though we cannot be sure that Jones read 'Serim', 'A Hymn to Ganga' indeed names Aurangzeb as 'a ruffian king'. A note in Scott's poem, citing Dow's *History*, emphasizes that during a period of dearth, the 'famous Mahometan tyrant' assumed a paternalistic responsibility towards his people, exerting himself 'to alleviate the distress of his subjects'.[56] While 'Serim' thus distinguishes between EIC indifference and Mughal charity, 'A Hymn to Ganga' erases both the native agency responsible for such relief efforts and the reality of native suffering itself. It invokes Aurangzeb as the antithesis of a recently deceased British hero, Augustus Cleveland, said to have pacified and begun to 'improve' the 'godless mountaineer[s]' (131) whose districts he oversaw, and in doing so it also counters Burke's well-known attack on 'English youth' in India as being 'without society and without sympathy with the natives'.[57]

Jones's emphasis on the connection between Orientalist knowledge and EIC power is most overt in 'A Hymn to Lacshmi' (1788), the Argument of which states that the 'wild fables' of Hindus should be attended to because the industry of those who believe them 'adds to the revenue of Britain' (154). The poem itself, more directly than 'A Hymn to Ganga', situates its praise of the deity it addresses within a narrative of Britain's providential role in India. After rehearsing a universal tribute to the natural abundance that Lacshmi brings, then in mystificatory fashion attributing drought and dearth to human 'vices', the poet entreats the goddess: 'Preserve thy vot'ries: be their labours blest!/ Oh! bid the patient Hindu rise and live' (162). In another shift towards the end of the work, he observes that 'the

Hindu' now sees 'beams' from 'western skies' that will 'Disperse th'unholy gloom!' in which he is shrouded (162–3). 'Though mists profane obscure their narrow ken,' the concluding couplet states, 'They err, yet feel; though pagans, they are men.'

Teltscher states that 'A Hymn to Lacshmi' finally 'redefine[s] the speaker and the audience', as Jones's native persona is 'banished by the condescending tones of assured Christian superiority'.[58] One further point to make here is that the poem may thus be seen as embedded in British abolitionist discourse as well as EIC Orientalism. If we again consider Jones in the company of his peers, it is clear that his reference to 'pagan' Hindus who 'err, yet feel' rehearses the conventions of representation by which African slaves are depicted in another 1788 poem, Hannah More's 'Slavery': More's work describes slaves as having 'heads to think, and hearts to feel,/ And souls to act, with firm, tho' erring zeal', despite their lack of exposure to the 'intellectual Sun' – analogous to Jones's 'beams, that western skies illume' (162).[59] 'A Hymn to Lacshmi' was composed four years after Jones arrived in Bengal, which suggests that his exposure to India did not entirely transform his cultural preconceptions. As is demonstrated by its thematic and lexical continuity with abolitionist verse, the work appears to be inflected by Jones's anterior concerns even as his encounter with the subcontinent is its direct inspiration. A radical Whig and a member of the Society for Constitutional Information, as well as a supporter of the American revolutionary cause, Jones may have invoked abolitionist rhetoric not just to emphasize the sympathetic underpinnings of Company rule but also to negotiate the 'crisis of liberty' facing Britons in the 1780s.[60] One way in which Jones squared his libertarian politics with the evident despotism of EIC authority was by styling his legal scholarship as a form of benefaction that restored to Indians, via the codification of 'their own laws', that portion of liberty that they were capable of enjoying.[61]

While 'A Hymn to Lacshmi' repudiates pagan error, the poem's beginning nonetheless salutes the goddess, in a detailed rendering of the creation myth of the Churning of the Sea of Milk. Teltscher notes that Jones styles himself both as 'Hindu devotee and colonial administrator' in the poem, and, as is the case with 'A Hymn to Camdeo', the narrator's 'subjective' flights are not straightforwardly contained by the preface and conclusion's 'objective' voice.[62] The poem might therefore be seen to instantiate the structural tension between 'absorption' and 'containment' that Leask identifies in later works such as Robert Southey's epic *The Curse of Kehama* (1810).[63] Contemporaries generally absolved Jones from the kind of criticism that would face Southey, however, as if accepting that he did enough to license his movement between stylistic registers and forms of subject matter. Southey himself acknowledged that it was difficult to accuse Jones of being compromised by his contact with Hindu mythology, and indicating how he sought to outdo his predecessor, he criticized Jones for having introduced the Hindu pantheon 'coldly and formally'.[64]

As he told Samuel Davis in 1786, Jones thought of his poetry as a 'relief' to his mind after 'severer employment in the discharge of . . . publick duty'.[65] 'A Hymn to Lacshmi' at once bears the imprint of Jones's sense of professional service and helps us to recognize how he could thus also conceive of poetry as a potentially liberating recreation. In the letter to Wilkins cited earlier, Jones declared that his friend's correspondence about his scholarly research was 'agreeable' to his 'second self', and Jones's invocation of a 'second self' prompts us again to think about different versions of Jones, identifiable at the level of self-representation as well as critical reception.[66] For Franklin, 'A Hymn to Lacshmi's' reference to Hindus as 'pagans' displays an 'uncharacteristic Serampore missionary mood' on Jones's part, appearing to anticipate the proselytizing projects pioneered by the Baptist missionaries who settled in the Danish colony in 1799.[67] In order to address the wide-ranging nature of the engagement with Jonesian Orientalism, the focus of the remainder of this chapter, however, it is most useful now to put to one side any question – implied by the adjective 'uncharacteristic' – as to the sympathies and the politics of the real Jones, and instead to think about the plurality of meanings offered by his writing.

While 'A Hymn to Lacshmi' shifts between the voices of 'devotee' and 'administrator', Jones's 1785 'A Hymn to Narayena' more directly explores devotional subjectivity, ostensibly transcending governmental imperatives and indeed any this-worldly concerns. The poet maintains the intensity of his first-person address throughout, from his initial hailing of the all-pervading 'Spirit of Spirits' (108) to his closing statement regarding his apparently 'total' absorption in this divine nature, such that he 'One only Being knows' (112).[68] Whereas 'A Hymn to Lacshmi' summons 'beams' from 'western skies' to counteract the gloom of Hindu error, 'A Hymn to Narayena' invokes an illumination prior to all existence, in the form of the 'glorious light' (108) that first directed the deity's omniscient power to exert itself. The poem's account of this refulgent magnificence is reliant on a familiar mediating text, *Paradise Lost*, but Jones nonetheless explored here a universal experience of devotion, and in doing so reiterated his earlier claims about the origin of poetry in religious ecstasy.[69] The poem's

Argument explicitly identifies the common ground between Vedic Hindu and Platonic traditions, presenting the material world of things as an ultimately illusory 'set of perceptions', a series of 'gay *pictures*' (106) occupying the space between God and his creation.

This same insight as to the compatibility of different traditions also informs 'A Hymn to Surya' (1786), a companion poem to 'A Hymn to Narayena'. Its Argument names Surya as equivalent to Phoebus, presenting 'enthusiastick admiration of the Sun' as fundamental to '*Egyptian, Indian*, and *Grecian* polytheism' (144). The poem arguably reads as a still more enraptured production than 'A Hymn to Narayena', and this may reflect the fact that it was composed after Jones discovered the 'new world' of Sanskrit, following his introduction to the language late in 1785.[70] The poet addresses Surya as the source of heat as well as light, styling himself as a votary of the deity 'Who with no borrow'd art/ Dares hymn thy pow'r, and durst provoke thy blaze/ But felt thy thrilling dart' (150). This passage offers an intertextual allusion to 'A Hymn to Camdeo' (which more cautiously solicits a 'warming' influence), and the obtrusive appeal to the temperature metaphor is again suggestive of a playful rejoinder to Collins's supposition regarding the perceptual and sympathetic limitations of British writers and readers. Jones's narrator identifies the essence of the natural religion breathing in '*Sanscrit* song', and if the conclusion of 'A Hymn to Lacshmi' intimates that Europeans may be the sole recipients of 'intellectual sun' (in More's phrase), 'A Hymn to Surya', like 'A Hymn to Narayena', offers a more inclusive vision, invoking at its close the 'great orb' which 'with all-enlight'ning ray/ Rulest the golden day' (152).

'A Hymn to Narayena' has been dubbed the most 'successful' of all Jones's Hindu hymns, because it appears to show him as a practitioner – rather than a theorist – of Romantic poetry, and 'A Hymn to Surya' is a similarly 'expressive' work.[71] By parading its author's knowledge of Sanskrit, however, it also invites us to think about other contemporary resonances of, and constituencies of interest in, its project of cultural translation. Immediately before his reference to the 'heav'nly truth' of '*Sanscrit* song', the poet draws attention to native recognition of his language skills, putting words into the mouth of the deity himself, who identifies Jones as one who 'lisping our celestial tongue,/ Though not from *Brahma* sprung,/ Draws orient knowledge from its fountains pure,/ Through caves obstructed long, and paths too long obscure' (151–2). This is a frequently discussed passage, and here I just want to acknowledge the broader significance of the 'reconstruction' of Hindu tradition to which it alludes – the work of a scholar-saviour very similar to the heroic figure of Jones's 1784 'Discourse', triumphant in spite of the obstacles in his way.[72]

Jones began to learn Sanskrit to help him to discharge his duties as a judge without being 'at the devotion' of Indian interpreters of legal texts; in contrast to his more conventional use of the term elsewhere, this kind of 'devotion' – dependence on native intermediaries – was a condition of which to beware.[73] The importance of Sanskrit to Jones meant that even as the composition of poems such as 'A Hymn to Surya' may have provided him with relief from daytime labours, it nonetheless remained on a continuum with his other, overtly 'interested' activities, notably the compilation of Hindu and Muslim laws. Whereas the metaphor of the fountain often encompasses notions of divine 'authorship' or literary inspiration in Jones's poetry, the phrase 'fountains pure' cited earlier, embedded in the discourse of the customary, refers to a deep indigenous wisdom that it is the task of the non-native scholar to recover. As Siraj Ahmed emphasizes, the process of 'drawing' knowledge that Jones describes alludes not to any abstract Saidian 'impulse to codify' but to the specific project of defining the 'traditional' Indian society that would be appealed to by the architects of the Permanent Settlement, which sought to establish a class of native property owners in Bengal so as to guarantee fixed land revenues for the EIC.[74] According to this contextualization of Jones's literary production, then, the 'renaissance' which he helped to initiate was distinctly Whig and civic humanist in its politics, since it aimed to restore Indian society to what was widely regarded in EIC circles as its virtuous agrarian foundation.[75]

As already acknowledged, however, this is not the only narrative of 'renaissance' in which Jones's diverse writings have been located. It is not possible here to consider the early nineteenth-century 'Bengal Renaissance' and the way in which native intellectuals adapted the 'Vedantic' construction of an essentially monistic Hinduism in EIC-sponsored Orientalist scholarship so as to provide a modernizing critique of Indian culture and society. It is useful briefly to return to Schwab again, though, and to recognize that while Jones's Sanskrit studies manifestly facilitated EIC governance, his literary works appealed to readers without such political imperatives. While 'it would be difficult to make a case that Indian cultural influences had sunk deep roots in Britain,' as P. J. Marshall states, audiences across Europe responded with great enthusiasm to Jones's translations of the classical dramas *Sakuntala* (1789) and *Gitagovinda* (1791).[76] One often-told story about Jones and his contemporaries concerns the way in which his discovery of the 'new world' of Sanskrit sparked a wave of

'Indophilia' that rivalled the intensity of responses to the *Arabian Nights* at the start of the century.[77] Jones's framing of Indian (sometimes more broadly 'Asiatic') antiquity as a site of human origins and universal truths instantiated, in Balachandra Rajan's paraphrasing of Schwab, 'a literary discourse of world humanism, ... free of Greco-Roman constraints'.[78] I say more about the way in which Jones's substantial influence on metropolitan literary production extended beyond the late eighteenth-century 'Orientalist' moment of British India. Before that, though, I want to introduce some more of Jones's contemporaries – those who appraised his legacy immediately after his death in April 1794.

'The Christian Rock'

The obituaries and elegies produced in the wake of Jones's death demonstrate that his legacy was as contested in his own time as it is today. In 'The Literary History of the Late Sir William Jones' (1795), delivered to the Asiatic Society shortly after Jones died, John Shore echoed Jones's account of his intellectual ambition, stating that the interests of his former colleague 'extended . . . to all languages, nations, and times'.[79] It is notable, though, that Shore declared that it would be 'unbecoming' to focus on Jones's poems and literary translations since Jones saw these 'lighter productions' simply as 'the elegant amusements of his leisure hours'.[80] What instead mattered most to Jones, Shore claimed, was his codification of Hindu and Muslim law, a scholarly project that took him 'far out of the road of amusement'.[81] Shore further emphasized Jones's seriousness by citing a scripture-focused passage from his 'Eighth Anniversary Discourse' of 1791 to prove his unswerving conviction as to the truth of Christianity. Shore more overtly looked for 'evangelical sympathies' in Jones's work in his longer memoir of 1804, as might be expected from someone who (as Lord Teignmouth) would become a prominent figure in the Clapham Sect.[82] Even if Shore's record of Jones's career may now seem misleadingly reductive, however, it still provided an introduction to Jones for many readers. Anna Maria Jones prefaced her 1799 edition of her husband's works with Shore's initial memoir, describing it as an 'admirable discourse' that offered 'the most accurate, and comprehensive account, yet extant, of [his] enlarged views and literary labours'.[83]

The Anglican clergyman and scholar Thomas Maurice provided a similarly partial memoir of Jones in his 'Elegiac and Historical Poem' of 1795, dedicated to Shore for his patronage of the author's *Indian Antiquities* (1792–6). This poem is another that sets its scene 'on the banks of the Ganges', staging an encounter between its narrator and the 'Sovereign Genius of the East', who performs a testimonial function akin to that of Scott's Brahmin, though instead he gives thanks for the arrival of Jones, avatar of 'freedom and science': 'To chase the tenfold gloom, my JONES, was thine,/ To cheer the Brahmin, and to burst his chains;/ To search for latent gems the Sanscreet mine;/ And wake the fervour of her ancient strains.'[84] Depicting Jones both as a scholar-hero and as a bearer of enlightenment and liberty (the abolitionist rhetoric of 'A Hymn to Lacshmi' is again evident in the reference to a bursting of chains here), Maurice's poem makes use of many of the tropes prominent in Jones's own writing. At the same time, though, the poem only minimally acknowledges the actual substance of Jones's learning, and in the Genius's account of 'Mohammedan' invasions of India, 'native' culture is represented by 'Veeshnu' alone. The poem makes no mention of any other figures in the Hindu pantheon, and when it states that Jones 'rent' the 'mystic veil, that wraps the hallow'd shrines/ Of India's deities', it credits him with helping to assimilate Hindu belief to the monotheistic understanding of his audience: thanks to Jones, the narrator declares, 'I see, sublime Devotion's noblest flame/ 'Midst Superstition's glowing embers burn!'[85] Later, in his *Indian Antiquities*, Maurice asserted that 'the Mosaic records and Christianity, far from being subverted by the *pretended antiquity* of the Brahmins, will derive a proud trophy from the *corroborative* testimony of their *genuine annals* and the congenial sentiments of their *primeval creed*.'[86] Maurice participated in what Marilyn Butler terms the 'Gothicization' of a corrupt Brahmanism, but additionally sought to distinguish between the merely 'traditional' authority of this priestly caste and the truth at the heart of a Hinduism that was essentially compatible with Christian revelation.[87]

The final response to Jones's death that I consider, William Hayley's 'Elegy on the Death of the Honourable Sir William Jones' (1795), was inspired by Maurice's poem, and displays continuities with Shore's prose memoir too. Like Maurice, Hayley emphasized the tearful sorrow of 'INDIA's mild sages' at the news of Jones's death, and like Shore he separated the different domains of Jones's research and writing: according to Hayley, Jones recognized the temptation of literary fame for the 'quicksand' that it was, and he 'gave the Muse [his] secondary love,/ Proclaiming Law [his] life's acknowledg'd queen'.[88] When read alongside his *Essay on Epic Poetry*, Hayley's elegy can further be seen to identify Jones as one of the honourable figures whose absence the earlier work laments. The poem alludes to John Flaxman's plans for a sculpture of Jones collecting information from native pandits, and, describing Jones as 'justly social' in his professional capacity, it celebrates him as a new kind of imperial hero. Jones 'searched what INDIAN wisdom could produce', the poem states, alluding to 'A Hymn to Surya', 'So hoards of knowledge from the lips of Age/ He drew, and fashion'd for the public use'.[89] Whether or not Hayley consciously redefined the idea of 'hoarding' in discourse on the Bengal famine, by projecting 'engrossment' onto Brahmins rather than EIC officials, the poem nonetheless offers another index of the purging of the scandal of empire in the final decade of the century. It is significant in this context that Hayley's reference to the 'social' Jones recalls Hannah More's claim about the 'social hands' of Captain Cook, who after his death in 1779 was so often seen to exemplify the possibility of a newly moralized, benevolent empire.[90] Just as Anna Seward's 'Elegy on Captain Cook' (1780) entreats Cook's widow to raise her thoughts above selfish grief, so Hayley's poem tells Anna Maria Jones that 'e'en in sorrow there's a virtuous pride,' since she can think of herself as 'The cherish'd partner of as clear a name,/ As e'er won glory in the toil of life'.[91]

Hayley's poem describes Jones as a 'Bright Genius!' imparting a 'lustre' to all around him, and the terms of this elevation of Jones as a hero of empire are reproduced in Franklin's account of Jones as a 'beacon' of enlightenment in our own dark times.[92] In addition to its lauding of Jones's exemplary patriotism, another distinctive feature of Hayley's elegy is its reflection on its subject's 'mild and rational piety'. The poem's final end note states that the syncretism of Jones's 'Discourse on the Gods of Greece, Italy, and India' may ultimately render a 'service to religion':

> He there points out what occurred to him as the only promising mode of converting the Mussulmans and Hindus to Christianity; and perhaps the most worthy honour, which the Asiatic Society could pay to the memory of Sir WILLIAM JONES would be to resume and realize his idea: the experiment is easy, and should it succeed in any degree, that success will form the noblest eulogy of the beneficent spirit, by whom it was suggested.[93]

This note stands out because in identifying the convergence between Jonesian comparativism and the future Christianization of India, it moves beyond both the idea that classical analogy might help to assimilate the difference of Hinduism and the claim that 'pure' Hinduism corroborated 'the system of Moses'. That Hayley was more emphatic even than Shore in this respect is perhaps surprising since – best known as a patron of

William Blake – he is not generally associated with evangelical cultural politics. Importantly, though, Hayley was able to see Jones's research in such terms, even if there is no evidence that Jones himself thought about his work in this manner.

Hayley's reference to the 'noblest eulogy' that could be given to Jones implies the existence of plural, potentially competing accounts of Jones's legacy, and there may be a defensiveness in this and other contemporary efforts to delimit Jones's 'true' achievement. Reviews of Jones's hymns to Hindu deities sometimes suggested that he failed to maintain a proper distance from his subject matter, and the *Monthly Review* in 1789 sarcastically declared that 'we have almost apprehension, that our excellent countryman had, with his situation, changed his religion.'[94] Another pioneering Orientalist scholar, Nathaniel Brassey Halhed, was by this time associated with a dangerous enthusiasm, after his testimony in support of the self-declared prophet Richard Brothers, and in the counter-revolutionary climate of the mid-1790s Jonesian Orientalism was among those scholarly discourses that were liable to be regarded as suspiciously unorthodox.[95] The anti-Jacobin T. J. Mathias, for example, stated that *Asiatick Researches* (the main conduit of Jones's scholarship before the posthumous *Works*) 'afforded the most curious and important facts', but he also added the qualification 'if applied with judgment and soberly investigated'. Just as Hayley alluded to other 'eulogies' of Jones, therefore, so Mathias recognized different possible uses to which Jones's work might be put.

In this *Dunciad*-inspired satire of the literary scene, 'The Shade of Alexander Pope' (1799), Mathias nonetheless credited Jones himself with the distillation of 'Truth' from 'Oriental dreams'.[96] In his *Pursuits of Literature* (1797), Mathias similarly expressed his confidence in the essential integrity and rectitude of Jones, as an exceptional figure who – reformist sympathies notwithstanding – had been uncorrupted by 'this *political* and *depressing* period': 'His mind collected, 'gainst opinion's shock',/ JONES stood unmov'd, and from the Christian rock,/ Coelestial brightness beaming on his breast,/ He saw THE STAR, and worshipp'd in the East.'[97] The apparent fastness of Jones's position on 'the Christian rock' renders him safe from any metaphorical 'drowning' in other civilizations or cultures. While it rather oddly aligns Jones with the magi who attended Christ's birth, this passage rehearses the terms of many of the works previously discussed, presenting Jones as a solitary scholar-hero whose intellectual quest, even after his death, still redounded to the honour of the nation and humanity at large. Mathias's Jones is no more the 'real' Jones than the transcultured savant preferred by others, however, and in the remainder of this chapter I say more about the widespread and often complex engagement with Jones in the work of later writers as well as contemporaries.

Afterlives

In her survey of Romantic-period Orientalism, Marilyn Butler refers to the 'aristocratic orientalism' of the 'ultra-liberals' who admired Hinduism 'as a type of paganism that offered to outdo Christianity in age, grandeur and sophistication': in his 'A Discourse on the Worship of Priapus' (1786), for example, Richard Payne Knight advanced the sceptical argument that Hindu mythology's sexual symbolism testified to the origin of religious faith in a primitive reverence for nature's procreative powers.[98] After its inception the Asiatic Society of Bengal largely took over the mediation of Indian antiquity from the metropolitan societies to which Knight and others belonged, and the natural philosopher Erasmus Darwin was one prominent intellectual who directly responded to its founder's writings. In his Linnaeus-inspired treatment of the process of plant reproduction, *The Loves of the Plants* (1789), Darwin drew upon Jones's similarly playful poem 'The Enchanted Fruit' (1784), based upon an episode in the Sanskrit epic *Mahabharata*. In a 'neo-aristocratic' – rather than 'radical Orientalist' – appeal to the rhetoric of sexual despotism, Darwin's poem presents 'the chaste MIMOSA' (of the Linnaean class 'Polygamia') as 'an eastern bride' processing to a 'mosque' to be sexually initiated: 'There her soft vows increasing love record,/ Queen of the bright seraglio of the Lord.'[99] Tim Fulford argues that Darwin brazenly eschewed the 'gentlemanly' mediation strategies of Jones's botanical writings, and Richard Polwhele's reference to the poem's 'prostitution of a plant' in his 'The Unsex'd Females' (1798) provides another example of anti-Jacobin wariness regarding the process by which such new knowledges were transmitted and 'applied'.[100]

While one British audience for Orientalist scholarship in the late eighteenth century was broadly 'elite', another was plebeian, although equally keen to explore the latent radical potential of Jones's work. David Weir presents William Blake as 'witness to the series of discoveries that later writers described under the rubric of the Oriental Renaissance', discussing Blake's engagement with Hindu mythology, as it is evident, for example, in *The Song of Los* (c. 1795).[101] Weir suggests that Blake may have encountered Jones's work either via his friends John Flaxman and William Hayley, or by reading related contributions to Joseph Johnson's *Analytical Review*, and while registering that the content of Blake's reading remains uncertain, he identifies areas of common ground between the 'enlightened' Jones and the 'prophetic' Blake.[102] For all the obvious differences between them and their writings, Blake ranged over similar terrain to Jones, whether by emphasizing the interconnection of world religions, by distinguishing between ideas of 'theological purity' and 'ritualistic practice', or by rejecting an Old Testament equation of 'disobedience' and sensual pleasure.[103]

The five editions of Jones's collected works that were published between 1799 and 1810 demonstrate the endurance of his reputation after his death, albeit that it is only quite recently that literary history has acknowledged Jones's centrality to the writing of this period. Traces of Jones's Hindu hymns are evident in numerous canonical poems, most famously perhaps Coleridge's 'Kubla Khan' (composed in 1797), in which the description of the river Alph echoes that of the Ganges in 'A Hymn to Ganga'. At a broader conceptual level too both the scholarly research done by Jones and others and Jones's poetry provided subsequent writers with a diverse range of intellectual and creative stimuli. In a 1797 letter to John Thelwall, Coleridge declared his readiness to 'adapt the Brahman creed, & say – It is better to sit than to stand, it is better to lie than to sit, it is better to sleep than to wake – but Death is the best of all! – I should wish, like the Indian Vishna, to float along an infinite ocean cradled in the flower of the lotos, and wake once in a million years for a few minutes – just to know that I was going to sleep for a million years more'.[104] While this casual identification with Vishnu exemplifies Coleridge's facility of Orientalist reference, it further testifies to his engagement with Wilkins's *Bhagvat-Geeta* as well as works produced by Jones; Coleridge's evocation of 'an intuitive sense of the unity of self and other resembl[es] the Hindu visions of oneness' that they described.[105] Although the religiously ortho-dox Coleridge would reject Indian pantheism as the product of a jejune misunderstanding, 'the vehemence of this later-life rejection,' Deidre Coleman argues, is 'closely tied up with his remembrance of the intensity of his original encounter with Indian texts.'[106]

In the case of Percy Shelley, Jones's influence is perhaps best described as silently informing. Whereas Southey and Thomas Moore (to whom I return) cited their sources – including works by Jones – in extensive footnotes, Shelley, as Leask argues, generally rejected Orientalist detail so as instead to provide poetic narratives available for 'universalist' reading, as is the case with *The Revolt of Islam* (1818), where 'Islam' stands for a generalized Eastern despotism.[107] Leask discusses the way in which *Prometheus Unbound* (1820) might be regarded as an exception to this

Shelleyan rule, because of the agency that it accords to the figure of Asia, who 'questions the self-proclaiming universalism of western truth by bringing down Jupiter and leaving his throne unfilled'. He suggests that the poem's composition may have been initiated by Shelley's reading of Rammohan Roy's reform-minded 'appropriation' of EIC-sponsored scholarship on Hinduism (including Jones's), and he thus presents 'the active role assumed by Asia' in her dialogue with Demogorgon as signalling 'the entry of [a] hybridized discourse into the heart of the western literary canon'.[108] *Prometheus Unbound* is not an 'Orientalist' poem, then, as its incorporation of an abstract figure by the name of 'Asia' makes plain, but neither is it an 'assimilationist' work in the manner of *The Revolt of Islam*, which more clearly aligns itself with the liberal imperialist argument that the East had to be made less Eastern.[109]

In all of Shelley's poetry, traces of Jones are perhaps most intriguingly evident in *Alastor, or, The Spirit of Solitude* (1816). Although the solipsism of the 'Alastor-poet' has been read in relation to Rousseau and Wordsworth, Shelley's description of his intellectual formation alludes to Jones as well, since we are told that in the poet's early days 'The fountains of divine philosophy/ Fled not his thirsty lips, and all of great,/ Or good, or lovely, which the sacred past/ In truth or fable consecrates, he felt/ And knew.'[110] The idea of 'fountains' of wisdom recalls the ubiquity of this metaphor in Jones's writing, and is given additional resonance by the fact that Shelley represents the poet's fascination with 'the sacred past' as impelling him into a state of voluntary exile, 'To seek strange truths in undiscovered lands' (72; l.77). The poet is thereafter depicted as an origin seeker (drawn to the 'secrets of the birth of time' [73; l.128]), who, again not unlike Jones in his 1784 'Discourse', entertains 'high thoughts' (73; l.107) as he encounters remnants of the great civilizations of the past, experiencing 'joy and exultation' (74; l.144) as he travels further East. Another measure of *Alastor*'s oblique engagement with Jonesian Orientalism is that the poet, in the 'loneliest dell' (74; l.146) of the 'vale of Cashmire' (74; l.145), subsequently dreams of a 'veiled maid' (74; l.151), an idealized creation who, via the figure of Sydney Owenson's Luxima in *The Missionary*, is descended from Jones's renderings of the goddess Lacshmi and the princess Sakuntala.[111] The nature of the poet's quest is transformed by this ambiguous moment of encounter, and his pursuit of the 'fleeting shade' (75; l.206) that had appeared to him comes to be driven by Thanatos rather than Eros, as he seeks a 'sepulchre' (80; l.430) in the natural world; it is telling that a later 'fountain' appears to him not as a source of recoverable knowledge but instead as 'searchless' (82; l.507), emanating from a 'stream' that is 'inaccessibly profound' (82; ll.502–3).[112]

Much has been written about Shelley's representation of the poet's initial traversal of symbolically vacant regions, and about the significance of his imagined encounter with the veiled maid, which Leask reads as a pioneering exploration of the 'psychopathology of empire'.[113] Interpreted in these terms, if *Alastor*'s 'emptying' of the East appears to make it available for colonization, the poem nonetheless undercuts the ideology of empire as 'civilizing mission', since the narcissistic poet – the voice of the veiled maid 'was like the voice of his own soul' (74; l.153), we are told – ends up being consumed by his own quest. Given my emphasis on Jones and his afterlives, however, I want to return to the mediation of Jonesian Orientalism in which Shelley's poem participated, and of which it is itself a product. *Alastor*'s basic narrative incorporates numerous motifs that are evident in 'Kubla Khan', and Coleridge's already discussed relation to Jones provides another instance of the characteristic intertextuality of Romantic Orientalist poetry – its ostensibly 'closed' and allusive, rather than referential, rhetorical economy; it seems fair to say, indeed, that Shelley engaged with Jones's work as much through others' responses to it as via his contact with the writing itself. I have mentioned that Owenson's *The Missionary* was an especially important intermediary text for Shelley, and I conclude by reading it as a fiction that stages the reception of Jonesian Orientalism, and which in presenting a complex, historically situated narrative of cross-cultural contact also sceptically reflects on the meaning of the openness to the East that is belatedly displayed by its title character.

'One Who Died in the Act of Prayer'

Critics have often noted that Owenson's Hindu heroine Luxima serves as a conduit for Jonesian ideas: she is said early on to look like 'the tutelar intelligence of the Hindu mythology, newly descended on earth, from the radiant sphere assigned her in the Indian zodiac', and the description of her theology is reliant upon Jones's essays.[114] The complexity of Owenson's engagement with Jones is signalled before this, however, when the Portuguese missionary Hilarion, en route to India, is portrayed in terms closely following those of Jones's 1784 'Discourse': 'through the clear bright atmosphere', we are told:

> the shores and mighty regions of the East presented themselves to the view, while the imagination of the Missionary, escaping beyond the limits of

human vision, stretched over those various and wondrous tracts, so diversified by clime and soil, by government and religion, and which present to the contemplation of philosophy a boundless variety in form and spirit (80).

What is especially striking here is that Hilarion is implicitly aligned with Jones even though at this stage he is an emphatically un-Jonesian figure, sailing eastwards with an 'insatiable thirst for the conversion of souls' (77). Hilarion invokes the 'powerful genius' of Tamerlane and then 'the Impostor of Mecca' and, 'awakening to a new impulse' (81), he considers how he might likewise gain ascendancy over others. He accuses himself of impiety after this flight of fancy, but – deliberately or not – the novel can nonetheless thus be seen to imagine alternative trajectories of the competitive sense of ambition often expressed by Jones.[115] '[D]isgusted' with the 'luxury and pomp' of early seventeenth-century Portuguese Goa (82), Hilarion conceives of his projected mission to 'Cashmire' as a fitting one for a 'higher order of genius' (83), and the language of 'penetration' that Owenson uses to describe this mission recalls the currency of the rape metaphor in metropolitan discourse on British India around the time that Jones was in Bengal.

In Lahore, on his way up country, Hilarion encounters a 'learned Pundit' (87) who suggests that he might best further his goal of proselytization by insinuating himself into the performance of Hindu devotional practice – submitting to 'prejudices which he could only hope finally to vanquish by previously respecting' (91). Spurred on by the pundit, Hilarion approaches the task of converting the famed Luxima as a challenge, imagining that his redemption of the 'Prophetess' would, in the pundit's words, 'operate like a spell on her compatriots' (96). It is Hilarion who comes to be entranced, however, and as it describes his possession by Luxima, the novel offers a retrospect on Jones's mediation of Hindu mythology: Owenson's portrayal of Luxima partly draws upon Jones's translation of Kalidasa's drama, and Hilarion is said to 'read the Shanscrit with ease and even with facility' (101). The novel accentuates the enthusiasm of Hilarion's response to Luxima so that his position on 'the Christian rock' (to recall Mathias's phrase) comes to be jeopardized. One measure of the seduction of Hilarion is that not long after he plans an 'attack [on] the birthplace of Brahma' (83), figured as an act of penetration, Owenson describes him as having had his own senses 'penetrated' by Luxima, as 'her dark and flowing tresses left an odour on the air' (111).

As if anticipating Schwab's humanistic vision of the coming together of hemispheres, the initial meeting of Hilarion and Luxima is presented as a joining of 'the noblest specimens of the human species, . . . ; she, like the

East, lovely and luxuriant; he, like the West, lofty and commanding' (109). While Owenson's earlier novel *The Wild Irish Girl* (1806) is in the background here, however, *The Missionary* departs from the conventions of 'colonial romance' that this tableau appears to rehearse. It does this not simply by scrambling Orientalist stereotypes (as the 'commanding' Hilarion comes to be awestruck by Luxima), but by presenting the relationship that develops between the pair as above all a source of inner conflict and turmoil. Hilarion and Luxima are initially presented as symbols of the faiths that they espouse, but as the novel progresses they gradually become estranged from their religious identities as, in David Simpson's words, 'the security of each is undermined by the desire for the other.'[116] First, Luxima is subjected to a Gothically rendered process of '*Brahminical excommunication*' (186) because of her contact with an infidel, then, having fled from Kashmir, Hilarion and Luxima are both later sentenced to be burned at the stake by the Spanish Inquisition in Goa.

The novel's climax sees Luxima's 'voluntary immolation' (246) on the pyre intended for Hilarion, who rescues Luxima only for her to be killed at the point of a dagger intended for the missionary himself; this sequence of events takes place against the backdrop of a rebellion of the local population, 'inflamed' by the treatment of their prophetess and echoing her cry of 'Brahma!' (249) – an exclamation that calls into question the status of Luxima's earlier 'conversion' (193) by Hilarion. There is much to say about this episode, but here I just want briefly to note the richly suggestive topicality of the novel's final scenes.[117] While readers would have understood Owenson's paralleling of the Inquisition and the customary practice of sati as compatible with the long-standing projection of the evils of empire onto Spain (the novel begins by presenting Portugal as in effect a Spanish colony), Hilarion's debate with a Jesuit from the Inquisition prior to this also brings out a much more contemporary resonance. The work was published during a period of debate about the renewal of the EIC charter (when the evangelical lobby successfully campaigned for a 'pious clause' permitting missionary activity in India), and it engages with this debate in a number of ways. Hilarion comes to accept Luxima's argument about the association of religious faith and cultural identity, and in his testy exchange with the Jesuit he emphasizes the gulf between precept and practice in missionaries' dealings with native peoples: 'We bring them a spiritual creed, which commands them to forget the world, and we take from them temporal possessions, which prove how much *we live for it*' (226). More directly, the text includes a footnote from Quintin Craufurd's *Sketches of the Hindus*

(1790) that brings the reader almost into the present, stating that 'the labours of the Missionaries for upwards of two hundred years' have produced 'not twelve thousand *Christians*' (226). A later footnote records how an insurrection akin to the one depicted in the novel took place in the South Indian city of Vellore in 1806, when 'the religious bigotry of the natives [was] kindled by the supposed threatened violation of their faith from the Christian settlers' (241).

As a result of such engagement with contemporary politics (I have to leave aside here the obvious resonance of the idea of 'religious bigotry' in an Irish context), *The Missionary* has often been read as a work that counters proposals to Christianize British India by aligning itself with the 'Jonesian' principle of respect for cultural difference, eventually recognized by Hilarion after his education by Luxima.[118] What complicates this reading of the novel's polemical thrust, however, is that Hilarion does not in fact undertake the new mission that the dying Luxima urges him to pursue. Rather than assume the role of a preacher of the 'spirit of peace' (257) to Christian and Hindu alike, as Luxima entreats him, Hilarion instead returns to Kashmir, to the site of their first meeting, where he becomes a recluse, 'equally avoided and avoiding' (260). Hilarion's inability to discharge any 'public' responsibility is partly a function of the work's historical setting, because Owenson records the rise of the Mughal emperor Aurungzebe, represented as a Muslim bigot and destroyer of Hindu shrines in Jones's 'Hymn to Ganga': 'While *Freedom* thus unfurled her spotless banner in a remote corner of the West' (as Portugal gained her independence from Spain), we are told, 'she lay mangled and in chains, at the foot of victorious tyranny in the East' (259). In its depiction of 'a universal human heart that struggles unsuccessfully to flourish in a hostile world', as Simpson puts it, however, the novel can also be seen to question the efficacy of individual virtue in environments that are not hospitable to it.[119] Though Hilarion cannot in any straightforward way be mapped onto Jones, it is striking here that the qualities of sympathy and toleration so often attributed to Jones are finally shown to be powerless in the face of power. The initial contact of Hilarion and Luxima is set up as if it constituted a symbolic reintegration of East and West, but Hilarion himself, for all his personal transformation, is in effect presented as a beacon that burns out – expiring 'at the foot of an altar which he had himself raised to the deity of his secret worship, and fixed in the attitude of one who died in the act of prayer' (261).

While *The Missionary* is manifestly a tragic tale about the lost possibilities of cross-cultural contact, the *Critical Review* distinguished it as a work which 'makes us as familiar and as sociable with those gay gentlemen, Brahma, Vishnu, and Co. as if we had been brought up under the same firm all our lives, as well as with Monsieur Camdeo ..., and a long *et cetera* of personages which make up the Indian mythology'.[120] This framing of the novel is arch rather than hostile, but its suggestion – as implied by the 'long *et cetera*' – that the Hindu pantheon may have begun to lose its novelty and interest invites us to think about the passing of the 'moment' of Jonesian Orientalism. The two most widely cited indices of a significant cultural shift taking place during this decade are the 1813 renewal of the EIC's charter, referred to earlier, and the 1817 publication of James Mill's *The History of British India*, which articulated, in Majeed's words, 'the liberal programme to emancipate India from its own culture'.[121] In the next chapter, however, I consider another way of approaching the literary Orientalism of the 1810s, following up on the *Critical*'s claim that the novel 'repays' the reader for its lengthy description of Hilarion's travels from Goa 'by setting us down in the delicious Garden of Eden, the vale of Cashmire'.[122] As well as being a source of inspiration for Shelley in *Alastor*, Owenson's Kashmir was a key reference point for Thomas Moore, who began the process of composing his poetic romance *Lalla Rookh* (1817) with a careful reading of *The Missionary*. 'Delicious' is an especially suggestive adjective for the *Critical* to employ, since it anticipates the way in which Moore would evoke a luxurious and splendid, familiar rather than challenging, milieu. In the second half of the next chapter I discuss *Lalla Rookh* as an inescapably allegorical work which at the same time, via its pastiche of an older idiom, succeeded in constructing a popular, consumable East. I begin, though, by looking at the epic poetry of Robert Southey, who with *Thalaba the Destroyer* (1801) idiosyncratically continued Jones's project of cultural translation.

Notes

1. To Montagu, 30 Sept. 1772, Forbes, *Life*, 1:234.
2. Montagu to Beattie, 5 Sept. 1772, ibid., 1:298.
3. Beattie, *Minstrel*, 5.
4. Schwab, *Renaissance*.
5. Hayley, 'Elegy', 9.
6. Franklin, *Orientalist Jones*, 79.

7. To Charles Wilkins, June 1784, *Letters*, 2:652.
8. Collins, *Persian Eclogues*, preface.
9. *Spectator*, 3:256.
10. Lowth, *Lectures*, 1:114–15.
11. *Selected Works*, 329. Further references appear as parenthetical citations in the text.
12. Sitter, 'Jones', 399.
13. Ibid., 388.
14. Jones, *Poems*, i.
15. Ibid., ii.
16. Fulford, 'Poetic Flowers', 117.
17. Cited in Rudd, *Sympathy*, 67.
18. Collins, *Persian Eclogues*, preface.
19. Byron, *CPW*, 4:145, l.408.
20. Dow, *Tales*, 1:viii.
21. Ibid., 1:iii.
22. Dow, *History*, 1:viii.
23. Ibid., 1:vi.
24. Ibid., 1:xxi–xxii.
25. Ibid., 1:ii.
26. Ibid., 1:i.
27. Scott, *Poetical Works*, 148. Further references appear as parenthetical citations in the text.
28. Ibid., 332.
29. Ibid., Advertisement.
30. Though see Mulholland, *Sounding Imperial*, 148–50.
31. Hayley, *Epic Poetry*, 109.
32. Ibid., 297.
33. Ibid., 109.
34. Nott, *Odes*, vii.
35. Ibid., v.
36. To Lee, Oct. 1786, *Letters*, 2:713.
37. Jones, 'Discourse', 10. Further references appear as parenthetical citations in the text.
38. Milton, *Paradise Lost*, 82; IV:159–63.
39. *Spectator*, 1:293.
40. Pratt, *Imperial Eyes*.
41. Schwab, *Renaissance*, 16.
42. Ibid., 18; De Quincey, *Confessions*, 72.
43. To the second Earl Spencer, Aug. 1787, *Letters*, 2:751.
44. *Miscellaneous Prose of Scott*, 4:193.
45. To Wilkins, June 1784, *Letters*, 2:652.
46. Franklin, *Orientalist Jones*, 22.
47. *Spectator*, 1:294.
48. *Letters*, 2:652.

49. Fulford, 'Poetic Flowers', 123; Dalrymple, *White Mughals*, 10.
50. Teltscher, *India*, 208.
51. Leask, '"Wandering through Eblis"', 177.
52. Franklin, *Orientalist Jones*, 360.
53. Scott, *Poetical Works*, 140.
54. Teltscher, *India*, 221.
55. Mulholland, *Sounding Imperial*, 132–3.
56. Scott, *Poetical Works*, 141.
57. Teltscher, *India*, 222; Burke, *Writings and Speeches*, 5:402.
58. Teltscher, *India*, 219.
59. More, 'Slavery', 5 and 1.
60. Brown, *Moral Capital*, 27.
61. Majeed, *Ungoverned Imaginings*, 42; to the second Earl Spencer, 19 Oct. 1791, *Letters*, 2:898–9.
62. Teltscher, *India*, 220.
63. Leask, '"Wandering through Eblis"'.
64. To Landor, 20 May 1808, *Life and Correspondence*, 3:147.
65. To Davis, 21 Sept. 1786, *Letters*, 2:705.
66. To Wilkins, June 1784, *Letters*, 2:650.
67. Franklin, *Orientalist Jones*, 293.
68. Rudd, *Sympathy*, 80.
69. Teltscher, *India*, 210.
70. To the second Earl Spencer, 12 Aug. 1787, *Letters*, 2:747.
71. Drew, *India*, 58.
72. Teltscher, *India*, 224; Franklin, *Orientalist Jones*, 319.
73. To Wilkins, March 1785, *Letters*, 2:666.
74. Ahmed, *Stillbirth*, 163.
75. Majeed, *Ungoverned Imaginings*, 30–1.
76. Marshall, 'British–Indian Connections', 60.
77. Franklin, *Orientalist Jones*, 251–86.
78. Rajan, *Under Western Eyes*, 86.
79. Shore, 'Literary History', 5.
80. Ibid., 8.
81. Ibid., 7.
82. Rudd, *Sympathy*, 122.
83. *Works of Sir William Jones*, 1: preface [n.p.].
84. Maurice, 'Elegiac and Historical Poem', Argument [n.p.] and 36.
85. Ibid., 36–7.
86. Cited in Rudd, *Sympathy*, 189.
87. Butler, 'Orientalism', 415; Rudd, *Sympathy*, 123.
88. Hayley, 'Elegy', 5.
89. Ibid., 16.
90. More, 'Slavery', 17.
91. Hayley, 'Elegy', 20.
92. Ibid., 17–18; Franklin, *Orientalist Jones*, 360.

93. Hayley, 'Elegy', 37–8.
94. *Monthly Review*, 81 (1789), 653.
95. Butler, 'Orientalism', 411.
96. Mathias, 'Alexander Pope', 72.
97. Mathias, *Pursuits of Literature*, 91.
98. Butler, 'Orientalism', 403.
99. Darwin, *Loves*, 32–3.
100. Polwhele cited in Fulford, 'Poetic Flowers', 127.
101. Weir, *Brahma*, 2.
102. Ibid., 57.
103. Ibid., 42, 89.
104. To Thelwall, 14 Oct. 1797, *Letters*, 1:350.
105. Vallins, Oishi, and Perry, eds., *Coleridge*, introduction, 3; Drew, *India*, 188–93.
106. Coleman, 'Coleridge', 54.
107. Leask, *British Romantic Writers*, 72.
108. Ibid., 150.
109. Ibid., 118; though see Warren, *Young Romantics*, 185–222.
110. *Shelley's Poetry*, 72 (ll.71–5). Page and line references appear as parenthetical citations in the text.
111. Drew, *India*, 255–8.
112. Warren, *Young Romantics*, 139.
113. Makdisi, *Romantic Imperialism*, 142; Leask, *British Romantic Writers*, 124.
114. Owenson, *Missionary*, 92. Further references appear as parenthetical citations in the text.
115. Butler, 'Orientalism', 423.
116. Simpson, *Stranger*, 222.
117. Wright, introduction to *Missionary*, 19–29.
118. Wright, *Ireland, India, and Nationalism*, 91–8.
119. Simpson, *Stranger*, 222.
120. Cited in *Missionary*, 299–300.
121. Majeed, *Ungoverned Imaginings*, 127.
122. Cited in *Missionary*, 299.

CHAPTER 5

'Imperial Dotage' and Poetic Ornament in Romantic Orientalist Verse Narrative

In comparison with Sir William Jones's work, much late eighteenth-century scholarly Orientalism was modest in its aims, mediating literary novelty as Jones had recommended in his 1772 'Essay on the Poetry of the Eastern Nations'. In his *Persian Miscellanies* (1795), William Ouseley, for example, undertook what he presented as the 'humble' task of removing the 'thorns and brambles' opposing readers' passage to 'the smiling garden of Persian Literature', while in his collection of *Romances* (1799) Isaac D'Israeli included a version of the renowned story of Mejnoun and Leila, based on Ouseley's translation.[1] D'Israeli's prose tale displays its roots in contemporary scholarship, but it also appeals to an older understanding of the East as a domain of romance rather than a sphere of political contention. D'Israeli indeed claimed that the tragedy of the couple surpassed any European analogue, since it concerned 'two fervid Orientalists, capable of more passion, more grief, and more terror', and in doing so he echoed William Collins's earlier description of 'Orientals'' greater capacity for passionate feelings.[2]

While it is necessary to keep in mind continuities in the metropolitan imagining of the East, however, Walter Savage Landor in his pastiche of *Poems from the Arabic and the Persian* (1800) pointedly eschewed the long-standing convention of publishing poetry actually or purportedly 'translated' from Eastern sources, declaring himself 'ignorant' of the languages referred to in his title.[3] By this time, moreover, Landor had already inaugurated the allegorical turn of Romantic Orientalism with *Gebir* (1798), a verse romance which obliquely reflects on the politics of the 1790s. In this narrative of the King of Gades's ill-fated attempt to conquer ancient Egypt, Landor drew inspiration from a pseudo-Oriental precursor text, Clara Reeve's 'The History of Charoba, Queen of Egypt' (1785), which was already an adaptation of an Arabian (though not *Arabian Nights*–style) romance. Landor took from Reeve the story of an imposing male protagonist who settles in Egypt aiming to marry the queen and to share her throne, only to fall prey to her superior cunning. His key innovation was to use a minimally substantiated Eastern setting as the basis for a complex fable of liberty and empire that intriguingly anticipated the French occupation of Ottoman Egypt in 1798; one marker of *Gebir*'s complexity is that it contrasts Napoleon and George III – respectively praised and damned – but that like many subsequent works, it additionally demonstrates the overlap between its critique of Oriental (also European old-regime) despotism and a new discourse of liberal imperialism.[4] It is important to recognize Landor as one of the numerous writers in the late 1790s who, though well aware of Jones, particularly engaged with a longer-established tradition of what Humberto Garcia terms 'Islamic republican-ism'. This was a branch of the 'radical Enlightenment' that conceived of Islam as 'a model and an idiom for the definition of political liberty', and which presented the prophet as above all a reforming legislator and republican – as for example Coleridge and Southey did in their unfinished poem 'Mahomet', which aligns his virtue and enthusiasm with an uncor-rupted non-Trinitarian Christianity.[5]

This chapter begins by discussing Southey's Islam-inspired epic *Thalaba the Destroyer* (1801) rather than *Gebir*, because it reached a much bigger audience than Landor's work, provoked fascinating critical responses, and in turn generated a significant act of authorial revision. *Thalaba* is an important text for my book as a whole since it both helped to establish the Orientalist epic poem as a medium of political engagement and in its own distinctive fashion extended the Jonesian project of cultural transla-tion. Contemporaries in fact seldom identified Southey's Bedouin hero as an agent of revolution, but they certainly acknowledged the way in which the poem confronted them with forms of otherness, especially via the eclectic register and 'ornament' of its main text and its copious and detailed footnotes. After considering the challenge thus offered to readers by Southey's work, I examine his *Roderick, the Last of the Goths* (1814) as a rewriting of *Thalaba*'s allegorical narrative that was also an attempt on Southey's part to redefine himself as a patriot poet and to re-familiarize the verse epic. *Roderick* is a poem that stages 'anxieties of empire', nonetheless, and contemporary works by Wordsworth and Byron, I show in what follows, at times offer comparable perspectives on the condition that Southey in *Thalaba* diagnosed as 'imperial dotage'.[6] The remainder of this chapter focuses on Thomas Moore's *Lalla Rookh* (1817) as a long poem made possible by Orientalist epics such as *Thalaba* (as is evident in two of its constituent tales, 'The Veiled Prophet of Khorasan' and 'The Fire-Worshippers'), but which also – the Irish allegorical resonance of these tales notwithstanding – to a large extent sidesteps the political concerns of precursor works. In contrast to *Thalaba, Lalla Rookh* is a text in which poetic ornament is detached from concerns about Asiatic luxury (or about the ethics of importing literary treasure), and bound up instead with a 'Regency Orientalist' culture of aristocratic magnificence and splendour. In the larger context of this study's focus on the relationship between Britain's imperial interests and Britons' cultural horizons, I discuss *Lalla Rookh* as a poem that recuperated verse romance as popular entertainment, albeit that its 're-enchantment' of the East, which many found so consumable, also sparked a significant critical backlash.

Thalaba the Revolutionary Destroyer

The question posed at *Thalaba*'s beginning, 'Who at this untimely hour/ Wanders o'er the desert sands?' (1.11–12), draws attention to the work's sense of its own difference from a 'desert' narrative such as D'Israeli's 'Mejnoun and Leila', in which the male protagonist Kais wanders alone after being separated from his lover. This question further establishes *Thalaba*'s departure from *Gebir*, because Thalaba – at this point accompanied by his mother, Zeinab – is a Bedouin youth and a Muslim, who may thus have been assimilated by readers to the prophet Mohammed. Though presented as a solitary figure rather than as the leader of a movement, Thalaba is the bearer of a revolutionary energy as he campaigns against the magicians of the Domdaniel caverns who had been responsible for his father's death. When he prays for strength to enable him to work God's will, 'and from the world/ Root up the ill-doing race' (3:178; XII:11–12), Thalaba identifies himself as a radical in the literal sense of the word. He also more specifically signals his Jacobin affiliations, since, desiring to be 'of all selfish passions purified' (3:178; XII:10), he channels, in Gregory Dart's words, 'Southey's belated enthusiasm for neo-Spartan principles'.[7]

Thalaba may be read as displacing Southey's political sympathies of the 1790s, then, although, like *Gebir*, it resists clear-cut allegorical construction. Thalaba is to some extent a Robespierrian figure, and the poem presents him combating superstition as well as luxury, as in book seven, for example, when, 'rooting up' the magician Aloadin's paradise garden, he vanquishes an enemy who had promised 'eternal joys' (3:110; VII:234) to the multitude following him; rewriting the idea of a 'smiling' Oriental garden, this episode underscores again *Thalaba*'s departure from the romance tradition recovered by Ouseley. If Aloadin's garden thus allegorizes a regime blinding its subjects into obedience, however, the depiction of the agents of temptation that Thalaba encounters sometimes calls to mind the anti-Jacobin caricature of insinuating radicals, as when another magician, Lobaba, attempts to divert Thalaba from his appointed task. Portrayed in a manner reminiscent of Milton's Satan, Lobaba here associates the promise of 'knowledge' with individual fulfilment and this-worldly pleasure, declaring that 'the powers which Allah/ Granted to man, were granted for his use' (3:65; IV:305–6).

One measure of *Thalaba*'s political complexity is the way in which the initial opposition between 'pure' desert and 'corrupt' garden becomes less straightforward as the work develops. At the outset, the hero comes across the figure of Aswad, who tells of how the ancient Arabian King Shedad planned 'A mighty work ..., / Here in the wilderness to form'(3:13; I: 227–8). Southey here sets up a defining contrast between the primitive Islam of Thalaba, for whom the desert is the anchor of his identity, and the 'Oriental' decadence represented by Shedad's grand designs. This distinction between simplicity and corruption structures much of the poem, as when Thalaba refers to his sharing of 'desert joys!' (3:108; VII:162) with his 'Arabian maid' Oneiza, and when prior to this, faced with the confusing spectacle of 'unveiled women' enticing him to 'merry-make with them' (3:101; VI:388–9) in Aloadin's paradise, he imaginatively transports himself to 'Deserts of Araby' (3:102; VI:393) to escape temptation. Elsewhere, however, desert wilderness stands for barrenness and vacancy as well as moral purity. Southey referred to 'the deserts that, to the disgrace of man, occupy so great a part of the world' in a letter of 1800, and in book five, after an account from the present of the now 'fallen' city of Baghdad, the poem looks ahead to when 'the Crescent from thy Mosques/ Be plucked by Wisdom, when the enlightened arm/ Of Europe conquers to redeem the East' (3:76; V:84–86).[8] This appeal to European powers of 'redemption' suggests that 'the East' might at once be freed from Islam's yoke and reclaimed for improvement. While *Thalaba* presents Babylon's 'imperial dotage' (3:78; V:134) in terms of a familiar discourse of luxury, it also demonstrates that its critique of Oriental corruption is compatible with the idea of an alternative imperial dispensation that would fill the blank spaces it evokes.

Southey's account of desert wilderness caught the attention of contem-poraries including Percy Shelley, whose tale fragment *The Assassins* (1814) and poems *Alastor* (1816) and 'Ozymandias' (1818) can be seen to present different Eastern spaces as 'empty', and thus potentially available for a colonization that also fulfilled revolutionary ideals of liberty.[9] For Shelley as for Southey,

Volney's polemic *The Ruins* (1791) spelt out the 'instruction' afforded by the desolation of the territory where glorious civilizations once flourished, and in his unpublished essay *A Philosophical View of Reform* (written in 1819–20) Shelley invoked 'the deserts of Asia Minor and of Greece' in an analogous manner to Southey in his letter to May.[10] The ironic self-consciousness of Shelley's imaginative writing means that it cannot be reduced to allegory, however, because even as *Alastor* sets up the idea of a 'ruined' and depopulated East it details how the 'Alastor-poet' is consumed by his own solitary endeavour. While there is no comparable broaching of transcultural desire in *Thalaba*, Southey's poem in a similar way undercuts any notion of civilizing improvement, since its hero is aware that his final triumph over his enemies also means his own end, as 'all [are] crushed' (3:192; XII:500) by the Domdaniel caverns' collapse. In a letter to Coleridge in 1799, after Napoleon's takeover in France, Southey stated: 'There wanted a Lycurgus after Robespierre, a man loved for his virtue, and bold, and inflexible and who should have levelled the property of France, and then would the Republic have been immortal, and the world ... revolutionized by example.'[11] With this analysis of contemporary politics in view, *Thalaba* appears both to stage Robespierre's uncompromising destructiveness and to register the 'want' of reformist agency in his wake: emphatically aligning deliverance and death, the poem is unable to represent a law-giving successor to its hero in the mould of the legendary Spartan.

Thalaba's proto-imperial politics are further complicated by the passage following Southey's digression about Europe's 'enlightened arm', when the poem imagines Baghdad's one-time 'Pomp', when 'The Merchants of the East and of the West/ Met in her arched Bazars', and 'Tigris on his tameless current bore/ Armenian harvests to her multitudes' (3:76; V:87–96). While commemorating the Abbasid Caliphate's 'Augustan' era, this passage's reference to a cosmopolitan congregation of traders and its georgic vision of river traffic respectively call up the twin symbols of London's boasted status as the hub of global commerce, the Royal Exchange and the Thames; a similar analogy is drawn when Lobaba tells Thalaba about Babylon's centripetal attraction as a city where 'from all the world/ Industrious merchants meet, and market ... / The World's collected wealth' (3:57; IV: 91–3). In paralleling Baghdad, Babylon and London, Southey implicated modern Britain in his account of the rise and fall of empire. *Thalaba*'s reference to Babylon is especially suggestive, since its 'imperial dotage' could at once be understood as the function of universally applicable laws of progress and decay, and, in line with contemporary millenarian rhetoric, as an impending fate facing Britain in particular. Southey wrote to John

May in 1797 that Britain was in the grip of an incurable contagion, as if it were a 'lazar-house ... that infects all within its atmosphere', and a discourse of commerce as infection continued to pervade Southey's work long after he ceased to identify with the radical cause.[12]

Ornament and Otherness

While one gauge of *Thalaba*'s political complexity is its ambivalent representation of desert wilderness, then, another is its combination of an enlightenment critique of superstition with a narrative of revolution as destruction identifying immanent decay within any advanced commercial society. The poem certainly confounded many critics, although this had less to do with its politics than with its lack of 'outside' perspective on the world it depicted: the *Monthly Magazine*, for example, presented *Thalaba* as a work that was 'marvellous' to a fault, where 'every incident is a miracle; every utensil, an amulet; every speech, a spell; every personage, a god; or rather a talismanic statue; of which destiny and magic overrule the movements, not human hopes and fears.'[13] Francis Jeffrey in the *Edinburgh Review* acknowledged that Southey produced 'vouchers', via his footnotes, for the poem's prodigies, and Southey imagined himself as a 'refiner' of his diverse raw materials: in an early note, he stated that '[a] waste of ornament and labour characterises all the works of the Orientalists,' and that the *Arabian Tales* which provided him with a source had been purged of 'metaphorical rubbish' by 'passing through the filter of a French translation' (3:194).[14] Southey also drew attention to *Thalaba*'s stylistic eclecticism, however, declaring in his preface that he chose an irregular rhythm for the poem as 'the *Arabesque* ornament of an Arabian tale' (3:3). If Southey responded to Jones's call for novelty in British poetry, he sought to rejuvenate modern verse in a more fundamental way than Jones had anticipated, experimenting both at the level of content and formal and metrical alternatives to Jones's neoclassical poetics; this – to some – inherently suspect innovation further explains critical hostility towards the work.[15]

Southey was concerned to be judged not just as a 'refiner', therefore, but as a literary pioneer in his own right. His seemingly contradictory references to a characteristically 'Oriental' 'waste of ornament' and to the '*Arabesque* ornament' with which he adorned his own work exemplify what has often been seen as the conflicted project of his epics from *Thalaba* onwards, namely that their main texts appear dependent on what their paratexts discredit. These references to 'ornament' are additionally significant since they differently frame the idea of 'Oriental' décor in terms of both a civic discourse which repudiates the corrupting effects of Asiatic luxury and a consumerist discourse which assumes the ready availability of the world's resources. Southey substantiated his disparagement of 'the works of the Orientalists' by recalling his own experience of intricately yet meaninglessly patterned objects popularly associated with the East: 'I have seen illuminated Persian manuscripts . . ., every page painted, not with representations of life and manners, but usually like the curves and lines of a Turkey carpet, conveying no idea whatever, as absurd to the eye as nonsense-verses to the ear' (3: 194). Reviewers of *Thalaba* sometimes also observed, however, that the poem was itself, in Jeffrey's words, an assemblage of 'disproportioned and injudicious ornaments' deriving from its author's 'imitation, or admiration of Oriental imagery'.[16] Addressing 'the materiality of Oriental discourse' in Southey's work, Diego Saglia discusses the way in which – at odds with Thalaba's own austerity – Southeyan Orientalism was embedded in an 'East of things'.[17] One rich example of Southey's imaginative engagement with this materiality is an 1801 letter to Coleridge, in which he playfully imagined the gustatory pleasures of an Eastern Grand Tour: 'if you and yours were with me, eating dates in a garden at Constantinople [we] would drink Cyprus wine and Mocha coffee, and smoke more tranquilly than ever we did in the Ship on Small Street.'[18]

Writing to William Taylor in 1805, Southey offered a more fantastical vision of imaginary travel, stating that '[y]ou will see my Hippogryff touch at Hindostan, fly back to Scandinavia, and then carry me among the fire-worshippers of Istakhar.'[19] Southey was famously ambitious in his writing plans, and his aspiration to produce an epic 'upon every poetic faith' appears to demonstrate the kind of 'imperial' ambition evident in Jones's 1784 'Discourse'.[20] The footnotes that Southey attached to his poems might in turn be seen to provide readers with an Olympian perspective comparable to that of his letter to Taylor. When focusing on Southey's 'command' of his materials, however, it is important to keep in mind the potentially fluid relation between narrative and annotation in these works. *Thalaba*'s opening episode gives an instructive example of this when the hero's mother invokes Job in her attempts to manage her grief, and Southey's note declares first that 'there can be no impropriety in making a modern Arab speak like an ancient one,' then that '[i]t had been easy to have made Zeinab speak from the Koran, if the tame language of the Koran could be remembered by the few who have toiled through its dull tautology.' For all that Southey's reference to the Koran is derisive, the interplay between note and text, as David Simpson argues, 'scrambles' the opposition between Christianity and Islam.[21] Southey's claim that the resignation associated with Job is 'particularly inculcated by Mohammed' emphasizes the proximity between the two faiths, with his subsequent point about resignation as 'the vice of the East' (3:193) being instantiated by the sublime Book of Job that Zeinab cites as much as by the 'dull' Koran.

While Southey was drawn to a material 'East of things', then, *Thalaba* also pursues an intellectual project exploring – again after Jones's example – the affinities and resemblances between different systems of worship and belief. Together with the poem's main text, Thalaba's notes offered a fund of possibilities for later writers: Marilyn Butler, for example, argues that Southey's 'anthropological' note on vampire legend 'fed or even created' the fascination with vampires evident in Byron's *The Giaour* (1813) and subsequent works.[22] Here, though, I want above all to emphasize, as others have, the significance of the great quantity and variety of annotation in *Thalaba*. Southey's notes often occupy more of the page than the text that they supplement, accumulating so as to constitute a mass of 'unrefined' information, drawn from heterogeneous sources. This information may be encyclopaedic in bulk and scope, but it provides readers neither with a proto-imperial position of objective knowledge, nor with 'consumer'-style access to pleasurable novelty. If Southey's letter to Taylor is suggestive of a facility of imaginary movement across the globe, *Thalaba's* notes 'ground' Southey's readers in a thickness of detail that is not straightforwardly compatible with any such survey mode. After citing Purchas (of 'Kubla Khan' fame) in his note on Aloadin's 'Paradise of Sin', Southey states that the story has been 'told by so many writers and with such difference of time and place, as wholly to invalidate its truth, even were the circumstances more probable' (3:259). Nonetheless, he references some of these writers anyway, as if to substantiate Simpson's point that *Thalaba's* notes invariably initiate 'an infinitely regressing pursuit of sufficient knowledge' rather than providing authoritative explanation.[23]

Southey's notes often explore forms of cultural comparison in a manner broadly analogous to Jones's writings. Whereas the comparative method of Jones is readily assimilable to a universalizing humanist vision, however, it is more difficult to incorporate the materials gathered by Southey into any such account of an inter-connected world. Instead, *Thalaba* might be seen to instantiate Schwab's 'dark sublime' by staging for its readers a 'significant otherness' too rich and multifarious to be available for easy comprehension or consumption. For this reason, Simpson reads *Thalaba* as the bearer of a 'prospective cosmopolitanism' that expands readerly horizons but refuses to make over the strange to the familiar.[24] Southey's notes participate in a process of 'foreignizing', Simpson argues, by 'taking over the page and claiming the typographic space as their own,' as 'what is supposed to become adjunct suddenly becomes primary.'[25] While we can only speculate as to how far readers may have been disorientated by this interplay of text and notes, *Thalaba*'s reviewers acknowledged the challenge that the poem thus presented, even if they did not respond to its demands. Southey retained this method of composition in his subsequent epics, although in *Roderick, the Last of the Goths*, he also rewrote *Thalaba*'s allegorical verse narrative as he sought more directly to work upon his audience.

Rousing the Reader

While *The Curse of Kehama*, like *Thalaba*, might be regarded as 'prospectively cosmopolitan', extending the Jonesian project of cultural translation, Southey's attempt to mediate Hindu culture for his readers was – unlike Jones's – widely viewed as a resounding failure. More obviously than *Thalaba*, *Kehama* reads like a poem divided against itself, demonstrating in its preface and notes Southey's increasing proximity to the evangelical lobby that campaigned to promote Christianity in India, yet displaying at points in its main narrative a fascination with Hinduism as a belief system as well as a fund of literary novelty. For numerous reviewers, Southey's rendering of Hindu mythology constituted an otherness beyond the possibility of assimilation; only if *Kehama* were 'translated into *Hindostanee*', the *Monthly Mirror* declared, would Southey 'obtain readers, who reverence and adore his deities'.[26] In another often-cited review, the Baptist minister John Foster offered a similarly definitive judgement on the 'utter desperateness' of Southey's project of incorporating Hindu mythology into British poetry.[27] The syncretism implicit in *Thalaba*'s opening scene went more or less unnoticed by critics, who were perhaps ready to accept the idea of affinities between Christianity and Islam. The suggestion of common ground between Christianity and Hinduism was another matter, however, and while the idea of such compatibility underpinned the evangelical project, it could not be entertained (so Foster argued) by a 'native poet' in 'the most Christianized country of Europe'.[28] Foster's analogy between Southey's work and 'a fine British fleet' returning from India with excrement from 'the lama of Tibet' frames Britain's connection with India as a potentially corrupting one, and extends the register of contamination to its limit. While Foster's analogy is calculated to accentuate the 'ludicrous' nature of the poem itself, it additionally provides a striking illustration of early nineteenth-century 'anxieties of empire', portraying the 'British fleet' not as the nation's 'wooden walls' but as the conduit of moral pollution.[29]

Southey staged such fears of 'the swamping of English propriety by grotesque oriental forms' in not dissimilar terms in his imaginary travelogue, *Letters from England* (1807).[30] He moreover appears to have anticipated *Kehama*'s hostile reception, as is evident in his acknowledgement that the work was 'too strange' to be successful, and in his handling of the subject matter of *Roderick, the Last of the Goths* (1814), begun well before *Kehama* was published.[31] Offering a long history of the Reconquest of Spain and thereby allegorizing the Peninsular War of 1808–14, *Roderick* is emphatically concerned with the attempt to forge an integral nationhood via the purging of foreign contamination. If *Roderick* may thus be understood as an exorcism of *Kehama*, however, I want to suggest that, above all in its representation of Islam, it rewrites *Thalaba* too. While *Thalaba* explores the theological continuities between Southey's own nonconformity and early Islam, *Roderick* is structured around a holy war between Spanish Christians and North African Muslims. Read alongside Southey's previous long poems, *Roderick* – at least at the level of its main text – thus familiarizes the experimental genre that he had helped to pioneer.

On its publication, *Roderick* was in some ways belated as well as derivative, its approach to the conflict in Spain overlapping with that of other authors – whether in portraying the patriot cause in chivalric terms (as Felicia Hemans did in 'England and Spain' [1808]), or adopting the traditional story that the eighth-century Moorish invasion of Iberia had been 'invited' by Count Julian, in revenge for the rape of his daughter Florinda by the Gothic king, Don Roderick (the basis of Scott's *The Vision of Don Roderick* [1811] and Landor's *Count Julian* [1812]). Southey's engagement with the history of Spain predated the war, however, and was considerably more detailed than that of his contemporaries. Southey demonstrated greater interest in the Moorish presence in Spain than they did, moreover, and this was an interest that for him went well beyond depicting Moors as proxies for Napoleon's armies.

Southey's *Chronicle of the Cid* (1808), a translation from Spanish of three biographies of the warrior-hero El Cid, illuminates the shift in his treatment of Islam from *Thalaba* to *Roderick*. In its introductory narrative of the rise of Islam, Mohammed is described as an empire-builder whose ambition was such that he accommodated himself to some of the degraded customs and manners he encountered. Southey's identification of Mohammed as an 'impostor', and his related claim that the prophet 'effected a revolution which ... still keeps in barbarism' large parts of the world, might be understood in terms of his attempt to distance himself from his earlier religious and political heterodoxy. His account of the prophet as a figure aiming 'only at his own aggrandizement' also presents Mohammed not as the inspiration for Thalaba but as a figure wanting in idealism by comparison. Instead of being an uncompromising 'destroyer' of corruption and immorality, Mohammed made no attempt to remodel the 'fabric of society'. 'The continuance of polygamy was his great and ruinous error,' Southey added, since 'where this pernicious custom is established, there will be neither connubial, nor paternal, nor brotherly affection: and hence the unnatural murders with which Asiatic history abounds. The Mahommedan imprisons his wives, and sometimes knows not the faces of his own children; he believes that despotism must be necessary in the state, because he knows it to be necessary at home.'[32]

This typifying reference to 'the Mahommedan' suggests that for Southey by this time Islam was a much less congenial – more essentially 'Eastern' – faith than it had been a decade earlier. Whereas in *Thalaba* Southey implicitly distinguished between 'primitive' and 'established' Islam, here the revolution initiated by Mohammed is assimilated to other – unspecified – 'Oriental revolutions', collectively likened to 'the casting [of] a stone into a stagnant pool', following which 'the surface is broken' only for 'green weeds [to] close over it again'. Another instructive instance of Southey's attempt to distance himself from *Thalaba* here is his ridicule of fatalism, now presented as a 'stupid patience' rather than, as is in *Thalaba*, a potentially noble stoicism in the face of God's will.[33] Especially striking for the modern reader is Southey's appeal to a 'clash of civilizations' rhetoric to accentuate the world-historical significance of past resistance to Moorish expansionism in Europe. In describing how the Cordoban Emir Abderrahman 'collected a prodigious army, and burst into France', Southey declared that '[t]he cause of civilized society has never been exposed to equal danger, since the Athenians preserved it at Salamis.'[34] Southey's reference to the Athenian defeat of Persian forces equates 'civilised society' with Europe, and his naming of Charles Martel, victor at Tours in 732, as the saviour of 'Christendom' just as directly presents Christianity as defining modern European civilization, even as the ongoing war on the continent belied any such notion of a unified Europe.

Southey identified the topicality of the rhetoric of holy war in a letter to Grosvenor Charles Bedford, telling him that the allied resistance in Spain was 'a crusade on the part of us and the Spaniards'; 'I love and vindicate the crusades,' he added.[35] Other poets similarly imagined the Peninsular War in such terms, but Southey went further than contemporaries, as is evident both in *Roderick*'s representation of scenes of conflict and its recuperation of crusading idealism. If Mohammed was, for Southey, 'inspired by no fanaticism', Roderick is energized by a Thalaba-like righteousness, from the moment when, at the outset of his penance for the rape of Florinda, he prays to be pointed towards 'Some new austerity, unheard of yet/ In Syrian fields of glory, or the sands/ Of holiest Egypt'.[36] This invocation of desert virtue recalls *Thalaba*, but Roderick's reference to a 'new austerity' also emphasizes the revision that the work enacts upon its precursor, as well as its rejection of the Oriental 'ornament' that critics found in it. Roderick imagines that he will 'barefoot seek Jerusalem' (2:27; II:151), and the poem indeed presents the beginning of the Reconquest of Spain as a kind of proto-crusade, because when the disguised Roderick addresses Pelayo, future founder of the Spanish monarchy, he urges him '[t]o wage heredi-tary holy war' until 'not one living enemy pollute/ The sacred soil of Spain' (2:102; XII:185, 187–8). Roderick denounces the Moorish yoke earlier in the same speech, referring to 'an impious foe/ [who] brings with him strange laws,/ Strange language, evil customs, and false faith' (2:102; XII:167–9), and a racialized discourse of contamination pervades the whole poem, with the Moorish hordes repeatedly likened to 'locusts' or 'vultures', flocking to 'that free feast which in their Prophet's name/ Rapine and Lust proclaim'd' (2:150; XX:13–14).

Even as Southey conceived of the peninsular conflict as a holy war, his frame of reference remained cosmopolitan. The antiquarian and scholarly detail of the poem's notes to some extent offsets the bellicosity of its main text, which itself testifies to other forms of social contact shadowing its main story of invasion and resistance. Though Count Julian refers to 'that liberty/ Of faith ... which the Prophet's law,/ Liberal as Heaven from whence it came, to all/ Indulges' (2:156; XX:247–50), however, *Roderick* affords little space to representing the tolerance alluded to here, and instead stresses the irreducible antagonism between mutually hostile camps. While the later history of Moorish Andalucía is now often elegized as a period of rich intercultural exchange, *Roderick* presents 'collaboration', as exempli-fied by Orpas, the former Archbishop of Seville, as an essentially treasonous consorting with the enemy. Boundary-crossing female characters such as Roderick's Queen, Egilona (who becomes 'chief' of the Moorish governor Abdalaziz's wives) are especially stigmatized because they 'combine sexual, national, and religious treachery'.[37]

The poem acknowledges that the Goths had themselves once been invaders, constituting one of many foreign yokes beneath which, as

Bishop Urban declares, 'the sons/ Of Spain have groan'd' (2:52; IV:268–9). Southey sought to circumvent the reality that Spain was always already impure, however, by displacing this impurity onto the Moorish other, and by presenting Pelayo as a figure capable of unifying the nation. In this imagining of nationhood, Southey made particular use of a gendered language of fall and redemption. Bedford stated in the *Quarterly Review* that he regarded the female patriot Adosinda – 'one of the few unhistorical figures in the poem', Saglia notes – as 'the person next in importance' to Roderick himself, because 'the evidence of her sufferings operates as a powerful call upon him to revenge them.'[38] Adosinda is the antithesis of sexual collaborators such as Egilona, and her account of slaughtering the Moor who had looked at her with 'libidinous eyes' (3:43; III:319) works 'like a spell' upon Roderick, reviving in him '[t]he pride and power of former majesty/ … but changed and purified' (3:44; III:361 and 370–1). The Moorish lust that Adosinda refers to here recapitulates Southey's claims about 'the Mahommedan' as a tyrant towards women (Roderick's act of rape, by contrast, is later presented as something for which Florinda blames herself). Adosinda recognizes that her display of patriotism 'rouses' Roderick, and the graphic violence of her tale of pre-emptive vengeance is subsequently reprised throughout the poem, as Spain regains its masculine virility in righteous conflict.

While Jeffrey in the *Edinburgh* expressed his distaste for its violence, it may have been precisely such violence that made others appreciate *Roderick* as an especially stirring work. Charles Lamb wrote that he regarded *Roderick* as 'a comfortable poem' which provided a 'firm footing' for the reader, because of the clarity of its opposition between 'Moors' and 'Christians'.[39] For John Taylor Coleridge in the *British Critic*, meanwhile, *Roderick* provided a welcome counter to the lack of 'enthusiasm in the character of the present age', and a reminder of the true '*chivalrous spirit*'. Coleridge added that, after his previous epics' mixed reception, Southey 'stands extorting respect from the scorner, and honourable acquittal from the judge', and he thus presented *Roderick* as a vindication of its author as well as its title character.[40] Part of *Roderick*'s initial appeal also stemmed from the fact that its narrative trajectory allegorized Britain's triumph over France after more than two decades of war. *Roderick*, as Saglia argues, 'avoids negotiations about the result of the conflict or the effective quality of Spanish patriotism which characterize the debate on the Peninsular War' – considerations informing Jeffrey's review – and instead offers 'confidence in victory, [and] a firm answer to the Whig "doctrine of doubt"'.[41] It is structured in a similar manner to Southey's earlier poems, but in contrast to *Thalaba*, the corruption that its hero fights is now figured as broadly Muslim, while the moral virtue by which he is energized is both Christian – albeit that Southey plays down the Catholicism of his Spanish characters – and patriotic in content. *Roderick* perhaps most clearly rewrites *Thalaba* by presenting its title character's agency as ultimately restorative rather than destructive. Roderick 'the Avenger' is modelled on Thalaba, and in the poem's final battle scene he is depicted, like Thalaba, as a figure 'seeking death' (2:203; XXV:563). Significantly, however, whereas Thalaba's asexual virtue only finds consummation in his own death, Roderick is an example to others, such as the future king Alphonso, who at the close is portrayed as '[r]ejoicing like a bridegroom in the strife' (2:193; XXV:175). If the poem could be seen as embodying a good 'enthusiasm', as John Taylor Coleridge put it, then, this was not a revolutionary fervour but rather a reinvigorating stimulus providing an antidote to 'imperial dotage'.

England in 1814

Roderick's 'renovatory' project is further illuminated when it is considered alongside Byron's *The Giaour* (1813). In a note regarding the fisherman's curse on the Giaour after his slaying of Emir Hassan, Byron refers to *Thalaba*'s notes on vampire superstition, while adding first-person testimony as to his own personal knowledge of the East. The curse itself more substantially engages with Southey, serving as, in Marilyn Butler's words, 'the analogue and answer to Southey's version of a Hindu curse in *Kehama*' (a poem which begins with the Rajah Kehama's curse on the Thalaba-like peasant Ladurlad, after he had killed the Rajah's son).[42] Byron obliquely intervened in the debate on the renewal of the EIC charter, responding to evangelical clamour for a 'pious clause' that would permit missionaries to operate in the subcontinent. He alluded to the long-running controversy about the customary practice of sati (the essence of Indian barbarity in evangelical discourse), and his poem's undercutting of its Venetian protagonist's heroism is key to its critical interrogation of missionary propaganda. Hassan's drowning of his harem slave Leila was done 'in the Mussulman manner', the Advertisement states, but after juxtaposing 'Muslim' barbarity and righteous 'European' revenge, the poem calls into question any idea of a 'Christian' moral superiority separating European men from their Eastern counterparts, most obviously when the Giaour admits that he would have acted no differently from Hassan had roles been reversed.[43] Even as the Giaour's fidelity to the memory of Leila differentiates him from Hassan, the poem presents the Giaour and Hassan as subscribing to the same code of masculine honour.[44]

The Giaour tells his story to a Christian friar who is presented in strikingly unsympathetic terms. An earlier note declares by implicit contrast that 'Charity and Hospitality are the first duties enjoined by Mahomet; and ... very generally practised by his disciples,' and in *The Giaour* as in the second canto of *Childe Harold's Pilgrimage* (1812), Byron's notes bear witness to the awe-inspiring spectacle of Muslim devotion.[45] One index of the way in which Southey's *Roderick* both rewrites the story of Byron's hero and responds to Byron's broadly respectful engagement with Islam is that from the beginning, when the monk Romano tells Roderick that never 'Hath such a contrite and a broken heart/ Appear'd before me' (2:21; I:216–17), it recuperates the concepts of confession and penance that *The Giaour* ironizes. Whereas *The Giaour* rejects the association of violence and redemption, because its hero remains a tortured figure, *Roderick* restores this connection, presenting its protagonist's bellicosity not just as atoning for his own sins but as inspiring others too. At the same time, *Roderick* endorses the crusading rhetoric that is treated with sceptical distance in *The Giaour*, where the poem's hero identifies himself as the killer of a 'Paynim' but nonetheless fails to find absolution, because he does not seek it.[46] Contemporaries complained that Byron's incorporation of Turkish voices served to 'other' the European hero – the Turkish term 'Giaour' might be seen as an equivalent to 'Paynim' – and, alluding to the fisherman's curse, the *New Review* declared its shock at hearing 'a raging turbaned-Turk ... calling a Christian infidel'.[47] Reviewers additionally complained about Byron 'disfiguring his pages with words that are not English', and such reaction to *The Giaour*'s provocation of its audience throws into relief Lamb's praise of *Roderick* as 'a comfortable poem'.[48] Lamb could inform Southey that he felt 'at home' in *Roderick* because its story of historical enmity between 'Moors' and 'Christians' was so reassuringly familiar, and so unambiguously offered a parable for the present.[49]

Addressing *Roderick*'s allegorical resonance, Tom Duggett argues that 'the redemptive plot of Roderick returning from exile to assist the "native" Pelayo invites ... [a] reading in which Roderick represents a formerly sinful Britain that now brings a fresh access of "Gothic Virtue" to Spain.'[50] What complicates Southey's representation of renovatory agency, however, is that while Roderick is an example to others, his status as 'last of the Goths' draws attention to the potentially precarious nature of 'Gothic virtue'. In an end note relating to the poem's scene-setting opening passage about how the Moorish yoke 'oppress'd and gall'd/ The children of the soil' (2:13; I:6–7) in Spain, Southey wrote that the invasion had been possible because the Spanish had 'ceased to be a warlike people': 'Habits of settled life seem throughout Europe to have effeminated the northern conquerors, till the Normans renovated the race, and the institutions of chivalry and the crusades produced a new era' (2:211). Southey's reference to the idea of Norman 'renovation' rather than to a despotic Norman yoke is continuous with his disavowal of his earlier radicalism, as he styled himself anew as a patriotic poet. In another respect, though, this claim that 'settled life' brought about a corruption that in turn demanded reform serves to demonstrate the consistency of Southey's political vocabulary from *Thalaba* to *Roderick* and beyond, since he once again alluded here to the seeming inevitability of decay in any developed society. That Southey understood 'renovation' with reference to distant historical – 'Gothic' or 'Norman' – precedent offers a perhaps surprising point of convergence between *Roderick* and *The Giaour*, which from the outset accentuates the gulf between a golden age of virtue associated with Themistocles (like Roderick, leader of the resistance to an 'Eastern' invasion) and the debased, unheroic present. Southey, unlike Byron, identified recent examples of heroic action, and in his *Life of Nelson* (1813) he described the 'glorious' death of the celebrated admiral in terms very similar to those that he would use to depict the death of Roderick. Nonetheless, even as Southey participated in the commemorative culture of empire, he continued to think with the concept of 'imperial dotage' broached in *Thalaba*.

Since modern commercial society tended towards 'dotage', and since renewal was necessarily short-lived and impermanent in its effects, in Southey's analysis, the process of national renovation had to be conceived of as constant. Influenced by Southey, Wordsworth in *The Excursion* (1814) addressed the question of national revival in a comparable way, and it is useful briefly to consider its exploration of the idea of an '*active* Principle', as articulated by the 'venerable Sage' at the beginning of book nine.[51] The poem argues for the necessity of state-sponsored education, 'so that none,/ However destitute, be left to droop/ By timely culture unsustained ... A savage horde among the civilised,/ A servile band among the lordly free!' (692; 9:303–10). In tandem with this vision of a national project of collective cultivation, the poem also suggests that Britain may need to 'cast off/ Her swarms' of surplus peoples so as 'to establish new communities/ On every shore whose aspect favours hope/ Or bold adventure' (693; 9:377–81). *The Excursion*'s final book thus offers an imperial narrative conjoining domestic and global civilizing missions. If it imagines the export of 'swarms' of surplus peoples, however, its reference to 'A savage horde among the civilized' (692; l.309) additionally signals its perception of the threat posed by the labouring classes within Britain itself. It is precisely because the poem presents this racialization of the poor in conditional terms – the danger is of them, without 'timely culture', *becoming* a 'savage horde' – that it also sees the nation's actual fulfilment of its 'glorious destiny' as such an urgent matter, 'needful to avert impending evil': 'The discipline of slavery is unknown/ Among us, – hence the more do we require/ The discipline of virtue; order else/ Cannot subsist, nor confidence, nor peace' (693; 9:351–4).

This sense of urgency informs Wordsworth's 'Essay, Supplementary to the Preface' (1815), a riposte to *The Excursion*'s critics in which Wordsworth returned to the question of authorial responsibility. The role of the poet was so important, he argued, because if the formative impact of a poem such as *The Excursion* was questionable, there was no doubt about the malign influence of bad poetry, especially upon young readers. Wordsworth's 'Essay, Supplementary' addresses the problem of a beguiled public, liable to 'run after' new works of 'popular' poetry 'as if urged by an appetite, or constrained by a spell!', and in the face of this susceptibility to dazzling novelty, it insists on the need to create a different taste that first requires a more self-disciplined audience to be brought into being.[52] This idea of the need for 'discipline' recalls *The Excursion*'s delineation of national imperatives, and distinguishes between an 'active' reading done by an audience whose taste has been 'invigorated and inspirited by [its] leaders' and the prevailing state of affairs in the literary marketplace. What is particularly significant for the current discussion is that the essay repudiates both 'absurdities, extravagances, and misplaced ornaments' and an explicitly Orientalized mode of passive reception – reading as sensual gratification – embodied by the figure of 'an Indian prince ... stretched on his palanquin, and borne by his slaves', who carry him 'like a dead weight'.[53]

Wordsworth probably had Byron's Turkish tales in mind here, and his sarcastic reference to readers 'thinking it proper that their understandings should enjoy a holiday' echoes Francis Jeffrey's less judgemental account of *The Bride of Abydos* and *The Corsair* as sources of imaginative recreation for readers who had become blasé about 'the pleasures of security'.[54] Referring to the 'westward' bias of his friend's writing, Barron Field later jested that Wordsworth wrote 'no oriental poems'.[55] The renowned 'Arab dream' passage in book five of *The Prelude* alludes to *Thalaba* (while making its solitary Bedouin lovelorn rather than a political agent), and in the same book the poet recollects his childhood encounter with the *Arabian Nights*. If Wordsworth thus signalled his sometime engagement with ideas of the East, though, he also subsequently produced critical rewritings of Byronic Orientalism, as for example in 'The Armenian Lady's Love' (1830), a revision of *The Corsair* in which the title character effects the escape from captivity of a Christian slave so that he can go home to his Medora-like wife. To return to the correspondence between Beattie and Montagu discussed in the previous chapter, it seems fair to say therefore that by the time of *The Excursion* and the 'Essay, Supplementary' Wordsworth envisioned primarily if not exclusively indigenous models for the revival of national literary culture. He credited Percy's *Reliques* (1765) with particular significance, both as a collection of 'native' balladry and as providing an instance of the kind of long-run impact that he sought to claim for his own writing: using a now familiar idiom, he stated that they 'absolutely redeemed' the nation's poetry.[56]

If Wordsworth identified Byron's Turkish tales as among those works 'which dazzle at first sight and kindle the admiration of the multitude', however, it is no less the case that Byron's poetry pre-emptively acknowledged the part it played in generating such corruption.[57] As Nigel Leask argues, Byron's Turkish tales are predicated on their heroes' transcultural desire for the East but also present this as a 'fatal attraction' that is corrosive of civic order and virtue.[58] If Byron would revisit such attraction more ironically in *Don Juan* (1819–24) especially, the poems to which Wordsworth responded offer their own distinctive staging of contemporary cultural anxieties just as much as *Roderick* or *The Excursion*.[59] While focusing on the Ottoman Near East, Byron's Turkish tales indirectly reflect on Britain's experience of Eastern empire, as, to cite Leask again, they acknowledge the nation's 'abandonment of an aristocratic, republican, civic, humanist heritage'.[60] For the present discussion, one particularly important difference of Byron's writing of the early 1810s from the works by Southey and Wordsworth cited earlier is that because it is so rooted in an understanding of honour and liberty as all but completely lost, it is unable to imagine redemptive possibility in the manner of *Roderick* or *The Excursion*: Byron's notes to *The Giaour* and *Childe Harold* often suggest that modern Greeks are too degraded to live up to the example of their heroic forbears. As already noted, Byron's Turkish tales insistently return to the scenario of 'frontier' contact that exposes the idea of principled activity as out of step with the modern world, and even – in the case of *Lara* (1814) – as itself corrupted beyond recognition.

It is useful briefly to consider *Lara* here, since while it can be read as depicting the problematic return home of Conrad or the Giaour, it additionally encroaches on the terrain of Southey's *Roderick*. Although *Roderick* had yet to be published when Byron completed *Lara*, it is an important intertext for Byron's poem because *Lara* employs a loosely Spanish setting and, more substantially, renders richly ambiguous the conditions of exile and homecoming that provide Southey's work with its narrative energy. Where Roderick becomes a Christian hero who in his crusading enthusiasm advances the campaign to purge Spain of an alien Moorish presence, the enigmatic Lara is personally transformed by his experience of the East, and also an agent of discord rather than unification in his native land, such that he helps to start a civil war. One tantalizing index of Lara's transformation is given after he collapses in the Gothic hall of his castle and speaks in a tongue that only his page Kaled can understand. The nature of Lara's implicitly homoerotic relation to Kaled remains unspecified, and it is no clearer either why Sir Ezzelin publicly accuses Lara of dishonourable conduct, or who it is that dumps Sir Ezzelin's corpse in a river prior to the duel that he had arranged to fight with Lara. This conclusion significantly alludes to Leila's drowning in *The Giaour*, however, in the process inviting us to recognize a trajectory of development in Byron's tales of 1813–14, as an act that is coded as 'Orientally' barbaric – the disposal of Sir Ezzelin's corpse after his clandestine murder – now takes place not in a distant frontier zone but in Europe itself.[61] In contrast to *Roderick*, violence is simply and straightforwardly brutal in *Lara*, without any larger purpose: 'What boots the oft-repeated tale of strife,/ The feast of vultures, and the waste of life?', the narrator states after the rising of Lara's serfs.[62] Having 'raised the humble but to bend the proud' by freeing his serfs, Lara is confirmed as lacking any Roderick-like motivation when, pointing east as if in the direction of 'some remember'd scene', he disdainfully rejects absolution just before he expires.[63] *Lara* has often been read as bringing this brilliant poetic sequence to a close, and in a much-cited letter of 1813 Byron in effect passed the baton of literary Orientalism to his friend Thomas Moore. I now focus on Moore's *Lalla Rookh* as a collection of verse narratives that largely sidesteps Byron's 'anxieties of empire'.

'The Finest Orientalism'

Byron advised Moore to 'Stick to the East' in his future writing, and dedicating *The Corsair* to Moore, Byron told his friend that his intended 'composition of a poem . . . laid in the East' would help him to emphasize the 'wrongs' of Ireland as much as India.[64] Moore's hugely successful *Irish Melodies* (1808–34) provided a template for the way in which Byron himself, in his *Hebrew Melodies* (1815), would identify with the suffering of the Jewish people and the condition of the modern Greeks, and indeed of all peoples dispossessed by the Congress of Vienna's redrawing of European territorial boundaries. While *Lalla Rookh*'s longest verse narratives are in the allegorical mode of Southey, however, the poem as a whole is politically more complex than has sometimes been claimed. As I argue in what follows, this complexity is evident in the way in which, against a backdrop of the apparent restoration of old regimes across Europe, so much of *Lalla Rookh* stages an 'Eastern' aristocratic splendour that rejects the 'austerity' of *Roderick* and instead recuperates the 'ornament' of *Thalaba*. Moore participated in the 'radical Orientalist' attack on the Prince Regent, but before he began to publish satires such as *Intercepted Letters* (1813), he had been part of his circle, attending his spectacular inauguration event at Carlton House in 1811; 'Nothing was ever half so magnificent; it was in *reality* all that they try to imitate in the gorgeous scenery of the theatre,' he wrote to his mother.[65] Hazlitt among others was cynical about how Moore sought to retain a sense of 'the intimacy of the great' well after he ceased to be 'familiar with Royalty'.[66] From its frame tale onwards, *Lalla Rookh* suggests that at the time of the work's production Moore may still have been absorbed in a culture of 'Regency Orientalism' (as most famously exemplified by the Royal Pavilion at Brighton), even as elsewhere he lampooned the Prince for the reactionary turn he took after rejecting his one-time Whig allies.

Moore's frame tale begins by situating the poem in 'the eleventh year of the reign of Aurungzebe'.[67] Although a footnote refers to how 'this hypocritical Emperor would have made a worthy associate of certain Holy leagues' (11), as if aligning the Mughal empire with European old regimes, Moore additionally associates him with a 'style of magnificent hospitality' (5) that is impressive even by Eastern standards. In a similar vein, it describes the Emperor's daughter Lalla Rookh as being 'more beautiful than Leila' or any other of the heroines who 'embellish the songs of Persia and Indostan' (6). This tale evokes an atmosphere of festive pageantry by describing the impending marriage, set to take place in the 'enchanting valley' (6) of Kashmir, between Lalla Rookh and the unnamed son of Abdalla, 'King of the Lesser Bucharia, a lineal descendant from the Great Zingis' (5). Readers are thus invited to consider this benign realm of romance in relation to the tragic Kashmiri episodes of *The Missionary* or *Alastor*. Moore's reference to the princess ascending 'the palankeen

prepared for her' (7) before travelling up country – recalling the carriage of
the 'Indian prince' in the 'Essay, Supplementary' – might be read as
a playful rejoinder to Wordsworth's critique of undisciplined reading.
The description of Feramorz, the young poet who accompanies the caval-
cade, holding 'a kitar; such as, in old times, the Arab maids . . . used to
listen to by moonlight in the gardens of the Alhambra' (18) similarly evokes
the idea of a passive, pleasure-seeking audience, as well as alluding to
a Moorish Spain very different from *Roderick*'s; the appeal to 'old times'
here affiliates *Lalla Rookh* with 'tales of the East' that predated Romantic
Orientalism. The differences between *Lalla Rookh* and Southey's epics are
also apparent from the outset at the level of the poem's – no less copious –
notes. *Lalla Rookh* cites many of the same sources as Southey in *Thalaba* or
Kehama, but its notes are subordinated to its main text and, as Simpson
states, 'do not open up arguments of their own or depart from the norm of
being largely illustrative'.[68] If the combination of text and notes in *Thalaba*
confronts readers with 'significant otherness', then *Lalla Rookh* appears to
present itself as an altogether more welcoming and undemanding work.

The starting point for the poem's first tale, 'The Veiled Prophet of
Khorassan', loosely set in the eighth century, is the revolt of its title
character Mokanna against the Abbasid Caliph Mahadi. Elevated by the
'blind belief/ of millions', Mokanna is a 'Prophet-Chief' who maintains
that the purpose of his silver veil is 'to hide from mortal sight/ His dazzling
brow, till man could bear its light' (19–20). Together with his eloquent
denunciation of the 'mockeries' of monarchical and priestly authority,
Mokanna's vision of a future 'reign of mind . . . on earth' clearly establishes
him as an agent of revolution. If he thus invokes a rhetoric of 'second birth'
(29), however, Mokanna is represented as a destroyer rather than
a reformer – a Robespierre but not a Lycurgus, to recall Southey's distinction – who vows to 'sweep [his] dark'ning, desolating way' (47), using man
as the 'instrument' of his evil ambition. The representation of Mokanna's
imposture is customarily read as offering a retrospect on the illusory
promise of the French Revolution, as well as, more topically, on the rise
and fall of Napoleon.[69] Even as he speaks the language of enlightenment,
Mokanna's actual goal is to prey on popular superstition and harness it to
his own ends: 'That Prophet ill sustains his holy call,' he states, 'who finds
not heav'ns to suit the tastes of all' (49).

Among Mokanna's followers are the warrior Azim, drawn to his
standard after returning from war against Byzantine forces, and his
former sweetheart Zelica, introduced as one of the prophet's 'chosen
maids' (30). Moore's representation of this 'once happy pair' (32)

provides another instance of the way in which his work departs from, even as in other respects it follows, *Thalaba*'s example, because their story provides a tonally ambiguous narrative surplus that confounds allegorical interpretation. Zelica is bound by oath into joining Mokanna's harem and her 'charnel-house' betrothal to the prophet alludes to the lurid subterranean scenes of *The Monk* (1796). Just as Lewis's work cynically accentuates the powerlessness of the victimized Antonia, so 'The Veiled Prophet' has Mokanna toy with Zelica: 'Thou'lt fly? – as easily may reptiles run', he tells her (57). Azim too, like Zelica, is depicted as a hapless figure, and his pursuit of Mokanna, once he is apprised of the impostor's crimes, has a blackly comic conclusion that makes a jest of his rage. While, like Thalaba, he is motivated by righteous feelings of vengeance, Azim finally succeeds only in killing the woman he loves, when, in a fatal consummation of their union, Zelica dons the dead Mokanna's veil and impales herself on Azim's spear during the tale's closing battle scene.

Moore's manipulation of his hero is especially evident in the extended temptation scene earlier in the poem, when Azim enters the chambers of Mokanna's harem in search of Zelica. 'Prepare thy soul, young Azim!', the poet-narrator declares at the start of this section of the tale, announcing a 'more perilous trial' now awaiting Azim than any that he had faced in Greece, as 'a dazzling host of eyes' replaces the 'phalanx' of 'Macedonian pikes' (64). Whereas Thalaba encounters and then flees from 'unveiled women' in Aloadin's paradise, the similarly unworldly Azim faces an all-round sensory assault from which it is almost impossible for him to escape. 'The Veiled Prophet' nods to *Thalaba* when the 'voluptuous place' (71) through which Azim wanders is likened to Shedad's palace, but if Moore's reference to 'the luxuries of that impious King' (70) might suggest a moralistic critique of overreaching excess, the intricate detail with which this luxury is evoked undercuts any such construction of it. As he begins to have his doubts about the prophet whose cause he has joined, Azim reminds himself that freedom flourishes in 'the bracing air/ Of toil, – of temperance' (71) rather than in the debilitating environment of the harem. His resolve soon fails, however, as we are told that 'ev'n while he defied/ This witching scene, he felt its witch'ry glide/ Through ev'ry sense' (72). If he begins this episode as a vigilant Thalaba-like figure, Azim involuntarily becomes a susceptible consumer of dazzling novelty. Having 'sunk upon a couch' and '[given] his soul up to sweet thoughts' (73), he is captivated by 'a group of female forms' (75) as they seductively perform to musical accompaniment. As others stare or sing, two 'lightsome maidens' are said to 'Chase one another, in a varying dance/ Of mirth and languor, coyness and advance' (79–80).

Ronan Kelly describes this episode's eroticism in terms of a cinematic idea of 'montage': *Lalla Rookh* provides 'vast crane-shot crowd scenes, starry close-ups on eyes, lips and jewels, and jump-cut editing throughout'.[70] In the context of the 'Regency Orientalism' referred to previously, Moore's distinctive production of aesthetic effects may also have a specific contemporary analogue in the architectural and interior decorative innovation of the Brighton Pavilion. The section of 'The Veiled Prophet' considered earlier is preceded by the frame tale's account of Lalla Rookh and her party camping overnight in a 'Royal Pavilion' which, like the structure designed by John Nash, generates pleasurable illusion from heterogeneous component parts: it is said to be surrounded by 'artificial sceneries of bamboo-work ... representing arches, minarets, and towers, from which hung thousands of silken lanterns, painted by the most delicate pencils of Canton' (61). Javed Majeed identifies Azim as a surrogate for the reader experiencing in the face of Oriental exoticism 'a mixture of puritanical distaste, and a desire to succumb irresponsibly to its soporific pleasures', and Azim's initially 'bewilder'd' response to the 'vast illuminated halls' of Mokanna's harem replicates the reaction of those visitors who disapproved of the Regent's frivolous architectural display.[71] *Lalla Rookh*'s reception history additionally demonstrates, however, that many approached Moore's work as if they were tourists visiting a literary palace of wonders. Canto five of Byron's *Don Juan* accentuates this aspect of *Lalla Rookh* when, alluding to the predicament of Azim in Mokanna's harem, it describes Juan in Gulbeyaz's palace being led 'room by room/ Through glittering galleries', before he encounters 'A dazzling mass of gems, and gold, and glitter,/ Magnificently mingled in a litter'.[72]

While some reviewers complained of its un-British gaudiness, *Lalla Rookh*'s rich and varied afterlife saw it adapted and excerpted in many different contexts, including that of lavish courtly spectacle. If the Brighton Pavilion was a product of 'the global circulation of elite and aristocratic cultures', as Greg M. Thomas states, the international appeal of Moore's poem was predicated on the existence of such a network.[73] Moore acknowledged this appeal in the preface to his 1841 *Poetical Works*, stating that a 'Divertissement' of 'Tableaux Vivans and songs' (xxiii) derived from *Lalla Rookh* had been performed at the Chateau Royal in Berlin in 1822, for the state visit of the Russian Grand Duke Nicholas, brother of and successor to Tsar Alexander I, who had helped to form the Holy Alliance in 1815.[74] With obvious satisfaction, Moore noted that the 'crowd of royal personages' present in Berlin played the parts not only of Aurungzebe, Lalla Rookh, Feramorz, and Fadladeen, but also of 'various denominations of Seigneurs et Dames de Bucharie, Dames de Cachemire, Seigneurs et Dames dansans a la Fete des Roses, &c' (xxiv). The extent to which Moore's poem came to be understood as embodying the idea of a fabulous Orient is further shown by the fact that it would become a reference point for travellers in India, when at their most enthusiastic to communicate the splendour of any (as they saw it) truly 'Eastern' scenes they witnessed: on first seeing the wives of the King of Oudh in 1828, for example, Fanny Parkes wrote that 'one was so beautiful, that I could think of nothing but Lalla Rookh in her bridal attire.'[75]

Moore incorporated reader response into his poem's frame tale, and via the interventions of the harem 'Chamberlain' Fadladeen, often seen as a figuring of Francis Jeffrey, he pre-emptively critiqued his own work. (Jeffrey described *Lalla Rookh* as 'the finest orientalism we have had yet', although this was an equivocal statement, since he regarded Moore's work, even more than Southey's *Thalaba*, as 'ornamental' to excess.)[76] At the end of the temptation scene discussed earlier, after Zelica has revealed herself to Azim as Mokanna's bride, it is Lalla Rookh's reaction that is recorded, however, as we are told that she 'could think of nothing all day but the misery of these two young lovers'; Moore also prefigures his frame tale's denouement here in noting that the Princess 'felt ... without knowing why, a sort of uneasy pleasure in imagining that Azim must have been just such a youth as Feramorz' (98). Lalla Rookh does not comment upon the allegorical narrative involving Mokanna (after the first section of the tale, she is likewise said to be 'occupied by the sad story of Zelica and her lover' [62]), and she responds throughout to Moore's work in a manner that is in keeping with its self-description as an 'Oriental Romance'.

Moore returned to Mokanna's revolt in the tale's final part, and in doing so depicted his hero Azim in the – to him – more congenial environment of 'streams of carnage' (109). Now defending the Caliph Mahadi against Mokanna's army, Azim turns the tide of battle in Roderick-like fashion, causing Mokanna to flee with Zelica; declaring that his banner shall remain '[t]he rallying sign of fraud and anarchy' (136), Mokanna then defiantly plunges into a bath of boiling acid, leaving Azim to avenge himself on an adversary who turns out to be his lover in disguise. The tale's politics are by this stage far from clear-cut, however, in part because Mokanna's followers are described as motivated by a sense of genuine 'oppression' in addition to misguided zeal. The ambiguity of the tale in this respect is thrown into relief when it is contrasted with Shelley's *The Revolt of Islam* (1818), sometimes read as a response to 'The Veiled Prophet'.[77] Shelley's Cythna parallels Zelica to the extent that she is captured and carried off by the Sultan Othman's men, then later raped, but where Moore's heroine is a cruelly tormented victim, Shelley's is an agent of revolution. If Zelica is captivated by the mystery of Mokanna's veil, Cythna proclaims the 'disenchanting' force of her own eloquence, stating that 'with strong speech I tore the veil that hid/ Nature, and Truth, and Liberty, and Love, – / As one who from some mountain's pyramid/ Points to the unrisen sun!'.[78] *The Revolt of Islam* stages the counter-revolutionary reaction against the uprising in Othman's capital, in a similar way to 'The Veiled Prophet', but even as it finally presents Laon and Cythna as martyrs to the cause of freedom, it frames its narrative of failed revolution in the larger context of a prefatory insistence that, in Marilyn Butler's paraphrase, 'the revolution is destined to repeat itself until it succeeds.'[79]

Considering 'The Veiled Prophet' alongside *The Revolt of Islam* alerts us to stylistic as well as political differences between the two works. The moral seriousness (and guarded optimism) of Shelley's conclusion, as Laon and Cythna are transported to another world, contrasts with the abrupt shift that takes place at the end of 'The Veiled Prophet', when we are informed that, after Azim's long vigil by the grave of his beloved, 'He and his Zelica sleep side by side' (142). The frame tale's account of the 'disappointments' that had befallen Fadladeen over the course of the wedding party's preceding journey provides a bathetic counterpoint to Azim and Zelica's tragic story, and the description of them at the same time maintains the 'ornamental' idiom that is characteristic of Moore's poem, and conspicuously absent from Shelley's. Following a reference to the failure of Fadladeen's couriers to 'secure ... mangoes for the Royal Table', for example, the narrator adds, with an absurdist attention to detail reminiscent of William Beckford's *Vathek*, that 'to eat any mangoes but those of Mazagong was, of course, impossible' (143). We are then told that 'in an unusual fit of liveliness', an elephant 'shattered ... to pieces' a set of 'fine antique porcelain' that was 'so exquisitely old, as to have been used under the Emperors Yan and Chun, who reigned many ages before the dynasty of Tang' (144). The place name 'Mazagong' and the proper names 'Yan and Chun' are footnoted by Moore, but there is perhaps something of Aravamudan's 'irresponsibility towards the cultural referent' here nonetheless, since these unfamiliar names remain detached from an explanatory context that would make them meaningful and instead signify only a generalized exotic opulence.[80]

While thus demonstrating that *Lalla Rookh* is embedded in an 'East of things', Moore's frame tale also has Fadladeen draw attention to the poem's status as a literary pastiche rooted in heterogeneous textual sources. Before being interrupted, Fadladeen states that to give his opinion of Feramorz's story, it would be 'necessary to take a review of all the stories that have ever [been written]' (145). As humourlessly literal-minded as Fadladeen shows himself to be here, he also pays tribute to the amount of reading undertaken by Moore as he built up his 'storehouse ... of illustration' (xvii) during the composition of *Lalla Rookh*. Fadladeen's later claim that the style of 'The Veiled Prophet' represents a pale imitation of the Persian masters more directly foregrounds the second-hand quality of Moore's work, its inability to rival 'the copious flow of Ferdosi, the sweetness of Hafez, [or] the sententious march of Sadi' (148). Even as Moore in this way avowed his reliance on source materials, however, he helped to develop a new kind of Orientalist aesthetic, characterized above all by the inclusivity – and, for the most part, accessibility – of its 'Eastern' reference.[81] Certainly, Moore offered 'samples of the finest Orientalism' (in Byron's phrase) without either the attendant recognition of the corrupting effects of Asiatic luxury that is sometimes apparent in Southey's *Thalaba*, or the self-accusation regarding complicity in a commercialized market-place that is evident in Byron's Turkish tales. If Fadladeen's function is to anticipate critical objection and therefore provide authorial disclaimers, as reviewers recognized, it is significant that when he harangues Feramorz, Lalla Rookh comes to the poet's defence, arguing that 'it is quite cruel that a poet cannot wander through his regions of enchantment, without having a critic for ever like the old Man of the Sea, upon his back!' (152).

Moore's princess here alludes to the fifth voyage of Sinbad in the *Arabian Nights* (where the Old Man of the Sea tricks a traveller into transporting him on his shoulders), and, revising Wordsworth's reference to the indolent 'Indian prince', she presents the figure of the critic rather than the palanquin-borne aristocrat as 'a dead weight' needing to be carried. Via the often stigmatized figure of the female reader (or in this case auditor), Moore therefore recuperates an idea of unsupervised, absorp-tive pleasure. As noted earlier, Moore inserted his poem into a story-telling tradition antecedent to Romantic Orientalism, not least by adopting a frame-tale structure which meant that Feramorz's tales could be under-stood by contemporaries as akin to 'poetical "Arabian Nights' Entertainments"'.[82] One of the most favourable reviews of *Lalla Rookh*, in the *Asiatic Journal*, praised the poem because it appeared to cater to an enduring appetite for the notion of an East seemingly detached from social reality, promising 'a renewal of the delicious moments of our childhood, when we first read those wondrous and golden tales'.[83] The tale of 'The Veiled Prophet' disappointed such expectations for this reviewer, as did 'The Fire-Worshippers'. As I now show, though, in 'The Fire-Worshippers' as well as in its two shorter verse narratives, 'Paradise and the Peri' and 'The Light of the Haram', *Lalla Rookh*'s combination of allegory and literary Orientalist enchantment both complicates its engagement with the politics of empire and offers its readers a consumable, because largely familiar, East.

Allegories of Empire: Moore, Ireland, India

At the end of 'Paradise and the Peri', *Lalla Rookh*'s second tale, Fadladeen once more criticizes Feramorz's story-telling, denouncing the poem as 'this flimsy manufacture of the brain, which in comparison with the lofty and durable monuments of genius, is as the gold filigree work of Zamara beside the eternal architecture of Egypt!'; directly rehearsing Wordsworth's argument against recent popular poetry, he also objects to the tale's 'lax and easy kind of metre' (86). Moore's story of the Peri's efforts to regain her place in heaven by offering gifts at its gates is less substantial than 'The Veiled Prophet', although it starkly refers to the pollution by 'human blood' of the 'sweet Indian land' that it describes, as 'man, the sacrifice of man,/ Mingled his taint with ev'ry breath/ Upwafted from the innocent flow'rs' (160–1). Any allusion to violence perpetrated in the present by EIC expansionism is ostensibly closed off by the naming of 'He of Gazna', the eleventh-century Turkish Sultan Mahmoud, as the guilty party: 'fierce in wrath/ He comes, and India's diadems/ Lie scatter'd in his ruinous path.' In describing the heroic resistance that is led by a 'youthful warrior' (162), whose last drop of blood is one of the gifts ensuring the Peri's readmission to heaven, the tale nonetheless looks ahead to its successor poem, which depicts opposition to 'Muslim' tyranny in a more extended and more overtly topical manner.

'The Fire-Worshippers' is set up by Feramorz's sighting of an ancient temple built by 'Ghebers or Persians of the old religion' – Zoroastrianism – before they 'fled ... from their Arab conquerors' (199). In a footnote referring to how Voltaire's tragedy *Les Guebres* 'alluded to the Jansenists', Moore declared at the tale's outset that it might be 'found capable of a similar doubleness of application' (201). Moore's 'Iran' – 'doom'd to bend/ Beneath' the yoke of 'fierce Arabia' (206) – ostensibly stands for Ireland/Erin, and the resistance led by the patriot Hafed against the Arab tyrant Emir Al Hassan thus allegorizes the Irish rebellions of 1798 and 1803. Given that the Emir is described as '[t]o carnage and the Koran giv'n' (204), and that Hafed claims to fight 'for happy homes and altars free' (237), Moore's tale often seems specifically to address this struggle through the lens of religion: in contrast to Southey's *Thalaba*, 'The Fire-Worshippers' depicts Islam as aggressively proselytizing rather than austerely pure, albeit that this framing of the history of Anglo–Irish conflict presents it in sectarian terms at odds with the secular nationalism of figures such as Robert Emmet and Moore himself.[84] In view of the growing influence of the evangelical lobby on the EIC during the 1810s, Moore's reference to the Emir as '[t]o carnage and the Koran giv'n' may at the same time allude to British policy in India as much as Ireland. 'The Fire-Worshippers' might therefore be seen to offer a broadly resonant parable as well as a particular 'national' allegory, its subject matter (as Majeed argues) the situation of all 'colonized cultures' rather than the case of Ireland alone.[85]

The allusiveness of 'The Fire-Worshippers' is in part a function of the model of 'colonial romance' that it derives from Sydney Owenson's novels *The Wild Irish Girl* (1806) and *The Missionary* (1811). 'The Fire-Worshippers' sets up such a plot when it introduces the Emir's daughter Hinda as one who, in her infatuation with Hafed, 'loves – but knows not whom she loves,/ Nor what his race, nor whence he came' (214). From an early stage, however, it is clear that the union of Hafed and Hinda is destined to be impossible; Lalla Rookh appears to realize this at the end of the tale's first section, when we are told that she 'could have wish'd that Feramorz had chosen a less melancholy story' (227). After he has been betrayed and his secret encampment has been penetrated by the Emir's forces, Hafed immolates himself on a blazing 'death-pile', while Hinda, seeing the flames of this pyre and realizing that 'Iran's hopes and hers are o'er' (318), throws herself from the boat on which she is making her escape. In a moment of bathos reminiscent of the end of 'The Veiled Prophet', Hinda is saluted by 'a Peri beneath the dark sea' who 'warbled' that 'No pearl ever lay, under Oman's green water,/ More pure in its shell than thy Spirit in thee' (319). The conclusion of 'The Fire-Worshippers' is over-determined as well as characteristically idiosyncratic, since Hafed's suicide calls up both the triumphant death of Thomas Gray's Bard, and therefore the domestic context of 'internal colonialism', and Luxima's immolation on Hilarion's pyre in *The Missionary*, therefore the Indian context of that novel, along with the struggle of colonized cultures in a more general sense.

In an Irish context, any sense of the subversive politics of 'The Fire-Worshippers' is qualified, however, by the fact that just as Hafed and Hinda's tragic end is signalled well in advance, so the Gheber defeat is anticipated long before it actually happens. Even before the Emir's army launches its assault on their hideout, Hafed and his men take a collective vow 'in Iran's injur'd name,/ To die upon that Mount of Flame – / The last of all her patriot line,/ Before her last untrampled shrine!' (247). This reference to the 'last of [a] patriot-line' echoes Gray again, and it perpetuates a mythology of heroic failure familiar from Moore's *Irish Melodies*; 'vainly brave', Hafed's 'last few' men pledge to 'die for the land they cannot save!' (245). Further to this, the frame tale of 'The Fire-Worshippers' foregrounds the way in which the sympathy that it elicits for 'the sufferings of the persecuted Ghebers' is contingent upon the failure of their rebellion: for Feramorz, it was 'impossible ... not to feel interested in the many glorious but unsuccessful struggles, which had been made by these original natives of Persia to cast off the yoke of their conquerors' (199–200). It is important here that not only is the liberal-minded Feramorz a Muslim – like the conquerors that he denounces – but that, as we later find out, he is also a monarch, his father having abdicated the throne. Together with the detachment that appears to be signalled by the idea of 'interest' in the idea of struggle in the quotation cited earlier, Feramorz's status frames the poem's sympathetic representation of an oppressed people as in part at least an elite concern, analogous to other contemporary forms of Whig cultural nationalism.

The tale's 'conciliatory' potential is perhaps best encapsulated by Hafed's plea to Hinda: 'When other eyes shall see, unmov'd,/ [Iran's] widows mourn, her warriors fall,/ Thou'lt think how well one Gheber lov'd,/ And for his sake thou'lt weep for all!' (224). This suggestion that love for individuals might in turn generate a larger sympathy for the communities to which they belong is itself complicated, however, by the poem's obtrusively graphic violence. The 'swarm' of the Emir's forces is compared to a 'locust cloud' (239), and Hafed is at times depicted as if he were, like Southey's Roderick, a righteous crusader knee-deep in the 'gushing gore' of Muslim dead; at one point he walks across a 'Tremendous causeway' (309) of corpses. The tale portrays Hafed and his men both as seeking death on the battlefield like Roderick ('his the best, the holiest bed,/ Who sinks entomb'd in Moslem dead!' [306]), and as equating violence and sexual initiation like Roderick's ally Alphonso: they rush to confront their enemies just 'as bridegrooms bound/ To their young loves' (304). There is a comparable representation of righteous bellicosity as a tumescent state shortly before this, when the idea that there is 'on Iran's neck a stain/ [that] Blood, blood alone can cleanse' is presented as a product of 'the swelling thoughts that now/ Enthrone themselves on HAFED's brow' (294).

The subsequent account of Hafed and his men offering 'terrible libations' to 'patriot vengeance' (308) may similarly suggest the tale's ambivalence towards bloodshed. Rather than pursue an 'Irish' reading of the poem (as many critics do), however, I want instead to return to the question of the relationship between political allegory and poetic 'ornament' in *Lalla Rookh*.[86] The complexity of this relationship is evident at the start of the tale's second section (just after Hafed has revealed his identity to Hinda), when the poet begins to set the scene as follows:

> The morn hath risen clear and calm,
> And o'er the Green Sea palely shines,
> Revealing Bahrein's groves of palm,
> And lighting Kishma's amber vines.
> Fresh smell the shores of Araby,
> While breezes from the Indian Sea
> Blow round Selama's sainted cape,
> And curl the shining flood beneath,–   (230)

While Jeffrey Vail suggests that the Irish associations of the colour green underscore the poem's 'doubleness of application', Moore's footnote cites Sir William Jones, for whom (in his 'Sixth Discourse on the Persians') 'the Green Sea' was the Persian Gulf.[87] The rest of the passage from which this quotation is taken alludes extensively to Jones's 1784 'Discourse', in which he recollected the pleasure he felt as he approached India by sea, and it is worth considering the function of such a classic Orientalist set piece in a poem that is often regarded as anti-colonial in its politics. In one respect it is no surprise to see such an engagement with Jones in *Lalla Rookh*, because Moore aligned himself with Jones's Whiggism. At the same time, however, the 'ornamental' Orientalism of the passage cited earlier (and of the poem as a whole) demonstrates how *Lalla Rookh* resonates in the context of British imperialism as well as Irish nationalism. While Majeed sees Moore as 'staging' an 'imperial sensibility' in playful and even subversive ways, a passage such as the one cited earlier, as much as it might be seen to mimic a Jonesian idiom, also evokes – without any obvious distancing strategy – a seductively sensuous Orient.[88] Noting that Moore's second son, Russell, briefly served the EIC in India (where he would die), Leask indeed suggests that Moore might most appropriately be viewed as a 'promoter' rather than parodist of Britain's 'fatal attraction' to the East in this period.[89]

Other critics, notably Vail, understand the 'ornamental' luxuriance of *Lalla Rookh* as part of a calculated strategy on Moore's part to entice a British audience into reading politically incendiary tales about Irish rebellion.[90] As is demonstrated by *Lalla Rookh*'s final tale, 'The Light of the Haram', it is nonetheless the case that Moore sometimes presented a perfumed, flower-strewn East, seemingly detached from any larger 'application', as a pleasurable destination in itself. With its story of the title character, Nourmahal's, reconciliation with her 'Imperial lover' (7:25), Sultan Selim, son of the sixteenth-century Mughal emperor Akbar, 'The Light of the Haram' anticipates the celebratory ending of Moore's frame narrative, which – as the party arrives in Kashmir – concludes on the festive note with which it began, when the poet Feramorz, 'having won [Lalla Rookh's] love as a humble minstrel' (7:68), is revealed to be her betrothed in disguise. The tale's 'Vale of Cashmire' setting is emphatically a happy valley, to the extent that even a 'minaret-crier' is said to issue a 'chaunt of glee' (7:16), and Moore's work reflexively draws attention to its enchanted atmosphere by describing Selim's capital during its annual 'Feast of Roses' as a 'City of Delight/ In Fairy-land' (7:22). Perhaps the most conspicuous marker of the tale's construction of a timeless and seemingly extra-political realm of romance is its lack of critical distance on the institution of the harem, which (as we have seen) was so often understood as a locus of class as well as gender conflict; the women in Selim's 'haram' are said to be 'inmates' but they 'smile' (7:42) regardless, and even without their crowning glory, Nourmahal, they comprise 'a living parterre/ Of the flow'rs of this planet' (7:21). 'The Light of the Haram', albeit knowingly, thus demonstrates that affinity for 'Eastern' magnificence and splendour which the poem as a whole so often displays. Francis Jeffrey regarded the 'excessive finery' of the tale as its greatest fault, but he paid tribute to the culture of Regency Orientalism in adding that '[i]ts finery . . . is not the vulgar ostentation which so often disguises poverty or meanness – but the extravagance of excessive wealth.'[91]

'The Real Truth'

It is useful to conclude by discussing *Lalla Rookh*'s reception, since reviews of Moore's poem illuminate the contest over Orientalist representation taking place during the 1810s and 1820s. In presenting such a 'happy' Kashmir, in marked contrast to more culturally specific or allegorically resonant depictions of the region, Moore harked back to an idea of the East as the domain of romance and imagination, as appealed to two decades earlier by William Ouseley and Isaac D'Israeli: D'Israeli's 'Mejnoun and Leila' indeed presents the figure of Kais reading to his mistress a Jones- as well as Ouseley-inspired tale of Kashmir as a garden paradise and 'land of love'.[92] In what was probably the most critical engagement with *Lalla Rookh*, however, the *British Review* seized upon what it presented as the poem's occlusion of the mundane social reality of the East:

> where we hear of nothing but of groves and baths and fountains, and fruits and flowers, and sexual blandishments, we are too apt to figure to ourselves a paradise of sweets; whereas the real truth is, that wherever these objects constitute the only or principal bliss or ambition or business of a people, there dirt and every disgusting impurity is sure to prevail, and there man tramples upon man in a series of cruel oppression down to the drooping wretchedness of the squalid populace, who have neither the reason nor rights of men.

With particular regard to the false impressions created by the poem's 'voluptuous homage ... to woman's charms', the reviewer complained of how 'foolish' female readers:

> devour these hyperbolical compliments of our amatory poets to the damask roses of their cheeks, the dark blue lustre of their eyes, and their thousand other charms, while they forget that in countries where these things are most celebrated in song, women are merchandize, and men are their proprietors, the reward of beauty is imprisonment for life, and those eyes, and cheeks, and thousand other charms, are the fading property of capricious lust.[93]

Against what the *Asiatic Journal* approvingly presented as *Lalla Rookh*'s channelling of the 'spirit' of the *Arabian Nights*, then, the *British Review* invoked a fixed idea of the bondage of Eastern women.[94] For the critic in question, it was this kind of 'common knowledge' as much as any actual evidence that exposed Moore as a fantasist, and it was a moral duty to emphasize what was at stake in such idealizing misrepresentation of the East.

Given the terms of the *British Review*'s hostility, it is all the more striking that others praised *Lalla Rookh* not just for the luxuriance of its imagery but for its truly Eastern authenticity. Ignoring the Irish allegorical resonance of 'The Veiled Prophet' and 'The Fire-Worshippers', *Blackwood's Edinburgh Magazine* suggested that Moore's native 'warmth of temperament' as well as his 'accurate and extensive reading' gave him a privileged understanding of the East.[95] In the 1841 preface to *Lalla Rookh*, Moore recorded his pleasure that eminent scholarly Orientalists such as Sir James Mackintosh and Sir John Malcolm identified the essential 'truthfulness' of his work. He related the anecdote of how the historian Mark Wilks had apparently once asked Mackintosh 'whether it was true that Moore had never been in the East', and when Mackintosh replied 'never', took this as proof 'that reading D'Herbelot is as good as riding on the back of a camel' (xvii–xviii). Moore here further signalled his 'pride and pleasure' that parts of the poem 'have been rendered into Persian, and have found their way to Ispahan' (xx). In a fictionalized autobiography of a native of Ispahan, as I later show, James Morier wrote against Moore and the EIC Orientalists who praised him: appealing to his own 'travelled' experience, Morier's authorial persona declares that while he had once imagined Persia as a 'land of poets and roses!', he now realizes that 'no country in the world less comes up to one's expectations'.[96] In the next chapter, though, I focus on avowedly second-hand forms of engagement with the East in the 'Cockney Orientalisms' of Leigh Hunt and Charles Lamb.

Notes

1. Ouseley, *Persian Miscellanies*, xxx.
2. D'Israeli, *Romances*, Advertisement.
3. Landor, *Poems*, preface.
4. Garcia, *Islam*, 126–56.
5. Ibid., 10.
6. Southey, *Poetical Works, 1793–1810*, 3:78; V:134. Page and line references appear as parenthetical citations in the text.
7. Dart, *Rousseau*, 17.
8. To John May, 18 Feb. 1800, *Life and Correspondence*, 2:52.
9. Leask, *British Romantic Writers*, 77.
10. Cited in Makdisi, *Romantic Imperialism*, 144.
11. To Coleridge, 23 Dec. 1799, *New Letters*, 1:211.
12. To May, 26 June 1797, *Life and Correspondence*, 1:316.
13. Southey, *Critical Heritage*, 67.
14. Ibid., 83.
15. Ibid., 78.
16. Southey, *Critical Heritage*, 84.
17. Saglia, 'Words and Things', 169.
18. To Coleridge, 11 July 1801, *Life and Correspondence*, 2:151.
19. Cited in Majeed, *Ungoverned Imaginings*, 53.
20. To Anna Seward, 28 May 1808, *New Letters*, 476.
21. Simpson, *Stranger*, 114–16.
22. Butler, 'Orientalism', 414.

23. Simpson, *Stranger*, 135.
24. Simpson, 'Limits of Cosmopolitanism', 148.
25. Simpson, *Stranger*, 134.
26. Southey, *Critical Heritage*, 134.
27. Ibid., 144.
28. Ibid., 142.
29. Ibid., 144.
30. Leask, *British Romantic Writers*, 4.
31. To Scott, 6 Nov. 1810, *Life and Correspondence*, 3:180.
32. Southey, *Chronicle*, xviii–xix.
33. Ibid., xx.
34. Ibid., xxv.
35. To Bedford, 17 Nov. 1808, *Life and Correspondence*, 3:186.
36. Southey, *Later Poetical Works, 1811–38*, 2:27; II:148–50. Page and line references appear as parenthetical citations in the text.
37. Bainbridge, *Visions of Conflict*, 184.
38. Southey, *Critical Heritage*, 180; Saglia, *Poetic Castles*, 87.
39. Southey, *Critical Heritage*, 186–7.
40. Ibid., 183–4.
41. Saglia, *Poetic Castles*, 82.
42. Butler, 'Byron', 74.
43. Byron, *CPW*, 3:39 and 3:73, ll.1062–3.
44. Leask, *British Romantic Writers*, 29.
45. Byron, *CPW*, 3:417–18 and 3:420.
46. Ibid., 3:73, l.1041.
47. *New Review*, 2 (Dec. 1813), 674.
48. *Eclectic Review*, 1 (Feb. 1814), 188.
49. Southey, *Critical Heritage*, 187.
50. Duggett, *Gothic Romanticism*, 116.
51. Wordsworth, *Poetical Works*, 689; 9: 3. Page and line references appear as parenthetical citations in the text.
52. Wordsworth, *Selected Prose*, 411.
53. Ibid., 389, 410.
54. Ibid., 389; *Edinburgh Review*, 23 (1814), 200.
55. Cited in Leask, 'Romanticism', 282.
56. Wordsworth, *Selected Prose*, 406.
57. Ibid., 412.
58. Leask, *British Romantic Writers*, 10.
59. Ibid., 63.
60. Ibid., 24.
61. Ibid., 62.
62. Byron, *CPW*, 3:244, ll.264–5.
63. Ibid., 3:244, 1.253 and 3:251, l.470.
64. To Moore, 28 Aug. 1813, *LJ*, 3:101; Byron, *CPW*, 3:148.
65. To his mother, 21 June 1811, *Letters*, 152.

66. Hazlitt, *Spirit of the Age*, 280.
67. Moore, *Poetical Works*, 6:5. Further references appear as parenthetical citations in the text.
68. Simpson, *Stranger*, 137.
69. Butler, 'Orientalism', 425.
70. Kelly, *Bard*, 283.
71. Majeed, *Ungoverned Imaginings*, 104.
72. Byron, *CPW*, 5:268; V:674–5 and 5:270; V:743–4.
73. Thomas, 'Chinoiserie', 245.
74. Kelly, *Bard*, 297.
75. Parkes, *Wanderings*, 77.
76. *Edinburgh Review*, 57 (1817), 1.
77. Leask, *British Romantic Writers*, 110.
78. Shelley, *Poems*, 2:207, ll.323–6.
79. Butler, 'Orientalism', 439.
80. Aravamudan, *Enlightenment Orientalism*, 100.
81. Rudd, *Sympathy*, 156.
82. *Monthly Review*, 83 (1817), 180.
83. *Asiatic Journal*, 4 (1817), 457.
84. Kelly, *Bard*, 291.
85. Majeed, *Ungoverned Imaginings*, 97.
86. Wright, *Ireland, India and Nationalism*, 91–108.
87. Vail, 'Moore', 321.
88. Majeed, *Ungoverned Imaginings*, 104.
89. Leask, 'Review', 247.
90. Vail, 'Moore', 323.
91. *Edinburgh Review*, 57 (1817), 33.
92. D'Israeli, *Romances*, 12.
93. *British Review*, 10 (1817), 31–2 and 34–5.
94. *Asiatic Journal*, 4 (1817), 457.
95. *Blackwood's*, 1 (1817), 279.
96. Morier, *Hajji Baba*, 5.

CHAPTER 6

Cockney Translation
Leigh Hunt and Charles Lamb's Eastern Imaginings

In a verse epistle 'To the Right Honourable Lord Byron on His Departure for Italy and Greece' (1816), Leigh Hunt expansively addressed the history of English poetry, stating that while 'our English clime' is supportive of 'ripe genius', Chaucer, Spenser, Shakespeare, and Milton all 'turned to Italy for added light', and found inspiration in Italian literary culture of a kind not to be had at home. After framing Italy's relation to England as that of 'woman's sweetness to man's force', Hunt's epistle then presents Italy as the site of sexual temptation, playfully cautioning Byron about the charms of 'lovely girls, that step across the sight,/ Like Houris in a heaven of warmth and light,/ With rosy-cushioned mouths, in dimples set,/ And ripe dark tresses, and glib eyes of jet'.[1] Hunt thus declared his intimacy with Byron while at the same time casually Orientalizing the Mediterranean. Whereas Hunt's contemporary J. H. Reynolds invoked 'ye Houries!' and asked them to 'smile' on his 'bold attempt/ With Eastern charms to decorate' his Byron-derivative *Safie: An Eastern Tale* (1814), Hunt here drew upon seraglio discourse in a more self-consciously worldly fashion, adopting a romance idiom comparable to that of Moore's *Lalla Rookh* and anticipating the terms of the 'witching scene' faced by Azim in 'The Veiled Prophet of Khorasan'.[2]

This chapter explores the emergence of forms of 'Cockney Orientalism' which in their engagement with Eastern otherness are at once familiar and unapologetically second-hand. It begins by considering the heterogeneous imaginative stimuli appealed to by Hunt's essay on the pleasures of solitary fireside contemplation, 'A Day by the Fire' (1812), an inaugural Cockney text.[3] In his work of the 1810s, the reformist Hunt understood English literature and English liberty as mutually imbricated traditions and, as I show in what follows, he lampooned 'Sultan' George the Prince Regent as the apex of an un-English system of corruption, invoking a 'radical Orientalist' rhetoric ostensibly at odds with the exoticism of his epistle to Byron. As is evident in his later poetry in *The Liberal* and in his subsequent prose writings, however, Hunt continued to be drawn to the idea of a seemingly extra-political 'dreaming with' the East.[4] It is thus tempting now to see Hunt as the purveyor of a progressive literary Orientalism predicated on its openness to Eastern others, although I seek to qualify such a reading, both by analysing the eagerness of his sympathetic identi- fication and by considering his denigration of China and things Chinese.

China is the main point of Eastern reference for Hunt's friend Charles Lamb, the other primary figure under examination here, and this chapter's second half begins by looking at how Lamb's Elia essay 'Old China' negotiates the challenge that Chinese difference presented to con- temporaries such as De Quincey, while also appealing to an idiosyncratic construction of 'China' as the basis for imaginative transport. 'A Dissertation on Roast Pig' offers a less genial if no less eccentric account of the idea of Chinese civilization, but it likewise exemplifies a Cockney Orientalism, I argue, because of the seemingly carefree way in which – Lamb's correspondence with Canton-based Orientalist scholar Thomas Manning notwithstanding – it parades its ignorance of China. Lamb understood that his work as a clerk at India House implicated him in the world of global commerce, and he reacted against this predicament not only by representing his service of the EIC as a state akin to thraldom but also by attempting to define a sense of self untroubled by 'strange beliefs or out of the way creeds or places'. In the context of this book's broader concern with the relationship between British imperial interests and Britons' cultural horizons, it might therefore be said that while Hunt in his diverse writings sought to project outwards so as to extend his imagi- native purview, albeit in a manner that did not involve engaging with 'significant otherness', Lamb, as in the letter cited earlier, appealed to the familiarity of 'old sympathies'.[5] Even if Lamb frequently chafed against the demands of his paid employment, however, in his first Elia essay, 'The South-Sea House', as I argue in conclusion, he also explored what he referred to elsewhere as the 'unseen' EIC, acknowledging how it might be possible for contemporaries to be 'at home' with empire while seeming to think very little about it.

Climate, Nature, and Genius

Hunt's 'A Day by the Fire' cites 'The Winter Evening' in William Cowper's *The Task* (1785), and its account of the 'creations of the eye' generated by fireside contemplation is further in dialogue with Coleridge's 'Frost at Midnight' (1798).[6] Whereas Coleridge's poem presents such contemplation as a function of silence and solitude, however, Hunt's essay portrays the fireside as a social milieu. It begins with the first-person declaration 'I am one of those that delight in a fireside,' and the figure of 'the Firesider' (225) whose recreation it describes maintains this sense of group identity, by sharing his hearth with others and imagining a kinship with 'the greatest and wisest' (231) who enjoyed similar meditative pleasures in the past. Even when Hunt focuses on the visionary transports of the lone individual, his delineation of such flights appears free from anxiety about the dissolution of the self, and while the essay acknowledges that these pleasures are vulnerable to outside interference, it makes no reference to the encroachment of external reality either. Hunt's engagement with Cowper throws this vision of home comfort into relief, since whereas 'The Winter Evening' begins with a post boy bearing news of defeat in America and India, 'A Day by the Fire' remains occupied with the sensual pleasure of merely holding a newspaper.

If the recurrent adjective 'snug' encapsulates the intimacy of 'domestic enjoyment' for Hunt, however, he associated such pleasure not so much with a state of private retreat from the world as with an outward-looking notion of creativity indigenous to Britain: even without 'the sunshine of the Southern countries', Britons still possessed an 'excursiveness of wit and range of imagination' (226). This play with the temperature metaphor as a gauge of inspiration is especially resonant, because Hunt here – implicitly at least – rejects William Collins's claim about the inability of the national 'genius' to appreciate the productions of hotter climes. Britain is blessed with creative potential irrespective of its actual weather conditions, for Hunt, not least because the effects of the sun are replicated by the fireplace in every home. It enjoys the best of both worlds, moreover, since its climate is conducive to a generalized idea of liberty – primarily associated with individual self-expression – which literary giants of the distant past would have found equally congenial.

One other manifestation of Hunt's 'snug notions' of liberty is the mixed sociability established by 'the knights and damsels of old' (226), which he illustrated with reference to Chaucer's 'The Knight's Tale'. While Hunt thus saw national literary tradition as embodying exceptional cultural resources, however, he also presented the fireside as facilitating considerably more exotic projections. The 'Let there be a cottage' passage in De Quincey's *Confessions* provides an instructive comparison in this respect, because De Quincey drew upon Hunt's essay as well as Cowper's poem, describing a state of seclusion which also constitutes a respite from the threat of the Malay who had earlier intruded upon him.[7] Rather than provide such a retreat from the world outside, the state of 'snugness' for Hunt allows the Firesider to imagine himself far removed not just from his immediate domestic environment but also from 'national' mooring in a larger sense. Coffee, not tea (central to De Quincey's tableau), is the catalyst for Hunt's pleasures of the imagination, because coffee is said to be 'more lively and at the same time more substantial' than tea, and since the associations it generates of 'the Turks and their Arabian tales' are 'infinitely preferable to ... Chinese ideas' (235). I say more later about Hunt and China, but here I want to emphasize a broader point about the centrality of such imaginary projection to so much of Hunt's writing. '[L]ike the king who put his head into the tub' (a reference to the story of Chec Chahabeddin in *Turkish Tales* [1708]), he states, 'I am transported into distant lands the moment I dip into the coffee-cup, – at one minute ranging the vallies with Sindbad, at another encountering the Fairies on the wing by moonlight, at a third exploring the haunts of the cursed Maugraby, or rapt into the silence of that delicious solitude from which Prince Agib was carried by the fatal horse' (235).

While Hunt presents a now domesticated commodity as the inspiration for these transports, his 'Eastern' frame of reference largely remains at a remove both from the material 'East of things' and from the insignia of a burgeoning imperial culture. Hunt here openly avows the casualness as well as range of his allusion, for example by crediting 'Turks' with the authorship of 'Arabian tales', and by naming the story of 'Maugraby' alongside better-known tales from the *Nights* itself. 'A Day by the Fire' brings together different folkloric as well as literary registers in a later passage that offers its clearest statement of the paradoxical sociality of solitary contemplation. After presenting the imagination as an ever-roaming faculty, Hunt describes a hearth-side moment in which 'the whole band of fairies, ancient and modern, – the daemons, sylphs, gnomes, sprites, elves, peries, genii, and above all the fairies of the fireside, the salamanders, lob-lye-by-the-fires, lars, lemurs, and larvae, come flitting between the fancy's eye and the dying coals'. Rewriting Coleridge's privatized reflection, Hunt celebrates the 'waking sense of disenthralment' (238) that enables and is in turn strengthened by communion with this heterogeneous band. 'Disenthralment', like 'Firesider', is a coinage of Hunt's, and it is a term that crystallizes his argument regarding the broadly emancipatory – rather than absorptive or anti-social – dimension of such imaginative flights.

I return to Hunt's claims about the significance of such reverie, but here I want to stress the diversity of the 'airy visitants' referred to earlier: 'peries' and 'genii', for example, would have been popularly associated with 'Eastern' fictions, whether in the form of translation or pastiche. Hunt's list of 'fairies' typifies the inclusivity of his cultural reference, and his readiness to confound the distinction between registers customarily regarded as separate from one another. Much has now been written about Hunt as a provocateur whose writings of this period perform self-consciously '"creolizing" manoeuvres', and the hostile critical response to Hunt's Dante-inspired *The Story of Rimini* (1816) was acutely attentive to this boundary-crossing aesthetic.[8] As is well known, *Blackwood's Edinburgh Magazine* led the assault on Hunt as the 'chief' of the new 'Cockney School' of poetry, classifying him as a man who could not help but disclose his lowly origins when he tried to write about anything outside of his limited knowledge. Its mockery of Hunt's efforts to pass as 'a poet eminently rural' is especially interesting here, since in noting Hunt's 'pretended' admiration for Wordsworth it states that it would be as 'impossible' for him to appreciate *The Excursion* 'as it would be for a Chinese polisher of cherry-stones, or a gilder of tea-cups, to burst into tears at the sight of the Theseus or the Torso'.[9] This jibe at once presents Hunt as lacking – and unable to attain – the cultural capital that would allow him properly to value Wordsworth's poetry or the Elgin Marbles, and, by aligning Hunt with a producer of ephemera who also happens to be Chinese, casts him as an alien, un-English figure, and therefore an outsider or interloper in a double sense.

Although 'Z' in *Blackwood's* made no explicit reference to Hunt's West Indian ancestry he sometimes insinuated that Hunt's work was marked by a degraded moral climate, describing him as a man who possessed 'not a single iota of the English character'.[10] This immorality was evident in Hunt's description of the rural pavilion in which, in *Rimini*, the consummation of Paulo and Francesca's illicit affair takes place: this structure was, for Z, little more than a 'bagnio', further proving Hunt's inability to evoke 'natural' outdoor scenes.[11] A later *Blackwood's* article again accused Hunt of sexualizing nature in his verse collection *Foliage* (1818), stating that 'Mr Hunt's "love of the country" . . . hangs on one great principle – [that] *every grove has its nymph*', and describing the group of female figures baring their limbs, in the poem titled 'The Nymphs', as 'a sketch of [Hunt's] seraglio'.[12] This Orientalization of Hunt converged with the widespread emphasis on his mean social origins, as Z and others made Hunt into the mouthpiece of a 'new mode of British urban vulgarity'.[13] Hunt was seen to be immersed in an artificial, inauthentic nature that was culturally and commercially mediated, hence Z's insistence on *Rimini's* 'pretence, affectation, finery, and gaudiness', and the recurrence of these terms and their cognates throughout *Blackwood's* articles on the Cockney school; Francis Jeffrey in the *Edinburgh* for his part distinguished the 'vulgar ostentation' of Cockneyism from the 'finery' of *Lalla Rookh*.[14] This discussion might be extended with reference to Keats, who was associated with a debased 'Oriental' aesthetic in a review of his *Poems* of 1817, and accused by *Blackwood's* of having 'outhunted Hunt'; Keats famously conceived of the receptivity of the imagination, in a state of 'diligent indolence', in a comparable fashion to Hunt.[15] I now, though, return to the question of Hunt's own sense of national belonging, considering in particular the Orientalizing strategies that he himself used in his critique of Britain's old regime.

Badex-Ampel

In his familiar essay 'A Now, Descriptive of a Hot Day' (1820), Hunt played up to the charges levelled against him, presenting a gallery of city dwellers and suburbanites about to succumb to indolence and take a siesta. While Hunt openly acknowledged the 'tropical blood' in his veins, however, he also conjoined ideas of indigenous literary creativity and native freedom.[16] Hunt recognized that the greats of English poetry had found inspiration in Italian literary culture, but he elsewhere associated them with an independence and lack of servility that he regarded as essentially English. In a letter 'To the English People' in the *Examiner*, for example, written after the suspension of habeas corpus in 1817, he addressed his audience as 'descendants of CHAUCER ... a Reformer in his day, [who] set his face both against priestly and kingly usurpation'. He invoked this inheritance against the 'oligarchy of the shallow' and those who 'neglect-[ed] any constitutional opportunity of putting an end' to its rule: 'There is not a youth who walks out of doors with a book, not a single scholar who has got beyond his syntax, not a reader of newspapers or reviews, not an individual, young or old, who loves to go to the theatre and hear SHAKESPEARE ... that ought not to blush at seeing a nation, renowned for every species of literature and greatness, governed 'gainst its will by a junto who neither feel what is English, nor can even talk it.'[17]

Together with Hunt's insistence on 'constitutional' opposition, this hailing of independent individuals – the youth, the scholar, and so on – demonstrates that Hunt was apprehensive of being tainted by the 'vulgarity' of popular radicalism, and anxious about the forms that collective action might take; as Kevin Gilmartin argues, Hunt's 'affiliative' gestures either tended to connect him with 'ancestors rather than contemporaries' or appealed to a sociability conceived of in conspicuously literary terms.[18] Even as Hunt used archaic terms such as 'oligarchy' or 'junto' – employed by the anti-Walpole opposition almost a century earlier – to describe the ruling elite, however, his critique of the unreformed status quo is marked by a rhetorical clarity and directness that derives from its appeal to languages of nation and race. The idea of 'shallow' oligarchy suggests that the governing class is unrooted in the traditions of liberty that are second nature to the 'English people' themselves, a claim underlined by the assertion that the ruling elite has no 'feel' for ('nor can even talk', or mimic) true Englishness. In the first of his essays on the suspension of habeas corpus, Hunt directly posed 'us' against 'them', contrasting 'the purity of our institutions' with 'the political existence of these men and their institutions'.[19] His denunciation of the Tory government in the name of the Englishness with which he held its authority to be incompatible further explains why *Blackwood's* sought in turn to castigate Hunt as an outsider, lacking in 'English character'.

Such appeals to a language of national belonging were a consistent feature of Hunt's writing throughout the 1810s, especially after he stepped up his criticism of the Prince Regent following the latter's abandonment of his one-time Whig allies. Whereas in his ostensibly friendly 'Letter of Strong Advice' of 1808, Hunt addressed 'his Royal Highness' as a 'a slave to [his] habits' who might be reformed if he kept better company, in the writings which led to his imprisonment for libel, and in works which he composed in prison, Hunt presented the Regent as a figure beyond rehabilitation.[20] As in the Eastern allegories that he published in the *Examiner* in 1813, either side of his sentencing, Hunt at times Orientalized the Regent's character and conduct, offering a civic humanist analysis of court vices. The first of these tales imagines a scenario in which luxury and corruption have brought about the nation's literal demise, depicting a group of fishermen who return home to find that their island of 'Hing-land', off 'the north eastern coast of China', has 'by some convulsion of nature disappeared' – perhaps, one speculates, because 'the inhabitants had been deserted by their favourite God, LI-BER-TEE'. The fishermen then meet a refugee named Whang, drifting alone, whose first words to them are that '"they are boring it"'.[21]

Whang refers to the 'dreadful secret' of the 'Lost Island', that its princes 'bore[d] holes to [its] bottom', and Hunt's allegory thus alludes to the 'Sinking Fund' by which the national debt was managed.[22] The size of the debt is directly connected with princely extravagance here, because Whang testifies as to how the 'folly and debauchery' of the corpulent 'CHIN-HUM' and his courtiers sapped 'the foundations of the country' by 'boring a hole by degrees through the heart and body of it'; in another demonstration of how Hunt and his antagonists vied to represent each other as un-English, it is striking that Hunt himself was accused (with *Rimini*) of attempting to 'sap the foundations of civil society and of social life'.[23] Recalling Chin-Hum's excesses in the same morally judgemental mode, Whang states that 'the word private was a sufficient reason for doing anything, however injurious; and you might have disseminated a pestilence, provided you did it between four walls.'[24] Hunt's essay therefore associates the Regent with an 'aristocratic' understanding of a protected private sphere, while in turn judging him by, in John Barrell's words, 'a more modern, middle-class expectation that the private life [of public men] would be understood as reflecting upon their public virtue'.[25]

In part two of his 'Sentence against the Examiner' essay, published just after his tale of 'Hing-land', Hunt introduced another 'fragment of an Eastern story', allegorizing his own encounter with state authority and directly referring to the Regent in impudently Cockney terms. The tale presents Sultan 'JEE-AWJ' of 'Ginnistan' as 'a *Raic*' who 'could sit up . . . night after night, drinking the forbidden liquor and eating bang', and it describes him as being 'fond of dress, delighting in sumptuous vests and drawers covered with gold', and sporting 'mustachios [that] were each of them six inches long'. Hunt's Jee-Awj 'did not know how to govern', however, and amused himself by 'scattering a . . . poison called Badex-Ampel in a river near his palace', the effects of which elicited protest from two fish with 'a knack of speaking their minds'.[26] As in the tale of 'Hing-land', Hunt alludes to the widely publicized revel at Carlton House in June 1811, at which the Prince of Wales celebrated his Regency's formal commencement. Unlike in the preceding tale, though, where this extravaganza portends a national calamity, the recently incarcerated Hunt here reimagines such a scenario to represent himself and his brother John defiantly exercising their instinct for free speech against the effects of princely dissipation; as Greg Kucich and Jeffrey Cox argue, indeed, this conceit of protesting fish may constitute Hunt's very first attempt at experimenting with an 'insolent' Cockney identity.[27]

Hunt published another Eastern allegory in the *Examiner* in January 1816, an 'Account of the Remarkable Rise and Downfall of the Late Great Kan of Tartary'. In it, he again referred to 'Hing-land', ruled by 'Prince JEE-AUGE' and his 'mandarins', but now narrated the national

struggle with 'NAH-PO-LEE-HUN', and the subsequent resurgence of
forces of conservatism in Britain and on the continent in the wake of his
defeat.[28] While numerous contemporary visual and textual satires of the
Regent figured him as an Oriental despot associated with absurd and
grotesque forms of display, as Gerard Cohen-Vrignaud shows, Hunt
addressed the Regent's behaviour in what was essentially an eighteenth-
century mode of literary Orientalism.[29] Hunt stated that '[p]eople are apt
to know themselves better by finding actions resembling their own in [the]
conduct and history of other nations,' and by thus focusing on 'bad
example' he wrote within a long-standing tradition of works addressing
the business of kingship and domestic government.[30] If the talking fish in
the tale of 'Ginnistan' signal again Hunt's intimate knowledge of the
Arabian Nights (specifically here the 'History of the Young King of the
Black Isles'), the brief narratives discussed earlier are all marked by their
satirical transitivity. By reviving a now archaic form, Hunt in effect harked
back to a period before Britain's turn to empire in the East and the more
scholarly, culturally particular Orientalisms that it helped to generate. He
thought that Sir William Jones's reformist 'political promise' had failed to
come to fruition because he had been side-tracked by 'the bad taste of
Indian literature', and in his own poetry, as I show in what follows, he
eschewed the literary innovations that Jones had helped to pioneer.[31] Hunt
circulated a lexicon of familiar 'Eastern' tropes (notably the figure of the
absolutist potentate), and his reiterated critique of political despotism
remained local in its scope, with his various allegories focusing their
attention on Britain alone.

Hunt was well informed about Britain's empire, and Deirdre Coleman
identifies him as 'a diligent observer and critic of British crimes in India'.[32]
In his *Examiner* essay, 'Necessity of Peace to Our Indian Possessions'
(1808), Hunt declared that he 'should behold our loss of India without
a sigh, were it not to add to the overgrown dominions of [France], who
would probably use the natives with the same tyranny as we have used
them'.[33] Hunt also described British involvement in India as a 'wen upon
our cheek', however, thus rehearsing the civic terms of anti-nabob discourse, according to which empire was understood primarily as endanger-
ing the imperial metropole; echoing the rhetoric of earlier writers such as
Goldsmith, he stated that 'the sun of India sucks up our seas to return to us
nothing but ... turbid and unprofitable showers.'[34] Hunt acknowledged
the condition of Indian subject peoples, then, but in claiming that the EIC
was as ever 'grinding' them, in a kind of business as usual, he summarized
the recent history of the nation's connection with India in terms of a single

narrative that, because it was so depressingly familiar, was easy and even desirable to forget. '[T]he people in England seldom even think of India,' he wrote a decade later:

> India only presents itself occasionally to their minds, as a great distant place with strange beasts and trees in it, where Brahmins meditate and Mussulmen keep seraglios, – where white people in regimentals are always fighting for some cause or other with the dark natives in vests and turbans, – and from which sallow elderly gentlemen are every now and then coming away to enjoy the large fortunes which they have acquired.[35]

In an 1817 essay on South America Hunt entertained the idea that revolution in Brazil might provide a catalyst for 'Reform all over the world'.[36] When he 'thought of' India, however, he recognized the problem which Burke more systematically addressed, that India might be too 'distant' and 'strange' for Britons' imaginations to apprehend. In his imagining of the East, Hunt eschewed both the scholarly particularism of Jones and the 'universalist' approach – sometimes associated with Shelley's *The Revolt of Islam* (1818) – which saw Asia as a future site of elemental struggle between forces of liberty and despotism. Hunt defended Shelley from the personal attacks that followed this poem's publication, but he was nonetheless ambivalent in his response to his friend's revolutionary allegory, admiring its idealism but questioning the means by which it sought to pursue its stated agenda: 'the book is full of humanity,' he wrote in *The Examiner*, 'and yet ... does not go the best way to work of appealing to it, because it does not appeal to it through the medium of its common knowledges.'[37] Hunt himself sought politically to engage with readers in a manner that was familiar to them, but in his Orientalist verse, as I now show, he was sometimes drawn to a seemingly extra-political realm of romance and imagination too.

'Good Kings Can Please a Liberal'

Although Hunt sometimes regretted the entanglement of literature and politics, he emphasized throughout his writings of the 1810s that *English* literary creativity was a product of the native genius for freedom which he invoked against Britain's old regime. Hunt appealed to a common understanding of this genius against what he saw as Shelley's mandarin tendencies, and as the basis for his optimism regarding future national renewal. 'It is high time ... for all of us,' he wrote in the preface to *Foliage* (1818), 'to look after health and sociality': 'We should consider ourselves as what we

really are, – creatures made to enjoy more than to know, to know infinitely
nevertheless in proportion as we enjoy kindly, and finally, to put our own
shoulders to the wheel and get out of the mud upon the green sward again.'
The individual indulgence of impulse in this account almost by default
constitutes part of a joint endeavour by which people combine to 'get . . .
upon the green sward again', and this 'again' emphasizes that such activity
allows those involved to regain access to a 'true' Englishness; once more
associating literary and libertarian inheritances, Hunt here identifies 'the
age of Shakspeare' as 'the most wise and lively, the most dancing, rural, and
manly period of our . . . history'.[38] *Foliage* thus illuminates 'the Politics of
Pan' in the writings of Hunt and his circle, for whom pleasure and play
provided an antidote to the gravity of works by Wordsworth and Coleridge
that conceived of national redemption in very different terms.[39] At the
same time, however, Hunt's preface additionally suggests how readily
'health and sociality' might – for 'creatures made to enjoy' – become
fulfilling ends in themselves, detached from any larger ameliorative project.
Hunt's own political trajectory cannot be straightforwardly plotted, but
taking into consideration his heterogeneous writings in the early 1820s it
seems fair to say that from around this period onwards Hunt increasingly
'renounced overt political designs' in his work, even as he insisted that
everything he wrote remained at least implicitly political.[40]

Hunt was involved in the production of *The Liberal* during the early
stages of his voluntary exile in Italy between 1822 and 1825, and some of the
miscellaneous poetry that he published in it took what was for him a novel
Orientalist form. One of these poems, 'Mahmoud' (1823), for example,
develops Gibbon's anecdote about the Turkish sultan 'Mahmoud the
Gaznevide', who ordered the execution of a sexually predatory soldier to
take place in darkness for fear that the offender might be his son, and
then – having proved his impartiality – offered a prayer of thanks that the
man in question was a stranger. Whereas the same figure in Moore's
'Paradise and the Peri' is himself violently rapacious, Hunt's Mahmoud,
unlike the Eastern princes of his earlier writings, is presented as offering
a good example. The poem gives itself as proof that 'Good Kings can please
a Liberal, even now,' differentiating Mahmoud from those who 'have
graced that drunken sphere,/ Which hurts the few whose brains can bear
it best'. This reference to princely dissipation calls up Hunt's earlier
political satires, and the fact that the poem's 'wild villain', prior to his
beheading, is said to be both a 'drunkard' and 'perhaps a lawless son' means
that the poem playfully entertains the idea of a 'good king' terminating the
life of an unworthy successor to his title.[41] As potentially incendiary as any

such implication would have been, however, Hunt's distinction between good and bad kings is less obviously rooted in a British context than his Eastern allegories in *The Examiner*, not least since the poem's exemplar of princely nobility is a Turk with no qualms about punishing wrongdoers by summary execution.

Hunt more clearly moved away from political allegory in his 1822 poem 'Cambus Khan', a free translation of Chaucer's unfinished 'The Squire's Tale', including its rich description of the presents with magical properties that the 'Tartar king' receives from a visitor to his court.[42] The poem inserts additional passages, derivative of *Lalla Rookh*, to fill out the Oriental milieu of the original, and in evoking the festivities that mark the twentieth anniversary of Cambus Khan's reign it gives an itemized list of Eastern effects – 'cushioned sophas', 'perfumes', 'dancing girls', and so on – that are largely absent from Chaucer's tale, and detached from any moral commentary on Oriental excess of the kind evident in Hunt's writings on the Regent.[43] This formulaic tableau provides a recognizable scene of another sort too, because after noting how the men at court were joined by 'the wives they thought the loveliest', the poet then interjects:

> You must not judge my Tartars by the tales
> Of nations merely eastern, and serails:
> The eastern manners were in due degree,
> But mixed and raised with northern liberty;
> And women came with their impetuous lords,
> To pitch the talk and humanize the boards.[44]

'Cambus Khan' accentuates the Orientalism of Chaucer's poem, then, but its account of 'northern liberty' tempering 'eastern manners' also to some extent familiarizes the Tartar court, presented as playing host to the mixed sociability that Hunt had celebrated in 'A Day by the Fire'; this hybridization of seraglio discourse significantly differentiates the poem from Moore's exoticization of the harem. Hunt's merging of the 'northern' and 'eastern' might be read as a politicized move, by which he playfully contested the Christianized Gothicism articulated by Wordsworth and Coleridge over the previous decade or more. Certainly, the idea of Englishness was always already cosmopolitan for Hunt, as is demonstrated by his 1819 *Indicator* essay 'Far Countries', which refers to 'the great Alfred' – here separated from the history of English liberty – as the translator of an unspecified 'book of geography' and the patron of travellers.[45] Jeffrey Cox argues that in a hostile political climate, Hunt and his circle turned to 'a localism that resists a coercive nationalism and a cosmopolitanism that seeks a non-imperial universalism', and 'Far Countries' ostensibly performs such an expansion of imaginative horizons.[46] It states that '[a]bout the same period' during which Alfred began to explore the wider world, 'Haroun al Raschid wrote a letter to the Emperor of the West, Charlemagne,' so as to bring about 'Arabic and Italian romance shaking hands in person!'[47]

Hunt's imagining of a cordial encounter between these world-historical figures, as representatives of literary traditions, is idealized to the point of self-parody. The larger political ramifications of this 'Cockney cosmopolitanism' may be more complicated than Cox suggests, however. The reference points of 'Far Countries' as well as 'Cambus Khan' remind us again that just as Hunt asserted his affiliation with 'ancestors rather than contemporaries', so his vision of the world beyond Europe tended to invoke distant historical figures (Haroun) and imprecisely defined regions (Tartary) ahead of matters of current concern.[48] As in his description of the crusades as voyages of intellectual discovery that 'pierced into a new world of remoteness', Hunt's accounts of cultural contact generally privilege life-enhancing forms of mutual exchange over any more difficult reckoning with the consequences of centuries of increasing global interconnection.[49] If Hunt can be seen to perform an engaging openness to the other, then, his global vision also displays an insouciant facility of reference. The heterogeneous allusiveness of so much of Hunt's work both denies the challenge of 'significant otherness' that (for example) 'Southeyan' Romantic Orientalist poetry presents to its readers and offers an implicit – perhaps distinctively Cockney – challenge of its own to the ease with which members of a cosmopolitan elite exhibited their cultural capital. Hunt's naming of 'my Tartars' in 'Cambus Khan' is especially significant in this respect. Keats wrote to his brother and sister in 1818 that he lived 'more out of England than in it', with 'Tartary ... a favourite lounge', and Hunt's possessive 'my' suggests that he too conceived of 'Tartary' as an easily inhabitable region that he was able to populate in a manner of his own choosing.[50]

Hunt's imaginative investment in 'Tartary' helps to illuminate his rejection of 'overt political designs' by distinguishing his version of 'The Squire's Tale' from his earlier writings which considered Chaucer's life and work in rather different terms. In Hunt's poetry in *The Liberal*, therefore, there are signs of a separation of the literary and libertarian inheritances that he had previously presented as mutually constitutive. Whereas Hunt's 1817 letter 'To the English People' on the suspension of habeas corpus hails its audience as 'descendants of Chaucer', 'a Reformer in his day', the 'wise wit' at the end of 'Cambus Khan' enjoins the reader to 'learn how to dream with Chaucer all day long'.[51] '[L]earn still better, if you can,' the 'wiser wit' continues, 'to make/ Your world at all times, sleeping, or awake;/ The true receipt, whether by days or nights,/ To charm your griefs, and double your delights.'[52] Hunt's poem finally addresses the reader not as part of a larger society, and thus one of many 'shoulders [at] the wheel' (to recall *Foliage*'s preface), but instead as an individual whose 'world' appears to be a circumscribed, though also almost limitlessly capacious, personal sphere.

'Araby, My First Love'

Rather than present 'Fancy' as a refuge from the harsh necessity of 'Fact', however, Hunt often declared that 'fancies are facts too,' as if the pleasures of the imagination had their own tangible life; for Hunt, in Gregory Dart's words, 'troubling over whether our imaginings were philosophically true ... was far less profitable than trying to ensure that they were sunny.'[53] Another of his contributions to *The Liberal*, 'The Book of Beginnings' (1823) is a poem about reading and writing poetry which also offers a retrospect on Hunt's career as an author to date, returning to the potentially uneasy relationship between literature and politics. It acknowledges the 'Tyrannous ills, ... / Slaveries, and slaughters, inequalities/ Extreme and insolent' that continue to 'Cause tears indeed, that from all human eyes/ Brave hands should seek to wipe', but then adds that if 'broad-eyed mirth' prevailed, ''Twould dry up all kind things, tears, smiles, and flowers,/ And make our hearts as withered as our bowers'. Hunt therefore suggests that the existence of 'Tyrannous ills' is actually necessary to make 'kind things' possible.[54] While he had insisted on the social dimension of imaginative transport in 'A Day by the Fire', 'The Book of Beginnings' undercuts this fantasy, because even as its narrator projects himself into numerous different roles, his constantly shifting self-identification is driven less by any attempt to 'commune' with others than by a voracious appetite for poetic 'light refreshment', wherever it is to be found. It is instructive in this regard to consider how the narrator at one point likens himself to 'a knight of old' pitted against 'tramplers of the right', in terms familiar from Hunt's earlier work, but then abandons this campaign with an abrupt 'Anon' – subsequently to become 'gentle as a morn of May/, ... all for flow'rs, and loving dreams at night'.[55]

After describing a period of 'repose' with 'My magic books', the poem's narrator indulges in several stanzas of free association, flitting from

'Arcady' to 'Tartary', and then randomly naming celebrated poets (Ovid, Spenser, Ariosto) and locales ('the Ganges', 'old Greece', 'Araby') in rapid succession.[56] The narrator's naming of Araby as 'my first love' is especially interesting here, at once occluding geographical and cultural specificity, declaring Hunt's sense of his 'true' literary vocation, and suggesting that the *Arabian Nights* embodies the pleasures of reading in an inimitably rich and memorable manner. 'I'm Giafar, I'm a "genie", I'm a jar,' he states, going on to identify with 'Sindbad', 'the Calendar', and then 'the prince, who shot his bow so far,/ And found that cellar, with a stock divine/ Of lips to kiss, still redder than the wine'.[57] While a note states that the phrase 'lips . . . redder than . . . wine' alludes to 'The Story of Prince Ahmed and the Fairy Peri Banou', Hunt's reference to a 'stock divine/ Of lips' also calls up both the 'paradise of lips' imagined by Keats's Endymion and *Lalla Rookh*'s harem scenes.[58] Hunt's adoption of something akin to Keats's 'camelion' persona in this poem nonetheless eschews any Keatsian exploration of the fluidity of selfhood.[59] Contemporaries similarly recollected formative early experiences of reading the *Nights*, but Hunt's poem is distinguished by its easy identification with Sindbad and others; as with 'A Day by the Fire's' summoning of 'the king who put his head in the tub', this intimacy of reference exemplifies a specifically Cockney Orientalism.[60] The casual personal familiarity and the literary underpinnings of Hunt's engagement with 'the East' are encapsulated in his 'A Rustic Walk and Dinner' (1842). Here, an authorial persona moves from declaring that 'Europe is home,/ And Christendom is home' to adding 'nay, Pagandom,/ Being of Europe; nay, the East itself, – / For who's a stranger in the Arabian Nights?'[61] Just as 'A Day by the Fire' expunges the problematic figure of the 'stranger' from the texts with which it is in dialogue, so this account of an always welcoming collection of tales bypasses any notion of potentially darker enchantment afforded by the *Nights* and the works that it inspired.[62]

Hunt sometimes acknowledged the tension between his instinct for writing in the first person and his political commitment to the ideal of community. In his *Examiner* essay 'I and We' (1824), for example, he conceded that the recurrence of 'this *I* of mine' in his work might compromise his goal of fostering sociality: 'it is difficult to be plural when talking of things singular.'[63] In the first of a sequence of articles in 1833 using the 'Wishing Cap' persona, however, Hunt also defended his habit of 'indulging in digression', presenting the wishing cap conceit as affording perpetual mobility, and so – enlisting readers on his side – access to 'every thing that we wish'. Hunt asked how 'consistency or *stationariness* [can] be expected of one, who, in as many seconds, can be in as many parts of the world, and of time', and he illustrated this capability with reference to, in Jane Stabler's words, a 'catalogue of some ninety-four flamboyantly diverse activities'.[64] The list begins with 'Smoking with the Turks', then takes in other 'occupations' such as 'Bowing with the Chinese', 'Vegetating with the Hindoos', 'Mythologizing with the Buddhists', and 'Loving with the Houris'. That these pursuits also include 'Monopolizing with the Tories,/ Compromising with the Whigs,/ [and] Reforming with the Radicals' perhaps especially captures the way in which the function of the list's breezy parallelism is to efface key differences between the constituencies to which it refers.[65]

The tagline of Hunt's *London Journal* (established in 1834) describes the periodical's project as being 'To assist the enquiring, animate the struggling, and sympathize with all'. In my conclusion I refer to Hunt's *London Journal* essay 'Genii and Fairies of the East, the Arabian Nights, &c.', but here I want to consider how Hunt's work from around the early 1820s onwards – when he 'renounced overt political designs' – invites us to recognize the limits of its apparently generous openness to the world.[66] If a poem such as Southey's *Thalaba* estranges difference, Hunt often seems to insist that nothing is strange. Even as he self-consciously defined himself against an elite, 'travelled' cosmopolitanism, his work demonstrates a comparable ease, at least to the extent that it frames its openness to the other in terms of the pleasurable experience of novelty rather than any kind of more disturbing or discomforting encounter. Where Hunt recognized that, to most Britons, the actual domain of the EIC's sovereignty was 'a great distant place', his personae from the 'Firesider' to the wearer of the 'wishing-cap' assume an unproblematic access to 'every thing that [they] wish', by virtue of the fact that, as the latter puts it, they are 'masters of time as well as place'.[67] It is therefore necessary to qualify any notion that the generosity of reference in the works discussed earlier might instantiate either a progressive 'Cockney Cosmopolitan' politics or a 'good', because horizon-expanding, literary Orientalism. This is in part because, as I have suggested, Hunt's avowed instinct for 'indulging in digression' calls into question the actual substance of a process of sympathetic identification that is constantly being diverted away from its object by the more appealing prospect of new 'beginnings'. As I now show, to conclude this discussion of Hunt, it is also because his diverse writings make brief but nonetheless frequent and significant allusions to forms of difference seemingly beyond the purview of authorial sympathy.

Hunt was one of the many early nineteenth-century writers prompted to engage with the subject of China by periodical coverage of the 'kowtow controversy' with which Macartney's 1792–4 diplomatic embassy became associated.[68] While 'A Day by the Fire' does not elaborate on its refusal to countenance 'Chinese ideas', a later Hunt essay in the *Examiner*, on the redecoration of Drury Lane theatre, is more direct in this regard. Written after the 1816 Amherst embassy had met with a similar fate to Macartney's, it refers to how the Chinese 'hustled us out of doors the other day' before then deriding the 'mummeries and monstrosities' of the theatre's new chinoiserie-style décor. The essay's presentation of 'Chinese deformities' as 'humiliating to the national taste' continues Hunt's critique of the Prince Regent's 'bad example', but where Hunt's *Examiner* allegories of 1813 invoked an entirely fictionalized 'China' for domestic satirical purposes, his later 'Chinese libels', as Kitson points out, additionally offer a particular 'idea of China and the Chinese'.[69] One such 'libel' appears in 'Far Countries', where a supposedly common knowledge regarding the Chinese 'contempt of other nations' (behind a 'mask of politeness') is presented as legitimizing a hostile response in kind. Writing against an earlier, broadly 'Enlightenment' Sinophilia, the essay bases its assessment of Chinese 'cunning' and self-satisfaction on the claim, now lodged in a collective memory of past humiliation, that '[they] have a great talent at bowing out ambassadors who come to visit them.'[70]

China therefore appears to represent an exception to the rule where Hunt's inclusive sympathies are concerned. One especially suggestive example of the anomalous status of China in Hunt's imagining of the East appears in his 1834 essay 'The Subject of Breakfast continued – Tea-drinking', which alludes to diplomatic encounters involving Macartney and Amherst before providing an assessment of the Chinese 'as a population'. This essay remains marked by the whimsicality that is characteristic of so much of Hunt's writing, and Hunt's claim to be following an 'irresistible' flight of fancy invites us to see similarities between the essay and 'A Day by the Fire', with both pieces invoking a domestic milieu as the locale for imaginative reverie. As he gives free rein to 'Chinese ideas', shifting from 'little-eyed' to 'little-footed' and 'little-minded' in his description of the Chinese and their 'tea-cup representations of themselves', Hunt nonetheless alludes to heavily freighted markers of difference that had already begun to acquire significance in the popular imagination.[71] There is a comparable conjunction of geniality and hostility in the work of Charles Lamb, who produced a porcelain-inspired reverie to which Hunt responded in the quotation cited earlier, although, as I now show, Lamb could be even more casually denigratory than Hunt in his engagement with China and 'Chinese ideas'.

Elian Perspectives

Before discussing Lamb's exercise in ekphrasis, 'Old China', it is useful to consider some other near-contemporary literary representations of the culture of chinoiserie. 'Chinese and Chinese-styled goods [were] naturalized within the eighteenth-century English interior,' in David Porter's words, but by the early nineteenth century they had also come to assume particular significance on a continuum with the decorative excess of the Prince Regent's Royal Pavilion at Brighton.[72] Maria Edgeworth invoked this meaning of 'Chinese' style in *The Absentee* (1812), where the designer Mr Soho's account of the heterogeneous Oriental interior that he envisages for Lord and Lady Clonbrony's London townhouse serves to illustrate his clients' susceptibility to 'English' aristocratic fashions and, by extension, their indifference to their Irish estates. Edgeworth's later story 'The India Cabinet' (1815) similarly accentuates the frivolousness of things Chinese. It describes the feelings of the young Rosamond on opening a drawer in a cabinet to find a set of clockwork toys including 'tumblers, tumbling head over heels down stairs, and performing various feats of activity'. Rosamond learns that commanding her curiosity provides greater pleasure than 'seeing Chinese tumblers, or any thing else', and while she is 'a little vexed' by her brother Godfrey's intervention, his soberly practical verdict on 'Chinese toys' provides the tale's final word: 'though [they] were very ingenious, he did not think that they were of any great use; . . . his father had shown him some machines, large *real* machines, which were much more useful, and which therefore he liked better.'[73]

Respectively aligning chinoiserie with aristocratic display and ephemeral miniaturism, these works by Edgeworth illuminate the Cockney coordinates of Lamb's essay 'Old China', published in *London Magazine* in 1823. If the fireside setting for the debate between Lamb's persona Elia and his cousin Bridget recalls that of Hunt's 'A Day by the Fire', Lamb unlike Hunt emphasizes the centrality of material objects to his narrator's flights of the imagination. Elia declares at the outset that '[w]hen I go to see any great house, I inquire for the china-closet,' and even as he thus associates the Chinese taste with a leisured social elite he announces his desire and capacity to partake of it. The essay registers that commodities such as porcelain had become everyday objects for people across the social spectrum, and in emphasizing the visual delight afforded by 'china jars and saucers', Elia celebrates his avowedly small-scale version of the Royal Pavilion's illusionist pleasures. With his opening line, 'I have an almost feminine partiality for old china,' Elia playfully acknowledges the gendering of consumption, yet at the same time, with the important qualifier 'almost', asserts his distance from the feminized figures by which he is captivated.[74] Elia meanwhile undercuts any moral perspective on his 'trifling' habit by representing Bridget's nostalgia for more austere times as no less of a fantasy than his own porcelain-inspired vision.[75]

'Old China' concludes with Elia's exhortation to Bridget to 'look at that merry little Chinese waiter holding an umbrella' (286), and Elia's dual emphasis on visual stimulation and sharing in the pleasures of the 'great' identifies him as a Cockney connoisseur. Elia's adoption of a mock-heraldic idiom to describe 'a cow and rabbit couchant' (281) on a piece of chinaware likewise represents an expression of the boundary-crossing aesthetic that *Blackwood's* censured in Hunt's work. Although Lamb was less concerned than Hunt to position himself in relation to the Lake School, 'Old China' parodically engages with two near-contemporary works also offering idiosyncratic 'Chinese' visions, Coleridge's 'Kubla Khan' and De Quincey's *Confessions*. 'Old China' makes a number of allusions to 'Kubla Khan', as in its reference to the *'speciosa miracula'* of figures 'upon a set of extraordinary blue china' (282), an echo of Coleridge's 'miracle of rare device' which draws an implicit parallel between teacup and pleasure dome and thus debunks 'Kubla Khan's' elevated register.[76]

Just as Elia's account of the intricate patterning of 'Chinese' bric-a-brac simultaneously 'miniaturizes' and domesticates Coleridge's pleasure dome, so it comically deflates De Quincey's lurid 'oriental dreams' too. Elia's statement of his 'almost feminine partiality for Old China' constitutes a confession of sorts, but whereas De Quincey describes himself being 'haunted' by Chinese furniture that is 'instinct with life', Elia maintains a position of spectatorial distance on the activity that he imagines in the 'world' represented by his china teacups.[77] De Quincey's account of his nightmare begins with the statement that 'the Malay has been a fearful enemy for months,' and he declares that, on being involuntarily 'transported' to China, he is 'terrified by the modes of life, by the manners, and the barrier of utter abhorrence, and want of sympathy'.[78] Elia refers by contrast to the pleasure of seeing 'my old friends – whom distance cannot diminish – figuring up in the air . . ., yet on *terra firma* still' (281), as if to negate De Quincey's sense of threatening strangeness.

What De Quincey regarded as '[t]he mere antiquity of Asiatic things, . . . institutions, histories, modes of faith, &c' was radically unsettling because it called into question his Eurocentric conceptions of time and space, and therefore the foundations of his own identity.[79] As exemplified by Elia's address to Bridget to 'just look at that merry little Chinese waiter' (286), 'old china' in Lamb's essay instead offers access to a benign, essentially comic realm in which 'little, lawless, azure-tinctured grotesques, . . . under the notion of men and women, float about, uncircumscribed by any element' (281). Elia's reference to the idea of 'floating about' recalls Coleridge's self-critical definition of his infrequent attempts to 'raise & spiritualize my intellect' against the 'Brahman Creed' exemplified by Vishnu, said 'to float about along an infinite ocean cradled in the flower of the Lotos, and wake once in a million years for a few minutes'.[80] The 'world before perspective' (281) imagined by Elia is broadly comparable to Coleridge's rendering of Vishnu's domain, and this phrase again invites us to see Lamb as responding to De Quincey, because it throws into relief the fact that Elia's vision of China is one where the relations of time and space that prove so disorientating to De Quincey are simply suspended, to amusing effect.

De Quincey's 'paranoid' mode is best illustrated by the nature of his response to Sir William Jones's 1784 'Discourse', an informing text for such a wide range of early nineteenth-century representations of the East. If for Jones the first-hand experience of being 'almost encircled by the vast regions of Asia' was exhilarating as well as 'provincializing', for De Quincey this encounter with the Oriental sublime was unambiguously overpowering.[81] De Quincey states that 'Vishnu hated me', as if contradicting Coleridge, and he describes the combination of different Eastern others against him.[82] Whereas Jones in his 'Discourse' maintains a stable spectatorial position even as he describes himself as being 'almost' surrounded, De Quincey imagines a kind of live burial and stages his own Orientalization, as has been widely discussed.[83] I say more about Lamb alongside Jones later, but here I want in particular to suggest that Lamb rewrote De Quincey's rewriting of Jones, such that, for the narrator of 'Old China' at least, 'Chinese ideas' come to supply familiar pleasures of the imagination.

'Old China' may offer a position of 'condescension' on porcelain and other Chinese-style goods, therefore, presenting them as the occasion for reverie and transport but at the same time providing readers with an index of their own modernity: 'Accompanying such reflections, as light-hearted as they may be,' as Porter writes, 'is the comforting reassurance that our own thoroughly rationalized, post-Renaissance visual world has advanced to the next level, and that we can recognize ourselves in this

difference.'[84] The apparent whimsicality of 'Old China' is atypical of
Lamb's writings, however, and in 'A Dissertation upon Roast Pig' (1822),
he more clearly acknowledged the fraught recent history of Sino–British
relations referred to earlier. At the same time, as Kitson suggests, he
offered a retaliatory response to the 'primal scene' of humiliation generated by the reception of the Macartney and Amherst embassies.[85]
While 'Old China' does not specify the precise origins of the cups and
saucers that Elia describes, and only minimally alludes to the large-scale
production of chinaware, 'Roast Pig' more fully (though still indirectly)
engages with the process of porcelain manufacture. Claiming to recount
a story from an ancient 'Chinese manuscript', the essay tells of how the
'great lubberly boy' (137) Bo-bo accidentally set fire to a wooden shed in
which his father's pigs were housed, and thereafter, again by chance,
became the first person ever to taste crackling. Elia exploits the rich
comic potential of his subject, going on to relate how long it took for
the Chinese to realize that the flesh of pigs could be cooked without
'consuming a whole house to dress it', and how 'a century or two' then
passed before – 'I forget in whose dynasty,' Elia states – 'the rude form
of a gridiron' was superseded by the spit (140).

This discovery narrative also has a less playful side, however,
because its tale of the time it took for more efficient roasting techni-
ques to be adopted rewrites the history of China, associating China
with a sluggish resistance to innovation that is contrasted with
Britain's more dynamic example. Lamb again rewrites De Quincey
here, since the 'sorry antediluvian make-shift of a building' (138) in
which Bo-bo's father keeps the family's pigs recalls De Quincey's
anxious sense of a 'young Chinese' as 'an antediluvian man
renewed'.[86] The readerly self-recognition identified by Porter is additionally evident, as Elia juxtaposes 'their great Confucius' (137) and
'our Locke' (140). Introduced as the author of 'Mundane Mutations',
Confucius is said to have memorialized the 'seventy thousand ages' in
which the Chinese 'ate their meat raw' (137), whereas Locke is the
point of comparison for the 'sage' who first saw an alternative to the
'custom of firing houses' (140). Fang claims that Lamb's hailing of
Locke reframes the process of 'firing' – hitherto central to the Chinese
domination of porcelain manufacture – as an industrial technique
which Britons understand better, and employ more effectively, than
Chinese.[87] This allusion to superior British invention chimes with the
conclusion of Edgeworth's 'The India Cabinet', and more specifically,
Fang claims, nods to the fact that the EIC had by this time begun to

export British-manufactured porcelain, alongside opium, to compete in Chinese markets.[88]

The essay's rhetorical movement is less straightforward than this allegorical reading allows, however, in part because Elia sets himself up as an epicurean whose passion for pig may come close to partaking of the savagery initially attributed to Bo-bo. That Elia is like Bo-bo in this respect draws attention to the universality of human appetites, and if we read pork as potentially standing for opium, the essay may be read as an addiction narrative alongside De Quincey's. In his reflections on 'taste' in the second half of the essay, Elia – having finished his 'Chinese' story – is non-committal about whether it would be justifiable to whip a pig to death in order to enhance its flavour, and thus challenges the reader to consider (in Felicity James's words) 'the cruelties even apparently civilized society can contemplate in the pursuit of its pleasure'.[89] Another measure of the essay's complexity is that while it certainly draws on and perpetuates current stereotypes about the 'true' scale of Chinese achievements, it also enjoys the creative license afforded by the idea of Chinese antiquity, just as Elia simultaneously displays 'condescension' towards and takes imaginative pleasure from the contemplation of a 'world before perspective'. Although Lamb's writing displays less attachment than Hunt's to *Arabian Nights*–style literary Orientalism, this essay, as Kitson suggests, offers an 'orientalized version of China ... in the manner of contemporary tales and pantomimes of Aladdin', accentuating the 'ostensible Chinese setting' of Galland's 'original' as it tells of how Bo-bo, like Aladdin, makes a lucrative discovery.[90]

What especially complicates any sense of an underlying imperial logic in either of Lamb's 'Chinese' essays is the way in which, most directly in his correspondence, Lamb reflected on his experience of working at the EIC's Leadenhall Street headquarters, where from 1792 he was a clerk in the accountant's department. Given my wider focus on British imperial interests and Britons' cultural horizons, Lamb is an important figure for this study, because he recognized that his living was dependent upon Britain's extended Eastern empire yet also displayed little obvious interest in Chinese actuality. Lamb maintained a correspondence with the Canton-based Thomas Manning, 'the preeminent expert on China in the Romantic period', but in referring to the channels of communication between London and Canton, he at times stressed both that China was 'so many hemispheres off', and that it was fundamentally alien and therefore likely to defy any attempt at imaginative comprehension.[91] Querying whether the Great Wall of China actually existed, and if so whether it was 'as big as London Wall', in the same letter to Manning, Lamb indeed complained how 'China – Canton – bless us – ... strains the imagination and makes it ache!'[92]

Such a notion of the problem of distance is a familiar one in this period: as already noted Hunt claimed that, for Britons, India was little more than 'a great distant place with strange beasts and trees in it'. Whereas Hunt emphasized his access to other more congenial – because essentially literary – 'Easts', however, Lamb in his correspondence with Manning, as David Higgins argues, presented the very contemplation of distance as compromising his 'obsessively localized' sense of self.[93] Lamb's comparison between the Great Wall of China and one of the remaining fragments of Roman fortification in London – the product of a less playful act of miniaturization than that performed in 'Old China' – demonstrates how he sometimes sought to negotiate the problem of the Oriental sublime, the antiquity and magnitude of 'Asiatic things', that was so destabilizing for De Quincey. If questions of age and (especially) scale are the subject of seemingly carefree and delighted reflection in 'Old China', the parade of ignorance in this letter, and in relation to Confucius or Chinese imperial dynasties in 'Roast Pig', is arguably more characteristic of Lamb's writing.

Even if Lamb's friendship with Manning gave him access to the latest Sinological research, then, his representation of China is often as derisive as Hunt's. Unlike Hunt, though, Lamb was often casually hostile towards the extra-European world more generally. He subsumed China under a general-ized notion of 'the East' when he told Manning that a 'new opera of "Kais"' (based on the romance of Mejnoun and Leila) would be appealing to him because it was 'all about Eastern manners' and described 'the wild Arabs, wandering Egyptians, lying dervishes, all that sort of people, to a hair'.[94] In a letter written on Christmas Day 1815, Lamb again teased Manning by suggesting that while in Europe '[e]mpires [had] been overturned, [and] crowns trodden into dust', his friend had been wasting his time in China, in a state of 'foolish voluntary exile'. Like his undiscriminating reference to 'that sort of people' in the earlier letter, Lamb's reduction of Manning's experience to 'settling whether Ho-hing-tong should be spelt with a – or a –' repudiates both scholarly Orientalism and 'travelled' cosmopolitanism.[95] Lamb's writing displays something of the familiarity of address evident in Hunt's work, therefore, but simultaneously demonstrates a wilful – if obviously affected – lack of awareness of or interest in the world outside of Europe.

'Official Confinement'

Writing to thank Southey for the gift of a copy of *Roderick*, Lamb referred to it as 'a comfortable poem', welcoming Southey's decision not to expose his readers again to the 'Oriental almighties' of *Kehama*:

> My imagination goes sinking and floundering in the vast spaces of unopened-before systems & faiths, I am put out of the pale of my old sympathies, my moral sense [is] almost outraged ... I am at home in Spain and Christendom. I have a timid imagination I am afraid. I do not willingly admit of strange beliefs or out of the way creeds or places. I never read books of travel, at least not farther than Paris, or Rome. I can just endure Moors because of their connection as foes with Xtians; but Abyssinians, Ethiops, Esquimaux, Dervises & all that tribe I hate. I believe I fear them in some manner ... I am a Christian, Englishman, Londoner, *Templar* – God help me when I come to put off these snug relations.[96]

There is much to say about this passage – for example its gathering of 'Abyssinians' and others into a single 'tribe', its nod to Hunt's idea of 'snugness', and its conjoining of hostility and timidity: in this last respect it is striking that Lamb speaks of 'hating' Abyssinians and their ilk, yet also registers both the defensiveness of a position in which 'old sympathies' constitute a 'pale' and the 'floundering' of his imagination before anything beyond that fastness.[97] In the context of my discussion of Lamb's engagement with a 'Chinese' commodity culture, however, I am particularly interested in the compatibility of the 'commercial cosmopolitanism' that Elia takes for granted and the performance of anti-cosmopolitan sentiments in this letter and across Lamb's work more generally. Jon Klancher glosses the idea of 'commercial cosmopolitanism' with reference to Cyrus Redding's account of London, in *The New Monthly Magazine*, as a 'vast storehouse for the mind' – a container 'perpetually increasing its contents' and 'delivering them to the multitude'.[98] Redding's sense of 'London as Cosmopolis' is in the tradition of writing about London as a world of its own, associated with *Spectator* 69, and Elia too sometimes invokes a comparable notion of the availability of pleasure and knowledge in the capital. Whereas Mr Spectator is so impressed by the spectacle of commercial intercourse at the Royal Exchange that he imagines himself 'a Citizen of the World', though, Lamb, in the letter cited earlier, defines his sense of self in hyperbolically parochial terms, in a manner almost exactly opposite to Hunt's movement from 'Christendom' to 'the East' in 'A Rustic Walk and Dinner'.

It is useful to refer to the *Spectator* here in part because doing so draws attention to some of the differences as well as similarities between the two writers that are this chapter's main focus. While for Hunt the *Spectator* provided a model for the journalistic personae that he employed, as well as – in *Spectator* 69 at least – for his vision of sympathy 'with all', for Lamb the disinterested and Olympian perspective that Mr Spectator claimed for himself was considerably harder to attain.[99] If the idea of spectatorial distance underpins 'Old China's' reveries, an earlier Elia essay, 'Oxford in the Vacation' (1820), situates such musing squarely within the context of the competing demands of work. In it, Elia further establishes his identity as an eccentric accounting clerk, declaring that it is sometimes his 'humour' when at work 'to while away … my time in the contemplation of indigos, cottons, raw silks, piece-goods, flowered or otherwise' (8–9). By thus recasting the business of ledger keeping as a 'relaxing' leisure-time activity, Elia seemingly presents his day job as continuous with, even subordinate to, his true writerly vocation. He suggests indeed that his desk-bound 'contemplation' prepares him for the writing that he does when he is not at work ('your outside sheets, and waste wrappers of foolscap do receive into them … the impressions of sonnets, epigrams, *essays*'), then adds that '[t]he enfranchised quill, that has plodded all morning among the cart-rucks of figures and ciphers, frisks and curvets so at its ease over the flowery carpet-ground of a midnight dissertation. – It feels its promotion' (8–9).

Ostensibly, then, Elia here imagines his late-night writing as a recreational pursuit that is creatively sustained by his daytime activity, or at least remains 'uncompromised' by that labour. His account of the seemingly fluid relationship between these forms of endeavour invites us briefly to consider Lamb alongside Sir William Jones. Both men were EIC employees, in London and Calcutta respectively, and both would become best known for the work they did beyond their primary occupation. Lamb, like Jones, seems to have conceived of a 'second self' that was not accountable to authority or responsible to others, and he imagined literary composition just as Jones saw scholarship, as (in the latter's words) a 'relief' from 'severer employment in the discharge of publick duty'.[100] There are obvious differences between Lamb and Jones too, though, and comparing them brings into sharper focus the distinctive character of Lamb's position as a metropolitan author whose professional work – a much more mundane form of 'writing' than the kind he aspired to produce – implicated him as a functionary in the business of empire. As the nature of his 'Chinese ideas' makes clear, Lamb rejected any Jones-like ambition to 'know' the East better than others. In addition, he sometimes referred to his service of the EIC almost as if he imagined himself as a colonial subject rather than, like Jones, someone able to couple 'delight and advantage'.

To return to the passage from 'Oxford in the Vacation' discussed earlier, Elia's reference to his 'enfranchised quill' invites the reader to consider the variety of terms that the obtrusive adjective might be defined against; the idea of a quill that 'frisks and curvets', as Higgins observes, presents desk work as 'a sort of slavery from which . . . writing, figured as a leaping horse, is delighted to escape'.[101] This connection of the necessity of paid employment with a state of un-freedom is repeated throughout Lamb's correspondence, and there is an obvious overlap between the concerns of Elia's essays and Lamb's letters. In a letter to the poet Matilda Betham in 1815, for example, Lamb exclaimed: 'Why the devil am I never to have a chance of scribbling my own free thoughts, verse or prose, again? Why must I write of Tea & Drugs & Price Goods & bales of Indigo[?]'[102] He more explicitly presented his work at India House as a kind of thraldom in a letter to 'Quaker poet' Bernard Barton in September 1822. Speaking as if he had been captured by Barbary pirates, in another figuring of the hostility that he imagined beyond the 'pale' of his sympathies, he stated that 'I am, like you, a prisoner to the desk. I have been chained to that galley thirty years.'[103]

Lamb sometimes had it both ways where his sense of the seemingly all-pervading world of mundane daily toil was concerned. In his Christmas 1815 letter to Manning, for example, he playfully asserted the insignificance of self-consciously 'serious' writing in relation to the trade in commodities that his labours helped to facilitate, telling his friend that Coleridge's 'forty thousand treatises in criticism and metaphysics' were 'destined . . . to wrap up spices'.[104] As much as Lamb sometimes deflated Coleridgean gravity in this way, he was nonetheless candid in his correspondence with both Wordsworth and Coleridge regarding the obstacles that his employment placed in the way of his personal happiness. 'My theory is to enjoy life, but the practice is against it,' he wrote to Wordsworth in March 1822, adding that 'I grow ominously tired of official confinement. Thirty years have I served the Philistines, and my neck is not subdued to the yoke.'[105] In an earlier letter to Wordsworth, Lamb lamented his inability to be as productive as his friend, complaining that 'these "merchants and their spicy drugs" . . . lime-twig up my poor soul and body':

I 'engross', when I should pen paragraph. Confusion blast all mercantile transactions, all traffick, exchange of commodities, intercourse between nations, all the consequent civilization and wealth and amity and link of society, and getting rid of prejudices, and knowledge of the face of the globe – and rot the very firs of the forest that look so romantic alive, and die into desks.[106]

As elsewhere, Lamb claims here that the need to perform one kind of apparently repetitive and mind-numbing writing stands in the way of him producing another of a more congenial variety; captured – literally, stuck – 'soul and body', he represents his employer's thwarting of his aspirations as all but absolute. Lamb also moves beyond his personal situation, however, because by quoting from a passage describing Satan's flight from Hell in *Paradise Lost*, he broaches a larger critique of global commerce as a fall from humankind's natural state – a descent figured by the contrast between the 'firs of the forest' and the 'dead' desks of accountants produced from them. While repudiating knowledge of the wider world in familiar terms, Lamb further denounces the whole network of exchange of which such knowledge is a by-product, ironically rehearsing the ideology of commerce which held that its agency united people in mutually beneficial interrelationship. When Lamb told Southey in 1818 that '[m]y bread and cheese is stable as the foundations of Leadenhall Street, and if it hold out as long as the "foundations of our empire in the East", I shall do pretty well,' he adopted a comparable rhetorical strategy, his use of quotation marks demonstrating a desire to distance himself from any 'official' legitimization of empire.[107]

It is instructive to consider Lamb alongside Thomas Love Peacock, who referred to the higher-ranking post in the Examiner's Office at India House that he acquired in 1819 as offering 'an employment of a very interesting and intellectual kind . . . in which it is possible to be of great service, not only to the Company, but to the millions under her dominion'.[108] In contrast to Peacock, Lamb often sought to dis-identify with the EIC, while also adopting a civic humanist language of opposition to empire more broadly. Lamb often invoked the idea of global trade as Fall, as in another letter to the Wordsworths in which he represented the 'pretence of Commerce allying distant shores, promoting and diffusing knowledge, good &c.—' as a Satanic ruse.[109] He employed a similarly mock-Miltonic register in referring to the 'Beasts' to whom he was responsible at India House, telling Mrs Wordsworth that while the 'dear abstract notion of the . . . Company, as long as she is unseen, is pretty, rather Poetical', he 'loathe[d] and detest[ed]' its actual manifestation as much as 'the Scarlet what-do-you-call-her of Babylon'.[110] This complaint against the EIC is expressed in characteristically hyperbolic terms, and the immediate occasion for it was outrage at the loss of a customary right (going home early on a Saturday) rather than any principled objection to empire. The idea of 'Babylon' invoked by Lamb nonetheless has a suggestive resonance, not just in connection with Milton's Orientalized Pandemonium, but by way of analogy for the condition of modern Britain.[111] Southey had referred to the 'imperial dotage' of Babylon, presented as a city-state akin to London, in *Thalaba*, and, as Dart notes, parallels between Britain and Babylon (visually explicit in John Martin's apocalyptic scenes) were to become especially frequent around the time of George III's death in 1820.[112]

At Home with Empire?

In much of Lamb's writing, then, efforts to conceive of an imaginative space free from the determinations of work appear bound up with a larger sense of (albeit implicit) resistance to the commercial empire that he served; certainly, Lamb's letters often take a sceptical view of any Peacock-style grand narrative of EIC-sponsored 'improvement'. In conclusion, however, I want to consider how Lamb might nonetheless be regarded as an 'imperial man', to the extent that he was – for all his protestations to the contrary – among those whose 'minds and skills were being applied to the government of a vast territorial empire as well as to the continuing management of an expanding trade'.[113] I want especially to explore the way in which Lamb's first Elia essay, 'The South-Sea House' (1820), stages a relatively new metropolitan understanding of a seemingly arm's-length relationship between Britain and its expanding Eastern empire. As I argue, its depiction of the South Sea House sets up a contrast between past and present which helps us to think about the 'unseen' EIC referred to by Lamb in the letter cited earlier.

The South Sea House was the headquarters of the South Sea Company, popularly associated with the 'bubble' of 1720. Elia describes this one-time 'house of trade' (1) as a 'magnificent relic!' (2) which – because it belongs to a different period of history – now provides a vehicle for pleasurable contemplation. He also presents it in terms that chime with Lamb's frequently expressed desire for freedom from the necessity of paid employment. '[T]o such as me, old house!', he writes, drawing attention to the peculiarity of his own sensibility, 'there is a charm in thy quiet: a cessation – a coolness from business – an indolence almost cloistral – which is delightful!' (2). Elia here adopts the language of Mr Spectator at the Royal Exchange, but the status of the South Sea House as 'a centre of busy interests' is registered in the past tense: 'The throng of merchants was here.' Though 'some forms of business are still kept up' (the South Sea Company continued to manage part of the National Debt), the 'soul' of the South Sea House is said to be 'long since fled' (1). The living death of the South Sea House and its status as a 'memorial' in 'the very heart of stirring and living commerce' (2) make it available to be read, as Higgins suggests, as a *'memento mori'* hinting at the future 'obsolescence and destruction that awaits the grandest imperial projects'.[114] In line with such a reading, Elia's account of his solitary pacing of the dust-layered premises appears to nod to a 'ruins of empire' text such as Anna Laetitia Barbauld's poem 'Eighteen Hundred and Eleven' (1812), in which the narrator traverses a Britain now vacated by the 'Genius' that had once presided over it.

The implicit comparison and contrast that the essay makes between South Sea House in the past and India House in the present also invites another reading of a less anxious lived experience of empire, however. Elia's recollection of his former colleagues initially seems at once affectionate and condescending, as when he states that the accountant John Tipp 'did ... scream and scrape most abominably' when he played his fiddle in his 'suite' (5) of rooms. But this eccentricity may also be understood in relation to William Hazlitt's account, in 'On Londoners and Country People' (1825), of the 'positive illusions' – not simply reducible to false consciousness – of the proud and self-possessed Cockney.[115] In view of Lamb's extensive reflection on the experience of work, in his correspondence and his essays, it is striking that Elia describes Tipp as protective of his leisure hours but 'quite another sort of creature' in the South Sea House, where he was the embodiment of a notion of professional service avowedly divorced from the world outside of the office. In Tipp's company, Elia states, 'all ideas, that were purely ornamental, were banished. ... The whole duty of man consisted in writing off dividend warrants.' Elia presents Tipp as one who regarded '"an accountant the greatest character in the world, and himself the greatest accountant in it"' (5), and his claim that, for Tipp, '[t]he fractional farthing' was 'as dear ... as the thousands which stand before it' nicely conveys the latter's understanding of figures on balance sheets as referring only to themselves. He goes on to add that Tipp never 'for lucre, or for intimidation, ... forsook friend or principle' (6), but this devotion to principle is defined as one that is restricted to the technicalities of accounting practice rather than concerning itself with any wider public sphere.

It might be argued that Tipp is depicted as functioning in a kind of asocial vacuum in this way because he is associated with the near-defunct South Sea Company, and therefore in effect could only ever have played at being an accountant. By virtue of his ethic of professional service and his clear demarcation of work and leisure time, however, Tipp intriguingly anticipates the much better-known figure of Mr. Wemmick in Dickens's *Great Expectations* (1861), someone able imaginatively to detach his suburban idyll from the less wholesome source of the income sustaining it. Albeit that Tipp is not a suburban Cockney of the same stamp as Wemmick, reading Tipp alongside Wemmick brings into focus Elia's description of him as upholding an ideal of 'commercial' honour – as in his careful treatment of 'the fractional farthing' (6) – yet also separating such duty from any consideration of the realities of the commercial exchange to which numbers on balance sheets correspond. Elia presents the annual balancing of books as occupying Tipp's 'days and nights for a month previous' (5), even though he yearned for busier times, and 'a return of the old stirring days when South Sea hopes were young!' (6). In view of what I have said about the idea of imaginative detachment, Tipp's apparent allusion to the pre-bubble period ('when South Sea hopes were young!') is especially suggestive, since it refers to a time when trading in slaves was one of the South Sea Company's key areas of activity.

Elia's recollection of another colleague, Henry Man, provides a further demonstration of how certain forms of nostalgic recollection may serve to distance troubling realities from current consideration; again Lamb here appears to be interested in exploring the broader question of the imperial metropole's imaginary relation to its colonial possessions. Elia presents Man as, unlike Tipp, curious about matters outside the workplace – 'great thou used to be in Public Ledgers, and in Chronicles,' he recalls – and he precisely situates him in the period of 'the war which ended in the tearing from Great Britain her rebellious colonies ... and such small politics' (7). Fang argues that Elia's 'aesthetic contemplation evacuates [the] formerly controversial history' of the slave trade as well as the scandal of the South Sea bubble, and a comparable 'evacuating' manoeuvre appears to be performed in the quotation just cited, via the double meaning of 'small politics'.[116] If this phrase functions as an ironic reference to the trauma of Britain's war with its American colonies and the loss of its 'first' empire, it additionally offers an appropriate recognition of how, taking a longer view, defeat in America did indeed come to seem a 'small' matter as Britain developed its 'second' empire in the East. This idea of 'small politics' moreover captures the way in which the very notion of empire itself became increasingly less controversial in metropolitan circles after the initial period of national introspection that followed the American war.

Lamb's essay certainly plays with the rhetoric of decline and fall, and in its account of the South Sea House as a 'magnificent relic' it may be read as presenting 'a London that is fundamentally shaped by imperial power and trade, but that is also haunted by the prospect of its own decay'.[117] Keeping in mind both the connection of the South Sea House to the slave trade and the depiction of Henry Man's obsession with the politics of the American war, however, the essay also arguably signals the transition from one phase of empire to another – where the former was (once) contentious but the latter appears more or less free from controversy, not least since it is imaginatively remote, though bound up with everyday life in the metropolis. Even as recollection of the past provides its core, the essay recognizes that its readers may be 'at home with empire' by virtue of taking it for granted.[118] It begins by addressing a 'Reader, in thy passage from the Bank' (1), and it goes on to position South Sea House 'in the very heart of stirring and living commerce, – amid the fret and fever of speculation – with the Bank, and the 'Change, and the India-house about [it], in the hey-day of present prosperity' (2). As much as the South Sea House itself is portrayed in terms of a 'ruins of empire' discourse, then, the essay here returns to the ur-text of eighteenth-century commercial empire, *Spectator* 69, to record the economic activity which flourishes around it. If Elia initially states of the South Sea House that 'the throng of merchants was here,' he acknowledges that his audience is habituated to a greater dynamism than this in the present.

Although a narrative of 'present prosperity' does not straightforwardly overwrite a narrative of decay, Lamb's essay at least offers a provisional negotiation of 'anxieties of empire', as if implicitly responding to Barbauld's claim in her earlier 'Epistle to Wilberforce' (1791) that 'British morals' have been 'changed' by 'foreign wealth'.[119] With Barbauld's formulation in view, we might say that not only does Lamb's essay contain the 'civic' narrative of decline and fall (because the South Sea House provides a pleasing spectacle), but it also registers the dynamism of an imperial metropolis which appears to bear no trace of the other. While it alludes to *Spectator* 69 in describing the City of London as 'the very heart of stirring and living commerce', its imagining of a network of empire eschews the cosmopolitanism of Addison's essay, in which the presence of international 'Ministers of Commerce' makes Mr Spectator identify as 'a Citizen of the World'.[120] We can only speculate now about the visibility to Lamb of the Indianized metropolitan community in London's 'Little Bengal'.[121] Lamb's essay helps us to think about how it may have been possible for Britons to conceive of a 'present prosperity' that was mentally separated from the 'unseen' global operations of the EIC, however, and albeit in a manner atypical of Lamb's writing, it stages an ideological formation which appears able to conjoin being imperial and not thinking very much about empire at all.

Notes

1. Hunt, *Selected Writings*, 5:131.
2. Reynolds, *Safie*, 8.
3. Dart, *Metropolitan Art*, 1.
4. Aravamudan, *Enlightenment Orientalism*, 8.
5. To Southey, 6 May 1815, *Works*, 6:465.
6. Hunt, *Selected Writings*, 1:232. Further references appear as parenthetical citations in the text.
7. De Quincey, *Confessions*, 58.
8. Kucich, 'Cockney Chivalry', 127.
9. *Blackwood's*, 2 (1817), 39–40.
10. Ibid., 3 (1818), 201.
11. Ibid., 2 (1817), 199.
12. Ibid., 6 (1819), 73.
13. Bewell, *Colonial Disease*, 174.
14. Jones, 'Suburb Sinners', 90; *Blackwood's*, 2 (1817), 39; *Edinburgh Review*, 57 (1817), 33.
15. Cited in Bewell, *Colonial Disease*, 172; *Blackwood's*, 19 (1826), xxvi; to Reynolds, 19 Feb. 1818, *Letters*, 62.
16. Hunt, *Selected Writings*, 6:79.
17. *Examiner*, 10 (9 Mar. 1817), 145–6.
18. Gilmartin, *Print Politics*, 209.
19. Hunt, *Selected Writings*, 2:100.
20. Ibid., 1:70.
21. *Examiner*, 6 (3 Jan. 1813), 1.
22. Ibid., 2.
23. Ibid., 3; *Blackwood's*, 3 (1818), 198.
24. *Examiner*, 6 (3 Jan. 1813), 3.
25. Barrell, *Spirit of Despotism*, 95.
26. Hunt, *Selected Writings*, 1:287.
27. Ibid., 1:283.

28. Ibid., 2:43–9.
29. Cohen-Vrignaud, *Radical Orientalism*, 121–37.
30. Hunt, *Selected Writings*, 2:43.
31. 'The Late Mr. Sheridan', *Examiner* (14 July 1816), [433–6].
32. Coleman, '"Voyage of Conception"', 92–3.
33. Hunt, *Selected Writings*, 1:47.
34. Ibid., 48 and 47.
35. Hunt, 'India', *Examiner* (20 Sept. 1818), 593.
36. Hunt, *Selected Writings*, 2:110.
37. Ibid., 2:160.
38. Ibid., 5:211–12.
39. Roe, *Dissent*, 71–87.
40. Gilmartin, *Print Politics*, 195–7.
41. Hunt, *Selected Writings*, 6:33.
42. *Liberal*, 1 (1822), 317.
43. Ibid., 326–7.
44. Ibid., 327.
45. *Indicator*, 1:96.
46. Cox, 'Cockney Cosmopolitanism', 246.
47. *Indicator*, 1:96.
48. Gilmartin, *Print Politics*, 209.
49. *Indicator*, 1:96.
50. To George and Georgiana Keats, 16 Dec. 1818 to 4 Jan. 1819, *Letters*, 167.
51. *Examiner*, 10 (9 Mar. 1817), 145; *Liberal*, 1 (1822), 330.
52. *Liberal*, 1, 330.
53. *Liberal*, 3 (1823), 103; Dart, *Metropolitan Art*, 41.
54. *Liberal*, 3 (1823), 114.
55. Ibid., 98.
56. Ibid., 99.
57. Ibid., 100.
58. Ibid., 118; Keats, *Complete Poems*, 123.
59. To Richard Woodhouse, 27 Oct. 1818, *Selected Letters*, 148.
60. Stabler, 'Aesthetics', 95–117.
61. *Monthly Magazine* (1842), 237.
62. Simpson, *Stranger*, 54–68; Warner, *Stranger Magic*, 87–159.
63. Cited in Gilmartin, *Print Politics*, 210.
64. *Tait's*, 2 (Jan. 1833), 436–7; Stabler, 'Aesthetics', 100.
65. *Tait's*, 2, 437.
66. Gilmartin, *Print Politics*, 196.
67. *Tait's*, 2, 435.
68. Kitson, *Romantic China*, 154.
69. *Examiner* (7 Sept. 1817), 570–1; Kitson, *Romantic China*, 178.
70. *Indicator*, 1:94.
71. *London Journal*, 1 (9 July 1834), 113.
72. Porter, *Chinese Taste*, 2.

73. Edgeworth, *Continuation*, 1:237, 240 and 245–6.
74. Lamb, *Elia*, 281. Further references appear as parenthetical citations in the text.
75. Porter, *Chinese Taste*, 9.
76. Fang, *Empire of Signs*, 55.
77. De Quincey, *Confessions*, 74.
78. Ibid., 72–3.
79. Ibid., 73; Leask, *British Romantic Writers*, 220–8.
80. To Thelwall, 14 Oct. 1797, *Letters*, 1:350.
81. Jones, 'Discourse', 4.
82. De Quincey, *Confessions*, 74.
83. Barrell, *Infection*.
84. Porter, *Chinese Taste*, 3.
85. Kitson, *Romantic China*, 157.
86. De Quincey, *Confessions*, 73.
87. Fang, *Empire of Signs*, 63.
88. Ibid., 63–4.
89. James, 'Manning, Lamb, and Oriental Encounters', 32.
90. Kitson, *Romantic China*, 169.
91. Ibid., 174; to Manning, 5 Dec. 1806, *Works*, 6:368.
92. Ibid. 6:364.
93. Higgins, *Romantic Englishness*, 130.
94. To Manning, 26 Feb. 1808, *Works*, 6:383.
95. To Manning, 25 Dec. 1815, *Works*, 6:481–2.
96. To Southey, 6 May 1815, *Works*, 6:465–6.
97. Higgins, *Romantic Englishness*, 130–2.
98. Cited in Klancher, 'Romantic Cosmopolitanisms', 74.
99. Gilmartin, *Print Politics*, 200.
100. Jones, *Letters*, 2:705.
101. Higgins, *Romantic Englishness*, 143.
102. To Betham, [n.d.] 1815, *Works*, 6:478.
103. To Barton, 11 Sept. 1822, *Works*, 7:572.
104. *Works*, 6:481.
105. To Wordsworth, 20 Mar. 1822, *Works*, 7:563.
106. To Wordsworth, 28 Apr. 1815, *Works*, 6:463.
107. To Southey, 26 Oct. 1818, *Works*, 6:516.
108. Cited in Bowen, *Business*, 146.
109. To the Wordsworths, 28 Sept. 1805, *Works*, 6:306.
110. To Mrs Wordsworth, 18 Feb. 1818, *Works*, 6:513.
111. Rajan, *Under Western Eyes*, 50.
112. Dart, *Metropolitan Art*, 164.
113. Bowen, *Business*, 149–50.
114. Higgins, *Romantic Englishness*, 134.
115. Hazlitt, 'On Londoners and Country People', *New Monthly Magazine* 6 (Aug. 1823), 173.

116. Fang, 'Consumer Imagination', 834.
117. Higgins, *Romantic Englishness*, 134.
118. Hall and Rose, *At Home*, 1–31.
119. Barbauld, *Poetry and Prose*, 126.
120. *Spectator*, 1:293–4.
121. White, *Little London*.

CHAPTER 7

'It Is Otherwise in Asia'
'Character' and Improvement in Picaresque Fiction

In the preface to *Hellas* (1822), Percy Shelley cited Thomas Hope's 'admirable novel' *Anastasius* (1819), subtitled 'Memoirs of a Greek', as a 'faithful picture' of corrupted Greek manners before the recent return of 'the flower of [Greek] youth, ... from the universities of Italy, Germany, and France, ... communicated to their fellow-citizens the latest results of that moral perfection of which their ancestors were the original source'.[1] This chapter begins by examining Hope's *Anastasius* and its protagonist's complex relation to his Greek cultural heritage. The novel displays obvious debts to Byron and Byronism, and as the quotation just cited demonstrates it indirectly at least addresses the question which both Byron and Shelley were to raise about whether modern Greeks might already be too debased to throw off the Ottoman yoke. Rather than discuss Hope's intervention in debates about Greek independence, however, I want instead here to consider some of the other implications of Shelley's claim that the novel offered a 'faithful picture' of manners. Anastasius was regarded by some as an irredeemably Orientalized figure, and situated in a broader literary-historical context, Hope's work can be seen as the prototype of a mode of fictionalized autobiography featuring native informants, written by men with experience of diplomacy and/or imperial administration such as James Morier, James Bailie Fraser, and William Browne Hockley.

The narrators of 'Oriental picaresque' fictions are sometimes depicted as at odds with their environment, so as potentially to invite cross-cultural identification with oppressed Eastern subjects, but, as I argue here, they are above all presented as objects of knowledge embodying particular, more or less unchanging, truths about the East. Other, more scholarly approaches to the contemporary condition of Eastern peoples continued to be adopted in this period, as in the writings of the EIC's Sir John Malcolm, but the Orientalist contextualization of cultural difference was increasingly contested by claims about the explanatory power of 'character' which the novels in question helped to circulate. As I show in what follows,

Morier's *The Adventures of Hajji Baba of Ispahan* (1824), even more than *Anastasius*, provides readers with a detached perspective on its protagonist as a figure exemplifying the larger realities of 'Asiatic manners' and life under a despotic government. Later fictions that I also explore here include Fraser's historical novels *The Kuzzilbash* (1828) and *The Persian Adventurer* (1830), likewise primarily set in Persia, and Hockley's *Pandurang Hari, or Memoirs of a Hindoo* (1826), the first such work to feature an Indian narrator.

Though avowedly supplying an antidote to romantic illusions about the East, these novels do not straightforwardly define themselves against older forms of literary Orientalism, since Morier's *Hajji Baba* and other works such as Thomas Henry Ottley's *Rustum Khan* (1831) remain indebted to the story-telling tradition of the *Arabian Nights*. I argue as well that in some cases metropolitan audiences saw these novels as caricaturing their protagonists, and indicated that they found *Lalla Rookh*'s idealized East more congenial instead. Nonetheless, in helping to establish the idea of 'the Oriental' as a unitary figure in the British imaginary, Oriental picaresque fictions were sometimes credited with evidential value, as for example by Sir Henry Bartle Frere, who in 1873 praised *Hajji Baba, The Kuzzilbash*, and *Pandurang Hari* for their insight into 'the inner life of Orientals'.[2]

The title characters of these novels are always already familiar, then, and they do not afford the cultural challenge of 'significant otherness' explored earlier. Even as they present actual or potential colonial subjects (and thus ostensibly subscribe to the liberal imperialist politics of James Mill and T. B. Macaulay), however, Oriental picaresque fictions shift between recognizing that their informant narrators are in want of education and suggesting that they may be incorrigibly roguish. To the extent that they seize upon character traits which appear innate and unreformable, I argue, these works may therefore be seen not only to invite scepticism about the prospect of imperial 'improvement', but also to accentuate for their readers the imagined distance of the 'Orientals' depicted.

'A Strange Dance over Land and Sea'

Thomas Hope was born in Amsterdam into a Dutch banking family, and he is best known today as the wealthy artist patron who helped to create the eclectic 'Regency style'. He was a cosmopolitan figure by virtue of his background and the range of his aesthetic tastes, and also because of his experience of the Levantine world, deriving from the Eastern tour he undertook between 1787 and 1795. Hope's status as a Regency taste maker might lead one to expect *Anastasius* to be as 'ornamental' as *Lalla Rookh*, but he emphasized that it was above all his familiarity with quotidian life in Egypt, Syria, and elsewhere that provided the basis for his 'minute' description. Hope also signalled his work's political resonance by announcing in its introduction that the 'ever interesting regions' it portrays had once been 'adorned by the Greeks', but now were 'defaced by the Turks'.[3] *Anastasius* traverses terrain to which Byron had already staked a literary claim, and it is derivative of Byron's writing in a number of ways, in the character of its protagonist as well as in some of the scenes of its action. If Hope drew upon Byron's Turkish tales, *Childe Harold's Pilgrimage*, and the opening cantos of *Don Juan*, however, his work in turn had a significant impact upon Byron, who introduced the Russo–Turkish war (1787–92) to *Don Juan* after reading *Anastasius*.[4] It is most accurate therefore to consider the mutual influence of Hope and Byron rather than to think of Hope simply as a lesser figure imitating Byron. Hope's for the most part cynical account of modern Greek patriotism echoed Byron's notes to *Childe Harold*'s second canto, but then Thomas Medwin claimed that Byron later 'out-anastasiused Anastasius in his view of the Greek character', even after he had decided to join the Greek cause.[5]

Anastasius introduces readers to a well-born protagonist who is a direct participant in – rather than, like Childe Harold, a detached observer of – the Levantine world. Even more emphatically than Byron's poetry, Hope's work presents this world as a free-for-all, where rival powers compete for influence and their representatives strive for personal advancement. Anastasius's story is as much one of accommodation as of defiance or rebellion, therefore, because while he chafes against the 'parental yoke' (1:18) he adeptly negotiates with other kinds of authority. After running away from his home in Chios when his lover, the French consul's daughter, becomes pregnant, Anastasius joins a Venetian brig, which is captured by pirates and then by 'the famous Hassan Capitan-pasha', a historical figure 'delivering the Morea from its Arnaoot oppressors': 'thus was I, hapless Greek', Hope's narrator states, 'compelled, in the space of five days, to bear the yoke of four different nations, – French, Venetians, Maynotes, and Turks' (1:24–5). Anastasius gains Hassan's protection by serving his Greek interpreter, and in the process establishes himself as 'a great favourite with the favourite of the favourite *par excellence*' (1:81). He refers to his success at working within the system of Turkish despotism and he later converts to Islam, becoming 'Selim Aga' in order to save his own life when (in another nod to *Don Juan*) his affair with a Turkish woman in Constantinople is discovered by her husband.

Despite his obvious selfishness, Anastasius may still sometimes be regarded as a sympathetic and redeemable figure; he reproaches himself when he hears of how his lover had died during childbirth, and he similarly regrets his treatment of another tragically devoted mistress, Euphrosyne. Anastasius responds with rapture to the sights and sounds of Chios when he returns there following his mother's death, and he intermittently expresses both his residual pride in his Hellenic heritage and his exasperation with his fellow countrymen. While the *Edinburgh Review* referred to Hope's narrator as 'our Oriental profligate', suggesting that he irreversibly 'turns Turk', Anastasius continues to appeal to the exceptionalist idea of noble 'Grecian blood' (1:277) even after his conversion to Islam.[6] Later in the novel, he attempts to legitimize his 'defiance' of 'morality and . . . law' by presenting his conduct as a means of escaping the condition of 'contented slavery' (2:144) in which others live.

If these glimpses of Anastasius's submerged idealism demonstrate Hope's indebtedness to Byron and the Byronic hero, however, Hope's novel also breaks new fictional ground, not least in its extension of its geographical reach beyond the primarily Aegean milieu associated with Byron. Although both Byron and Shelley read the novel through the lens of the Greek struggle for independence, it often departs from this immediate political context, as when Anastasius encounters a Cretan, Aly, who tempts him with the 'irresistible attractions' of Egypt, which, he claims, 'always welcomed . . . wanderers who had no predilection for any particular soil, or attachment to any particular home' (1:280). Anastasius subsequently sails for Egypt, where he cures the Bey of Cairo of a mystery illness, and is then rewarded with high office and marriage to his new patron's daughter. In one of the numerous moments where he invites the reader to celebrate his upward mobility ('behold me now' is a recurrent phrase), Anastasius proudly exclaims: 'Here am I, the youngest son of a petty drogueman in an island of the Archipelago . . . become the master of a host of slaves, the son to a Bey of Egypt, and the governor of a province; . . . occupying a station far beyond what once my most sanguine dreams durst have promised me' (2:60).

Anastasius precisely situates his narrative in 1784 here, noting that 'the times . . . admitted not of nice distinctions between friends and foes' (2:80). As if to substantiate this observation, he fights both for and against the Egyptian Mamelukes in their conflict with the Ottoman Turks. He also later fights on the Turkish side against Russia's Austrian allies in the

Russo–Turkish war, while indicating that he is motivated by an instinct for 'martial discord' (2:278) rather than political principle. The *Quarterly Review* complained that Hope's novel becomes increasingly hard to follow as it thus leads its protagonist 'a strange dance over land and sea', attributing this difficulty in particular to the way in which it immerses the reader in detail 'which is neither important nor impressive' – whether of 'Caliphs, ... Sultans, ... Beys and ... Mamelukes', or of 'unprofitable squabbles ... in the wilds of Wallachia and Moldavia'.[7] The hybrid historical-picaresque form of *Anastasius* might be read as symptomatic of the regional instability of the period. This state of flux is alluded to by the Smyrna-based Italian Cirico, who presents the French Revolution as the harbinger of worldwide transformation, and it is further illustrated by the episode in which Anastasius gets caught up in the Wahhabi rebellion against an Ottoman empire 'tottering to its base' (3:134). Shortly before his experience of Wahhabi society, Anastasius records how 'Babel's ancient confusion of tongues still seems to prevail at Bagdad,' with 'Turks, Persians, Indians, Jews, Egyptians, Greeks, and Arabs ... constantly vying, which ... should outbawl the other' (3:136). We are often reminded in such a way that the numerous different characters in the novel move in a near-anarchic but at the same time cosmopolitan and multilingual sphere, and the frequently disorientating experience of reading Hope's work is an effect of this cultural complexity as well as of the political disorder in which Anastasius finds himself embroiled.

Its familiar Byronic associations notwithstanding, then, the specificity of *Anastasius*'s reference presented much that was strange to its initial audience. Here, though, I want to emphasize that at least some of Hope's readers were able to assimilate his work as a vehicle for already established truths about a static Eastern realm and an unchanging Oriental character. Hope's narrator to some extent licenses such an approach when, in preparing to renounce Islam and return to Europe for the sake of his son Alexis, towards the novel's close, he distinguishes between the 'habits' and 'manners' of 'the East' and 'the system of the West'. It is clear that for Anastasius, this return to Europe actually involves a significant loss: 'The people of Europe seemed heartless, the virtues of the Franks frigid, the very crimes of the West dull and prosaic, and I was like a plant which, reared in all the warmth of a hothouse, is going all at once to be launched into all the inclemency of an atmosphere ripe with chilling blasts' (3:354). Ignoring this equivocal comparison of 'East' and 'West' on the part of Hope's narrator, however, the *Edinburgh Monthly Review* was adamant that the diverse Eastern regions which he traversed prior to this moment constituted a degraded as well as homogenous domain, and ascribed this degradation to the sway of Islam. While 'Mahometans in a poet's hands are poetical personages,' the reviewer claimed, citing both the *Arabian Nights* and Byron's Turkish tales, 'the *every-day* of the dull Moslemin ... is insupportable,' and the 'vices, tyrannies, and crimes' of the novel's characters are 'stamped for ever with a disgusting identity': 'Constantinople, Cairo, Bagdad, Damascus, vary locally but not morally, and the surly, selfish, proud, cruel, sensual Muslemin, is the same in all.'

The same critic referred to the 'grand mistake' that Hope made in writing *Anastasius*, suggesting that this kind of narrative represented a literary dead end.[8] *Anastasius* was nonetheless an influential work, as already noted, and others recognized both its novelty and its potential appeal. The *Monthly Review*'s account of Hope's work is especially interesting, because it argues that *Anastasius* hails an audience to some degree aware of its geographical settings via their 'youthful reading' of fictions in the romance mode, and that it then re-educates them as to the mundane reality of life in the East: if the Eastern regions depicted in the *Nights* and elsewhere were once 'the seats of early civility, freedom, and luxury', the reviewer declared, these ostensibly 'smiling' lands were now 'paying usurious retribution for their former glory in the lowest prostration and debasement of nations'.[9] This decline was still attributable to a failure of political authority that was potentially applicable to contemporary Britain too: reading *Anastasius* in the context of the Peterloo massacre and its aftermath, the *Edinburgh Review* stated that 'Turkey ... is in that condition to which we are steadily approaching.'[10] The *Monthly* ignored any such domestic resonance, however, and moreover downplayed any idea that readers might identify with Anastasius as a victim of despotism, emphasizing instead the novel's evidential value as a portrayal of the Turkish government's 'crimes and deformities'. The story of Anastasius (as revealed at the close) takes the form of a deathbed confession, with Hope's protagonist offering his life as a moral narrative about how providence remained 'mindful of my sins when I had forgotten them' (3:397–8). For a range of reviewers, though, if the work was a moral narrative its real subject was as much the Ottoman empire, or the East more generally, as it was the life of Anastasius himself. The *Monthly*'s verdict that 'We do not recollect a work which more forcibly illustrates the vices of the Turkish government' captures the way in which *Anastasius* could be understood as a source of information that was at once 'new' and authoritative.[11] I discuss later the representation of the relationship between individual and 'government' in the 'Persian' *Hajji Baba* novels of James Morier, but in order to contextualize Morier's writing more fully I first consider the field of Orientalist scholarship relating to the Near East, especially Persia, in the 1810s and 1820s.

'The School of Experience'

As well as publishing *Anastasius*, John Murray in 1819 issued the first volume of *Antar: A Bedoueen Romance*, an abridged version of the legend of the titular hero, translated by the diplomat Terrick Hamilton. The *Monthly Review* suggested that most readers of this tale would need to demonstrate 'Christian' patience of a similar kind to the indefatigable translator's, but it also acknowledged a more discriminating audience able to appreciate *Antar* on its own terms, in the context of the 'history of the human mind, through the different periods of its social and moral progression'. Whereas *Anastasius*, for some, represented an 'Oriental' (or Orientalized) character as it had been corrupted by despotism, *Antar* depicted 'real Arabs ... in their native simplicity', offering a generally applicable insight as to the manners of a pristine society.[12] This assertion that the state of all pre-commercial societies could be read off from *Antar*'s representation of Arabia demonstrates the enduring purchase of Scottish Enlightenment conjectural history for those seeking to assimilate the difference of other peoples and cultures. Jane Rendall emphasizes both the quantity and the range of the Orientalist research conducted in the decades after Sir William Jones's death, complicating any idea of the straightforward ascendancy of utilitarian and evangelical ideologies of 'improvement' in this period. The EIC servants that Rendall discusses were 'India-centric' in their focus, but policy imperatives and personal curiosity meant that their interests extended well beyond the subcontinent, and that they plotted a variety of Eastern societies on the stadial trajectory from rudeness to refinement.[13]

While Mountstuart Elphinstone was fascinated by evidence of 'clan' society in Afghanistan, Sir John Malcolm provided extensive commentary on neighbouring Persia, its decadence often juxtaposed with Afghan vigour.[14] Even as Persia, like Afghanistan, assumed an increasing strategic importance as Britain extended its authority in India (Malcolm travelled to Tehran as an EIC envoy), Persian antiquity, especially the ruins of Persepolis, continued to hold an aura for such scholar-diplomats. Malcolm acknowledged that the 'dazzling glories' of Persian antiquity were in the distant past, and that the 'happiness and prosperity' enjoyed by people 'under the rule of ... ancient kings' was 'far beyond what they have ever since experienced'.[15] If he regarded modern Persia as despotic, however, Malcolm contextualized the nature of Persian government, understanding it in relation to the realities of tribal society and Shia clerical authority, and in comparative terms rather than as simply 'Eastern' in character.[16] It is instructive therefore to consider some of Malcolm's diverse writings alongside the picaresque fictions which are this chapter's primary focus.

Malcolm began 'Persia: A Poem' (1814) by recommending that anyone doubting the blessings of British liberty would 'learn the value of his matchless home' by going to Persia.[17] In his *History of Persia* (1815), Malcolm declared that in Persia as in the Islamic East more generally, 'the tale of despotism, which is the only one they have to tell, is always the same.'[18] While Malcolm concluded that no country appears 'less altered in its condition' than Persia over the previous two millennia, however, he also qualified this account of Persian despotism in important ways, by acknowledging forms of restraint on the Shah's authority and by considering the population's quotidian experience.[19] He declared that 'no ... Mahometan nation [had] attained a high rank' yet he added that 'he who has travelled over the greatest space will be most struck with the equal dispensation of happiness and misery,' and that 'we should not assume too great a superiority over those who continue in a more barbarous state.'[20] Though he enumerated the obstacles in the way of improvement, Malcolm also sometimes recognized progressive energies in the present that were incompatible with any idea of a 'stationary' society. Even as the main text of Malcolm's poem 'Persia' rehearses a formulaic lament about Ispahan's 'faded splendour', an accompanying footnote refers to how it 'continues to be the first commercial and manufacturing city' in the kingdom.[21]

In his more informally written retrospect on his career as a diplomat, *Sketches of Persia* (1827), Malcolm again modified his claims about the effects of despotic government by attending to the lives of ordinary Persians. Recalling a debate with a Persian friend, Jaffier Ali Khan, about the condition of women in Persia, for example, he recorded how his interlocutor accused the 'English' of taking their 'ideas of the situation of females in Asia from what [they] hear and read of the harems of kings, rulers, and chiefs'.[22] Shortly after this, Malcolm referred to a similar debate with another figure, Mirza Aga Meer, who, disputing the frequency of polygamy in Persia, appealed to the evidence of Abu Taleb's travels in Britain in order to assert that 'a great proportion of your females and their offspring are in a much more miserable and degraded state than any in our country!'[23] By incorporating dialogue into his work and emphasizing the transactional dimension of his own experience in this way, with reference to named individuals, Malcolm interrogated his readers' preconceptions. Looking back to an earlier time when rival powers were competing for influence, he was disdainful of others' plans to 'improve' Persia, stressing the need for travellers to be governed by a 'spirit of humility' and to question their judgments, rather than to 'pronounce on a superficial glance, that every thing is wrong, that does not accord with [their] own habits and feelings'.[24]

Malcolm here also intervened in debates about the government of British India, and he was clearly aware that his ideas of 'almost imperceptible' change in Persia contested the modernizing agenda of James Mill's *History of British India* (1817): complaining that his appeals to experience had been dismissed by others as a defence of 'prejudice', he signalled his familiarity with the liberal imperialist critique of 'native' custom.[25] Malcolm shared Mill's intellectual inheritance, but whereas the utilitarian Mill argued that it was necessary to 'emancipate India from its own culture' (in Javed Majeed's words), Malcolm, with the history of the French Revolution in mind, was much more wary of any such vision of progressive social transformation.[26] He argued instead for a policy of minimally interventionist 'indirect' imperial rule, and it was axiomatic for him that good government adapted itself to existing customary practices.[27]

Malcolm wrote that he gained his knowledge of India and Persia from 'the school of experience', and it is illuminating now to contrast Malcolm's display of his authority as a commentator with the appeal to experience made by a man with whom he may have crossed paths in Persia, James Morier.[28] Morier produced two accounts of his travels as secretary to the Crown envoys, Sir Harford Jones and Sir Gore Ouseley, as – on rival missions to the EIC embassies in which Malcolm was involved – they attempted to negotiate a treaty with the Shah that would help to protect India from French or Russian attack. Published in 1812 and 1818, these narratives 'through Persia, Armenia, and Asia Minor' are illustrated volumes which incorporate drawings done by Morier himself, both of the ruins of ancient sites and of contemporary scenes. If Morier's work thus upholds current travel writing convention, however, there are also signs here of a more idiosyncratic style of personal observation on Morier's part. He wrote to his mother in 1812 that 'I am sick of Persia & every thing belonging to it,' and his *Journeys* intermittently offer a similarly jaundiced perspective on the 'depression of spirits' likely to be felt by the European traveller, accustomed to 'neatness, cleanliness, and ... convenience in the exteriors of life', but having in Persia to face 'the very contrary'.[29] While Morier, like Malcolm, included passages of dialogue in these two narratives, this most often took the form of conversations with downtrodden people complaining about their 'governors' and entreating 'you Europeans [to] come and take this country from us'.[30] Even as he thus appeared to attend to what Persians had to say for themselves, Morier began here to explore the ventriloquizing strategies that he would later employ in *The Adventures of Hajji Baba*.

'Our Friend Hajji'

Morier was born in Smyrna, and his background has much in common with Thomas Hope's. Morier's Swiss-born father, a merchant of Huguenot descent, was consul-general of the Levant Company at Constantinople, and like Hope, Morier was a peripatetic and cosmopolitan figure. Unlike Hope, however, Morier was also directly associated with the world of British diplomacy, becoming secretary to Sir Harford Jones in 1806, then serving as an aide to the Persian ambassador Mirza Abul Hasan when he came to London to finalize the treaty that Jones had sought to establish with the Shah. He accompanied Abul Hasan back to Persia in 1810, travelling with Sir Gore Ouseley's mission to ratify this treaty, and he was subsequently involved in drawing up the revised Treaty of Tehran, which reflected Britain's new entente with Russia and the diminished French threat to India. Morier's *Second Journey* of 1818 offers an amused distance on Abul Hasan as a figure vainly obsessed with his public image. Morier notes, for example, that once in the company of other Muslims in Bombay, en route to Persia, Abul Hasan rediscovered the abstemiousness which he had put aside in London: 'At the several public entertainments which were given to him at Bombay, he courageously did penance with plain water, although champagne was offered to him as grape water.'[31]

Abul Hasan returned to London in 1819, and this second mission, coupled with *Anastasius*'s success, may have prompted Morier to revisit his travels in Persia and his interaction with Abul Hasan. *Hajji Baba* frames its protagonist's first-person narrative with an introductory epistle from Morier's authorial persona, the English traveller 'Peregrine Persic', to 'the Rev. Dr. Fundgruben', 'Chaplain to the Swedish Embassy at the Ottoman Porte', and Morier here emphasizes the authenticity of his experience, and the critical purchase afforded by it, in a manner continuous with that of his two *Journeys*; as if echoing Morier's letter to his mother, cited earlier, Persic declares that 'I will not say . . . that the years I passed in Persia were years of happiness.'[32] Persic recalls how his addressee had once observed that 'no traveller had ever satisfied [him] in his delineation of Asiatic manners' (2), and he outlines his own qualifications for success in this regard, defining his worldliness against the Orientalist antiquarianism of his Swedish friend, whom he praises for his authorship of 'that very luminous work ... *The Biography of celebrated Mummies*' (1).

Morier's surrogate further establishes his authority by presenting it as the hard-won product of initial disappointment. Persic states that if he had once considered the kingdom of Persia as 'that imaginary seat of Oriental splendour! That land of poets and roses!', the years which he spent there made him see how 'perhaps no country in the world less comes up to one's expectations' (5). This period was redeemed a little, however, he adds, by his chance re-encounter with Mirza Hajji Baba, whom he had once 'seen much of ...', owing to his having been in England, whither, in quality of secretary, he accompanied the first ambassador which Persia had sent in modern times' (8) – a reference to the embassy of 1809–10; Morier had himself met a Persian student in London named Hajji Baba Afshar.[33] Persic introduces his former acquaintance as an indigenous informant whose life story provides privileged access to the reality of 'Asiatic' manners. By making Persic appeal to the explanatory power of individual experience – both his own and Hajji Baba's – in such a way, Morier distanced his work from the scholarly projects of cultural translation considered earlier; significantly, Persic says that he 'refrained' (14) from adding scholarly footnotes to Hajji Baba's narrative, despite being eminently qualified for the task. At the same time, Morier undercut the argument which he rehearsed about the prospective benefits of cross-cultural exchange, because even as Persic points to the gains that might derive from 'a more general intercourse' between '"the nations who wear the hat and those who wear the beard"', he claims that the continuation of an entrenched mutual suspicion between Christians and Muslims is 'most certain' (13).

Persic refers to Hajji Baba's narrative as a window on 'Persian', 'Asiatic' (or 'Oriental'), and 'Mohamedan' manners, and his use of these varying though overlapping descriptors prepares the reader to view Hajji Baba as a representative other. From the start of his story, however, Hajji Baba is individuated and familiarized too. While he closely resembles Hope's Anastasius, his account of his 'tricks and frauds' (87) also to some extent converges with the domestic 'chronicles of crime' from which the Newgate novel developed in the late 1820s. Hajji Baba explains that his name itself testifies to a successful act of deception, because he had not earned the right to the 'Hajji' prefix by undertaking a pilgrimage to Mecca. This initial deception sets the tone for the work, as 'our friend Hajji' – as the *Quarterly Review* dubbed him – displays a roguish resourcefulness and unscrupulous entrepreneurialism in almost all of his dealings with others.[34] His story is one of constant self-reinvention, as he leaves his family and his father's barbershop and goes on to assume, among other roles, the occupations of a scribe, a water carrier, a tobacco seller, a pupil of the Shah's physician, an assistant to the chief executioner, a dervish, a merchant, and, finally, a diplomat, who at the close is on the point of travelling to Britain. Hajji Baba's actions are throughout informed by his determination to seize upon any chance of 'advancing myself in life' (87), to the extent that after he and his first master have been taken prisoner by Turcomans, he helps to lead a raid on the caravanserai where his own father's business is located. During his brief spell as an executioner, Hajji Baba claims in mitigation to be the victim of a system of despotism overpowering the will of the individual. Immediately after attempting to attribute his conduct to 'the example of others', he nonetheless accommodates himself to 'all the importance' of his new position, his expression of pride echoing the 'behold me now' refrain of Hope's Anastasius: '"In short, I am somebody now", said I to myself, "formerly I was one of the beaten, now I am one of the beaters"' (177).

Episodes such as this suggest that Morier participated in the critical backlash against the Orientalist exoticism of *Lalla Rookh*. As the story of Hajji Baba's love affair midway through the novel demonstrates, however, Morier's work is not straightforwardly an 'anti-romance' seeking to break the spell cast by Moore. Hajji Baba is not a libertine like Anastasius, and after his first sight of the veiled figure of Zeenab, a Kurdish slave in the harem of his physician master, he develops a passionate attachment to her, imagining himself 'a Majnoun, and she a Leilah' (162). The tale of the two lovers has a tragic ending when the physician gives Zeenab as a gift to the Shah, who has her thrown from a tower when he finds that she is pregnant. Albeit briefly, it establishes Hajji Baba as a protagonist whose potentially noble aspirations are thwarted by despotic authority, thus further differentiating him from Anastasius, who is almost always culpable for the unhappy fate of the various women who love him. While Hajji Baba goes on to marry again, the strength of his devotion to Zeenab shows him, for a time at least, to be at odds with his environment, and therefore perhaps both more enlightened and more sympathetic than those around him.

Morier's relation to 'Eastern' forms of narrative is also more complicated than might first appear to be the case because, unlike *Anastasius, Hajji Baba* is steeped in the *Arabian Nights*. Its title alludes to the celebrated story of Ali Baba, and the Baba/barber pun at the outset – 'My father . . . was one of the most celebrated barbers of Ispahan' (15), Hajji Baba's first sentence states – moreover calls up the *Nights'* story of the Barber and his six brothers. The novel at times incorporates embedded tales such as the 'Story of the Baked Head' (261), and Hajji Baba himself, during his spell as a story-telling dervish, offers a pastiche of a *Nights'* tale that begins '[i]n the reign of the Caliph Haroun al-Rashid' (77). The partialness of Morier's appreciation of the *Nights* is nonetheless suggested by Persic's description of the collection as offering 'the truest picture of the Orientals' (2), and the *Quarterly Review* indeed suggested that Morier carefully situated his work in relation to the *Nights* even as he rejected the 'improbabilities and extravagance' of many of its stories. His successfully accomplished aim, it alleged, was to reach an audience already imaginatively attached to the *Nights*, and then, 'rejecting all pretence of formal instruction, to communicate the authentic but scattered results of travelled observation and experience, through the medium of a connected and amusing story'.[35]

If Hajji Baba's narrative was seen as affording pleasurable instruction, however, my account of the novel so far suggests that Morier offered different – even potentially contradictory – forms of knowledge regarding Persia and its people. The 'vicissitudes' (3) of his life demonstrate Hajji Baba's ability to adapt to change, but are also presented as a function of an all-enveloping 'atmosphere' (177) that determines the conditions in which he can exert his agency, channelling his energies towards specific selfish ends. As is exemplified by his relations with women, 'our friend Hajji' might therefore be seen both as a mobile, modern protagonist and as an archetypal Persian (or 'pure Asiatic' [3]): while his tragic affair with Zeenab makes him a sympathetic figure, as suggested earlier, his later adoption of an assumed character to gain the hand of the wealthy Turkish widow 'Shekerleb, or Sugar-lips' (389) re-establishes him as a rascally opportunist. Morier's representation of Hajji Baba as at different times improvable and incorrigible helps us in turn to consider the novel's reflection on the state of Persian society more generally. Whereas Malcolm thought that the modernization of Persia had to be gradual, Morier argued for a much more thoroughgoing transformation: 'the Mahomedan will continue to hold to his bigoted persuasion, until some powerful interposition of Providence shall dispel the moral and intellectual darkness which, at present, overhangs so large a portion of the Asiatic world' (13–14). Morier's emphasis on the necessity of 'improvement' chimes with the liberal imperialism of James Mill, and in terms similar to Mill – though, unlike him, invoking

the authority of personal experience – he presented the irrational superstition of 'the Mahomedan' as an index of a social backwardness that could
only be transcended with the aid of external stimulus.

'Boundless Difference'

Shortly after his imposture as a Turkish Aga is exposed by Shekerleb's
family, Hajji Baba meets the Persian ambassador to Turkey, Mirza Firouz
(commonly identified as a figuring of Abul Hasan), who revels in his
account of the initial deception that he had perpetrated. Hajji Baba's
encounter with Mirza Firouz introduces him for the first time to the efforts
of 'rival dogs' (421) – Britain, France, and Russia – attempting to forge
strategic alliances with the Qajar monarchy. Tasked with providing further
information about Europe that Mirza Firouz might pass on to the Shah,
Hajji Baba gains a reputation for perspicacity that leads to his further
advancement. Hajji Baba here enters the learned sphere of 'Persianate
Europology', but the novel presents the scholars in whose circles he
moves as unable to make informed cross-cultural comparison.[36] Whereas
Malcolm noted that his interlocutors already had a critical perspective on
British customs and manners deriving in part from the circulation of
writings by travellers such as Abu Taleb, Morier has his protagonist fall
in with a scribe, who, bewildered by what he has heard about their political
system, sees Britons as untranslatable: 'how can you and I understand the
humours of such madmen?' (426–7), he states. Referring to the upright
appearance and conduct of the 'English Elchi' (436), perhaps modelled on
Sir Harford Jones, Hajji Baba later declares that '[i]t would be taking up
the pen of eternity ... to describe the boundless difference that we
discovered between the manners and sentiments of these people and
ourselves' (437). Morier wrote in his *Second Journey* that 'there is still no
line of separation between any two Eastern nations so strong, as that ...
between Europeans and Asiatics,' and his Hajji Baba fictions sometimes
offer readers such a perception of unbridgeable distance from the 'Persian'
side too.[37]

Mirza Firouz says of 'the Franks' in Persia that '[t]hey pretend to be
actuated by no other principle than the good of their country ... words
without meaning to us' (441), and Hajji Baba adds of the 'English' in
particular that '[o]ne of the most remarkable features in [their] character
[is] their extreme desire to do us good against our own inclination' (442).
Morier's representation of advances in medicine as an index of improvement further produces this distinction between Persians who look out for

themselves alone and Britons who are altruistically concerned with others' welfare. After contrasting an 'infidel' (97) doctor seeking to publicize a vaccine for smallpox and the Shah's physician who regards the disease as 'a comfortable source of revenue' (98), the novel refers to another doctor in the English ambassador's party who is zealous 'to renew the practice of the cow medicine', stating that 'this blessing must be spread throughout the world' (442–3). The ambassador himself subsequently announces his desire to give to Persians 'a cheap and comfortable article of food' (444), in the form of the potato. *Hajji Baba* again departs from *Anastasius* in these episodes, because while Hope's novel presents only a single Briton – a Birmingham button maker – whose efforts to advance himself in Constantinople prove him to be little different from those with whom he competes, Morier's work presents its 'English' characters as honourable men operating above the fray of self-interest.

Hajji Baba's adventures culminate in him preparing to accompany Mirza Firouz on a diplomatic mission to Britain, modelled on those undertaken by Abul Hasan, and his excitement at this prospect provides the point of departure for the novel's sequel: 'If any of my readers know what we Persians are,' he declares, 'they will readily ascertain the reasons of my exultation.'[38] Morier stated that the idea of a mission from the Shah's court offered him the means of 'illustrating Persian manners by contrast with those of England', a goal which he archly referred to as 'the direction of my Mecca' (1:xxx). He further presented *Hajji Baba in England* as a contribution to the improvement of Persia, arguing in his introduction that '[i]n talent and natural capacity, the Persians are equal to any nation in the world' (1:xxiii), and that he aimed to offer 'strong incentive to reflection' (1:xxiv) by which they might begin to question themselves. As an example of how this process of self-analysis might work, Morier cited a letter supposedly written to him by Mirza Firouz, complaining at his previous depiction of Persians. Even as Morier's introduction interprets Mirza Firouz's angry reaction as the first phase of his enlightenment, however, it also conveys its author's palpable enjoyment of the comic idiom in which this protest is rendered. Morier's delight in 'Persian English' is still more apparent when his authorial persona responds in kind, enlisting readers in the mockery of his correspondent for being unable to take a joke: '*You say Hajji Baba all lies. To be sure all lies. Thousand and One Nights all lies. All Persian story-books lies; but nobody angry about them. Then why for you angry with me?*' (1:xxv).

A similar condescension is evident throughout the novel, as when the Persian embassy's English guide states that 'we look upon etiquette now as child's play,' only to add that 'in consideration of your being Persians, and knowing no better, we do not hesitate in giving you as much of it as you please' (1:246). The Shah's grand vizier in turn organizes 'presents' with which to impress King George and his court, assembling among other things a number of female slaves and a harem superintendent, prompting the embassy's English guide to tell him that there is no slavery in Britain and that the monarch only has one wife. This episode is a predictable one, offering a frisson of exoticism while inviting Britons to congratulate themselves, but what is especially significant here is Morier's emphasis on the gulf of understanding between the Persians and their guide: 'How can I explain,' the latter states, 'that which to you must be so difficult of comprehension?' (1:29). The novel emphasizes both that its Persian characters have much to learn about Britain and that they do not grasp the scale of their knowledge deficit. The inflated sense of self-importance that Morier attributes to his Persians parallels the self-delusion so often projected onto the Chinese – likewise seen as etiquette-obsessed – in contemporary British writing. Just as hostile accounts of a fossilized Chinese civilization may be read as a product of Britain's failure to make China respond to its commercial overtures, so Morier's representation of ignorant and intractable Persians probably reflects something of the British frustration at the failure to exert political influence over Fat'h Ali Shah.

Hajji Baba in England works in a long-established genre, and like texts such as Goldsmith's *The Citizen of the World* it satirizes Britons' misapprehension of, and readiness to exoticize, cultural difference. While he plays along with the error when he is designated a 'prince', Hajji Baba protests at Britons' 'extraordinary ignorance . . . with respect to us and our religion' (2:315), and he challenges Orientalist stereotypes, telling one man that Persians use handkerchiefs not for throwing at women but for wiping their hands. If Hajji Baba complains of being 'laughed at by the infidels', however, he presents this 'daily mortification' as something almost inevitable, the function of a near-universal reflex on the part of his hosts, 'whenever they discerned anything in our habits of life that differed from theirs' (1:134). (Goldsmith's work, by contrast, distinguishes between the cultural insensitivity of its 'ladies of distinction' and the enlightened openness of the man in black.) This reflex may indeed derive from British arrogance, but such a self-opinion is not without justification, the novel suggests, because it is grounded in the actual distribution of power and knowledge across the globe. *Hajji Baba in England* is a differently balanced – and more rhetorically straightforward – work than its precursors, therefore, because it repeatedly and un-ironically impresses the technological and other achievements of modern Britain on its narrator and his countrymen. While a discourse of 'wonder' also informs near-contemporary 'Persianate' travel writing on Europe, in Morier's novel Persian amazement at the steam engine, British naval power, or EIC authority in Asia comes almost entirely unqualified by the critical questioning so evident in Abu Taleb's work.

Hajji Baba's narrative does converge with Abu Taleb's *Travels* in an episode towards the end when, prior to returning home, he visits the Englishwoman with whom he had fallen in love, Bessy Hogg, now finding that she is about to submit to an arranged marriage to a wealthy merchant: 'force alone,' he states, 'had made her marry this ill-bred possessor of gold and sugar' (2:317). In a moment of relativizing commentary somewhat reminiscent of Abu Taleb's 'Vindication of the Liberties of Asiatic Women', Hajji Baba ironizes the earlier claim of his party's guide that '[o]ur women are under no control' (1:31), stating that 'these English after all ... are a bad race [whose] souls sleep in money. They marry, they separate, they fight, they make peace, for money' (2:317). Elsewhere, however, the text offers a more straightforward account of 'Persian' sexual politics, as in its portrayal of the Circassian slave who accompanies the ambassador: Morier here referred to an actual relationship which he derisively 'transformed' by dubbing the ambassador's wife 'Delfarib' (Persian for 'Heart's Dis-ease') rather than – her actual name – Delaram ('Heart's Ease').[39] With the state of diplomatic negotiations by now in the background, the embassy's return to Persia closes down the interrogative potential which the story of Bessy Hogg's marriage appears to display. *Hajji Baba in England*'s difference from its predecessors in this respect is illuminated by the passage in which Mirza Firouz acknowledges Persian deficiencies in the sphere of 'science and learning', telling the astrology-fixated Mohamed Beg that '[y]ou have only read your own books; but see, these people have read both ours and theirs!' (2:128). Whereas Goldsmith's Altangi offers a utopian vision of the mutual benefits likely to accrue should the enlightened of all countries meet on equal terms, Hajji Baba and others often display a cultural deference towards Britain (absent from actual Persian travel writing of this period), while at the same time puffing themselves up in the anecdotes that they later share with their countrymen. Torn between his recognition of British prowess and his desire to rise yet further in the Persian social hierarchy, Hajji Baba diplomatically tells the Shah at the novel's close that 'there can be no comparison' between Britain and Persia. The Shah's response, 'what is there in the world like our Iran?' (2:340–1), undercuts Morier's introductory claims about the Persian capacity for self-reflection, again insinuating that Persia may be impervious to the 'improvement' that is initially held up as desirable and even necessary by each of his Hajji Baba fictions.

Persian Adventurers

After *Hajji Baba in England* Morier went on to write other novels set in Persia and surrounding regions, including *Zohrab the Hostage* (1832) and *Ayesha, the Maid of Kars* (1834). They were generally well received, in part because they managed, in the *Quarterly Review*'s words, 'to transplant . . . European forms of composition into another soil'.[40] In *Zohrab*, for example, the title character, son of a rival to Aga Mohamed Shah, falls in love with Princess Amima, the Shah's niece, only for the accession of Fat'h Ali, depicted rather differently from in *Hajji Baba* and its sequel, to ensure a comic rather than tragic resolution. According to *Fraser's Magazine*, *Zohrab* surpassed the 'frothy publications of slip-shod authors', because notwithstanding its conventional storyline, it provided 'insight into the manners of the East'.[41] The *Quarterly Review* suggested that Morier's post-*Hajji Baba* works were inspired by Sir Walter Scott's *Waverley* and *Rob Roy*, and the latter's 'intermingling [of] civilized English personages among the wild creatures of the Highlands' offered a model in particular for *Ayesha*, which tells of the adventures of the English Lord Osmond, 'bitten by . . . *turcomania*', as he traverses lands 'not . . . kept under control by either the Sultan or the Shah'.[42]

Morier wrote in the wake of both Byron and Scott here, but in broadening his repertoire he may also have responded to James Baillie Fraser's first novel *The Kuzzilbash: A Tale of Khorasan* (1828), itself assimilated by reviewers to *Anastasius* and *Hajji Baba*. Fraser wrote two travel narratives recording his early 1820s' expedition from Bombay to Persia, and like Morier he used his travels as raw material for his fiction. Fraser's *Narrative of a Journey into Khorasan* (1825) displays numerous points of overlap with Morier's *Journeys* and his Hajji Baba novels, taking as its opening premise the 'very erroneous impression [which] appears to prevail regarding the character and value of the Persian nation'.[43] Fraser presented these 'false impressions' as the product of 'the Eastern tales that delighted our youth, [with] scenes of wonder, voluptuousness, and inexhaustible riches', and which thereby '[threw] over this quarter of the globe an illusion of magic and magnificence, that can hardly fail to envelope it for ever, unless dispelled by cold and accurate realities'.[44] Along with Morier, Fraser identified a range of unflattering 'national' traits among the people he encountered, and he provided a disenchanted retrospect on earlier British diplomatic overtures, arguing that the time and money expended on trying to make Persia an ally had produced no lasting benefit.

Substantiating his claim that hitherto no one had conveyed 'the true and full extent of [Persia's] misery and wretchedness', Fraser asserted that previous authors referred 'chiefly to ... the sovereign and his immediate attendants, the rich and powerful', and correspondingly ignored 'the state of the people, or the face of the country'.[45] Whereas 'Khorasan' in *Lalla Rookh* is a remote and largely incidental backdrop for an allegorical narrative, which begins by evoking, with reference to Sir William Jones, 'that delightful Province of the Sun', Khorasan for Fraser is a realm of 'poverty, depravity, and weakness'.[46] Fraser's emphasis on Khorasan's wretched state is especially significant because it both rejects the idealization of *Lalla Rookh* and contests the literary Orientalist association of 'desert' space with either austere moral virtue (as in Southey's *Thalaba*) or raw human emotion (as in the story of Mejnoun and Leila). Khorasan offered possibilities as a novelistic setting for Fraser because, ungoverned and all but ungovernable, it was a site of collision and dispute. As much as Scott's historical fiction was a model for Fraser, as it was for Morier, Fraser described a much more specifically realized milieu than the 'Syrian' desert of Scott's *The Talisman* (1825), prompting Scott in turn, in his 1832 introduction to that novel, to pre-empt criticism of his 'ignorance ... as regards Eastern manners'.[47]

The narrator of *The Kuzzilbash*, Ismael Khan, offers an Anastasius-type retrospect on his life, writing as a witness to 'what passes in this changing world'.[48] When Ismael's home village is attacked, he is seized and taken to the camp of a Sunni Turcoman chieftain, where he strikes up a close friendship with his new master's son, Selim, and falls in love with one of his daughters, Shireen. Forced to flee when Shireen becomes pregnant, Ismael is then attended by a Sufi Dervish who tells him that his fate is yoked to that of Nader Shah, 'whom Providence has destined to be exalted high in fame, as Iskunder, as Chengiz, or as Timoor'.[49] Following the Dervish's entreaty that he associate only with 'Kuzzilbashes' ('redheads' – soldiers belonging to a militant Shia elite) of his own kind, Ismael earns a position in Nader's personal guard. Having assisted in the recapture of the holy city of Mashhad from its Afghan occupiers, however, he is corrupted by his first experience of urban life, and gets caught up in ultimately tragic intrigues with the harem beauty Fatimah and her servant Zeebah. The Dervish reappears to tell Ismael to rejoin Nader so as to atone for his waywardness, and towards the end of the novel Fraser's protagonist is reunited with Selim and Shireen, now prisoners of the increasingly powerful chief. Ismael intercedes on their behalf and he is restored to his first love, although this seemingly satisfying resolution comes with a cautionary postscript: 'our hero, possessed of competence and rank, as well as of his long-lost mistress, might with us, have had a fair prospect of ease and happiness for the rest of his days. But it is otherwise in Asia.'[50] Even as Ismael Khan displays a vigorous energy and warrior virtue that differentiate him from the city-dwelling Hajji Baba, therefore, he is – like Morier's protagonist – unable to transcend his degraded environment, which Fraser refers to in generically 'Asiatic' terms irrespective of his attention elsewhere to the specifics of ethnic and cultural difference.

Fraser all but dropped the story of Ismael and Shireen from his sequel, *The Persian Adventurer* (1830), but he similarly presented its content as evidence of things being 'otherwise in Asia', priming the reader at the start for 'strong delineations of atrocity'.[51] The novel describes events of the late 1730s including Nader's expulsion of Afghans and Ottoman Turks from Persia, his coronation as Nader Shah, and his invasion of northern India. After its graphic portrayal of the sack of Delhi and the massacre perpetrated there by Nader's forces, *The Persian Adventurer* then culminates in a depiction of the later revolt against Nader, who, giving freer rein to his despotic instincts on returning from India, proves unable to maintain a united kingdom. The novel accentuates Persia's implosion in the wake of Nader's murder, as the men of his army go their separate ways and return to their former lives as free-booting plunderers. 'Before noon of the following day,' Fraser concludes, 'nine-tenths of that mighty host, which had subdued the whole of Persia, Affghanistan, and India, . . . had melted like hoar-frost when the sun breaks forth and drinks it up; and with it the magnificent empire which it had formed and upheld, crumbled in a moment into dust!'[52]

In developing the figure of the mobile 'Eastern' narrator, then, Fraser did more than Hope and Morier to situate his protagonist's life in relation to specific historical actors and events, to the extent that Nader Shah rather than Ismael Khan might be regarded as the 'Persian Adventurer' of Fraser's second novel. What is especially significant, however, is that by presenting Greater Persia in this way, Fraser additionally offered perspectives on the rise and fall of empire of a kind not evident in *Anastasius* or *Hajji Baba*. The scope of Fraser's novels is such that they refer not just to Persia but also to the interconnected histories of Mughal India, Ottoman Turkey, and Afghanistan. *The Kuzzilbash* and *The Persian Adventurer* say nothing explicit about the history of Nader Shah in relation to the history of British India, leaving it to the reader to make the association between the decline of Mughal authority hastened by Nader Shah and the EIC's later emergence as a consolidating power across the subcontinent. Fraser's depiction of Nader Shah as a figure 'destined to be exalted high' is nonetheless suggestive in this respect, not least since so many contemporaries appealed to a providential idiom in order to make sense of Britain's position as a successor to previous invaders of India. Although the story of his demise potentially indicated the fate of all empires (including Britain's), Fraser presented it as testimony to the post-Nader weakness of Persia, which, he wrote elsewhere, would 'fall to the first attacking power' minded to invade.[53] He most clearly conjoined the histories of Persia and British India in his introduction to *The Kuzzilbash*, when he described how he first became interested in Nader Shah's life, evoking the scene of his work's composition by recalling how, during his residence in India, his 'old Moonshee' gave him the manuscript history of Ismael Khan.[54] With reference again to the representation of individual experience of 'life on the ground', and of authorial interaction with indigenous informants, I now turn to the Indian picaresque fiction of William Browne Hockley.

'We Must Submit to What We Cannot Avoid'

While *Pandurang Hari*'s subtitle, 'Memoirs of a Hindoo', nods to *Anastasius*, Hockley styled himself as a successor to Morier, presenting himself in his introduction as a worldly observer who had seen through the pleasing illusions by which others had been snared. Whereas Morier sought to debunk the 'Oriental splendour' pastiched by *Lalla Rookh*, however, Hockley wrote against the 'Orientalism' identified by James Mill as a credulous enthusiasm about Indian antiquity and the enduring richness of its civilization. If Mill's work in effect put 'Hindu' civilization and society on trial, then *Pandurang Hari* ostensibly presents itself as a witness for the prosecution. Hockley declared that 'Hindoo simplicity of character has been praised', when in fact 'from the rajah to the ryot', the natives of India are 'ungrateful, insidious, cowardly, unfaithful and revengeful'.[55] This was not necessarily a permanent state of affairs, since 'in a country governed for ages by ... despotic barbarians,' Hockley claimed, '[m]eanness, cunning, cowardice, and self-interest' constitute a kind of evolutionary adaptation, 'almost necessary ... to carry on existence' (I:xii). There is nonetheless a striking multiplication of negative 'Hindoo' characteristics in these sentences, and as in both Mill's *History* and Morier's fiction there is throughout Hockley's work a slippage between the explicit statement that native character is an effect of bad government and the implicit claim that this character is innate. While the apparent bitterness of Hockley's prefatory remarks may be attributed in part to his personal situation (he lost his post as a judge in the Company's Bombay Presidency in 1824), it is notable that the author offers no pretence of a past friendship with Pandurang Hari, instead beginning with the uncompromisingly direct assertion that '[n]othing can be more irksome to the European than the society of the inhabitant of Hindustan' (1:v).

The novel starts by setting up its foundling plot, as Pandurang describes his memory of being rescued by a man who, recognizing him to be of high caste, saved him from a roadway where he had been abandoned. His deliverer is an army commander in the service of Maratha chieftain Holkar, and Pandurang speaks of being 'gradually initiated in Mahratta roguery' in the early years of his life, when he learns that 'there is nothing in this world equal to rupees' (1:9). Pandurang's unscrupulousness trumps even that of Morier's protagonist. Employed by his new master as a secretary receiving civil complaints, he extorts bribes from one petitioner only to ignore his case and then to expropriate his wealth after the desperate man had murdered the adversary from whom he had initially sought protection. Pandurang is subsequently responsible for framing another man whom he knows to be innocent of the murder charge against him, his motivation in this instance being to settle a past score as well as to earn personal reward. He passes as a magician in order to lend authority to his fatal accusation, playing to the superstition of his auditors, and he is insulated from the consequences of his imposture when, prior to being trampled by an elephant, his victim has his tongue cut out.

Even as he is a more overtly cynical figure than Hajji Baba, however, Pandurang Hari is still, like Morier's narrator, to some extent redeemed by his love for a woman. While wandering around Poona, Pandurang comes to the aid of an injured orphan named Sagoonah, left for dead by men working on behalf of a subordinate of the 'Peeshwa' (chief minister) who had sought to cover up the fact that, instructed to procure Sagoonah for his master, he had unsuccessfully propositioned her on his own behalf. The hunting of Pandurang and Sagoonah takes up much of the remainder of Hockley's intricately constructed novel, and Pandurang sometimes thinks of himself as a victim, the prey of 'powerful and violent men' (2:204) who are much worse than he is. It emerges that the key agent of Pandurang's persecution, the wandering mendicant Gabbage Gousla, is in fact his uncle, Gunput Rao, who regards Pandurang as an obstacle in the way of his occupation of the contested throne of Satarah. Pandurang, we learn, is actually the lawful successor to this title, and had in his infancy been betrothed to Sagoonah, whom Gunput Rao wanted to marry to his own son. There are shades of *Lalla Rookh* here, as an apparently impossible union between two lovers turns out to have been preordained all along. Pandurang is reunited with his father, and his knowledge of his family history all but makes him a different person, such that he exclaims 'I now felt like a new man' (3:285). Hockley's narrator presents the story of his life as a moral lesson, but at the same time – unlike Anastasius, for example – he claims to have learned the error of his previous ways.

Pandurang's description of the 'tranquil and secure haven' (3:397) in which he ultimately arrives captures the generic shift from picaresque to romance that takes place over the final pages. The account of Pandurang's marriage to Sagoonah comes without a *Kuzzilbash*-type disclaimer that things are 'otherwise in Asia', and the memoirs of Hockley's narrator might therefore be seen to resist the 'representative' claims that are initially made for them. Importantly, however, the novel also emphasizes that the atypical stability of the novel's concluding settlement is made possible by the guaranteeing presence of British power: 'the British resident presided as umpire' (3:289) over the competing claims to the throne of Satarah, we are told, while 'English officers' attend the durbar held by Pandurang's father following the confirmation of his succession (3:316). The novel alludes both to battles of the Second Anglo–Maratha War (1803–5) and to the restoration of Raja Pratap Singh to the principality of Satarah after the end of the Third Anglo–Maratha War in 1818, when most Maratha territory was annexed to the Bombay Presidency. Running throughout it is a contrast between the flux of native society and the order that is brought and upheld by EIC authority. While a range of different figures commit themselves to driving the 'Topee Wallas' out of India, the dating of the novel's action signals that such efforts have come to nothing, and the forward-looking Pandurang accommodates himself to the inevitability of the break-up of the Maratha confederacy that the novel stages. In response to what he has learned about the increasing sway of the 'English', Pandurang states that: 'we shall find ourselves more peaceable, and they who will labour will have their reward. The thieves and turbulent will be kept quiet: we must submit to what we cannot avoid' (2:276).

Hockley's representation of the EIC as a stabilizing force is complicated by a brief episode at the end of the novel that acknowledges the violence by which its authority is maintained. A former travelling companion of Pandurang's testifies that, when imprisoned in Ahmednagar 'upon a false charge', he witnessed a Sepoy-led massacre of his fellow inmates – 'poor, naked, defenceless men', who were 'fired upon . . . as they were begging for mercy' (3:390). 'How the magistrate would have been able to justify himself to the government, I cannot tell,' he states, adding sarcastically that 'perhaps the silence may be attributed to the known modesty of our conquerors, who never indulge themselves in anything like a boasting, even of their most valiant acts' (3:393–4). Pablo Mukherjee notes that for a brief moment here, 'the authorial control over the ventriloquist strategy of colonialism is relinquished and the recording and confessing "eye" constitutes a "native" view of the colonial regime.'[56] In response to this story Pandurang himself comments that he 'could not conceive such a dreadful example would have been made, by those who pride themselves upon their humanity' (3:390), and it is as if he struggles to come to terms with the gulf between British precept and practice that is disclosed by the news that he hears.

If, as Pandurang states, an Englishman he later spoke to about this event 'shewed great reluctance' (3:393) to talk about it, such a minimal (and also second-hand) portrayal of the workings of EIC rule nonetheless remains consistent with the 'off-stage' role of 'English Government' throughout the novel. From Pandurang's observation that 'those English are large powerful men' (1:89) to his account of being 'brought . . . back from the brink of the grave' (3:38) by an English doctor, Hockley's work often has its narrator report on the superior capabilities and achievements of Englishmen yet at no stage gives an English character any direct speech. The larger significance of this silence is thrown into relief towards the end, when the death sentence against Gunput Rao is commuted on condition of him confessing his crimes. The advantage of preserving Gunput's life and making him speak, we are told, is that 'the English would thus become masters of the full extent of the treasonable conspiracy at Poona in all its ramifications, and be thereby the better enabled to crush any minor associations to which it might have given rise' (3:319).

Gunput Rao's story may have provided a model for Philip Meadows Taylor during his composition of the pseudo-autobiographical *Confessions of a Thug* (1839), based on his experience as the Nizam of Hyderabad's Assistant Superintendent of Police. There is no space to discuss this work here, but I want to suggest that it might be regarded as a culmination of the lineage considered thus far as much as it helped to establish a new, linguistically richer Anglo-Indian fiction.[57] For all that the idea of 'confession' appears to indicate a formal departure from the narration of 'adventures', *Confessions of a Thug* remains in the picaresque mode, retracing the movements of its peripatetic antihero. It can be read as a text that is both thematically and generically related to *Pandurang Hari*, because the Thug scare which it records and exploits was in large part consequent upon the demise of the Maratha confederacy. While the extent of Ameer Ali's criminality is greater than that of his fictional precursors (he claims to have committed more than 700 murders), in other respects he demonstrates similarities to them, not least because of the manner in which he sometimes comes across as potentially sympathetic: Taylor's protagonist is monogamously attached to the two women that he loves, he grieves for his dead son, and he can be seen as a modernizer of sorts, at odds with a corrupt and venal society. More emphatically than is the case in Hockley's or Morier's works, Taylor's introductory narrative signals what is at stake in attempting to understand 'the native', and the 'Sahib' who listens (and occasionally responds) to Ameer Ali's story is a shadowy figure rather than, like Peregrine Persic, someone who enjoys a bantering relationship with his informant. The Sahib's near silence invites readings both of his omniscient authority over his captive and his uncertainty as to the quality and reliability of the testimony he provides. Whether or not we read *Confessions* as a novel which betrays a state of 'information panic', however, it is significant that it establishes a distance between its authorial surrogate and his source, just as *Pandurang Hari* does.[58] As Javed Majeed argues, Ameer Ali's narrative 'ensures that the author does not become creolised', but instead 'vicariously experience[s]' India, 'without it subverting [his] persona as a British official'.[59]

New Stories for Old?

At this point it is important to complicate my argument thus far about the emergence of a new kind of fiction focusing on the 'character' of informant narrators. While Hockley went on to write works including *Memoirs of a Brahmin* (1843), in which the narrator, Bapoo Brahmin, laments the 'blindness of the English Governors who will not believe ... in the depravity of a Brahmin's heart', shortly after *Pandurang Hari* he also published a work of a rather different kind, *The Zenana; or, A Nuwab's Leisure Hours* (1827).[60] Its collected tales could still be seen to exhibit 'the workings of the baser passions [in] the Asiatic mind', as the *Monthly Review* put it, and Hockley even has a high-caste Hindu narrator refer to the 'cruel Hindoos' as an 'ignorant and superstitious people'.[61] Nonetheless, the assembled stories, told by men from different occupational backgrounds, are also derivative of the *Arabian Nights*, and Hockley positioned his work within the long-established tradition of Eastern-style fictions which developed out of the *Nights*. His preface begins with the conceit of its narrator, an authorial persona, assembling his household staff to tell tales in order to help him to gain a better knowledge of colloquial Persian and Hindi, and in the long frame tale, the 'Nuwab' of the title, a mid-eighteenth-century viceroy of Surat, is likewise presented as an auditor of stories. The Persian princess who initially evades the Nuwab's attempts to make her his wife manages to persuade him not to doom 'one in every thousand to death' in frustration at his thwarted desires, but instead to request entertaining tales from the 'chief' of each profession in the city.[62] This scenario recalls the story of Schahriar and Scheherazade, and its centrality to *The Zenana* demonstrates how Hockley here modified *Pandurang Hari*'s introductory focus on an essentially corrupt native character, inviting his readers as well as the Nuwab to find 'amusement in *their* leisure hours'.[63]

Thomas Henry Ottley's *Rustum Khan* (1831) likewise brings together new conventions of testimonial and an older story-telling tradition. In a similar manner to the poetry of contemporary Anglo-Indian writers such as Sir Charles D'Oyly, Ottley's preface and opening chapters detail some of the 'poignancies [and] absurdities of quotidian life in colonial society'; his preface registers a range of familiar Anglo-Indian complaints, most notably about the cost of keeping up appearances and the resulting necessity of reliance on Indian creditors.[64] If the novel sometimes provides derisive commentary on Hindu character, however, it does not in any straightforward way align itself with the 'anti-orientalist burlesque' of a work such as D'Oyly's poem *Tom Raw the Griffin* (1828).[65] Where D'Oyly's Tom Raw is a cadet seeking preferment in the EIC Civil Service, Ottley ('Lieut H.C.S' on the novel's title page) styles himself as a military man, more comfortable with the sword than the pen, who decides to write a novel for want of anything better to do in times of peace. Even as Ottley's authorial persona rehearses the weariness with the subcontinent that is another recurrent feature of Anglo-Indian literature of the period, he displays an affinity, as a fellow soldier, with the novel's Muslim title character. This affinity is demonstrated most clearly when Rustum Khan gloomily foresees 'the total overthrow of Mahommedan power in India', and Ottley's narrator joins him in contemplating the ruins of Ahmedabad (one-time provincial headquarters of the Mughal empire), asking 'who would not sigh to see such a heritage wrested from his possession?'[66]

The narrator notes how 'the hand of improvement had . . . been active in the extreme' in and around Ahmedabad, but he is nonetheless unimpressed by scenes of cultivation and industry under British authority, describing them as 'more fit for the cool calculator, than the military youth' (1:239).[67] Rustum Khan meanwhile declares that he has no quarrel with the current British rulers of this region, since his hostility is reserved for the Marathas who had displaced Mughal authority and destabilized customary social relations. The two men to a large extent share an understanding of Hindu character and Maratha treachery (overlapping with that of *Pandurang Hari*), and Ottley's protagonist is presented more sympathetically than any of the other various native informants discussed so far. The main thread of his story concerns his attempt to overcome obstacles in the way of his love for Mao Saheb Bebee, with whom he is finally united at the end of the novel, although the couple 'knew no happiness' because she had been forced to become another man's wife prior to her rescue by Rustum Khan, 'which rendered [his] kind action . . . a curse'. Rustum Khan concludes his narrative by thanking his 'Saheb' interlocutor for being 'an interested hearer', and Ottley's narrator in turn states that he 'derived much pleasure' from this experience.[68]

The 'fourteen nights' of Ottley's subtitle refers to the number of evenings over which Rustum Khan delivers his story to his companion. While Ottley thus offered only a perfunctory engagement with the *Nights*, the gesture is significant because it demonstrates again that texts from this period which sometimes presented themselves – and/or were regarded – as offering access to truths about native character did not simply reject older forms of literary Orientalism, even where they sought to provide a corrective to what readers thought they knew about the East; the emphasis on the 'vicissitudes' of life in the East which structures picaresque fictions such as *Hajji Baba* might actually be seen as faithful to those stories in the *Nights* which tend towards social realism rather than 'fabulous' Orientalism. Other forms of literary Orientalism also remained current at this time, and it is important to emphasize that even as the picaresque mode appears to have been ascendant in the decades after *Anastasius* – it structures historical romances such as the anonymous *Oriental Wanderings, or The Fortunes of Felix* (1824) and R. R. Madden's *The Mussulman* (1830), as well as novels of Anglo-Indian life such as *The Adventures of Naufragus* (1827) – numerous works eschewed the scenarios of cross-cultural encounter which provide a starting point for most of the fictions discussed earlier.

The *Quarterly Oriental Magazine*'s review of *Pandurang Hari* noted that to 'the greater portion of the public in England, . . . Indian transactions are nearly as strange as the wars of the Crusaders', and the most prominent author of the period, Sir Walter Scott, played with this notion of the imaginative distance of colonial affairs in the preface to *The Surgeon's Daughter* (1827).[69] In it, Scott's narratorial persona receives encouragement, now that the topic of domestic conflict has become exhausted, to turn to the work of historians so as to gather the raw materials for a narrative set in India 'fifty years back': when he says that he has never been to the subcontinent, his friend reassures him that '[y]ou will tell us about [India] all the better that you know nothing of what you are saying.'[70] The 'wars of the Crusaders' were just as much of a subject as 'Indian transactions' for Scott in his work of the late 1820s, and (as noted earlier) he carefully presented himself, in his 1832 introduction to *The Talisman*, as not competing with contemporaries who had first-hand experience of the East. As is well known, some of the most renowned and widely discussed examples of literary Orientalism from the 1820s – for example Percy Shelley's epic *Prometheus Unbound* (1820), Byron's play *Sardanapalus* (1821), and Mary Shelley's *The Last Man* (1825) – were much less concerned with questions of accuracy or authenticity than with the philosophical, political, or symbolic possibilities afforded by Eastern settings. Other 'Easts' in this period, such as Byron's in the 'harem cantos' of *Don Juan*, may alternatively be read as a response to the 'imaginative provocation' which the mythology of sultans and seraglios continued to provide, and there is a rich and diverse history of nineteenth-century literary and visual representations of the harem that is beyond the scope of this study.[71] Also beyond my scope here is the increasing prominence in this period, especially in popular theatre, of different kinds of Chinese subject matter, as China increasingly came to be understood as a rival empire which presented Britain with distinct strategic challenges and opportunities.[72]

Rather than explore the diversity of Orientalist representation in the 1820s and 1830s in any more detail, I want to conclude this chapter by following up on the *Quarterly Oriental Magazine*'s claim about the 'strangeness' of Indian affairs, so as to consider the respective assumptions and concerns of metropolitan and colonial audiences. The *Quarterly Oriental Magazine* was a periodical produced in Calcutta, and in its review of *Pandurang Hari* it accepted Hockley's assertion that Pandurang was a figure beyond any sympathetic identification on the part of readers: the public 'must expect none of that interest which is connected with sentiment', it cautioned, but instead recognize that 'there are no two people in the world who have less in common than the Englishman and the Hindoo.'[73] Displaying the same kind of worldly realism as Morier's

Peregrine Persic, this reviewer declared that 'European readers who have no personal acquaintance with the Indian character ... will be greatly surprized at the description of Hindoos contained in these volumes,' though those 'who reside in this country ... cannot deny that there are few people in the world more generally flagitious'.[74] Against this endorsement of Hockley's unflinching portrayal of his protagonist, the review of the novel by the *Oriental Herald* (a periodical devoted to Indian affairs, but established in London) by contrast presented Pandurang Hari as a grotesque caricature. For this reviewer, any author who could present Indians in such a way had to be possessed of a 'jaundiced vision' and to know 'little of human nature' or of India itself.[75]

I do not want to overstate this contrast between metropolitan and colonial perspectives on the figure of the roguish Oriental, not least because as the *Quarterly Oriental Magazine*'s reviewer notes, *Pandurang Hari*'s precursors, *Anastasius* and *Hajji Baba* (also first published in London), were 'greedily purchased by the English Public'.[76] Rather than offer a strictly 'metropolitan' response to Hockley's work, the *Oriental Herald*'s reviewer disputed the knowledge of India it displayed; a decade earlier, conversely, lack of first-hand experience of India was no bar to James Mill pronouncing on 'leading features in the character of the Hindus' in a way which may have influenced Hockley.[77] It remains the case, however, that some of the works discussed earlier may potentially have offered different meanings in different contexts. Where *Confessions of a Thug* is concerned, for example, if it drew attention to 'the role of surveillance and information-gathering for the maintenance of imperial authority and legitimacy', as Majeed argues, its 'appalling disclosures' (in Taylor's phrase) about the apparent criminal conspiracy of Thuggee caught the imagination of the domestic public for a broader range of reasons.[78]

To return to *Pandurang Hari*, it is important to emphasize moreover that some metropolitan readers acknowledged the newness of the Oriental picaresque as a form but nonetheless signalled their preference for a more familiar style of literary Orientalism. The *Monthly Review*, for example, credited Hockley's work as 'the first sketch we have received of Hindostanee life', but also criticized it as an 'unrelieved picture of enormous and incredible villainy' which it found wanting in relation to near-contemporary works including the enormously popular 'second-hand' verse narrative written by Thomas Moore, who had only 'visited ... in fancy the climes of the East': 'Here we have none of that nice keeping of sentiment, idea, and phrase, which in Hajji Baba was so wholly and thoroughly eastern; nor of that perfect orientalism which, in Lalla

Rookh, was yet more extraordinary.'[79] Appearing to signal an habituated preference for Moore's romance mode (for old stories rather than new ones, in other words), the *Monthly*'s reviewer suggested that a work written from the vantage point of first-hand 'experience' might in fact provide too much information – too much in the way of specific detail – for an audience at home to digest: 'it is almost impossible for the English reader to follow with any interest the ... rapid transitions of political intrigue, which are made to lead to the recovery of the rights of Pandurang and his father to the *musnud* of Satarah.'[80]

The reception of such picaresque fictions therefore demonstrates again that the history of 'British Orientalisms' across this period was one of an ongoing process of contestation in which different modes of reading were exercised as well as different creative possibilities explored or accentuated. That said, even if some metropolitan readers (in particular) were unreceptive to tales of Oriental roguery, the novels I have discussed in this chapter may still be regarded as culturally important, because of the way in which they developed out of and helped to perpetuate a revisionist perspective on older and more romantic notions of the East, and thereby offered a reference point for subsequent commentators. Something of the formative cultural work performed by such fictions is suggested by the Indian colonial governor Sir Henry Bartle Frere's introduction to a new edition of *Pandurang Hari*, published in London in 1873. In it he recollected his 'gratitude to a friend who recommended it to me, with "Hajji Baba" and the "Kuzzilbash", as the only books he could find which gave any idea of what would now be called the inner life of Orientals'. Bartle Frere read *Pandurang Hari* as 'a series of photographic pictures from the past generations of a great Indian nation', presenting it as a source of valuable evidence in part because it gave contemporaries an index of how much had changed for the better in British India over the previous fifty years.[81] What is especially significant for my purposes here is that even as Bartle Frere approached *Pandurang Hari* as a text demonstrating its author's informed first-hand knowledge of India and its peoples, he bracketed it together with picaresque fictions rooted in other specific contexts.

It is instructive at this point to refer back to my introductory account of the distinction drawn by Richard Owen Cambridge in 1761 between the generic 'Orientalism' of the past, circulated by 'ideal stories' that were 'works of the imagination', and the new register of Eastern difference with which Britons came to be acquainted as a result of the Seven Years' War.[82] While the idea of 'Orientalism' post-Said may broadly be understood as a rhetoric which rehearses an unexamined 'common knowledge' rather than informed awareness based on experience and understanding, Bartle Frere's casual reference to 'the inner life of Orientals' notably instantiates an Orientalism which is no less generalizing but which is nonetheless confidently assertive about its accuracy and truth. As I hope to have shown in this chapter, the diverse texts under discussion, from *Anastasius* to *Confessions of a Thug*, are more ambivalent than a reading such as Bartle Frere's suggests, not least because of the way in which they sometimes shift between, on the one hand, a commitment to the improving agency of empire and, on the other, a more cynical perspective on the capacities of actual or potential colonial subjects. Seen in relation to fictional travellers discussed earlier in this study such as Goldsmith's Lien Chi Altangi, however, the informant narrators of Oriental picaresque fictions illuminate a significant shift in the way in which Britons – now seemingly much less reflexively 'open' to the East – saw themselves in relation to their others over the course of this period. In the conclusion to this study which follows, I say more about, and to some extent qualify, this idea of a cultural shift, paying particular attention to the ideology of improving empire and different forms of both metropolitan and colonial resistance to it.

Notes

1. *Shelley's Poetry*, 409.
2. Preface to *Pandurang* (1873), v–vi.
3. Hope, *Anastasius*, 1:vi. Further references appear as parenthetical citations in the text.
4. Cochran, 'Hope's *Anastasius*', 76–90.
5. Cited in ibid., 81.
6. *Edinburgh Review*, 35 (1821), 100.
7. *Quarterly Review*, 24 (1821), 519, 518, and 521.
8. *Edinburgh Monthly Review* (1820), 444.
9. *Monthly Review*, 91 (1820), 4.
10. *Edinburgh Review*, 92.
11. *Monthly Review* (1820), 140.
12. *Monthly Review*, 94 (1821), 277–8.
13. Rendall, 'Scottish Orientalism', 44.
14. Ibid., 65–6.
15. Malcolm, *History*, 1:263.
16. Harrington, *Malcolm*, 88.
17. Malcolm, 'Persia', 2.
18. Malcolm, *History*, 1:276.
19. Ibid., 2:621.

20. Ibid., 2:619.
21. Malcolm, 'Persia', 4 and 25.
22. Malcolm, 'Sketches', 2:39.
23. Ibid., 2:47.
24. Ibid., 2:162.
25. Ibid., 2:160.
26. Majeed, *Ungoverned Imaginings*, 127.
27. Harrington, *Malcolm*, 133–4.
28. Malcolm, *History*, 2:628.
29. Cited in Johnston, *Morier*, 179; Morier, *Second Journey*, 45.
30. Morier, *Second Journey*, 77 and 52.
31. Ibid., 18.
32. Morier, *Hajji Baba*, 6. Further references appear as parenthetical citations in the text.
33. Green, *Love of Strangers*, 35.
34. *Quarterly Review*, 30 (1823), 203.
35. Ibid., 199–200.
36. Tavakoli-Targhi, *Refashioning Iran*, 35–53.
37. Morier, *Second Journey*, viii.
38. Morier, *Hajji Baba in England*, 1:4. Further references appear as parenthetical citations in the text.
39. Eskandari-Qajar, 'Persian Ambassadors', 26.
40. *Quarterly Review*, 48 (1832), 392.
41. *Fraser's Magazine*, 6 (1832), 576.
42. *Quarterly Review*, 51 (1834), 485; Morier, *Ayesha*, 1:9 and 15.
43. Fraser, *Khorasan*, v.
44. Ibid., 158–9.
45. Ibid., 159.
46. Moore, *Poetical Works*, 6:19; Fraser, *Khorasan*, v.
47. Scott, *Introductions*, 393.
48. Fraser, *Kuzzilbash*, 1:12.
49. Ibid., 1:192.
50. Ibid., 3:332.
51. Fraser, *Persian Adventurer*, 1:viii.
52. Ibid., 3:388.
53. Fraser, *Khorasan*, 185.
54. Fraser, *Kuzzilbash*, 1:1–2.
55. Hockley, *Pandurang* (1826), 1:xii and 1:xiv. Further references appear as parenthetical citations in the text.
56. Mukherjee, *Crime*, 64.
57. Majeed, 'Confessions', 86–110.
58. Bayly, *Empire*, 173.
59. Majeed, 'Confessions', 98.
60. Hockley, *Memoirs*, 1:vii.
61. *Monthly Review* n.s., 6 (1827), 171; Hockley, *Zenana*, 2:156.

62. Ibid., 1:274.
63. Ibid., 1:viii.
64. Leask, 'Anglo-Indian Poetry', 57.
65. Ibid., 55.
66. Ottley, *Rustum Khan*, 1:216 and 1:224.
67. Ibid., 1:239.
68. Ibid., 2:378–9.
69. *Quarterly Oriental Review*, 89.
70. Scott, *Chronicles*, 155.
71. Yeazell, *Harems*, 13.
72. Kitson, *Romantic China*, 221–40.
73. *Quarterly Oriental Magazine*, 6 (1826), 76.
74. Ibid., 86–7.
75. *Oriental Herald*, 8 (1826), 82.
76. *Quarterly Oriental Magazine*, 76.
77. Mill, *British India*, 1:305.
78. Majeed, '*Confessions*', 87; Taylor, *Confessions*, 5.
79. *Monthly Review* n.s., 1 (1826), 84, 89, and 83 [ch.].
80. Ibid., 89.
81. Preface to *Pandurang* (1873), v–vi.
82. Cambridge, *Account of the War*, v.

Conclusion
British Orientalisms, Empire, and Improvement

At the beginning of his 1840 essay 'Lord Clive', Macaulay lamented that 'the great actions of our countrymen in the East should, even among ourselves, excite little interest'.[1] Macaulay's various writings and speeches on India in many respects provide an appropriate end point now, not least because they recognize the significance of the era of the Seven Years' War with which this book began. Echoing Richard Owen Cambridge's reference to how 'a handful of Europeans' subdued 'a multitude of Asiatics', Macaulay in his 1833 speech on the renewal of the EIC charter described the remarkable conquest of India by 'a handful of adventurers from an island in the Atlantic' who 'subjugated a vast country'.[2] He reprised this story of Britain's accession to power in Bengal in his essays on Clive and Warren Hastings, while at the same time accentuating the claim which he made in his earlier speech that the 'character' of 'Hindoos' qualified them only to be the subjects of an enlightened despotism. Adapting the typificatory discourse of Hockley's *Pandurang Hari*, Macaulay declared in his essay on Clive that 'the Bengalee … shrinks from bodily exertion; and though voluble in dispute, and singularly pertinacious in the war of chicane, he seldom engages in a personal conflict, and scarcely ever enlists as a soldier.' The conclusion which Macaulay drew from this sketch of 'Bengalee' effeminacy was that '[t]here never, perhaps, existed a people so thoroughly fitted by nature and by habit for a foreign yoke.'[3]

Macaulay emphasized the importance of the revolution in Bengal eighty years earlier, and as is indicated by this point about 'Hindoos' or Bengalis (if not Indians more generally) being 'fitted' for subjection, he acknowledged the contemporary reality of British sovereignty across much of the subcontinent. Regretting the 'little interest' now shown in the deeds of Clive and his successors, however, Macaulay additionally suggested that others were less aware of the realities of empire, and that metropolitan Britons had in the past failed to keep up – or were not concerned in the first place – with what was actually happening elsewhere in the world. In his essay on Hastings, for example, he referred to the 'interval between the time in which [Indians] became our subjects, and the time at which we began to reflect that we were bound to discharge towards them the duties of rulers'.[4] Macaulay memorably defined these duties in his 'Minute on Indian Education' (1835), in which he called upon Britons to effect the transformative modernization of India.

Macaulay's reference to Britons' – belated – recognition of their duties as 'rulers' in the late eighteenth century suggests that his understanding of imperial responsibility was at least partly rooted in the thinking of Burke, who defended empire on the basis of its potential to improve the lives of subject peoples. The most famous or notorious line in Macaulay's 'Minute', that 'a single shelf of a good European library was worth the whole native literature of India and Arabia,' also demonstrates, however, his emphatic rejection of the Burkean (or Jonesian) project to extend the sympathies of Britons and to make them better informed about their colonial subjects.[5] Macaulay saw India as, in Balachandra Rajan's words, 'a place of exile where self-understanding is to be defended and not extended'.[6] While Cambridge in 1761 recognized that national extroversion made Britain newly open to the East, and Sir William Jones a decade later welcomed such openness as providing much-needed creative stimulation, Macaulay (as Saree Makdisi puts it) 'scorned Jones and anyone who [sought] inspiration . . . from . . . the backward and thoroughly degenerate East'.[7] In an earlier work that is likewise often taken to signal a pivotal shift in Britons' orientation towards India, his *History of British India* (1817), James Mill provocatively called upon Jones as a source of evidence about the vices of Indian character that he enumerated: "'Perjury'", said Sir William Jones, to the Grand Jury at Calcutta, "seems, to be committed by the meanest, and encouraged by some of the better sort among the Hindus and Mussulmans, with as little remorse, as if it were a proof of ingenuity, or even a merit'".[8]

I have tried thus far to use literary history to illuminate Britons' changing sense of themselves in relation to their Eastern others during the three-quarters of a century following the Seven Years' War, and both Jones and Mill are essential reference points in this enquiry. Whereas Jones, one of the key figures in this study, appears to have been energized by a will to know, Mill in effect rejected what I have presented, following David Simpson, as 'the challenge of the other' to British cultural horizons. As Uday Singh Mehta and Jennifer Pitts argue, Mill understood 'the stranger' not in the context of Simpson's dialectic of hospitality and hostility but rather as exemplifying a state of developmental infancy that in turn helped to provide a new alibi for empire. Mehta states that for Mill and others, 'the political and imperial gaze is never really surprised by the stranger,' and in the picaresque fictions discussed in the previous chapter, the typification of the 'Hindoo' (or 'Persian') appears to bear out Mehta's account of the stranger as a 'child/deviant' whose difference must be 'assimilated'. The reconceptualization of the stranger in the nineteenth-century liberal tradition mobilized a family metaphor that indicated at once colonial government's 'commitment to tolerance' and its insistence on the legitimacy of well-intentioned violence, and the idea of empire as a process of mentoring would be a very familiar one up until the end of the century and beyond.[9]

If it is broadly fair to say that British culture was significantly less self-critical and reflexive at the end of the period covered by this study than at the beginning, however, in what remains I want briefly to complicate any notion of the straightforward ascendancy of an ideology of improving empire emanating from the metropolis, by referring to three different kinds of response to it. The first of these responses is implicit in the claim made by the narrator of T. H. Ottley's novel *Rustum Khan* (1831), cited earlier, that scenes of cultivation in areas under EIC authority were 'more fit for the cool calculator than the military youth'.[10] While it is important to recognize, following Makdisi, that a Macaulay-style critique of 'Orientalism' could have domestic as well as colonial implications (since Britain still had to be 'made Western'), it is necessary to acknowledge too that the idea of improvement in a colonial context was itself contested.[11] Catherine Hall questions the actual influence of Macaulay's 'Minute', and Hall and others point to the gulf between Macaulay's liberal agenda and the actual Tory bias – as demonstrated by Ottley's narrator – of colonial administration.[12] The 'liberal project' of empire remained unstable, more-over, Hall argues, since one effect of 'naming and demarcating the "pecu-liarities"' of those who would be made into colonial subjects was 'to disseminate notions of ... difference ever more widely'.[13] Even as the picaresque fictions discussed earlier depict seemingly representative others as objects of a governmental agenda, they precisely stage the tension that Hall identifies between the language of modernizing improvement (which assumes that colonial subjects will be incorporated into a kind of extended family) and ideas of a seemingly permanent national 'character' which may be beyond reform.

The second response to the ideology of empire-as-improvement that I want to consider comes from those who in seeking to define improvement on their own terms rejected any unidirectional model of authority or influence originating in the imperial centre. I have not been able to give space in this study to the work of important and increasingly widely discussed figures such as the liberal reformer Rammohum Roy (proponent of a 'Hindu Unitarianism') or the mixed-race poet Henry Derozio – Bengali intellectuals who, as Daniel E. White argues, conceived of 'an alternative modernity that cannot be reduced to the reactions of groups peripheral to the metropolitan centre of power and culture'.[14] To return to the point that I made in the final chapter about varying critical responses to fictions such as *Pandurang Hari*, I would, however, like to emphasize that even ostensibly straightforward works manifestly committed to the improvement of actual or potential subject peoples may have appealed to different audiences in surprisingly different ways.

Morier's *Hajji Baba* is especially interesting in this respect, because while readings such as Bartle Frere's suggest that it may be seen as 'Orientalist' in a Saidian sense, providing knowledge in the service of imperial power, other audiences seized upon alternative kinds of potentiality in it. *Hajji Baba* was translated into Persian from French by the exiled intellectual Mirza Habi Isfahani (d. 1893), and a Persian edition of the novel was published in 1906, at the start of the revolution which resulted in the establishment of constitutional monarchy in Iran. As Kamran Rastegar demonstrates, ambiguity about its actual authorship as well as about the identity of its translator facilitated *Hajji Baba*'s appropriation by a 'secondary readership' able to reimagine for their own purposes the novel's embeddedness in a proto-colonial discourse of 'knowing'.[15] These readers responded to its 'mapping of an Iranian social space', Rastegar argues, and they were 'historically positioned so as to be able to ... translate for themselves the imaginary spaces of the book as relating to the material struggles they were engaged in'.[16] While the novel was thus congenial to reformist Iranians seeking better to know (and to direct the future of) their own nation, the figure of Hajji Baba would also have been assimilable, Rastegar claims, as a 'socially mobile' and 'flat' character of a kind already familiar from indigenous literary modes.[17] Rastegar's identification of *Hajji Baba* as a 'transactional text' captures both this story of its afterlife and the way in which the novel in its original form was already steeped in a Persian idiom and a Persian as well as more broadly 'Eastern' story-telling tradition. More generally by the late nineteenth century, as Mansoor Moaddel states, 'the issues raised by Morier's criticism and ridicule of Iran's traditional social order became ... more clearly the fundamental points of contention among diverse ideological producers in India, Egypt, and Iran.'[18]

The final way in which I want to qualify claims about the cultural ascendancy of a new ideology of improving empire demonstrates again the plurality of British Orientalisms across the period covered by this book, and returns us as well to the concept of 'openness to the other' which has been so productive for recent critical analysis of actual or virtual encounters with the East. I referred earlier to Gerard Cohen-Vrignaud's study of a 'radical Orientalism' which encompassed not just the widespread use of an Orientalist lexicon in the critique of Britain's old regime but also appeals to the East as a realm of imaginative licence 'where the liberal dictates of self-control and social duty could be escaped'.[19] In the latter context figures who would reward attention include William Beckford, who sometimes identified with the overreaching villain-hero of *Vathek* (1786), Charlotte Dacre, who in *Zofloya* (1806) explored the transgressive sexual aura of her Moorish title character, and Byron, whose verse drama *Sardanapalus* (1821) details what Cohen-Vrignaud describes as its protagonist's 'orgiastic self-dissipation'.[20] To conclude, though, I want to go back to Leigh Hunt, and in particular to his 1834 essay on 'Genii and Fairies of the East', a very different kind of book-ending text from Macaulay's 'Minute'. Hunt had likened the Prince Regent to Sardanapalus in the article that led to his imprisonment for libel in 1812, but in this piece, albeit that it focuses on nothing more hedonistic than reading, he breezily defended a form of pleasure seeking that was seemingly untrammelled by any sense of social responsibility:

> Hail, gorgeous East! Hail, regions of the coloured morning! Hail, Araby and Persia! – not the Araby and Persia of the geographer, dull to the dull, and governed by the foolish, – but the Araby and Persia of books, of the other and more real East, which thousands visit every day – the Orient of poets, the magic land of the child, the uneffaceable recollection of the man.
>
> To us, the Arabian Nights are one of the most beautiful books in the world: not because there is nothing but pleasure in it, but because the pain has infinite chances of vicissitude, and because the pleasure is within the reach of all who have body and soul, and imagination.[21]

This recollection of readerly pleasure past and present confirms the enduring attraction of the 'old' domain of literary Orientalism, long after British exploits in Asia had begun to introduce readers to a more culturally specific register of Eastern reference. Viewed alongside Macaulay's 'Minute' and in the context of the 'radical Orientalist' repudiation of 'social duty', Hunt's essay might be read as offering an implicit 'resistance to modernization' (in Makdisi's phrase), because it conceives of childhood not – in the terms of contemporary liberalism – as an immature developmental stage, but rather as a domain of authentic experience to which it is necessary to maintain a connection.[22] This essay is especially interesting to consider at this point because of the idiosyncratic way in which it conceives of openness to the 'gorgeous East' as a conduit to a 'magic land' that remains a source of 'uneffaceable recollection' to readers in adult life. It describes the way in which reading fabulous Eastern narratives 'makes people go out of themselves', and in thus invoking the ubiquitous trope of 'transport' it seeks to pre-empt any charge that this experience might be regarded as absorptive and anti-social: such romances, Hunt writes, 'keep a region of solitude and sweetness for us in which the mind may retreat and recreate itself, so as to return with hope and gracefulness to its labours'.[23]

At the same time, however, Hunt appears to refuse any connection between the world of the reader and wider social reality, since he distinguishes between 'the Araby and Persia of books' and 'the Araby and Persia of the geographer', as if the two spheres were completely separate from each other; in Hunt's knowingly paradoxical formulation, indeed, the literary sphere is 'more real'. Hunt's recuperation of romance and wonder here could be interpreted as a riposte to Morier's assault on the idealization of Persia as a 'land of poets and roses!'; by the same token, Hunt might be seen to defend the example of Moore's *Lalla Rookh*, which was read by some as offering a 'renewal' of childhood pleasures.[24] Hunt nonetheless implicitly endorses the revisionist perspective of Morier and others when he states that the real 'Araby and Persia' are beyond the interest and sympathy of readers: 'dull to the dull, and governed by the foolish'. I began this book by arguing for the need to historicize the terms on which Britons may have regarded themselves as 'open' to the East during the long aftermath of the Seven Years' War, and Hunt's essay is a good place to conclude because it indirectly reflects both on the question of how metropolitan Britons lived their empire and on the moral and ethical purchase of displays of openness to Eastern others. Hunt may present himself as 'at home' with the East here, but this is a familiar imaginary realm that is pleasing precisely because it is insulated from the encroachment of sordid reality, whether of British material interests or of actual Eastern cultures and societies. Though his celebration of the 'gorgeous East' as 'the magic land of the child' may carry a broadly oppositional potential, Hunt's performance of sympathy in this essay – because it so clearly detaches itself from engagement with the wider world – challenges us to interrogate its substance. Hunt's case further prompts us to consider the way in which, by the end of our period, openness to the East may have come to offer a release from social responsibility and the cares of the world as much as a horizon-expanding encounter with otherness.

Notes

1. Macaulay, *Poetry and Prose*, 306.
2. Ibid., 699.
3. Ibid., 329.
4. Ibid., 380.
5. Ibid., 722.
6. Rajan, *Under Western Eyes*, 179.
7. Makdisi, *Making England Western*, 192.
8. Mill, *British India*, 1:305–6.
9. Mehta, *Liberalism*, 33; Pitts, *Turn to Empire*, 123–33.
10. Ottley, *Rustum Khan*, 1:239.
11. Makdisi, *Making England Western*.
12. Hall, *Macaulay*, 228.
13. Ibid., 237–8.
14. White, *Little London*, 15.
15. Rastegar, 'Unintended Gift', 253.
16. Ibid., 261 and 262.
17. Ibid., 259–62.
18. Moaddel, *Islamic Modernism*, 50.
19. Cohen-Vrignaud, *Radical Orientalism*, 37.
20. Ibid., 146.
21. *London Journal*, 1 (1834), 233.
22. Makdisi, *Making England Western*, 166.
23. *London Journal*, 1 (1834), 233 and 236.
24. *Asiatic Journal*, 4 (1817), 457.

Bibliography

Periodicals Consulted

Asiatic Journal
Blackwood's Edinburgh Magazine
British Review
Eclectic Review
Edinburgh Monthly Review
Edinburgh Review
European Magazine
The Examiner
Fraser's Magazine
Leigh Hunt's London Journal
The Liberal
Monthly Magazine
Monthly Review
New Monthly Magazine
New Review
Oriental Herald
Quarterly Oriental Magazine
Quarterly Review
Tait's Edinburgh Magazine

Selected Primary Sources

Alexander, William, *The History of Women, from the Earliest Antiquity to the Present Time*, 2 vols. (London: W. Strahan and T. Cadell, 1779).
Arabian Nights' Entertainments, ed. Robert Mack (Oxford: Oxford World's Classics, 1995).
Arabian Tales: Being a Continuation of the Arabian Nights Entertainments, 4 vols. (Edinburgh: Bell & Bradfute, 1792).
Bage, Robert, *The Fair Syrian*, 2 vols. (New York, NY: Garland, 1979).
Mount Henneth, 2 vols. (London: T. Lowndes, 1782).

Barbauld, Anna Laetitia, *Selected Poetry and Prose*, ed. William McCarthy and Elizabeth Kraft (Peterborough: Broadview, 2002).

Beattie, James, *Dissertations Moral and Critical* (London: W. Strahan and T. Cadell, 1783).

The Minstrel, in Two Books (London: Charles Dilly, 1784).

Bhagvat-Geeta, trans. Charles Wilkins (London: C. Nourse, 1785).

Bickerstaff, Isaac, *The Sultan, or A Peep into the Seraglio* (London: Charles Dilly, 1787).

Burke, Edmund, *The Writings and Speeches of Edmund Burke*, vol. 5, ed. P. J. Marshall (Oxford: Clarendon Press, 1981).

The Writings and Speeches of Edmund Burke, vol. 6, ed. P. J. Marshall (Oxford: Clarendon Press, 1991).

Byron, *Complete Poetical Works*, ed. Jerome J. McGann, 7 vols. (Oxford: Clarendon Press, 1980–93).

Cambridge, Richard Owen, *An Account of the War in India* (London: T. Jefferys, 1761).

Coleridge, Samuel Taylor, *Collected Letters of Samuel Taylor Coleridge*, ed. Earl Leslie Griggs, 2 vols. (Oxford: Clarendon Press, 1956).

Table Talk, ed. Carl Woodring, 2 vols. (Princeton, NJ: Princeton University Press, 1990).

Collins, William, *Persian Eclogues* (London: J. Roberts, 1742).

Cowley, Hannah, *A Day in Turkey; Or, The Russian Slaves* (London: G. G. J. and J. Robinson, 1792).

Darwin, Erasmus, *The Botanic Garden, Part II. Containing the Loves of the Plants, a Poem*, second edition (London: J. Johnson, 1790).

Day, Thomas, *Reflections upon the Present State of England, and the Independence of America*, third edition (London: J. Stockdale, 1783).

D'Israeli, Isaac, *Romances* (London: Cadell and Davies, 1799).

Dow, Alexander, *The History of Hindostan*, 2 vols. (London: T. Becket and P. A. De Hondt, 1768).

Tales, Translated from the Persian of Inatulla of Delhi, 2 vols. (London: T. Becket and P. A. De Hondt, 1768).

Edgeworth, Maria, *Continuation of Early Lessons*, 2 vols. (London: J. Johnson, 1815).

Forbes, Sir William, *An Account of the Life and Writings of James Beattie*, 2 vols. (Edinburgh: Archibald Constable, 1806).

Fordyce, James, *The Character and Conduct of the Female Sex* (London: T. Cadell, 1776).

Fraser, J. B., *The Kuzzilbash. A Tale of Khorasan*, 3 vols. (London: Henry Colburn, 1828).

Narrative of a Journey into Khorasan, in the Years 1821 and 1822 (London: Longman et al., 1825).

The Persian Adventurer, 3 vols. (London: Henry Colburn and Richard Bentley, 1830).

Gibbes, Phebe, *Hartly House, Calcutta*, ed. Michael J. Franklin (New Delhi: Oxford University Press, 2007).

Goldsmith, Oliver, *Collected Works of Oliver Goldsmith*, ed. Arthur Friedman, 5 vols. (Oxford: Clarendon Press, 1966).

The History of England, from the Earliest Times to the Death of George II, 4 vols. (London: T. Davies and others, 1771).

An History of England, in a Series of Letters from a Nobleman to His Son, 2 vols. (London: J. Newbery, 1764).

Hamilton, Elizabeth, *Translation of Letters of a Hindoo Rajah*, ed. Pamela Perkins and Shannon Russell (Peterborough: Broadview, 1999).

Hayley, William, 'An Elegy on the Death of the Honourable Sir William Jones' (London: T. Cadell and W. Jones, 1795).

An Essay on Epic Poetry (London: J. Dodsley, 1782).

Hazlitt, William, *The Spirit of the Age* (Plymouth: Northcote House, 1991).

Hockley, W. B., *Memoirs of a Brahmin*, 3 vols. (London: Newby & Boone, 1843).

Pandurang Hari, or Memoirs of a Hindoo, 3 vols. (London: Geo. B. Whittaker, 1826).

Pandurang Hari, or Memoirs of a Hindoo, 2 vols. (London: Henry S. King, 1873).

The Zenana; Or A Nuwab's Leisure Hours, 3 vols. (London: Saunders and Otley, 1827).

Hodges, William, *Travels in India, during the Years 1780, 1781, 1782 & 1783* (London: J. Edwards, 1793).

Hope, Thomas, *Anastasius: Or, Memoirs of a Greek*, second edition, 3 vols. (London: John Murray, 1819).

Hunt, Leigh, *The Indicator, and the Companion*, 2 vols. (London: Henry Colburn, 1834).

Selected Writings of Leigh Hunt, ed. Michael Eberle-Sinatra and Robert Morrison, 6 vols. (London: Pickering & Chatto, 2003).

Hurd, Richard, *Letters on Chivalry and Romance* (London: A. Millar, 1762).

Inchbald, Elizabeth, *The Mogul Tale; or, The Descent of the Balloon* (London: F. Powell, 1796).

Jardine, Alexander, *Letters from Barbary, France, Spain, Portugal, &c.*, 2 vols. (London: T. Cadell, 1788).

Johnson, Samuel, *The Plan of a Dictionary of the English Language* (London: J. and P. Knapton and others, 1747).

The World Displayed, 20 vols. (London: J. Newbery, 1759–61).

The Yale Edition of the Works of Samuel Johnson, 21 vols. (New Haven, CT: Yale University Press, 1955–).

and Ellis Cornelia Knight, *The History of Rasselas, Prince of Abissina and Dinarbas: A Tale*, ed. Lynne Meloccaro (London: J. M. Dent, 1994).

Johnstone, Charles, *Chrysal, or The Adventures of a Guinea*, ed. Kevin Bourque, 2 vols. (Kansas City, MO: Valancourt Books, 2011).

The History of Arsaces, Prince of Betlis, 2 vols. (London: T. Becket, 1774).

The Pilgrim: Or, A Picture of Life, 2 vols. (London: T. Cadell, 1775).

Jones, Sir William, 'A Discourse on the Institution of a Society for Enquiring into the History, Civil and Natural, the Antiquities, Arts, Sciences, and Literature of Asia' (London: T. Payne, 1784).

The Letters of Sir William Jones, ed. Garland Cannon, 2 vols. (Oxford: Clarendon Press, 1970).

Poems Consisting Chiefly of Translations from the Asiatick Languages (Oxford: Clarendon Press, 1772).

Selected Poetical and Prose Works, ed. Michael J. Franklin (Cardiff: University of Wales Press, 1995).

The Works of Sir William Jones, 6 vols. (London: G. G. and J. Robinson, 1799).

Keats, John, *Complete Poems*, ed. John Barnard (Harmondsworth: Penguin, 1988).

The Letters of John Keats, ed. Jon Mee (Oxford: Oxford World's Classics, 2002).

Knox, Vicesimus, *The Spirit of Despotism* (London, 1795).

Lamb, Charles, *Elia and the Last Essays of Elia*, ed. Jonathan Bate (Oxford: Oxford World's Classics, 1987).

Lamb, Charles and Mary Lamb, *The Works of Charles and Mary Lamb*, ed. E. V. Lucas, 7 vols. (London: Methuen, 1903).

Landor, Walter Savage, *Poems from the Arabic and Persian* (Warwick: H. Sharpe, 1800).

Langhorne, John, *Solyman and Almena* (London: H. Payne and W. Cropley, 1762).

Logan, John, *A Dissertation on the Governments, Manners, and Spirit of Asia* (London: J. Murray, 1787).

Lowth, Robert, *Lectures on the Sacred Poetry of the Hebrews*, trans. G. Gregory, 2 vols. (London: J. Johnson, 1787).

Lyttelton, George, *Letters from a Persian in England, to His Friend at Ispahan*, second edition (London: J. Millan, 1735).

Macaulay, T. B., *Poetry and Prose*, ed. G. M. Young (Cambridge, MA: Harvard University Press, 1970).

Mackenzie, Henry, *The Man of Feeling*, ed. Stephen Bending and Stephen Bygrave (Oxford: Oxford World's Classics, 2001).

Malcolm, Sir John, *The History of Persia, from the Earliest Period to the Present Time*, 2 vols. (London: John Murray, 1815).

'Persia: A Poem' (London: John Murray, 1814).

Sketches of Persia, 2 vols. (London: John Murray, 1827).

Mathias, T. J., *The Pursuits of Literature: A Satirical Poem, Part the Fourth* (London: T. Becket, 1797).

'The Shade of Alexander Pope on the Banks of the Thames' (London: T. Becket, 1799).

Maurice, Thomas, 'An Elegiac and Historical Poem Sacred to the Memory and Virtue of the Honourable Sir William Jones' (London, 1795).

Memoirs of a Gentleman, Who Resided Several Years in the East Indies (London: J. Donaldson, 1774).

Memoirs of the Revolution in Bengal, Anno Dom. 1757 (London: A. Millar, 1760).

Mill, James, *The History of British India*, 3 vols. (London: Baldwin, Cradock, and Joy, 1817).

Millar, John, *The Origin of the Distinction of Ranks*, third edition (London: J. Murray, 1779).

Milton, John, *Paradise Lost*, ed. Scott Elledge (New York, NY: Norton, 1975).

Moore, Thomas, *Letters of Thomas Moore, vol. 1: 1793–1818*, ed. Wilfred S. Dowden (Oxford: Clarendon Press, 1964).

Poetical Works, 10 vols. (London: Longman *et al.*, 1841).

More, Hannah, 'Slavery, a Poem' (London: T. Cadell, 1788).

Morier, James, *The Adventures of Hajji Baba of Ispahan*, ed. C. W. Stewart (London: Oxford University Press, 1910).

The Adventures of Hajji Baba of Ispahan in England, 2 vols. (London: J. Murray, 1828).

Ayesha, or The Maid of Kars, 3 vols. (London: Richard Bentley, 1834).

A Second Journey through Persia, Armenia, and Asia Minor (London: Longman *et al.*, 1818).

Mulligan, Hugh, *Poems Chiefly on Slavery and Oppression* (London: W. Lowndes, 1788).

'The Nabob: Or, Asiatic Plunderers' (London: J. Townsend, 1773).

Nott, John, *Select Odes from the Persian Poet Hafez* (London: T. Cadell, 1787).

O'Keeffe, John, *The Little Hunch-Back; or, A Frolic in Bagdad* (London: J. Debrett, 1789).

The Orientalist: A Volume of Tales after the Eastern-Taste (Dublin: James Hoey Jr, 1764).

Ottley, T. H., *Rustum Khan; or, Fourteen Nights' Entertainment at the Shah Bhag*, 3 vols. (London: W. Sams, 1831).

Ouseley, William, *Persian Miscellanies* (London: Richard White, 1795).

Owenson, Sydney, *The Missionary*, ed. Julia M. Wright (Peterborough: Broadview, 2002).

Paine, Tom, *Rights of Man*, ed. Eric Foner (Harmondsworth: Penguin, 1985).

Parkes, Fanny, *Wanderings of a Pilgrim in Search of the Picturesque*, ed. Indira Ghose and Sara Mills (Manchester: Manchester University Press, 2001).

Percy, Thomas, *Reliques of Ancient English Poetry*, fourth edition, 3 vols. (London: F. and C. Rivington, 1794).

Plays by Samuel Foote and Arthur Murphy, ed. George Taylor (Cambridge: Cambridge University Press, 1984).

The Poems of Shelley, vol. 2: 1817–1819, ed. Kelvin Everest and Geoffrey Matthews (Harlow: Longman, 2000).

Porter, Sir James, *Observations on the Religion, Law, Government, and Manners, of the Turks*, 2 vols. (London: J. Nourse, 1768).

Price, Richard, *Political Writings*, ed. D. O. Thomson (Cambridge: Cambridge University Press, 1991).

De Quincey, Thomas, *Confessions of an English Opium-Eater*, ed. Grevel Lindop (Oxford: Oxford World's Classics, 1985).

Reynolds, J. H, *Safie: An Eastern Tale* (London: James Cawthorn, 1814).

Ridley, James, *The Schemer: Or, Universal Satirist* (London: J. Wilkie, 1763).

Tales of the Genii: Or, The Delightful Lessons of Horam, the Son of Asmar, 2 vols. (London: J. Wilkie, 1764).

Russell, William, *Essay on the Character, Manners, and Genius of Women in Different Ages*, 2 vols. (London: G. Robinson, 1773).

Scott, Helenus, *The Adventures of a Rupee*. A New Edition (London: J. Murray, 1782).

Scott, John, *Poetical Works* (London: J. Buckland, 1782).

Scott, Jonathan, *Bahar-Danush; Or, Garden of Knowledge. An Oriental Romance*, 3 vols. (Shrewsbury: J. and W. Eddowes, 1799).

Scott, Sir Walter, *Chronicles of the Canongate*, ed. Claire Lamont (Harmondsworth: Penguin, 2003).

　　Introduction and Notes from the Magnum Opus: Ivanhoe to Castle Dangerous, ed. J. H. Alexander (Edinburgh: Edinburgh University Press, 2012).

　　The Lives of the Novelists (London: Oxford University Press, 1934).

　　The Miscellaneous Prose Works of Sir Walter Scott, vol. 4 (Edinburgh: Robert Cadell, 1843).

Shebbeare, John, *The History of the Excellence and Decline of the Constitution, Religion, Laws, Manners and Genius of the Sumatrans*, 2 vols. (London: G. Kearsley, 1760).

Shelley's Poetry and Prose, ed. Donald Reiman and Sharon Powers (New York, NY: W. W. Norton, 1977).

Shore, Sir John, 'The Literary History of the Late Sir William Jones' (London: Edward Jeffery, 1795).

Smith, Adam, *Wealth of Nations*, ed. Kathryn Sutherland (Oxford: Oxford World's Classics, 1993).

Smollett, Tobias, *The History and Adventures of an Atom*, ed. Robert Adams Day (Athens, GA: University of Georgia Press, 1989).

Southey, Robert, *Chronicle of the Cid* (London: Longman *et al.*, 1808).

　　The Critical Heritage, ed. Lionel Madden (London: Routledge and Kegan Paul, 1972).

　　Later Poetical Works, 1811–1838, ed. Tim Fulford and Lynda Pratt, 4 vols. (London: Pickering & Chatto, 2012).

　　New Letters of Robert Southey, ed. Kenneth Curry (New York, NY: Columbia University Press, 1965).

　　Poetical Works, 1793–1810, ed. Lynda Pratt and Tim Fulford, 5 vols. (London: Pickering & Chatto, 2004).

Southey, C. C., ed., *The Life and Correspondence of the Late Robert Southey*, 6 vols. (London: Longman *et al.*, 1850).

The Spectator, ed. Donald F. Bond, 5 vols. (Oxford: Clarendon Press, 1965).

Starke, Mariana, *The Sword of Peace; or, A Voyage of Love* (London: J. Debrett, 1789).

Stuart, Gilbert, *A View of Society in Europe, in Its Progress from Rudeness to Refinement* (Edinburgh: John Bell, 1778).

Voltaire, *Candide and Other Stories*, trans. Roger Pearson (Oxford: Oxford World's Classics, 1998).

Weber, Henry, *Tales of the East*, 3 vols. (Edinburgh: John Ballantyne and others, 1812).

Wollstonecraft, Mary, *Works of Mary Wollstonecraft*, ed. Janet Todd and Marilyn Butler, 10 vols. (London: William Pickering, 1989).

Wordsworth, William, *Poetical Works*, ed. Ernest De Selincourt (Oxford: Oxford University Press, 1990).

    Selected Prose, ed. John O. Hayden (Harmondsworth: Penguin, 1988).

Selected Secondary Sources

Ahmed, Siraj, *The Stillbirth of Capital: Enlightenment Writing and Colonial India* (Stanford, CA: Stanford University Press, 2012).

Aravamudan, Srinivas, *Enlightenment Orientalism: Resisting the Rise of the Novel* (Chi ago, IL: University of Chicago Press, 2012).

Bainbridge, Simon, *British Poetry and the Revolutionary and Napoleonic Wars: Visions of Conflict* (Oxford: Oxford University Press, 2003).

Ballaster, Ros, *Fabulous Orients: Fictions of the East in England, 1662–1785* (Oxford: Oxford University Press, 2005).

Barrell, John, *English Literature in History, 1730–1780: An Equal, Wide Survey* (London: Hutchinson, 1983).

    The Infection of Thomas De Quincey: A Psychopathology of Imperialism (New Haven, CT: Yale University Press, 1991).

    The Spirit of Despotism: Invasions of Privacy in the 1790s (Oxford: Oxford University Press, 2006).

Bayly, C. A., *Empire and Information: Intelligence Gathering and Social Communication in British India, 1780–1870* (Cambridge: Cambridge University Press, 1996).

Belcher, Wendy Louise, *Abyssinia's Samuel Johnson: Ethiopian Thought in the Making of an English Author* (Oxford: Oxford University Press, 2012).

Bewell, Alan, *Romanticism and Colonial Disease* (Baltimore, MD: Johns Hopkins University Press, 1999).

Bohls, Elizabeth A., *Romantic Literature and Postcolonial Studies* (Edinburgh: Edinburgh University Press, 2013).

Bolton, Carol, *Writing the Empire: Robert Southey and Romantic Colonialism* (London: Pickering & Chatto, 2007).

Bourke, Richard, *Empire & Revolution: The Political Life of Edmund Burke* (Princeton, NJ: Princeton University Press, 2015).

Bowen, H. V., *The Business of Empire: The East India Company and Imperial Britain* (Cambridge: Cambridge University Press, 2006).

Brown, Christopher Leslie, *Moral Capital: Foundations of British Abolitionism* (Chapel Hill, NC: University of North Carolina Press, 2006).

Butler, Marilyn, 'Byron and the Empire in the East', in *Byron: Augustan and Romantic*, ed. Andrew Rutherford (Basingstoke: Macmillan, 1990), 63–81.

    'Orientalism', in *The Penguin History of English Literature: The Romantic Period*, ed. David Pirie (Harmondsworth: Penguin, 1994), 395–447.

Chakrabarty, Dipesh, *Provincializing Europe: Postcolonial Thought and Historical Difference* (Princeton, NJ: Princeton University Press, 2000).

Clark, Anna, *Scandal: The Sexual Politics of the British Constitution* (Princeton, NJ: Princeton University Press, 2004).

Cochran, Peter, 'Why Did Byron Envy Thomas Hope's *Anastasius?*', *Keats-Shelley Review* 24 (2010), 76–90.

Cohen-Vrignaud, Gerard, *Radical Orientalism: Rights, Reform, and Romanticism* (Cambridge: Cambridge University Press, 2015).

Coleman, Deirdre, 'The "Dark Tide of Time": Coleridge and William Hodges' India', in *Coleridge, Romanticism and the Orient*, ed. David Vallins, Kaz Oishi, and Seamus Perry (London: Bloomsbury, 2013), 39–54.

'"Voyage of Conception": John Keats and India', in *India and Europe in the Global Eighteenth Century*, ed. Simon Davies, Gabriel Sanchez Espinoza, and Daniel Sanjiv Roberts (Oxford: Voltaire Foundation, 2012), 79–100.

Colley, Linda, *Britons: Forging the Nation, 1707–1837* (New Haven, CT: Yale University Press, 1992).

Cox, Jeffrey N., 'Cockney Cosmopolitanism', *Nineteenth-Century Contexts* 32 (2010), 245–59.

Dalrymple, William, *White Mughals: Love and Betrayal in Eighteenth-Century Britain* (London: Flamingo, 2003).

Dart, Gregory, *Metropolitan Art and Literature, 1810–1840: Cockney Adventures* (Cambridge: Cambridge University Press, 2012).

Rousseau, Robespierre, and English Romanticism (Cambridge: Cambridge University Press, 1998).

De Bruyn, Frans and Shaun Regan, eds., *The Culture of the Seven Years' War: Empire, Identity, and the Arts in the Eighteenth-Century Atlantic World* (Toronto: University of Toronto Press, 2014).

Dirks, Nicholas, *The Scandal of Empire: India and the Creation of Imperial Britain* (Cambridge, MA: Belknap Press, 2006).

Drew, John, *India and the Romantic Imagination* (Oxford: Oxford University Press, 1987).

Duggett, Tom, *Gothic Romanticism: Architecture, Politics, and Literary Form* (Basingstoke: Palgrave, 2010).

Eskandari-Qajar, Manoutchehr, 'Persian Ambassadors, Their Circassians, and the Politics of Elizabethan and Regency England', *Iranian Studies* 44 (2011), 251–71.

Fang, Karen, 'Empire, Coleridge, and Charles Lamb's Consumer Imagination', *Studies in English Literature 1500–1900* 43 (2003), 815–43.

Romantic Writing and the Empire of Signs: Periodical Culture and Post-Napoleonic Authorship (Charlottesville, VA: University of Virginia Press, 2010).

Festa, Lynn, *Sentimental Figures of Empire in Eighteenth-Century Britain and France* (Baltimore, MD: Johns Hopkins University Press, 2006).

Franklin, Michael J., *Orientalist Jones: Sir William Jones, Poet, Lawyer, Linguist, 1746–1794* (Oxford: Oxford University Press, 2011).

ed., *Romantic Representations of British India* (London: Routledge, 2006).

Fulford, Tim, 'Coleridge and the Oriental Tale', in *The Arabian Nights in Historical Context: Between East and West*, ed. Saree Makdisi and Felicity Nussbaum (Oxford: Oxford University Press, 2008), 213–34.

'Poetic Flowers/Indian Bowers', in *Romantic Representations of British India*, ed. Michael J. Franklin (London: Routledge, 2006), 113–30.

Garcia, Humberto, *Islam and the English Enlightenment, 1670–1840* (Baltimore, MD: Johns Hopkins University Press, 2012).

Gilmartin, Kevin, *Print Politics: The Press and Radical Opposition in Early Nineteenth-Century England* (Cambridge: Cambridge University Press, 1996).

Green, Nile, *The Love of Strangers: What Six Muslim Students Learned in Jane Austen's London* (Princeton, NJ: Princeton University Press, 2016).

Grenby, M. O., 'Orientalism and Propaganda', *The Eighteenth-Century Novel* 2 (2002), 215–37.

Guest, Harriet, *Small Change: Women, Learning, Patriotism, 1750–1810* (Chicago, IL: University of Chicago Press, 2000).

Hall, Catherine, *Macaulay and Son: Architects of Imperial Britain* (New Haven, CT: Yale University Press, 2012).

and Sonya O. Rose, eds., *At Home with Empire: Metropolitan Culture and the Imperial World* (Cambridge: Cambridge University Press, 2006).

Harrington, Jack, *Sir John Malcolm and the Creation of British India* (Basingstoke: Palgrave, 2010).

Hawes, Clement, 'Johnson and Imperialism', in *The Cambridge Companion to Samuel Johnson*, ed. Greg Clingham (Cambridge: Cambridge University Press, 1997), 114–26.

Higgins, David, *Romantic Englishness: Local, National, and Global Selves, 1780–1850* (Basingstoke: Palgrave, 2014).

Hoeveler, Diane Long, and Jeffrey Cass, eds., *Interrogating Orientalism: Contextual Approaches and Pedagogical Practices* (Columbus, OH: Ohio State University Press, 2006).

Hudson, Nicholas, *Samuel Johnson and the Making of Modern England* (Cambridge: Cambridge University Press, 2003).

James, Felicity, 'Thomas Manning, Charles Lamb, and Oriental Encounters', *Poetica* 76 (2011), 21–38.

Johnston, Henry Mckenzie, *Ottoman and Persian Odysseys: James Morier, Creator of Hajji Baba of Ispahan, and His Brothers* (London: British Academic Press, 1998).

Jones, Elizabeth, 'Suburb Sinners: Sex and Disease in the Cockney School', in *Leigh Hunt: Life, Poetics, Politics*, ed. Nicholas Roe (London: Routledge, 2003), 78–94.

Joseph, Betty, *Reading the East India Company, 1720–1840: Colonial Currencies of Gender* (Chicago, IL: University of Chicago Press, 2004).

Kaul, Suvir, *Eighteenth-Century British Literature and Postcolonial Studies* (Edinburgh: Edinburgh University Press, 2009).

Kelly, Ronan, *Bard of Erin: The Life of Thomas Moore* (London: Penguin, 2009).

Kitson, Peter J., *Forging Romantic China: Sino–British Cultural Exchange* (Cambridge: Cambridge University Press, 2013).

Klancher, Jon, 'Discriminations, or Romantic Cosmopolitanisms in London', in *Romantic Metropolis: The Urban Scene of British Culture, 1780–1840*, ed. James Chandler and Kevin Gilmartin (Cambridge: Cambridge University Press, 2005), 65–82.

Kucich, Greg, 'Cockney Chivalry: Hunt, Keats, and the Aesthetics of Excess', in *Leigh Hunt: Life, Poetics, Politics*, ed. Nicholas Roe (London: Routledge, 2003), 118–34.

Leask, Nigel, *British Romantic Writers and the East: Anxieties of Empire* (Cambridge: Cambridge University Press, 1992).

'Elizabeth Hamilton's *Translation of Letters of a Hindoo Rajah* and Romantic Orientalism', in *Repossessing the Romantic Past*, ed. Heather Glen and Paul Hamilton (Cambridge: Cambridge University Press, 2006), 183–202.

'Kubla Khan and *Orientalism: The Road to Xanadu* Revisited', *Romanticism* 4 (1998), 1–21.

'Review of Javed Majeed', *Ungoverned Imaginings, History Workshop Journal* 36 (1993), 242–9.

'Romanticism and the Wider World', in *The Cambridge History of English Romantic Literature*, ed. James Chandler (Cambridge: Cambridge University Press, 2009), 271–92.

'Towards an Anglo-Indian Poetry? The Colonial Muse in the Writings of John Leyden, Thomas Medwin and Charles D'Oyly', in *Writing India: The Literature of British India*, ed. Bart Moore-Gilbert (Manchester: Manchester University Press, 1996), 52–85.

'"Wandering through Eblis": Absorption and Containment in Romantic Exoticism', in *Romanticism and Colonialism*, ed. Tim Fulford and Peter Kitson (Cambridge: Cambridge University Press, 1998), 165–88.

Mahmoud, Fatma Moussa, 'Orientals in Picaresque: A Chapter in the History of the Oriental Tale in England', *Cairo Studies in English* (1961–2), 145–88.

Majeed, Javed, 'Meadows Taylor's *Confessions of a Thug*: The Anglo-Indian Novel as a Genre in the Making', in *Writing India: The Literature of British India*, ed. Bart Moore-Gilbert (Manchester: Manchester University Press, 1996), 86–110.

Ungoverned Imaginings: James Mill's The History of British India *and Orientalism* (Oxford: Clarendon Press, 1992).

Makdisi, Saree, *Making England Western: Occidentalism, Race, and Imperial Culture* (Chicago, IL: University of Chicago Press, 2014).

Romantic Imperialism: Universal Empire and the Culture of Modernity (Cambridge: Cambridge University Press, 1998).

William Blake and the Impossible History of the 1790s (Chicago, IL: University of Chicago Press, 2003).

and Felicity Nussbaum, eds., *The Arabian Nights in Historical Context: Between East and West* (Oxford: Oxford University Press, 2008).

Marshall, P. J. 'British–Indian Connections c.1780-c.1830': The Empire of the Officials', in *Romantic Representations of British India*, ed. Michael J. Franklin (London: Routledge, 2006), 45–64.

Mehta, Uday Singh, *Liberalism and Empire: A Study in Nineteenth-Century Liberal Thought* (Chicago, IL: University of Chicago Press, 1999).

Moaddel, Mansoor, *Islamic Modernism, Nationalism, and Fundamentalism: Episode and Discourse* (Chicago, IL: University of Chicago Press, 2005).

Moore-Gilbert, Bart, ed., *Writing India, 1757–1990: The Literature of British India* (Manchester: Manchester University Press, 1996).

Mukherjee, Pablo, *Crime and Empire: The Colony in Nineteenth-Century Fictions of Crime* (Oxford: Oxford University Press, 2003).

Mulholland, James, *Sounding Imperial: Poetic Voice and the Politics of Empire, 1730–1820* (Baltimore, MD: Johns Hopkins University Press, 2013).

Neill, Anna, *British Discovery Literature and the Rise of Global Commerce* (Basingstoke: Palgrave, 2002).

Nussbaum, Felicity, *Torrid Zones: Maternity, Sexuality, and Empire in Eighteenth-Century English Narratives* (Baltimore, MD: Johns Hopkins University Press, 1995).

Ogborn, Miles, *Global Lives: Britain and the World, 1550–1800* (Cambridge: Cambridge University Press, 2008).

O'Quinn, Daniel, *Staging Governance: Theatrical Imperialism in London, 1770–1800* (Baltimore, MD: Johns Hopkins University Press, 2005).

'Theatre, Islam, and the Question of Monarchy', in *The Oxford Handbook of the Georgian Theatre 1737–1832*, ed. Julia Swindells and David Francis Taylor (Oxford: Oxford University Press, 2014), 638–55.

Orr, Bridget, 'Galland, Georgian Theatre, and the Creation of Popular Orientalism', in *The Arabian Nights in Historical Context: Between East and West*, ed. Saree Makdisi and Felicity Nussbaum (Oxford: Oxford University Press, 2008), 103–29.

Pitts, Jennifer, *A Turn to Empire: The Rise of Liberal Imperialism in Britain and France* (Princeton, NJ: Princeton University Press, 2005).

Pocock, J. G. A., *Virtue, Commerce, and History* (Cambridge: Cambridge University Press, 1985).

Porter, David, *The Chinese Taste in Eighteenth-Century England* (Cambridge: Cambridge University Press, 2010).

Ideographia: The Chinese Cipher in Early Modern Europe (Stanford, CA: Stanford University Press, 2002).

'Sinicizing Early Modernity: The Imperatives of Historical Cosmopolitanism', *Eighteenth-Century Studies* 43 (2010), 299–306.

Pratt, Mary Louise, *Imperial Eyes: Travel Writing and Transculturation* (London: Routledge, 1992).

Rajan, Balachandra, *Under Western Eyes: India from Milton to Macaulay* (Durham, NC: Duke University Press, 1999).

Rastegar, Kamran, 'The Unintended Gift: The Adventures of Hajji Baba Ispahani As Transactional Text', *Middle Eastern Literatures* 10 (2007), 251–71.

Rendall, Jane, 'Scottish Orientalism: From Robertson to James Mill', *Historical Journal* 25 (1982), 43–69.

'Tacitus Engendered: "Gothic Feminism" and British Histories, c.1750–1800', in *Imagining Nations*, ed. Geoffrey Cubitt (Manchester: Manchester University Press, 1998), 57–74.

Roberts, Daniel Sanjiv, 'A "Teague" and a "True Briton": Charles Johnstone, Ireland and Empire', *Irish University Review* 41 (2011), 133–50.

Roe, Nicholas, *John Keats and the Culture of Dissent* (Oxford: Oxford University Press, 1997).

ed., *Leigh Hunt: Life, Poetics, Politics* (London: Routledge, 2003).

Rothschild, Emma, *The Inner Life of Empires: An Eighteenth-Century History* (Princeton, NJ: Princeton University Press, 2011).

Rudd, Andrew, *Sympathy and India in British Literature, 1770–1830* (Basingstoke: Palgrave, 2010).

Saglia, Diego, *Poetic Castles in Spain: British Romanticism and Figurations of Iberia* (Amsterdam: Rodopi, 2000).

'Words and Things: Southey's East and the Materiality of Oriental Discourse', in *Robert Southey and the Contexts of English Romanticism*, ed. Lynda Pratt (Aldershot: Ashgate, 2006), 167–86.

Scherwatzky, Steven, 'Johnson, *Rasselas*, and the Politics of Empire', *Eighteenth-Century Life* 16 (1992), 102–13.

Schwab, Raymond, *The Oriental Renaissance: Europe's Rediscovery of the East, 1680–1880*, trans. Gene Patterson-Black and Victor Reinking (New York, NY: Columbia University Press, 1984).

Sharafuddin, Mohammed, *Islam and Romantic Orientalism: Literary Encounters with the Orient* (London: I. B. Tauris, 1996).

Simpson, David, 'The Limits of Cosmopolitanism and the Case for Translation', *European Romantic Review* 16 (2005), 141–52.

Romanticism and the Question of the Stranger (Chicago, IL: University of Chicago Press, 2012).

Sitter, Zak, 'William Jones, "Eastern" Poetry, and the Problem of Imitation', *Texas Studies in Literature and Language* 50 (2008), 385–407.

Stabler, Jane, 'Leigh Hunt's Aesthetics of Intimacy', in *Leigh Hunt: Life, Poetics, Politics*, ed. Nicholas Roe (London: Routledge, 2003), 95–117.

Tavakoli-Targhi, M., *Refashioning Iran: Orientalism, Occidentalism and Historiography* (Basingstoke: Palgrave, 2001).

Teltscher, Kate, *India Inscribed: European and British Writing on India 1600–1800* (Delhi: Oxford University Press, 1995).

Thomas, Greg, 'Chinoiserie and Intercultural Dialogue at Brighton Pavilion', in *Qing Encounters: Artistic Exchanges between China and the West*, ed. Petra Ten-Doesschate Chu and Ning Ding (Los Angeles, CA: Getty Research Institute, 2015), 232–47.

Vail, Jeffrey, 'Thomas Moore: After the Battle', in *A Companion to Irish Literature*, vol. 1, ed. Julia M. Wright (Oxford: Wiley-Blackwell, 2010), 310–25.

Vallins, David, Kaz Oishi, and Seamus Perry, eds., *Coleridge, Romanticism, and the Orient* (London: Bloomsbury, 2013).

Warner, Marina, *Stranger Magic: Charmed States and the Arabian Nights* (London: Chatto & Windus, 2011).

Warren, Andrew, *The Orient and the Young Romantics* (Cambridge: Cambridge University Press, 2014).

Watts, Carol, *The Cultural Work of Empire: The Seven Years' War and the Imagining of the Shandean State* (Toronto: University of Toronto Press, 2007).

Weir, David, *Brahma and the West: William Blake and the Oriental Renaissance* (Albany, NY: State University of New York Press, 2003).

White, Daniel J., *From Little London to Little Bengal: Religion, Print and Modernity in Early British India, 1793–1835* (Baltimore, MD: Johns Hopkins University Press, 2013).

Wilson, Kathleen, *The Island Race: Englishness, Empire and Gender in the Eighteenth Century* (London: Routledge, 2003).

The Sense of the People: Politics, Culture, and Imperialism in England, 1715–1785 (Cambridge: Cambridge University Press, 1995).

Wright, Julia M., *Ireland, India and Nationalism in Nineteenth-Century Literature* (Cambridge: Cambridge University Press, 2007).

Yeazell, Ruth Bernard, *Harems of the Mind: Passages of Western Art and Literature* (New Haven, CT: Yale University Press, 2000).

Index

CAMBRIDGE STUDIES IN ROMANTICISM

General Editor
JAMES CHANDLER, *University of Chicago*

9 781108 460101